Caribbean Literature and the Environment

Caribbean Literature and the Environment

BETWEEN NATURE AND CULTURE

Edited by Elizabeth M. DeLoughrey,
Renée K. Gosson, and George B. Handley

New World Studies

A. James Arnold, editor

University of Virginia Press

Charlottesville and London

The University of Virginia Press
© 2005 by the Rector and Visitors of the University of Virginia
All rights reserved
Printed in the United States of America on acid-free paper
First published 2005

9 8 7 6 5 4 3 2 1

Library of Congress Cataloging-in-Publication Data

Caribbean literature and the environment : between nature and culture /
edited by Elizabeth M. DeLoughrey, Renée K. Gosson, and George B. Handley.
      p. cm. — (New World studies)
   Includes bibliographical references and index.
   ISBN 0-8139-2373-5 (cloth : alk. paper) — ISBN 0-8139-2372-7 (pbk. : alk. paper)
   1. Caribbean literature—20th century—History and criticism. 2. Ecology in
literature. 3. Nature in literature. I. DeLoughrey, Elizabeth M., 1967- II.
Gosson, Renée K. III. Handley, George B., 1964- IV. Series.
PN849.C3C29 2005
809'.933556'09729—dc22

2005007615

In memory of M. Dorothy MacDonald (1910–2004)
For Joan Price, Leo Gosson, and Lee Gosson
And for Bill Handley

Contents

viii *Contents*

Acknowledgments

A COLLABORATIVE project of this kind owes debts to many individuals for their efforts. We benefited initially by being brought together serendipitously on a 2001 MLA panel, "Caribbean Literature and the Environment," where we discovered our mutual passion for the subject and our complementary areas of specialty. We would like to thank William Slaymaker for having the insight to organize that panel and thus facilitate our fruitful discussions that followed. At Brigham Young University, Roger Macfarlane, former chair of the Department of Humanities, Classics, and Comparative Literature, and Jeffrey Ringer, director of the Kennedy Center, both generously covered many of the unseen costs of conference calls, printing, and photocopying, funds that enabled a meeting in person in Ithaca (including Indian food supplied by Chris and lessons on how to pronounce "DeLoughrey" properly), as well as funds to hire research assistants Rex Nielson, Bethany Beyer, James Krause, and Rachelle Woodbury, who helped with bibliographic matters in a selfless and diligent manner.

We would also like to thank the anonymous readers and the exceptional editorial staff at University of Virginia Press, especially Cathie Brettschneider and James Arnold. We have felt consistently encouraged and guided by the highest standards of professionalism and scholarship. Proper study of the Caribbean cannot be done alone, and we appreciate the wide range of coverage that was made possible by our talented, patient, and outstanding contributors. Our only regret was that so much of our communication was not in person but over numerous emails. We feel fortunate to have had the opportunity to work with Antonio Benítez-Rojo. His contribution to this collection exemplifies his ability to push us into new frontiers and to do so with social and intellectual grace. We deeply regret that he did not live to see its completion. Finally, we have so enjoyed our association as coeditors; mutual hard work, graciousness, and laughter made this a true labor of love.

Elizabeth DeLoughrey would like to thank the Center for Cultural Studies at the University of California, Santa Cruz, for providing an interdisciplinary intellectual environment in which this project could be completed.

One of her primary inspirations for this project has been the work of Wilson Harris; she'd like to acknowledge the importance of his ecological vision as well as his kindness in corresponding with her during the conceptual stages of this project. Most important, she is the most grateful for Chris and Grendel, her guiding stars and grounding earth.

Renée Gosson would like to thank Raphaël Confiant for his reflections regarding Martinicans' indifference to their landscape as a symptom of assimilation and alienation. She is also grateful to Solenne Langelez and Jahman N'daw for their transcription of this interview, and to her friend, colleague, and codirector Eric Faden, whose idea to make a film in Martinique—where the landscape itself plays the leading role—has added a visual dimension to her research. She would also like to express her appreciation to Bucknell University for its untenured faculty leave, which allowed her the time to focus on this project. And finally, she is indebted to her partner, Simonne, who continually reminds her of the nature beyond ecocriticism, in the hills of Pennsylvania, Vermont, and Oregon.

George Handley would like to thank Derek Walcott for inviting him to St. Lucia and for graciously allowing an extensive interview. He is indebted to Scott Slovic, Sandra Lubarsky, David Orr, and the Ponderosa Group at Northern Arizona University for having helped him to catch the vision of environmental work in academia. As always, he would like to thank his brother, Bill, for his friendship and his outstanding example of scholarship and intellectual integrity; his parents, Ken and Kate, for their undying encouragement; and, of course, his wife, Amy, for fifteen years (and counting) of happiness.

Caribbean Literature and the Environment

Introduction

Elizabeth M. DeLoughrey,
Renée K. Gosson, and George B. Handley

Hay que aprender a recordar
Lo que las nubes no pueden olvidar

You've got to learn to remember
what the clouds cannot forget
—Nicolás Guillén, "Elegía"

NICOLÁS GUILLÉN's insight, from his 1947 poem "Elegía," captures one
of the central paradoxes of Caribbean literature. He states plainly, "hay
que aprender," which implies a more generic mandate than the English
translation can provide. "One must remember" or "we must all remember"
or "it must be remembered" are all possible translations of the imperative
to record and to commemorate a history that has no surviving witnesses
except nature itself. The vague subject of the imperative is appropriate,
since it is not clear who will be capable of remembering what the clouds
alone seem to remember. Despite this uncertainty, the mandate remains;
the past must not be ignored even if it cannot be known. Nature's muted
voice can neither be fully reclaimed nor entirely suppressed. The clouds
have witnessed the devastation of indigenous populations, the violence of
the Middle Passage, and a host of other human atrocities in the Caribbean,
yet there remains a palpable separation between natural phenomena,
human history, and their mutual articulation.

Guillén's work, like that of many other authors in this volume, might
be read as a response to the fact that there is probably no other region in
the world that has been more radically altered in terms of human and
botanic migration, transplantation, and settlement than the Caribbean.
This unique and troubled history has caused theorists such as Édouard
Glissant to conclude that the dialectic between Caribbean nature and
culture has not been brought into productive relation. He determines
that the Caribbean "landscape is its own monument: its meaning can only
be traced on the underside. It is all history" (*Caribbean Discourse* 11).

The title of our collection, *Caribbean Literature and the Environment: Between Nature and Culture,* takes Glissant's observations as a starting point and is the first volume to examine literary narratives that engage with Caribbean and ecocritical studies in the four major language areas of the region. While we make no claims that this book is representative, we hope to create a dialogue between the growing field of environmental literary studies, which has primarily been concerned with white settler narratives, and Caribbean cultural production, especially the region's negotiation of complex ethnic legacies.[1] Our objective is to bring Caribbean and ecocritical studies together by exploring the ways in which the history of transplantation and settlement has contributed to a sense of place and an environmental ethic in the Caribbean.

Our contributors explore the relationship between human and natural history, or, in Glissant's terms, texts that produce a "language of landscape" (*Caribbean Discourse* 146). Overall, we begin with the premise that nature is already acculturated by the human process of rendering meaning, which is not the same thing as saying that nature does not exist outside of culture. In its exploration of the relationship between nature and culture, this collection addresses four overlapping themes: how Caribbean texts inscribe the environmental impact of colonial and plantation economies; the revision of colonial myths of Edenic and natural origins; connections between the process of biotic and cultural creolization; and finally, how Caribbean aesthetics might usefully articulate a means to preserve sustainability in the wake of tourism and globalization.

Although North American ecocritics often inscribe an idealized natural landscape that is devoid of human history and labor, the colonization and forced relocation of Caribbean subjects preclude that luxury and beg the question as to what might be considered a natural landscape. Against the popular grain of U.S. ecocritical studies, we argue that addressing the historical and racial violence of the Caribbean is integral to understanding literary representations of its geography. As Wilson Harris reminds us, this is "a landscape saturated by traumas of conquest" (*Whole Armour* 8). Like Guillén, Glissant also suggests that the land is a mute historical record of a "fight without witnesses" (*Discours antillais* 177), so that a gesture of destruction against land becomes an act of violence against collective memory. The land, states Beverley Ormerod, is the past's "only true guardian . . . history waits, latent, in Caribbean nature, which is filled with sorrowful reminders of slavery and repression" ("French West Indian" 170). While the brutality of the plantation system produced a particular relationship to the natural world, it is important to consider those sites that served as vital repositories of indigenous and African beliefs and assertions of rebellion against plantation capitalism. This is most evident in the history of indigenous and slave resistance in which mountain ranges, mangrove swamps, provision grounds, and other sites of environmental opposition to the plantocracy provided vital alternative communities.

There are dangers in attempting to tell a muted story. Excessive historicity often leads to blaming the victim, in many cases the land itself, when the past is elusive. In 1930, Antonio Pedreira wrote his famous invective against his own Puerto Rico, blaming the land's tolerance for the historical and racial confusion that resulted from colonialism. Oddly, the culprit is the island itself: "Isolation and diminutive geography have condemned us to live in perpetual submission, having as our only defense not aggression but patience" (115). Similarly, V. S. Naipaul has argued that "the history of the islands can never be satisfactorily told," not simply because of the "brutality" but, notoriously, because "history is built around achievement and creation; and nothing was created in the West Indies" (*Middle Passage* 29). Although much has been written about Naipaul's charge, few have pointed out that the landscape itself seems to have "invited" its degradation: "There were only plantations, prosperity, decline, neglect: *the size of the islands called for nothing else*" (27; our emphasis). Naipaul's literary oeuvre contradicts the "natural" futility he perceives in the landscape, yet he raises an important question about the ways in which assumptions about historiography are embedded in geography. As is the case for many writers of the region, "geography serve[s] as a metaphor for history —as well it might in islands whose history has been so deeply influenced by geographical factors" (Rohlehr 235).

Literature's challenge to speak of this history must resist not only the silencing effects of the Caribbean's colonial legacies on Amerindian, African, and Asian peoples but also what Derek Walcott calls nature's own "vegetal fury" (*The Bounty* 13). Ecological processes of death and regeneration are indifferent to, though certainly not independent of, the human story. As Guillén suggests, literature must do the impossible: it must remember a human history that has been buried by the tremendous tropical indifference of the Caribbean environment.

While this collusion of human violence and natural regeneration obstructs access to history, it also presents particular poetic and environmental opportunities. It means that in the battle against amnesia induced by colonialism's erasures, the deterritorialization and transplantation of peoples, and even natural disasters, the Caribbean writer often seeks nature as an ally. For this reason, writers have often articulated a poetic relation with land that is consistent with the highest aims of sustainability, although not always couched in the language of environmentalism. Glissant explains:

> The relationship with the land, one that is even more threatened because the community is alienated from that land, becomes so fundamental in this discourse that landscape in the work stops being merely decorative or supportive and emerges as a full character. Describing the landscape is not enough. The individual, the community, the land are inextricable in the process of creating history. Landscape is a character in this process. Its deepest meanings need to be understood. (*Caribbean Discourse* 105–6)

Thus, poetic imagination in the Caribbean is simultaneously oriented toward the racial and biotic history of displacement, even though the latter has not received due attention.

If it is true that the current global environmental crisis is in part due to human alienation from nature and inattention to history, as many have argued, Caribbean literature has a vital contribution to make. Following the lead of ecocritic Lawrence Buell, we position Caribbean texts as "environmentally oriented work[s]" in that they demonstrate that "the nonhuman environment is present not merely as a framing device but as a presence that begins to suggest that human history is implicated in natural history" (*Environmental Imagination* 7–8). However, like most ecocritics, Buell bases his study on U.S. landscapes and has not considered the more tumultuous aspects of (island) colonization. If we reposition Buell's definition of the environmental imagination in the Caribbean context, we might very well ask if the transplantation of sugarcane and the millions of slaves across the Atlantic to cultivate this crop could be called "natural," even if cane, breadfruit, coffee, nutmeg, ackee, mango, and countless other staple crops of the region have become deeply *naturalized*. Unlike the white settler production of nature writing, Caribbean writers refuse to depict the natural world in terms that erase the relationship between landscape and power. Foregrounding the discourse of power assures an interrogation of the ways in which the multiple ethnicities of the Caribbean have constituted the local environment, just as the history of enslaved and indentured women's labor helps to expose the Northern conceit of conflating women's bodies with passive nature. Ultimately, the complex diasporas of plants and peoples in the Caribbean, and these writers in particular, problematize the notion of natural history and its segregation from human agency.

Unlike the masculine Anglo-American insistence that alienation from nature is caused by excessive mobility and transience, here we see that there are various causes for alienation from nature that differ according to the historical conditions of peoples in the wake of the violence of Western expansion. As recent work in environmental justice demonstrates, answers to ecological problems are possible only through a close examination of such specificities.[2] Postcolonial literature has given more attention to this problem than has U.S. nature writing; placelessness in the former tends to be seen more as a particular political problem rather than as a universalized moral one, as in the latter. Wendell Berry, one of the foremost voices of environmentalism in the United States, believes, for example, that for the modern American, "geography is artificial; he could be anywhere, and he usually is" (53). While this may be true of many white male Americans, it is certainly a harder argument to make for immigrants, women, and/or people of color. As Melvin Dixon has argued, slavery's legacies of geographical containment have necessitated an interest among African American writers in preserving and/or reinventing the self against the delimiting forces of history and oppression. Consequently, geography does not remain fixed outside of time and language as it might in white settler narratives; rather, "verbal invention [turns] figures of the landscape into settings for the performance of identity" (6).

، Although ecocriticism overlaps with postcolonialism in assuming that deep explorations of place are vital strategies to recover autonomy; postcolonial criticism has given little attention to environmental factors. On the other hand, ecocriticism's opposite tendency to understate the social and historical specificities of place has been tempered by postcolonial and environmental justice studies. By bringing these fields together in the context of Caribbean literatures, we hope to reflect a postcolonial investment in what Fiona Barnes calls "the cultural and political ramifications of geography, the so-called sense of place" and a sustained ecocritical focus on the ways in which race, gender, and other social vectors help constitute environmental experience (150).

Natural Histories

The yoking together of the terms "natural" and "history" would seem to suggest a common recognition of the ways in which the nonhuman world has manifested change over time. But more often than not this phrase is generally understood as the narrative practice of humans, particularly Europeans, in their empirical observations of biotic phenomena—what Michel Foucault calls "the transference of a rationality formed elsewhere" (*Order of Things* 130). The colonization of the New World tropics, as Richard Grove has pointed out, has been integral to the European rendering of the taxonomy of flora and fauna and has provided the epistemological "roots" of discourse and legislation on environmental conservation. To foreground the ways in which colonialism has radically altered and transplanted the Caribbean environment is to call attention to how natural histories are deeply embedded in the world historical process, to highlight the organicist assumptions of what might be deemed "natural," and to underscore the difficulties posed to European and Caribbean writers alike in rendering a history of the environment.

Despite the intense scrutiny and narrative interpellation of tropical environments, these landscapes continue to be misunderstood for reasons that can be traced to the early Caribbean colonists. European travelers had already discursively fashioned Asia through the classical lens of Herodotus, so it was hardly surprising that voyagers to the Caribbean incorporated this "popular vocabulary for constituting 'otherness.'" (Hulme 21).[3] Conflating texts of the broader Mediterranean with the startling difference of the New World, European reports rendered the landscape in a binary between the similarity to the writer's homeland and its radical differentness (Gerbi 6). The novelty of Caribbean flora and fauna caused a shift in European conceptions of human and nonhuman difference and raised questions about whether this newness could in fact be rendered as historical at all.[4]

From this tension arose an unprecedented interest in the science of natural history. Since Columbus's early journals, Europeans marveled at the "variety and newness" of the islands' flora and fauna, their "eternal greenness," the lack of deciduous trees, and the staggering absence, to European eyes, of a dormant winter season (Gerbi 48). This in turn led to hyperbolic misinterpretations of tropical fecundity. As early as 1494, armchair travelers proclaimed that one could plant any seed in Guadeloupe, "for the soil rejoices . . . and never reject(s) anything that you throw in it; it accepts nothing without giving it back much more abundantly and with great increase" (Nicolò Scillacio quoted in Gerbi 28–29). Gendering the soil as a receptive woman's body that "rejoices" at the insertion of male seed, the language of even the earliest colonists helped to naturalize what later would become the Caribbean plantocracy.

This myth of fertility confused plant diversity with an extraordinary yield for food, leading readers and many a current-day tourist to assume that one need not labor in tropical climates for sustenance. But when the Spanish forced indigenous laborers into the mines and disrupted their agricultural systems, countless died of starvation (Lowenthal 15). As David Lowenthal has argued, the West Indies with "their infertile, dry, or poorly

drained soils, precipitous slopes, and long history of soil erosion and depletion contrast sharply with the stereotype of lush tropical gardens that will
bear fruit if one just pokes a stick in the ground" (15). In reality, the
islands' formation and climate diversity have produced many soils that
"are notably deficient in nutrients" (Watts 36).

While debates about the social and religious practices of native Caribbean peoples prevailed,[5] sustained documentation of the flora and fauna
didn't appear until Gonzalo Fernández de Oviedo y Valdés's encyclopedic
Historia general y natural de las Indias in 1535. Well before Enlightenment taxonomies of nature, Oviedo prided himself on his experience in
the field in collecting ethnographic and botanical information (Gerbi 225).
Here the relationship between ethnography, natural observation, and narrative production was forged and was deeply entangled with notions of
spatial difference and colonial violence. The flora, fauna, and humans
that were captured and transported lifeless to European metropoles for
analysis, documentation, and display attest to the epistemic violence of
the production of "natural" knowledge. Janet Browne has shown that the
new histories of nature drew their language from the discourse of empire
and increasingly from incipient nation-building, inscribing biotic "colonists" and natural "kingdoms" (32–57). With the systemization of natural
history in the eighteenth century, particularly Linnaeus's standardization of
plant nomenclature, a new science emerged that contributed to the erasure
of indigenous knowledges while erecting a hierarchy of racial "species"
and gendered difference.[6]

Scholars have documented a shift from the utopian representation of
tropical nature to concerns about its generation of hypersexuality, disease, and moral decay in the eighteenth century.[7] However, they have not
linked this to a possible social catalyst: the increased transplantation of
Africans to the American neotropics. We suggest that these social and
environmental changes are an important, if overlooked, factor in discourse
of the Caribbean. During the height of plantation slavery, Europeans
began to separate "culture" from its epistemological root, "cultivation,"
and attribute degeneracy to those involved in tropical agriculture. Reinvigorating classical texts, Montesquieu and travel writer Alexander von
Humboldt argued that the soil fertility of the tropics "retards the progress
of nations towards civilization" and degenerates "intellectual faculties"
(Humboldt quoted in Stepan 42). Even as Humboldt drew from Caribbean
nature to construct "nations of plants" (see Browne 32) and to theorize
"a new kind of planetary consciousness" (Pratt 120), these were already
deeply entangled in colonial hierarchies.

Thus a legacy continues in the split between the *natural*—often rendered as unmediated tropical flora and fauna outside the all-too-human hand of plantation agriculture—and an anthropocentric *history* that would focus exclusively upon the social layering of settlement in the colonial context. Perhaps this is why the first European novel written in the Caribbean, Fernández de Oviedo's chivalric romance *Claribalte* (1514–15),[8] does not draw from the local landscape. Although he completely obscured the tropical and colonial spaces from which European naturalists drew their specimens, Foucault determined that their genre depends on "a history restored to the irruptive violence of time," as well as "the common affinity of things and language with representation" (*Order of Things* 132).

Drawing upon Glissant, we argue that it is only by foregrounding the New World's "*irruption into modernity*" (*Caribbean Discourse* 146) that we might integrate the polarization between the social and natural, as well as the temporal and the spatial. This framework is vital to understanding one of the region's first colonial epics, James Grainger's "The Sugar Cane: A Poem, In Four Books" (1764). As an amateur historian and physician, Grainger attempted to reconcile the irreconcilable: the natural flora of the Caribbean with the racial hierarchies of the plantation. His georgic ode to that "Supreme of plants" (1:22–23), the sugarcane, is a dual and conflicted text: copious footnotes on the islands' natural history anchor and often overwhelm idyllic lines of verse. Grainger adopts Linnaean classifications of flora and fauna, records local botanical history, ethnographic observations of African religious and social practices, medicinal use of plants for venereal and other diseases, advice for the treatment of slaves, the usefulness of slave provision grounds, and the problem of insects and disease that affect the harvest. Inviting spectatorship of "cultured soil" that "charms the eye" (3:538, 539), and devoting extraordinary detail to "imperial cane," Grainger's abolitionist contemporaries were horrified by the contradiction of celebrating "the beauty of the island" by suppressing "the miseries of the slaves" (Anonymous 327). Kamau Brathwaite rightly observes that "when Grainger contemplates "Nature," the specificity of the Caribbean "disappears" (*Roots* 140); the "tyranny of the model" of georgic idyll prevents a local engagement with the Caribbean environment as well as a meaningful representation of its people (141). Yet the text's failure is instructive; the irruptive history of Caribbean colonization disrupts facile natural metaphors.

The difficulty in reconciling the natural aesthetics of a landscape that has been so dramatically altered with the violence of colonial history has proven a continuing paradox for Caribbean writers. For instance, in the

French-Caribbean literary tradition, the first black writers perpetuated the European romanticization of the landscape.[9] The rise of Marxist frameworks of interpretation for the histories suppressed by colonialism, and a body of literature that formed around the plantation and social realist novel understandably had far more investment in reclaiming a historical Caribbean subject than engaging with the natural environment. Wilson Harris has sustained the most vocal critique of the ways in which the adoption of a realist history for the Caribbean novel has prevented an engagement with the "numinosity" of the landscape, in which one might find "the legacies of the past in the present" (*Selected Essays* 207). In response to Grainger's epic, Derek Walcott laments, "no historical collection acknowledges the fact that the beauty of the Caribbean islands could have helped the slave survive," and suggests "there was some separate benediction in the stupendous dawns and sunsets that had nothing to do with the boring evil of their servitude" ("Frowsty Fragrance" 61). Cane, in the words of Sam Selvon, "is bitter," but there is more to the Caribbean environment than the plantation complex.

In an effort to decolonize Caribbean historiography, the revitalization of folk culture, including religious practices, has provided a regenerative framework for both human and natural histories in the Caribbean. For instance, Aimé Césaire has drawn extensively from botanical history to inscribe African and Arawakan "roots" on his "calabash of an island" (*Collected Poetry* 47), while Eric Roach's poetry explores the "glorious landscapes of the soul" (71) and positions rural plantation labor as a means to know "the spirit of the place" (80). Although this relationship to land has often been troubled by exile, Brathwaite's seminal work on "nation-language" specifically links the Caribbean "folk/metaphysical mind" to arboreal and other natural images derived from "African symbolism" and religion (*Roots* 221). Andrew Salkey observes of the peasant in Haiti: "The land . . . is his own way of claiming to have a history which includes past and present and insures the future" (35). More recent Caribbean writing has directly admonished those early naturalists, "the great plant appropriators" who "simply go out and take someone else's beauty for themselves" (Kincaid, *My Garden [Book]*: 102, 119), while others have produced "rewrites" of the botanists' journeys into the heart of (Caribbean) darkness.[10]

Over thirty years ago, Sylvia Wynter characterized the region's history by the ideological and geographical split between the plantation and the provision ground; this dichotomy remains "the distinguishing characteristic" of Caribbean narrative (99). Africans imported crops such as yam, ackee, gourds, and other staples into the Caribbean. By growing these items alongside indigenous cultigens, the slave provision grounds and their internal markets contributed a vibrant, alternative economy to the monoculture of the plantocracy.[11] This tension between the ideologemes of plantation capitalism and maintaining a space for Caribbean agency and sustenance encapsulates some of the major concerns of our contributors in this section. Although in other works he has drawn upon one of the productive outcomes of natural history, chaos theory, in "Sugar and the Environment in Cuba," Antonio Benítez-Rojo provides an overview of this island's complex botanical history, arguing that much of Cuba's cultural memory is embedded in its environment; thus violence done to the land becomes a simultaneous assault on human memory. Derek Walcott's "Isla Incognita," written in 1973 and published for the first time here, is an intimate portrait of the poet's struggle to represent the landscape without the alienated and taxonomic lens of colonial naturalists. The essay provides evidence that his critique of the "muse of history" that would be published the next year begins with the interaction of the writer with the natural world. In a similar vein, "Shaping the Environment: Sugar Plantation, or Life after Indentured Labor," writer Cyril Dabydeen explores the paradox of rebuilding Indian diaspora culture upon the ruins of the plantation system, revisiting the ecological triumphs and disappointments of postindependence Guyana. Imagining that sugar might fuel the writer's lifeblood, Dabydeen raises powerful questions about the recuperative qualities of the artistic imagination. Finally, Trenton Hickman's essay, "Coffee and Colonialism in Julia Alvarez's *A Cafecito Story,*" explores the plantation system in order to provide a trenchant reading of the neocolonial aegis of U.S.-initiated environmentalist movements in the Caribbean. Together these essays move beyond the plantation complex to suggest the indispensability of localized cultural responses to environmental history.

Myths of Origins

Inquiry into the natural history of a region inevitably leads to questions about origins, a topic that has fascinated both European and Caribbean writers alike. From colonial interpellations of tropical island Edens to the legends of El Dorado, the narrative teleology of conquest has produced a utopic counterpart that often positions itself outside of the Euclidean violence of the plantation system. The notion of Caribbean origins is tied to a long history of mythologizing nature in a region that Peter Hulme has succinctly described as a unique "discursive entity" (5). Hulme shows that in their reliance upon Mediterranean antiquity, European inscriptions assimilated the Caribbean into an already established discursive relation between isolated islands and inquiries into philosophical and natural origins.[12] Of course, an assumed one-to-one relationship between woman and land (and island) was one of the originary tropes of colonial Caribbean discourse. Centuries later, few of these ideologemes have disappeared; the gendering of Caribbean nature, as well as idealizing its utopian contours, continues to the present. For example, twentieth-century histories of the French Caribbean perpetuate the Edenic myth: "All in all we have a vision of enchanted shores and happy islands" (Antoine 352). Such idealizations have inspired many Caribbean authors to recapture a more "Adamic" and perhaps more originary claim to the significance of their landscapes in a way that destabilizes the colonial gaze; these gestures to a naturalized archaeology include revisions of colonial myths and the natural sciences.

To the first Europeans, biblical and classical texts of the broader Mediterranean were vital to formulating their understanding of the Caribbean's newness. One finds ample testimonies from Christopher Columbus, Amerigo Vespucci, and Fernández de Oviedo likening the Antilles to the Greek "Blessed Isles" and the earthly Paradise. Fernández de Oviedo also put forth an argument that the Caribbean islands were in fact the Hesperides, already known to the ancient Spaniards in their (spurious) Greco-Roman antiquity (Gerbi 271). Generally speaking, the greater the writer's classical and theological education, the deeper the connections that were wrought between the islands of the ancients, landscapes of the Bible, and the New World. From reports of mermaids, Amazons, giants, and anthropophagites, "creatures from the ancient myths invaded the newly discovered lands and seas" (Gerbi 21). This led to the reconfiguration of the region through classical and Christian toponyms such as the Virgin Islands, the Antilles, and Brazil.[13]

Hulme points out that the image of America as woman reflects an anxiety about the novelty of the New World that can be traced in "the relationship between European, native, and land" in which case the latter two are handily conflated in a naked and visually accessible woman's body (xii). As Carolyn Merchant has argued, this prelapsarian Eve would eventually fall once Europeans discovered the unruly wildness of the New World, but this would only further inspire the attempt to tame nature into a recovered Eden. Consequently, the colonial machine would produce a refurbished "Mother Eve," or nature as an "improved garden, a nurturing earth bearing fruit" ("Reinventing" 137). The search for an original state of nature outside of industrialized Europe (even while the Caribbean provided the labor and raw materials for this industrialization) hid the effects of environmental violence behind the guise of gendered metaphors of the feminized and maternal "womb" of Caribbean landscapes. As such, this produced a gendered division between the space/time of Europe and the feminized, "primitive" tropics that erased the historical depth of the New World and helped to perpetuate the myth of European innocence in the hemisphere.

Due to colonial and tourist views of the islands as ahistorical, passive, and idyllic landscapes, Caribbean writers have had to recover a sense of historicity. As early as the 1960s, Wilson Harris noted that "the theme of origins" was vital to West Indian writing and was being mediated through social and geological sciences (*Selected Essays* 140). Many writers have re-visioned a more "natural" and thus originary Caribbean archipelago by turning to biogeography. As Chris Bongie points out, "the topos of the island" lends itself to "the absolutely particular" on one hand and, on the other, "a fragment, a part of some greater whole from which it is in exile and to which it must be related" (18). To make regional claims to the broader archipelago and Americas, Brathwaite has asserted that the islands' "unity is submarine" (*Contradictory Omens* 64). In an attempt to desta-bilize the colonial balkanization that segregates the region into colonial language groups, these writers have turned to a precolonial and originary vision of the region's formation. In the words of Jean "Binta" Breeze, "under this ocean / we hold hands" (77).

Curiously, the biogeography of the Caribbean presents one of the more difficult challenges to questions of human and natural origins. In an effort to explain the simultaneous existence of apparently much of the same flora and fauna over large stretches of islands, scientists appeal to a com-bination of at least two theories. One, known as dispersal theory, argues that the islands were once connected to a common mainland by a land bridge and that subsequent continental drift and rising sea levels separated the islands. Biota were carried off on islands, like drifting rafts, separated from their island cousins. But vicariance theory argues that the islands were autonomously created by volcanic activities on the ocean floor. Given this Brathwaitian postulation of geographical autonomy with submarine unity, the only explanation for commonalities would be a series of com-plex biotic migrations facilitated by bird flight, by large pumice "rafts"— fragments created by volcanic activity—or by large masses of floating vegetation that spread biota from one island to another.[14] As such, these migration and settlement patterns have proven to be powerful metaphors of the shared experience of diaspora, settlement, and adaptation. Given the geological diversity of the Caribbean islands, these two paradigms are insufficient to explain Caribbean origins, just as cultural theory has been unable to settle on singular continental explanations for Caribbean roots and has instead turned to theories of fragmentation and grafting.

These theories may sound more like poetic imagination than science, and indeed Caribbean biogeographers readily admit that "it is plain beyond all argument that we all suffer under the burden of ignorance" (Ernest Williams 32). On the basis of the complexity and uncertainty of these theories, Benítez-Rojo, Glissant, Harris, Kincaid, and Walcott, among others, have defended the role of literature in forging an environmental imagination in the Caribbean and in prioritizing spatial/natural relations. They place land and seascapes within a temporally dynamic human story and insist that Caribbean literature must not be balkanized by its presumably insignificant size but must be addressed in its island, oceanic, and continental complexity.[15] Precisely because literature's rhetorical stance is one of imagined relations, it is well suited to the task of responding to History's presumed absence in the region.

This need for a poetic imagination capable of rising to the challenge of historiography's lacunae is also relevant to the search for precolonial human origins. While most of the indigenous people of the Caribbean were decimated, this has not precluded indigenous cultural survivals, nor has it discouraged writers, nationalist literatures, and scientists from excavating their originary presence. But like biogeography, archaeology is not able to give a simple answer about origins. The Caribbean islands have seen various waves of human immigration from about 5000 BCE; while Edenic colonial narratives might have placed these migrants in a state of unaltered nature, Richard Grove explains that "rapid and extensive transformations in the natural environment" occurred long before Europeans arrived (16). For example, indigenous peoples introduced agouti, dogs, guinea pigs, and opossum from the mainland; they also developed the first fishing economy in the region (Wing 140, 143; Watts 41–77). Significantly, the learning curve of island peoples may have of necessity been sharper than that of their mainland counterparts, since large-scale nomadic hunting and gathering were not possible and spacious expanses were not as likely to shield them from the immediate environmental effects of their economic activities. The limited space and natural resources of island geographies made them vital and primary registers of ecological change and helped to "heighten awareness of man as an environmental agent" (Grove 475–76). Both Brown and Grove have explained that the dynamism of these same islands allowed scientists to understand the threat of species extinction in the late eighteenth century.

The Caribbean's fossil records are not as scarce as Derek Walcott once claimed when he wrote that the Arawak "leaves not the lightest fern-trace / of his fossil to be cultured / by black rock" (*Collected Poems* 114), but archaeological and biogeographical science has been slow to establish a sufficient record (Perfit and Williams 73). If we are limited by an epistemology that cannot acknowledge its limitations, we are led to the perpetuation of myth; in this case, the myth that islands have no historical or temporal depth. This would belie the fact that as islands they bear witness to and participate in a history of migrations over land and sea, as Charles Darwin and Alfred Wallace first noted. Thus, rather than gardens emptied of history, islands are registers of a complex dynamic between the land and the sea, the indigenous and the immigrant, and the constant threat/anticipation of arrival.[16]

This leads to a kind of Glissantian poetics, close to what biogeographers call "retrodiction": "the use of the possibly distorted information about the present day as a means to extrapolate to the truth of the long past" (Perfit and Williams 73). Where the biogeographical and geological record is incomplete, all that is conclusive is that "biology and . . . geology must share common histories" even if we can't know their common story (Ernest Williams 14). The chief difference between this science and poetics, however, is the willingness to admit the unknowability of the past. To Glissant, a poetics imagines a whole that cannot be known, whereas science would seem to insist on knowing a whole that therefore need not be imagined. This rhetorical knowledge, we claim, functions as an effective countermyth to the virginal Eden of the European imagination because it is more self-conscious and self-critical. With important implications for ecocriticism, Glissant claims that human and natural history are the rightful territory of creative narrative: "Literature for us will not be divided into genres but will implicate all the perspectives of the human sciences" (*Caribbean Discourse* 65).

Literature is by no means the only way to establish a sense of place, but its rhetorical recovery of a *sense* of history, especially when historical memory is fragmented, can play a crucial role in establishing sustainable belonging in the land. According to Glissant, all cultural zones formerly organized by plantation systems have in common a preoccupation with cultural amnesia and the loss of origins. As a result of this loss, "[i]t is necessary to establish the legitimacy of the inhabitant in the land in anchoring him/her in a sense of permanence or of recovered time" (Degras and Magnier 15). As Walcott explains, nostalgia over a lost history, whether African, European, or any other, will lead us ultimately to a "rejection of the untamed landscape" ("Muse of History" 42), and will thus lead the Caribbean writer to lament and disparage the present and the immediate environment. The postcolonial subject must somehow acknowledge loss; a sense of place will have to come from sources more mythical and poetic than deep historical knowledge.

How have Caribbean writers negotiated these myths of origins? Shona N. Jackson's essay, "Subjection and Resistance in the Transformation of Guyana's Mytho-Colonial Landscape," warns that myths of origins stage the reprisal of colonial legacies unless they are sufficiently reimagined. She traces a disturbing nationalist revamping of the El Dorado myth in Guyana, in which Amerindian and women subjects are trapped in a neo-colonial fantasy of expansion and desire. The myth of Eden is no less relevant to contemporary Haiti, as explained in LeGrace Benson's essay, "A Long Bilingual Conversation Concerning Paradise Lost," or to the broader anglophone Caribbean, as detailed in Jana Evans Braziel's "'Caribbean Genesis.'" Benson situates Wilson Bigaud's 1951 *Paradis Terrestre,* reproduced on the cover of this volume, within the tradition of Haitian landscape painting. This Garden of Eden at the moment of the Fall already contains evidence of a dynamic and complex meeting of African and European cultures and thus leads us to reflect upon how this encounter impacted the environment and artistic expression alike. Braziel reminds us that like race, myth is an inherited structure of colonial discourse, and argues against the balkanization of humans and environment through a Glissantian "poetics of (eco)relation" that draws from multiple creative geneses. The writers addressed in these two essays articulate the value of a consistent return to the story of land and to a disavowal of human claims on it, so as to revise Old World myths of Caribbean origins. In George B. Handley's interview, "'The Argument of the Outboard Motor,'" Derek Walcott insists on praising the Edenic Caribbean while also acknowledging the dangers of using such nakedness for appropriation and consumption. Direct experience with nature can teach, shape, and hopefully amend the human story, and this is perhaps the reason why, to invoke Walcott's interview, "the argument of the outboard motor" is fallacious, or, as Shona Jackson ultimately insists, the El Dorado myth does not completely erode the land's own natural dynamism. Consequently, attention given to nature's narrative may serve to ameliorate the effects of Edenic longings through increased knowledge and understanding.

Hybridity and Creolization

Glissant has argued that "composite peoples . . . those who could not deny or mask their hybrid composition, nor sublimate it in the notion of a mythical pedigree, do not 'need' the idea of Genesis, because they do not need the myth of pure lineage" (*Caribbean Discourse* 141). The destabilization of atavistic origins inevitably provides a framework for discussing hybridity and creolization. Long before postcolonial studies popularized these two terms, Caribbean writers were theorizing the complex and often violent histories of interaction in the primarily bounded island spaces of the region. Since colonial sciences, based largely on the Caribbean context, had established a hierarchy of racialized species that encoded intermixture as evolutionary degeneracy, it would seem that hybridity would have to be one of the first ideological battlegrounds in the region. While there are notable differences between the terms transculturation, métissage and mestizaje, Créolité, and nation-language, they share an engagement in cultural practices—from language to epistemology—that help characterize the complex layering of Amerindian, European, African, Indian, East Asian, and Middle Eastern settlement over time.

As Robert Young details, the concept of hybridity was first utilized in European science of the natural (nonhuman) world. With the visible presence of racial mixture in the nineteenth-century West Indies, Europeans erected a science that argued for the degeneracy and ultimate infertility of the offspring of mixed-race sexual unions. As much as this science established a taxonomy of race, it also encoded normative heterosexual and gender relations. As Nancy Stepan has explained, the European male was catapulted to the top of the masculinist hierarchy, non-European men were feminized, and the bodies of women of color were interpellated as the site of reproductive response and responsibility. Carolyn Cooper has argued that the notion of black (women's) amorality or "slackness" has been key to the degradation of Creole languages. As such, race, gender, language, and cultural production are deeply intertwined. Although the natural world largely has been bracketed out of these discussions, the tropical environment, invoking sensuality and languor to Europeans, was key to the denigration of creolization, just as it has been vital to its redefinition.

Caribbean writers have redefined these colonial myths by destabilizing the discourse of colonial desire and excavating the continued indigenous and African presence in the region, but this process has tended to emphasize the human rather than the natural dimensions of creolization. Yet one needs only to consider Fernando Ortiz's 1940 thesis regarding transculturation to realize the interweaving of racial and environmental histories. His theory relied as much on racial differences as it did on the differences between the cultivation of tobacco and sugar, the latter an imported and hybridized staple crop of plantation slavery that came to be known as "Creole Cane." Alejo Carpentier's 1949 articulation of America's "marvelous reality" was based in large measure on the notion of a Caribbean environment with "incredible intertwining of plants and its obscene promiscuity of certain fruit" and the "magic of tropical vegetation" that surpassed Western expectations (85). His theory was no more easily separated from the environmental history of his homeland than it was from his tendency to sexualize the "virginity" of the landscape and to racialize the "Faustian presence of the Indian and the black man" (88).

Because ample scholarship has been produced on the multiple forms of creolization in the region,[17] here we'd like to pick up on a neglected point made by Glissant:

> Creolization as an idea is not primarily the glorification of the composite nature of a people: indeed, no people has been spared the cross-cultural process. The idea of creolization demonstrates that henceforth it is no longer valid to glorify "unique" origins that the race safeguards and prolongs . . . Creolization as an idea means the negation of creolization as a category, by giving priority to the notion of natural creolization. (*Caribbean Discourse* 140)

Glissant's use of the term "natural creolization" is useful for two reasons. First, it dismantles the colonial binary between the presumed purity of Europeans and their hybrid others, and second, it returns to the broader language of *naturalized* acculturation and, by extension, the nonhuman world.

To engage Glissant on these two points, we might start by emphasizing the *circuitous* pattern of what Alfred Crosby called the "Columbian exchange." To do so would invigorate an understanding of the process of creolization on both sides of the Atlantic and beyond and would draw attention to what Young (through Raymond Williams) explains as the rhizomatic chain between the Latin word *cultura* and its etymological offshoots: culture and colony and, by extension, land, soil, and cultivation (*Colonial Desire* 30–31). To examine European culture at its root symbolism—its cultural/cultivated crops—uncovers a history of colonial exchange and begs the question of "natural creolization." We destabilize the authenticity of national culture when we realize that its icons, such as the potato in Ireland, the tomatoes of Italy, and the sugar that sweetened the tea of England all either derive from the New World or were imported through colonial routes. Words and cultural objects from hurricane to cannibal to hammock and barbeque derive from indigenous Caribbean sources. The staple crops of the Caribbean—including sugarcane, coffee, and nutmeg—were all introduced through colonial trade networks or, in the case of the national fruit of Jamaica, the ackee, like the yam, across the Middle Passage.[18]

The colonial process involved a simultaneous uprooting of plants *and* peoples, reminding us that the etymological root of the word "diaspora" is "seed." Often the same ships contained flora and fauna as well as human beings for transplantation to colonial botanical gardens and sugar plantations across the Atlantic. In fact, the first ship of Bengali indentured laborers sent to Trinidad, the *Fortitude,* also brought nutmeg trees (Ragatz 76). In the Caribbean, the island landscape into which these laborers were acculturated was as routed in trade networks as the human arrivants. To quote from Jamaica Kincaid:

> What did the botanical life of Antigua consist of at the time . . . [Christopher Columbus] first saw it? To see a garden in Antigua now will not supply a clue. The bougainvillea . . . is native to tropical South America: the plumbago is from southern Africa; the croton is from Malaysia; the hibiscus from Asia and East Africa; the allamanda is from Brazil; the poinsettia is from Mexico; the bird of paradise is from southern Africa; the Bermuda lily is from Japan; the Flamboyant Tree is from Madagascar; the casuarina comes from Australia; the Norfolk Pine comes from Norfolk Island; the tamarind tree is from Africa and Asia. The mango is from Asia. The breadfruit is from [Tahiti]. (*My Garden [Book]:* 135)

The wake of plantation economies has necessitated daring natural adaptations of a wide variety of plants and animals. If diaspora constitutes much of the human experience in the Caribbean, it also constitutes the experience of plants and animals, a literal spreading of seeds, and the resultant adaptations that became necessary for survival.

This is not to unduly celebrate the process of "natural creolization," lest we forget that the horses, dogs, and disease introduced to the Caribbean by European carriers had devastating and violent consequences for Amerindian and African peoples, just as colonial contact increased rates of syphilis and malaria among Europeans (see Crosby). This exchange was hardly mutually beneficial or even equitable. But emphasizing the transatlantic circuits of creolization destabilizes a presumed European purity and stability. In the Caribbean context, the discourse of creolization not only has served to emphasize the inevitable fragmentation of racial memory in the region, but it has helped to conflate human and natural histories, a welcomed shift that warns against the pretension that human societies can act independently of ecosystems. For even while tropical landscapes represent the most diverse flora and fauna on the planet, their diversity is all the more threatened. In fact, more Caribbean faunal species have disappeared in the last century than in any other habitable environment on earth (Watts 40).

Hybridity and creolization have been central terms to the various formulations of Caribbean cultural theory but have not yet figured prominently in the environmental philosophies of recent decades.[19] Thus these essays engage with the hybridity of cultural and natural landscapes, proposing new directions for ecocritical theorization. For instance, Renée K. Gosson's interview with the Martinican novelist Raphaël Confiant compares the homogenizing transformation of the landscape of his island-department of France to a deeper-seated and less perceptible cultural standardization that strives to erase the possibilities of Créolité. Isabel Hoving's "Moving the Caribbean Landscape" explores the axes of gender, sexuality, and ethnic hybridity in Shani Mootoo's novel of incest, *Cereus Blooms at Night*. Arguing that an acceptance of the ambiguity of Caribbean nature is vital to reclaiming the island environment for postcolonial ecology, Hoving reads Mootoo's vivid landscapes as the key to a necessary revolution in human ontology. In "'Rosebud is my mama, stanfaste is my papa,'" Natasha Tinsley explores the creole landscapes and sexualities of Surinamese oral literature in order to insist on the inextricability of social and natural discourses. She provides a broad and startling picture of how the European colonial system upheld expectations of normative "nature" that sought to discipline not only unruly tropical landscapes but also transgressive social practices pertaining to sexuality, gender, and race. Finally, Lizabeth Paravisini-Gebert turns to African-based religious practices in "'He of the Trees,'" demonstrating the vital role they have played in forging an environmental imagination in the Caribbean that fosters community, sustainability, and local food production. She highlights how writers from Alejo Carpentier to Mayra Montero have imagined the relationship between Afro-Caribbean religion and nature and insists that historically—and most recently in the floods in Haiti—Caribbean nations have failed politically to realize this vision of environmental and social well-being. Collectively, these essays suggest inextricable links between the history of human and botanical transplantation, the region's cultural and social hybridity, and the fate of the landscape's biodiversity.

Aesthetics of the Earth

Although the geographies and social histories of the Caribbean are diverse, many of the writers discussed in this volume suggest that a shared aesthetic response to colonial violence sustains regional unity. As Edward Said suggests about postcolonial representation, "the land is recoverable at first only through the imagination" (225). Caribbean writers observe the need for deeper historical knowledge but recognize that the search often leads to discontinuity in the historical archive, an obstacle that archaeology or biogeography may never overcome. For example, the attempt to recover Africa in its original wholeness, for example, although alluring, has led to facile attempts to smooth over the inherent discontinuities of New World history; consequently the equation between greater historical knowledge and a deeper sense of place is perhaps untenable. The Créolistes explain, "afraid of this uncomfortable muddle, we tried in vain to anchor it in [the] mythical shores" of "mother Africa, mythical Africa, impossible Africa" (Bernabé, Chamoiseau, and Confiant 88, 82). They maintain that a "violent and paradoxical therapy, Negritude, replaced the illusion of Europe by an African illusion" (82). Historically, constructing a sense of place has taken many forms: from the Mediterranean topos imported by Europeans (re-visioned by writers such as Carpentier and Walcott),[20] to a return to African and East Indian cultural landscapes. Glissant refers to this as an alienating and "unfulfilled desire for the other country" that is only mitigated "when one rediscovers one's landscape" (*Caribbean Discourse* 234).

These writers suggest that one's cultural identity and sense of place are not to be pursued with a singular perspective. To use John Elder's ecological metaphor, fragmentation is not necessarily cause for lament since it can also represent a "composting, fermentive pattern . . . Only with the detritus of the past can soil be made to sustain the cycle of life into a new present" (30–31). In Wilson Harris's words, this means an engagement with "the native and phenomenal environment of the West Indies," which is characterized by a divide between "broken conceptions" of the pre-Columbian landscape and "misconceptions of the residue and meaning of conquest" (*Selected Essays* 140).

A sense of belonging in the Caribbean is conditioned by an always-incomplete knowledge of natural and human histories and therefore necessitates recreating a sense of place in the present. As Glissant explains, the Caribbean subject faces the rather paradoxical "obligation to remake oneself every time on the basis of a series of forgettings" ("Creolization"

273), since every step forward in forging a new identity and sense of place from the fragments created by New World experience means leaving behind an imagined whole. Consequently, all cultural and natural signs that are intended to communicate our sense of belonging to a place must be read backwards, metonymically reaching to a presumed wholeness of which the sign is simply a part.

Given the multiple ethnic settlements in the Caribbean, and the continuing pattern of diaspora and outmigration, how does a writer achieve a sense of place? Or in the bemused words of Phyllis Allfrey, "Living in sunless reaches under rain / How do the exiles from enchanted isles / tend and sustain their rich nostalgic blaze?" (1). Glissant's *Poetics of Relation* outlines a useful distinction between atavistic and composite cultures that suggests a way to find rootedness in the (literary) landscape without the concomitant problems of either ethnic nationalism or a devaluation of local place. Atavistic cultures, which reify ethnic genealogy and origins, claim a "faultless continuity" in the land by rejecting creolization (*Traité* 196). Land thus becomes "territory" (*Poetics* 45). Composite or creole cultures, on the other hand, have developed "a relationship with the natural surroundings" (145), a "defense" of Creole language, and a commitment to a "protection of the land." These components lead to "an ecological vision of Relation" (146). Consequently, a sense of place is established through a cross-cultural and synchronic aesthetic that is capable of imagining competing claims, lost histories, as well as a deep attachment to the natural environment in the present.

For composite cultures, belonging in the Caribbean landscape means engaging in historical reconstructions that may largely be an act of imagination or desire for a wholeness that is not achievable. This might reflect the tension between Caribbean subjects and the local landscape that undergirds narratives as diverse as Alejo Carpentier's *The Lost Steps,* Jean Rhys's *Wide Sargasso Sea,* George Lamming's *In the Castle of My Skin,* Maryse Condé's *Crossing the Mangrove,* and Jamaica Kincaid's *Annie John.* We become aware, then, not so much of the concrete historical density embedded in nature but of our own participation in creating a sense of place. That is why that wholeness often appears in *imaginative* literature; in representing the historical past of our landscapes, literature points to our desire for place. Derek Walcott expressed this redemptive value in his Nobel speech: "Break a vase, and the love that reassembles the fragments is stronger than the love which took its symmetry for granted when it was whole" ("Antilles" 69). Such has become the attitude of many Caribbean authors toward the natural world since recovery of its primordial wholeness and historical innocence is not feasible. They do not have to accept environmental degradation as inevitable, but precisely for that reason many writers refuse to argue from a position of invisibility or moral purity. Learning to read the evidence of where human and natural histories have joined together is perhaps the best and only hope. This allows the Caribbean imagination not only to find the roots of its nature but to establish grounds for cross-cultural relations.

An aesthetics of the earth, then, not only forges a sense of place that is open to competing and fragmented histories of the Caribbean but also gives incentive for environmental conservation. The naturalist Aldo Leopold argued in 1949 that the environment was threatened by commodification of land and of recreation and that a "conservation aesthetic" would help to stay the hand of capitalist consumption of nature. Nature, runs his argument, can be protected if we have increased powers of perception and rely less on technology to transform the environment. Similarly, Octavio Paz once claimed that the "aesthetic impoverishment" of the market's so-called progress directly threatens the well-being of the land precisely because the market knows no values and makes blind decisions regarding local ecologies (157). While the market "is highly efficient . . . it has no goal." The result is the "contamination of lakes, rivers, seas, valleys, forests and mountains." Like Wilson Harris, Paz argues that the aesthetic relation to land that poetry teaches "is the antidote to technology and the market" because it aids in "reminding us of certain buried realities, restoring them to life" and helps us to hold "contrary or divergent realities in relationship" (159, 158).

Glissant has joined in the attack against the "international standardization of consumption" by which local economies, cultures, and ecologies are sacrificed for the sake of neocolonial gain (*Poetics* 150). While he calls for a return to an "aesthetics of the earth," he specifically insists that such an aesthetics would necessarily begin with a "passion for the land where one lives" so as to resist this "affective standardization of peoples" and of nature (148). This market-driven force, so typical of tourism, would blindly convert all islands into a "mini Miami," to quote from Walcott's interview in this collection (150, 151). At the same time, however, this aesthetics must resist the reactionary and "obsolete mysticism" of much environmentalism, which yearns for the sacred root, or the "sectarian exclusiveness" of atavistic cultures (147). An aesthetics of the earth, for Glissant, does not stem from a simple appreciation of beauty, especially since so much of the environment of composite peoples has long since been ravaged by colonial violence. But it is precisely the seeming inappropriateness of aesthetics in the context of waste and rupture that can enable a regenerative response. By reorienting a people to a "love of the earth— so ridiculously inadequate or else frequently the basis for sectarian intolerance," Glissant hopes that Caribbean literature can teach the political force of ecology (151); that is, that literature can recapture ecology's radical articulation of "the relational interdependence of all lands, of the whole Earth" (147). In this sense, aesthetics becomes a source of healthy "disruption and intrusion" into discourses of sacred claims to legitimacy and into the market itself.

While Caribbean landscapes can hardly be said to be untouched by human hands, learning an aesthetic appreciation of nature's otherness may help to preserve local particulars and resist the seduction of what Wilson Harris calls the "progressive realism" of First World teleology and technological power (*Radical Imagination* 73). The region's chief environmental problems at present stem from the aesthetic impoverishment of these neocolonial forces that first began, according to Harris, with Cortez. Colonialism's disregard for nature's otherness "has consistently broken [the life of the imagination] by making passive creatures of the very earth on which we move, by making the animals subject to our rages and our lusts and our greeds" (79). That we continue to believe that "mechanical adjustments" alone will solve the problem of ecological degradation is evidence of how profoundly the contributions of literature have been ignored.

Today IMF and World Bank–defined development means that ecological conservation plays second fiddle to immediate economic benefits. As Stephanie Black's film *Life and Debt* documents, transnational corporations, like the plantation economies before them, continue to exploit Caribbean agriculture and labor in the interests of Northern capital. Population pressures, exacerbated by limited geographical space, have led to struggles with waste removal and sewage treatment.[21] Many Caribbean nations are dependent on food imports, despite the rich agricultural promise the islands once held. Martinique, a country that formerly had a thriving system of provision grounds, imports over 98 percent of its food supply. In the interview included in this volume, Raphaël Confiant explains that the transformation of the Martinican landscape into shopping malls represents another chapter in the continuum of colonial occupation of his island. Glissant too has denounced the destruction of the agricultural economy of Martinique and its replacement by welfare-dependent consumerism.

The culture of tourism has become crucial to the economies of most of the islands. Most Caribbean states are forced to maintain tourist and service sectors that are remarkably like exploitative plantation economies. Kamala Kempadoo points out that by 1996 "formal tourism employment" (exempting a vast informal network) represented over 25 percent of the Caribbean region and was one of fastest growing sectors (20). Alarmingly, between 70 and 90 percent of foreign capital earned in tourist industry is not invested in the Caribbean itself but is extracted through foreign goods and services (21). Like the plantation system, the tourist industry does little to sustain the local economy while fattening the coffers of industrialized Northern states and multinational corporations. Mimi Sheller explains, "following in the footsteps of the explorers, the planters, and the armed forces, the tropical 'holiday in the sun' became a safe new means of consuming the Caribbean environment" ("Natural Hedonism").

Tourism initiated this "second-invasion of land-snatchers" (Pattullo 178), but instead of clearing land for monocrop production, this international market force is clearing coastlines, destroying coral reefs, creating waste and water pollution, and ruining mangrove swamps and other wetland areas. Despite the tourist's presumed love of nature, the fact remains that mountains, rivers, cities, and historical sites do not hold the appeal of denuded paradises of white sand. The irony is that "what the tourist came to enjoy no longer exists in its pristine condition" simply because environmental concerns are consistently overlooked by Caribbean governments in the interest of obtaining the tourist dollar (Pattullo 179).

Caribbean writers have not always succeeded in having a voice in such matters. For instance, Hilton Corporation built the Jalousie Resort and Spa between the famous Piton peaks in St. Lucia in the early 1990s despite protests from the likes of Derek Walcott. Instead of turning it into a national park, the government allowed the land to be sold to Hilton where now only guests of this very exclusive spa—typically foreigners visiting the Caribbean—are allowed entrance. This occurred despite the fact that an environmental impact study recommended against the construction of the spa. Tragically, archaeological artifacts were destroyed in the construction.[22] Walcott vehemently protested the building of the spa, which earned him criticism from many of the local working class who viewed the development as a much-needed economic opportunity. He and the others who joined him to form the St. Lucia Environmental Awareness Council were cast as "Johnnie-come-latelies," outsiders who merely wanted the mountains for their own privileged pleasure.

This reaction against one of St. Lucia's most celebrated native sons demonstrates that without a strong tradition of local consumption, many of the otherwise noticeable effects of misguided environmental policies go unnoticed on small islands because the hegemonic forces of tourism and neocolonialism have been adopted on the local level. It is this "passive consumption" and "non-critical adoption" that Aarón Ramos has in mind when he writes of the "deep-seated tension" between "contradictory inclinations" in islands such as Martinique, caught between "the preservation of social and economic gains, and the consolidation of the cultural community" (xvii). While transnational corporations develop land for economic profit without regard for long-term ecological health, some argue that there is an overall "deep-rooted indifference to the environment" in the Caribbean. This stems from the "culture of plantation management, which continues to prevent the majority from owning land in the countryside, [and which] has alienated people from environmental issues" (Beckles 193). Local Caribbean governments often lack sufficient expertise to adequately regulate environmental behavior, and local educational initiatives on behalf of environmental issues have been rare (Pattullo 181).

That is not to say that there have been no green successes in the Caribbean. One needs only to consider the recent cease-fire of naval bombing on the island of Vieques in Puerto Rico, for example, or the still-experimental development of ecotourism in the region. But in the face of continued environmental and cultural exploitation, more change is needed. To this end, Caribbean writers have consistently offered aesthetic representations of natural and human history that have insisted upon greater political change. The authors discussed in this final section offer distinct visions of the nature of such aesthetics and their relevance to ecological degradation.

Helen Tiffin's exploration of the vexed relationship between cultural belonging and place in "'Man Fitting the Landscape:' Nature, Culture, and Colonialism" explores how, through writing, Jamaica Kincaid and V. S. Naipaul dis-alienate themselves from their local and colonial topoi, achieving a "re-cognition" of literary landscapes inherited through the British canon. In "Flashbacks of an Orchid," Heidi Bojsen demonstrates how Patrick Chamoiseau's *Biblique des derniers gestes* similarly critiques the nineteenth-century French Romantic ideas of nature and nation in order to challenge their applicability to the creolized history and ecology of Martinique, especially in nationalist narratives lobbying for independence. Ineke Phaf-Rheinberger's "Landscapes, Narratives, and Tropical Nature: Creole Modernity in Suriname" traces the conflict between the Amazonian interior and Creole modernity as it emerged in the visual arts and how contemporary novelists—Cynthia McLeod, Clark Accord, and Astrid Roemer—revisit these colonial appropriations of the tropics. Her readings demonstrate that the crisis of Creole modernity is essentially a persistent and unresolved ambivalence in the contemporary Surinamese metropolis toward nature, specifically the wildness of the tropical interior.

In "The Uses of Landscape," Eric Prieto demonstrates how post-Négritude writers from Martinique have used aesthetics to justify increasing engagement with "real-world" environmental problems. Using the "Manifesto for a Global Project" as an example of this activism, Prieto claims that ecocriticism would be wise to follow this model in exploring the interrelation between theoretical ideals and environmental realities. Finally, in "From Living Nature to Borderless Culture," Hena Maes-Jelinek explores the ways in which Wilson Harris's formative expeditions into the Guyanese interior catalyzed an ecological imagination that ranges from the deep history of geology to the frenetic energy of quantum physics. Covering the span from his earliest novels to *The Dark Jester,* her essay elucidates the ways in which Harris recovers the depths of Caribbean history and charts a path for the future through the living presence of dynamic inner and outer landscapes. Aesthetics, then, emerges in these essays as a vital strategy for resisting the predictions of colonial environmental discourse and resituating the perceiver within the particulars of the immediate environment. This in turn opens the possibility of understanding the relation between one's place and the larger shared history of the Caribbean region.

Caribbean Literature, Ecocriticism, and the Environment

Despite the history of ecological imperialism, the vital role the Caribbean islands played in the evolution of modern environmentalism, and a rich literary inscription of local landscapes, ecological concerns seem surprisingly absent in Caribbean criticism. Perhaps one reason for this inattention is the perception that environmentalism is chiefly a politics that protects urban social privilege, particularly within the United States. Many U.S. ecocritics have acknowledged this possibility and have urged a broadening of ecocritical inquiry but have not always recognized the "implicit imperialism in this globalizing move" (O'Brien paragraph 3).

The discourse of the "American Adam," which was so critical to the initial identification and critique of U.S. exceptionalism, and even its more recent rejection in the so-called "New American Studies," have largely ignored the Caribbean and Latin America, or have only touched upon authors in exile or of immigrant extraction within the United States. Ecocriticism arose from questions first raised by the work of Leo Marx, R. W. B. Lewis, Henry Nash Smith, and others about the environmental imagination of empire's westward expansion in the United States. That the Caribbean has been bypassed is even more disconcerting considering that the roots of the current environmental crisis can be found in the age of conquest that begins in the region. Others have, of course, since revised their visions of America's ecology, especially within the environmental justice movement, but they have scarcely left the geopolitical boundaries of the United States to gain a more comparative understanding, despite lip service to the expanding borders of "American" studies. Ironically, a field that upholds the environment as the predominant spatial focus of analysis has quite rigidly adhered to that which is most inimical to ecology itself: a bounded national frame.

This has led to the tendency to uphold white, masculine settlers as normative subjects and to erase Native American, African American, Asian American, and Hispanic historical presence in the New World. This is especially apparent when one considers that love of nature, or defense against its destruction, has been articulated from the point of view of settlers who offer themselves as sole representatives of culture and history, while Amerindians and other racialized subjects are relegated to ahistorical beings whose political claims upon the land are rendered invisible by their very "naturalness." Unfortunately, the global claims of environmentalism have provided an all too easy justification for white privileged subjects to elide the complex issues of historical and social inequity. For instance, in his introduction to *The Green Studies Reader,* Laurence Coupe claims that "class, race and gender are important dimensions" of environmentalism, but "the survival of the biosphere must surely rank as even more important, since without it there are no issues worth addressing" (5). With this homogenizing sleight of hand, discourses that claim protection of nature come at the cost of ignoring histories of social stratification; since threats to ecology cannot be separated from their social causes, such dichotomous views prove ineffective in the face of such concomitant problems. As T. V. Reed notes, "pretending to isolate the environment from its necessary interrelations with society and culture has severely limited the appeal of environmentalist thought, to the detriment of both the natural and social worlds" (146).

While we are cautious, as U.S.-based editors of this volume, about the risks of "grafting" ecocriticism onto a Caribbean context, we believe that there are benefits from bringing the two fields into dialogue. Even though the social issues we have highlighted are elided in much ecocriticism, it would not be accurate to say that critics of Caribbean literature have generally ignored environmental concerns due to a conscious rejection of ecocriticism's limitations. There is no reason to believe that Caribbean critics are any less vulnerable to the effects of modern alienation from nature; nature is often not "seen" simply because of a lack of ecological awareness. We hope this volume gives ecocritics a deeper appreciation for the voices of Caribbean literature and critics of the Caribbean incentive to pay more attention to environmental sustainability. We anticipate that these generalizations about both groups will eventually prove inaccurate. With the authors of this volume, we suggest that literature can play a vital role in reshaping human attitudes toward the natural world and that the natural world bears the marks of the best and worst of human behavior. We share Jack Corzani's belief that there is "a place for literature in a world where people are hungry and where the beaches, coconut trees and armchairs are reserved for the tourists" and that sometimes "poetic action can have a greater effect than practical and immediate action" (1–2).

Environmentalism's highest hope is manifest in its reorientation of human ethics toward what Aldo Leopold once called a "land ethic" that considers the well-being of all biota, including humans. Such an ethic involves a shift in our cultural imagination, "a reinhabitory commitment," writes Lawrence Buell, that "entails extension of moral and sometimes even legal standing to the nonhuman world" (*Writing* 170). Literature is crucial to guiding us in this process of "reinhabitation" since it shapes our imaginative responses to pain, loss, and suffering of human and nonhuman life and potentially leads us "toward alternative futures" (2). To this end, Wilson Harris calls for writers to "deepen our perception of the fauna and flora of a landscape of time which indicate the kind of room or space . . . in which whole societies conscripted themselves" ("Composition" 48). In so doing, however, Caribbean representations of nature will never be without risk. A poetics that imagines what Buell has named the "environmental unconscious" may serve to rekindle our environmental awareness that has been lost since the advent of industrialization, urbanization, and the cash economy (*Environmental* 22), but it may also simultaneously serve to reflect the prisonhouse of colonialism. But perhaps the Caribbean's colonial legacies enable writers to perceive more clearly their own limitations so that nature's dynamism becomes more apparent. In this way, history and human possibility both remain open. It is the role of ecocriticism, and the aim of this volume, to identify this dynamism at work in literature so that the biogeographical realities that underlie Caribbean cultural discourse can be acknowledged and thus help to mitigate against environmental indifference.

To this end, we conclude the volume with the region's foremost philosopher and writer of the complex entanglement between conquest, literary representation, and ecological sustainability. In his epilogue, Wilson Harris asks us to "visualize the ever-changing mobility of the earth, a mobility, a vulnerability, a curious infirmity . . . that is born of land and water and fire and cloud through which we may create doors or windows." By building architectures of a spatial imagination, "the life of the earth" might be "seen *in fiction* as sensitively woven into the characters that move upon it, whose history . . . reflects a profound relationship to the earth." This allows us to "speak of a humanity whose feet are made of mud or land or water or any other element to attune us to our being on an earth that moves as we move upon it." In his engagement with chaos and quantum theory, Harris's "Theatre of the Arts" builds a cross-disciplinary bridge between contemporary natural sciences, histories of conquest, and our ecological futures, envisioning new directions for Caribbean literature and the environment.

Notes

Unless otherwise noted, all translations into English are by the authors.

1. There are obvious gaps in the geographies covered in this collection that reflect an uneven response to our call for papers rather than a lack of scholarship about particular parts of the region.

2. See Adamson, Evans, and Stein's *The Environmental Justice Reader,* which moves beyond the "wilderness-based, white-authored nature writing, and advocates a more inclusive, class- and race-conscious ecocriticism that articulates the complex human relationships to environment expressed in culturally diverse literature" (9).

3. See also Gerbi 125–26; and O'Gorman.

4. See Arnold 9–38; Gerbi 258–59; and O'Gorman 29–34.

5. For example, Bartolomé de las Casas's *Historia de las Indias* is almost exclusively concerned with ethnography rather than natural history.

6. See Schiebinger; Stepan, *The Idea of Race in Science*; and Young.

7. See Stepan, *Picturing Tropical Nature* 48.

8. See Gerbi 202–5.

9. See Corzani.

10. This is a play on Mayra Montero's *Tu, la oscuridad* (*The Palm of Darkness*), a revision of Conrad's famous tale with a Haitian setting. See also Dabydeen's *Dark Swirl*.

11. In addition to being a stepping stone toward liberation, the slave gardens were also a powerful site of creolization. Slaves grew "a staggering array of crops" that included cashews, bananas, calabashes, calalu, okra, oranges, and other fruits and spices (Berlin and Morgan 9). See also Parry; and Tomich.

12. See also Loxley; Bongie; and DeLoughrey, "The Litany of Islands."

13. For a discussion of the classical refashioning of the Caribbean, see O'Gorman; Gerbi; and Hulme.

14. On the theory of pumice rafts, see Perfit and Williams 60.

15. See Philip on the shift from island to "I-land"; and DeLoughrey, "Tidalectics," on the role of the sea in the regional literary imagination.

16. See DeLoughrey, "Litany of Islands."

17. In addition to Brathwaite; Glissant; and Ortiz, see Shepherd and Richards, eds., *Questioning Creole*.

18. On the indigenous Caribbean, see Hulme. On botanical transplantation, see Crosby's works as well as the collection by Viola and Margolis, eds., *Seeds of Change*.

19. In *Roman marron,* Richard D. E. Burton identifies a botanical shift in the different natural metaphors used to express French West Indian identity and culture. He traces an evolution in Martinique's three main identity movements (Négritude, Antillanité and Créolité) from the single tree rooted in the landscape of Négritude, to the tangled paradigm of the rhizome and mangrove swamp, which—according to Glissant and the Créolistes—more accurately symbolizes the complexity of Creole identity.

20. See Dash's chapter, "A New World Mediterranean," in *The Other America* on Carpentier and Walcott's *Omeros*.

21. Barbados and Haiti, for example, are the two most densely populated nations in the Americas (Arthur 152).

22. "Hands Off Piton; Walcott Threatens to Get Physical."

PART 1

Natural Histories

Sugar and the Environment in Cuba

Antonio Benítez-Rojo

Translated by James Maraniss

I IMAGINE CUBA passing rapidly through the geological ages . . . Jurassic . . . Oligocene . . . Miocene . . . The land rises and sinks as though the universe's time were shuffling it . . . Pliocene, eleven million years. A tectonic cataclysm sculpts the Sierra Maestra . . . Pleistocene, only a million years. The ebb and flow of the waters is cutting out, more and more precisely, the Cuban archipelago; little by little the unmistakable lizard shape of the main island stands revealed. Peninsulas, gulfs, bays, cordilleras. and adjacent keys now come out to be recognized in spite of their primeval state. Now huge birds of prey are seen. They land atop the royal palms (*Roystomea regia*), the ceiba trees (*Ceiba pentandra*), the pines (*Pinus tropicalis*), and soon they change into fossils (Marrero 1:29–37). I'm still in the Creation's Fifth Day.

My look slows down to take in all of Eden's landscape: Cuba before Good and Evil. It is a magnificently pristine land: imposing forests of mahogany, ebony, cedar, *magagua,* quebracho, *acana, granadillo, guayacán, dagame;* plains colored with fruits, flowers, butterflies. In the foothills of the Sierra de los Órganos, I see some bearded monkeys with long tails; they're hunting refuge in a stand of trees. We're dealing here with *Paralouatta varonai,* whose existence none knew about until recently (MacPhee 4–6). If we except the alligators, Cuba's fauna hardly could be more pacific; it's more decorative than anything else. I have looked with a naturalist's curiosity at the motionless iguana, at the elephantine manatee, at the *pájaro mosca* (*Mellisuga helenae*), at the tropical seal (*Monachus tropicalis*), at the parakeet (*Aratinga euops*), the parrot (*Amazona leucocephala*), the macaw (*Ara tricolor*), all of them now endangered or extinct (Silva Lee 19–148).

I undertake a quick tour of the other Edenic islands. Of all the Antilles, Cuba is not just the oldest, it is the freshest, too, the shadiest, most irrigated, most varied in its landscapes; its ecology the most complex. I come back instilled with a remote nationalism. (In seventy centuries I'll be born in Havana, yet an impossible point in the island's wet green wilderness.) Of the megafauna in the Pleistocene, one of the last birds that's going to

disappear is the giant owl (*Ornimegalonyx oteroi*). Too voluminous to
fly, it chases a hutia (*Capromys*) with huge strides, captures it with one peck
and ducks into a cave to feed its young (MacPhee 11–13). Its skeleton—in
particular the strong thigh bones—astonishes the Ancient Ones, naked
and broad-faced, who had come from the south and west around 4000
BC. With their repeated migrations to the Cuban archipelago, the names
they will receive are various: Guanahatabeyes, Aguanabeyes, Ciboneyes-
Guayabo Blanco, and Ciboneyes-Cabo Redondo (Dacal Moure and Rivero de la Calle). None of them knows how to grow things. They go from
here to there, hugging the coast, dwelling in caves and leaving abstract
pictographs and conch tumuli, fish spines and crab and tortoise shells.
For thousands of years their craftsmanship would be limited to bone and
stone; they barely will discover pottery. Beside their dead, some of them
would place modest utensils and ornaments; also minutely worked quartz
balls, perhaps the price of a calm voyage to the other world. Their diffuse
confederacy of gatherers, hunters, and fishermen will hardly leave a trace
in the natural world, although it will indeed exterminate the ground sloth
(*Megalocnus rodens*), a 450-pound mountain of vegetation-eating meek-
ness (Marrero 1:35).

Around 1250 AD, some others come to settle. Their canoes are longer,
sturdier than those their predecessors used. They come in from the east,
from the isle they call *Haití*. Their great epic has not yet been written. It
begins thousands of years earlier on the Andes' eastern slopes; it ends
abruptly in Cuba, not finishing the conquest of the Ancient Ones or the
island's total occupation. It was up to the white man to apply the word
"ending." During the legendary odyssey, they would learn to cultivate
yucca and sweet potato, to domesticate the dog, to spin cotton, to smoke
tobacco, and to bake pottery. I think for an instant about their ragged
route through the rivers of Amazonia. All of a sudden the discovery of
the Orinoco, the Father of Waters, then the travel by canoe across the
Guianese forests, the delta's aquatic labyrinth, the decision to take to
the sea, the first island, the second, the third . . . and finally, around 1250, the
Cuban archipelago, and there they will repeat the roofs of the *bohíos,*
the dances of the *arieto,* the *batey* for their ceremonies and their ball
games. Columbus will call them *taínos,* "good" or "noble" in the Arawak
dialect that they spoke (Rouse).

The Taino Machine

There's no doubt that these new inhabitants modified the nearly virginal
natural world that they found in Cuba. This is so much the case that we

can speak of a Taino machine, an adaptation of the Amazonian model used by their ancestors. It functioned on human energy, and its production, hardly diversified, centered on the transformation of bitter yucca (*Manihot utilissima*), a poisonous tuber, into a principal food source. A patch of vegetation burnt to ashes—so began the planting stage in symmetrical mounds of earth, a technique that would contribute to the greatest yields in the yucca plantations. After between twelve and eighteen months, it was harvest time. Then the rhizomes' hairy crust would be smoothed with scrapers made of seashells, and, once peeled, they would be scoured and washed, their white pulp introduced into a sleeve of stitched palm fiber and hung from a tree. At this stage of chemical change, the sleeve was squeezed; the poisonous liquid dribbled out between the fibers and dripped into a bowl. Afterward, the flour would be molded into cakes, which were baked on a kind of ceramic tray set over some rocks. The finished product was called, and is called still, *casabe*. It is considered to be one of the most enduring, useful breads that mankind has produced (Marrero 1:58–63).

The question now arises: from an ecological point of view, was the Taino millennium harmful to Cuba? A study undertaken by the Jesuit Fathers in 1518 found that 800,000 mounds of sown yucca produced enough *casabe* to feed 7,000 Tainos for a year (Marrero 1:63). Taking into account that Cuba's population at the moment of conquest is estimated at some 80,000 people, 12 million mounds would feed them all. Given the fact that Cuba's surface area is 110,922 square kilometers and that 72 percent of it consisted then of forested areas, the annual rate of deforestation was insignificant (Marrero 1:32; Díaz-Brisquet and Pérez-López 141).[1]

In addition to yucca, the Tainos introduced—either the species or its cultivation—cotton, sweet potatoes, the root vegetable called *malanga*, pineapples, tobacco, peanuts, maize, peppers, beans, and squash. I think that, given their proverbial frugality and modest demographic significance, rather than affecting the ecological system negatively they contributed toward making it more complex. Concerning the fauna, it is true that they fished as much as they could and they hunted reptiles, birds of all kinds, and several species of mammals, but all of these were found in great abundance by the European conquistadors. It's easy to see that the Taino machine (made of wood, shells, plant fibers, stone, and baked clay), upon being coupled to the Iberian machine (moved by animal energy and made with metal gears and leather pulleys), would suffer a fatal overload. In just a few decades, there were only a few remnants left of the Taino machine and those who operated it: a list of proper names (like *canoa*, *bohío, hamaca, guayaba, jutía,* and *iguana*), most of them designating local flora and fauna; a few habits (like smoking tobacco and eating yucca); and a rich toponymya (Cuba, Habana, Camagüey, Masí, Guahanacabibes, Toa, Moa, Jatibonico, Mayabeque, Yumurí, Saramaguacán, Guamuhaya, Cacoyuguin, Tánamo, Hanabanilla, Guaniguanico, Macaca, and many more), proving that they were the true colonizers of the island (Zamora). Although this is not the place to reflect upon this cultural cemetery, one cannot but lament the destruction of Taino society and the way their saga of exploration and settlement fell into oblivion.

The Iberian Machine

The introduction of this new machine seems to have been a matter of fate, although there are those who find historical reasons for it. Unlike the case with the anonymous Tainos, one can be exact about the name of the one who implanted it in Cuba, as well as the date and place where it was done. (Don't think it was Christopher Columbus; his participation in this business was of a purely exploratory nature, although he never tired of eulogizing the island's natural endowments.) The place was a Taino village called Baracoa, on Cuba's eastern end; the year, 1512; the person, Diego Velázquez, a veteran of the Italian campaigns and the "pacifier" of the southwest of Hispaniola, who had been now named governor of Cuba. The title of this model's series, Nuestra Señora de la Asunción de Baracoa, illustrates the coupling or copulating of Iberian technology—generally masked with pious names—to and over that of the Taino. At any rate, during the three years that Velázquez and his three hundred men spent exploring the island, another six machines were turned on: San Salvador del Bayamo, Nuestra Señora de la Santísima Trinidad, Sancti Spíritus, Sancta María del Puerto de Príncipe, San Cristóbal de la Habana, and Santiago de Cuba, each one in the town that bears its name. Considering that these are all today machine-cities, one might think that their first models had some resemblance to the present-day ones. Nothing could be further from the truth. Velázquez's settlements never grew beyond small military encampments intended to conquer the indigenous villages and find gold deposits. With the drift of centuries, following a few shifts in placement and thanks to the changes that history brings, these seven towns would become what they now are.

Given that the Iberian machine was installed nearly everywhere in the Americas during the sixteenth century, and that it marks the end of prehistory in these vast territories, its workings have been investigated, studied, analyzed, and commented on multitudinously and in every way possible. From the beginning it had its detractors (Bartolomé de las Casas) and admirers (Gonzalo Fernández de Oviedo), in a polemic that continues today. However, all I want to do here is to speak about the ecological consequences deriving from its going to work in Cuba. To note, for instance, that during the fifteen-day stay of one of Velázquez's lieutenants in an indigenous village, his men ate more than 10,000 parrots, "the most beautiful in the world, and it was a pity to kill them," says las Casas (Marrero 1:71). Or to mention the kind of South American dog, introduced by the Tainos, whose last exemplars disappeared (eaten?) in Velázquez's times.

But, as one would imagine, the object of the conquest of Cuba was not to exploit exotic sources of alimentation. By that time nobody remembered Columbus's first voyage in search of Oriental spices. The magic word was gold, and the Iberian machine applied itself to its production for three decades, making use of forced indigenous labor. By midcentury, there were scarcely one hundred Tainos left. They had been wiped out by European diseases, overwork, ill-treatment, hunger, and mass suicides. There wasn't any gold left, either (the first breach of the original geological order), and, since the island's richness was now defined only in terms of agricultural profit, the productive capacity of the Iberian machine was oriented in that direction. Thus the crops, plantains, sugarcane, pasture, horses, donkeys, cattle, sheep, hogs, goats, chickens, dogs, cats, and bees introduced by Velázquez from Hispaniola, accompanied by rats, ticks, and other vermin, would proliferate admirably as at the same time they radically modified the ecological system (Silva Lee 23). Soon the forests would fill up with pigs, wild dogs, and rats that decimated the native fauna, as was the case with the *almiquí* (*Soledonon cubensis*).

The exploitation of the forest began timidly with the founding of settlements and took on commercial importance before it ended the century with the resulting deforestation of certain areas. Given the scarcity of wood in Spain, Cuban mahogany and ebony were employed in the building of bookcases, furniture, and ornamentation for the Spanish palaces and monasteries, the Escorial among them (Marrero 1:121). Legislation intended to protect the forests around Havana was passed in 1551, but no protective measure could hope to succeed. A few years later, when the shipbuilding industry was founded there, expeditions would have to be sent out in search of wood to the north coast of what is now the province of Pinar del Río.

Thanks to its geographical situation and the magnificent bay next to which it had been set, Havana came to be the obligatory gathering place for the Spanish ships that traded with the American colonies. Promoted to be the island's capital in 1603 (until then it had been Santiago de Cuba), it would have for many years the privilege of being the only Cuban port authorized to trade with Spain. Its continuous development—demographic, economic, military, urban, administrative—had created the conditions for the extension of agriculture and the raising of cattle and poultry, for an increase in the number of fortifications, for the growth of an active shipbuilding industry, and for a guaranteed abundance of water by means of an aqueduct that connected the city with a nearby river, today called the Almendares. At the end of the sixteenth century, there was not anywhere on the island a more appropriate place for the foundation of the sugar-making industry, already begun in Hispaniola several decades before. The chance was not missed. A group of local investors, with financial help from the Crown, took on the construction of the first sugar mills (Marrero 1:315).

Slowly sugar production grew in importance; along with leather and tobacco, it would constitute the island's principal export during the sixteenth century. Unlike its rival goods, however, sugar brought two great evils along, one of them social and the other ecological. The first one was the enslavement of Africans, needed because of the lack of cheap manpower on the island; the second was deforestation and the contamination of the rivers. Slavery and its evils are not the subjects of the present work. As to deforestation, it ought to be said that wood was at that time—and was to be for many years—the only fuel used in sugar production; furthermore, cultivating sugarcane required vast land clearing, which resulted in destruction of forests and impoverishment of biodiversity (MacPhee 16). The "nature preserves" adjacent to the city had been threatened by the 1630s. One of them was the *Monte Vedado* (Forbidden Woods), now a Havana neighborhood, so named because it was forbidden to walk in it, even though its woodland riches had begun to shrink with the clandestine logging that went on there (Marrero 3:245). The other was the Almendares River, where the waters served not just to turn the wheels of the sugar and saw mills built on its banks but also as a dumping ground for industrial waste and mule and horse excrement (Marrero 4:21).

In spite of the complaints and regulations put up against the expansion of the sugar industry, economic realities triumphed over good sense. The English occupation of Havana (1762–63) left behind as payment the introduction of 5,000 slaves and an increase in sugar production (Marrero 10:138). Thirty years later, as a consequence of the great slave rebellion in Saint-Domingue (now Haiti), sugar and coffee prices would climb extraordinarily, a situation that landowners of Havana would seize upon to acquire from the Crown all sorts of privileges favoring the development of their plantations. Very soon the great Iberian socioeconomic machine (sum of all the island's machines) had to make room for a new machine: a Creole machine. But before discussing that, one must say that toward 1775–80—after two and a half centuries of populations and depopulations, births and deaths. and legal and illegal introductions of slaves— the 80,000 exterminated Tainos had been replaced by an equal number of persons of color, among them 50,000 slaves; the white population had grown from Velázquez's 300 men into some 100,000 inhabitants (Marrero 9:175); to the seven original villages there had been added some forty urban and semi-urban nuclei; the number of sugar mills in Havana had grown from 16 to 136 (to a total of 484 for the whole island); the farms, plantations, tobacco fields, and big cattle ranches came to about 8,000 (Marrero 10:87). According to Moreno Fraginals's estimates, during that period the deforestation rate was over 6,700 hectares per annum (Moreno Fraginals, *Cuba/España* 155). Baron Alexander von Humboldt, in his work on Cuba, gives an account of a strange use for hardwood: "[The *habaneros*] had the odd idea of making pavements [of the streets] by means of the union of great tree trunks . . . Quite soon they abandoned this project and returning travelers saw with surprise the most beautiful mahogany trunks buried in Havana's ravines" (Humboldt 99). Even with this and everything else, as the eighteenth century ended, 65 percent of the island's total surface was forested (Díaz-Brisquets and Pérez-López 141).

The Creole Machine

The social differences between the *peninsulares* (Spaniards) and the Creoles (people born in the colonies) had already been well defined in the Americas by the middle of the eighteenth century. According to the Spanish empire's usual practice, the former held the highest administrative, military, and ecclesiastical positions, as well as the job of handling commercial and financial activities. The Creole, as a second-class citizen, was entrusted only with the spheres of money-making agriculture and cattle-raising, the exercise of professions and trades, and the minor duties that colonial society held out. Nevertheless, Cuba presented a different picture. With the way opening gradually because of the Spanish empire's economic ineptitude, there arose in Havana a class of rich landowners that, already by the end of the eighteenth century, could be regarded as a local oligarchy— self-made, producing sugar and coffee, with proud families that intermarried and protected one another. Thanks to their knowledge of the land

and modern ideas and to their enterprising character (in the capitalist sense), they had gained access to free trade, including the free introduction of slaves. Soon they were buying titles of nobility and gaining influence in both administrative and military circles. It was this astute and ambitious social class that completed the construction of the Creole Machine, a plantation machine, one of the most powerful and devastating to the environment of any the world has seen. It has loomed so disproportionately in the past three centuries' socioeconomic picture that it might be said that the history of the Caribbean—and most particularly Cuba—was written by it until quite recent years (Benítez-Rojo 8–10).

It is possible to observe in short order the demolishing stride of the sugar mill through the length and breadth of the island. Here, however, our only alternative is to move along through the calendar in great leaps. Spreading along the roads that led out of Havana, the sugar plantations extended toward the west, the south, and the east of the city. With my imagination working again, I'll take the southern road toward the valley of Güines: in 1780, I see the chimneys of only two sugar mills; by 1792, there are nine of them; by 1804, twenty-six; in 1827, I count forty-seven; in 1846, seventy-six; in 1859, the entire region is smoking with the fire of eighty-nine chimneys (Moreno Fraginals, *El ingenio* 1:140). Now I take the road west, toward Matanzas. In 1798, I see that the place must have some five hundred houses, all of them with thatched roofs. It's a poor village; surely the production of its three sugar mills lacks all significance. I come back in 1825, with the population grown considerably, in both white men and slaves; the number of houses has also grown, and some of them are large, with red tile roofs; there are several dozen mills, and their owners take pride in producing 25 percent of the island's sugar. In 1837, the region's wealth can be seen in the number of new towns that have sprouted on the plain; one of them is Colón. In 1857—my last imaginary voyage—the sugar of Colón, Matanzas, and Cárdenas (now incorporated cities) represents more than 55 percent of Cuba's total production. The land that this sugaring enclave occupies measures some 227,000 hectares (Moreno Fraginals, *El ingenio* 1:141). The first-growth forest now covers only 40 percent of the island's surface (Díaz-Brisquets and Pérez-López 141).

Independent of the progress of the machine through the western part of the island, there is sugar production in the central (Trinidad) and eastern (Santiago de Cuba) regions. Except in the eastern sugar mills, sugar-making technology has been improving steadily; following several advances, it has gone from the mill powered by oxen to a mechanized one, steam-powered.

With the aim of reducing the cost of moving sugar to the port for shipping, the Havana-Güines railroad is established in 1837 (the world's fourth). Twenty years later, rails connect all of the sugar-producing areas of Cuba, and the Morse telegraph is starting to operate in the most modern mills. In 1860, there are 1.365 mills, 70 percent of them steam-powered (Dye 183). As the century ends, with slavery now abolished, there are radical changes in the sugar-making agribusiness complex. The new productive unit is given the name "central," acknowledging the consolidation of great stretches of land surrounding a much more productive mill (Dye 87–101). The rhythm of deforestation speeds up.

> The burning of the Cuban forest was a daily spectacle in the countryside. The toponym *quemados* (burnt), alone or in a compound name, appears on Cuban maps as the most common on the island. Wherever its name appears there is a memory of a forest in flames . . . The Havana-Matanzas plain, where the great Cuban plantation arose, was soon a treeless land. The death of the forests was also, in the medium term, the death of the island's fabulous fertility. With the trees cut down, with sugar cane sown in the humus that the centuries had accumulated, the first harvests gave astonishing yields. Later, production began to slip, the terrible soil erosion got started, and miles of streams dried up. (Moreno Fraginals, *Cuba/España* 156)

Yes, certainly, the development of sugar in Cuba in the nineteenth century was spectacular. There were periods in which the annual increase in sugar production was 25 percent. The ecological cost, however, cannot be measured in money. Perhaps one could make a very general estimate of the wood that was lost, but how can one put a value on the irrecoverable disappearance of plant and animal species, the quick evaporation of the soil's moisture to the point of sterility? Furthermore, how can one put a price on the lives of hundreds of thousands of Africans whose forced labor made of Cuba the richest plantation island in the world?

The Republican Machine

Toward the second half of the nineteenth century, the impossibility of integrating the Cuban into the Spanish economy begins to align the export business toward the United States. In 1894, 91.5 percent of sugar exports went to the neighbor to the north (Moreno Fraginals, *El ingenio* 3:77). So, in the 1890s, although Cuba remained, politically, a Spanish colony, it was economically dependent on the United States. This circumstance contributed to Washington's taking advantage of the war of liberation from Spanish rule, which broke out in 1895, to make war against Madrid in

1898. As everyone knows, the Spanish defeat was rapid, decisive, and humiliating not only for Spain.

After four years of U.S. military occupation, Cuba obtained a relative independence, a kind of freedom hampered substantially as much by the Platt Amendment, which authorized the U.S. government to intervene at will on the island, as by that country's economically powerful groups (Ayala 79–101). This close dependence, along with the advent of the second industrial revolution, led to there being an increase in U.S. capital investment in Cuban sugar. In 1924, U.S. sugar investments represented 63 percent of total U.S. agricultural investments worldwide, and the sugar produced by American companies in Cuba represented 63.53 percent of Cuba's total production (Ayala 77, 100).

There's no doubt that these big investments aided the reconstruction of the island—leveled by three years of scorched-earth warfare—and its modernization, but they also generated serious problems, among them that of closing off Cuba's economic development as anything but a single-industry country. Given the existence of enormous stretches of plains and woods available in the central and eastern regions, most of the new mills were built in the provinces of Camagüey and Oriente. Those mills were called *colosos* (colossal) because of their enormous production. They brought together all of the technological advances that then drove the mass production of consumer goods in the developed countries. In 1877, 1,190 mills produced 516,268 tons of sugar (Dye 183; Moreno Fraginals, *El ingenio* 3:37). But in 1929, 163 mills produced 5.4 million tons (Dye 183; Moreno Fraginals, *El ingenio* 3:39). This, naturally, was possible thanks to a corresponding increase in deforestation. From 1905 to 1925, the annual rate of deforestation was over 80,000 hectares (Díaz-Brisquet and Pérez-López 141). In the 1940s, when production averaged some 4 million tons, the forests still covered 18 to 21 percent of Cuba's surface; in 1959, as production reached more than 6 million tons, availability had diminished to around 14 percent, although what remained of the original vegetation was in marginal areas or ones hard to exploit economically such as swamps, mountains, and mangroves on the coasts and keys (Moreno Fraginals, *El ingenio* 3:40; Díaz-Brisquet and Pérez-López 141). Regarding the death of the forest, Manuel Moreno Fraginals informs us:

> Today, of the Cuban forests, of the legendary mahoganies, almost nothing is left. Still in 1962, along the Sagua River, the *palanqueros* were poling the river. The waters slid calmly along through the treeless lands. The *palanqueros* carry a long lance with an iron tip. With it they go along stabbing the riverbed until

they know that they've struck wood. Then they come alive, pull it up and take
it to the shore . . . And so, day after day, they extract from the river's depths
what remains of the trees that sugar has destroyed. They live off the forests'
cadavers. (Moreno Fraginals, *El ingenio* 1:163)

In 1962, when Moreno Fraginals visited the Sagua River, Cuba's forested
area represented only 900,000 hectares, that is, 8 percent of Cuba's surface (Díaz-Brisquet and Pérez-López 141). Bartolomé de las Casas assures
us that in his time, when the woods covered 72 percent of the island, it
was possible to traverse the island east to west beneath the shade of the
trees (Marrerro 1:29). If he were to have tried it in the early 1960s, he
might have died of acute despondency.

The responsibility for this ecological catastrophe lies primarily with the
sugar-making machine. But a machine is an ensemble of indifferent parts
moved by a motor. It has no consciousness; it can't be brought before the
bar of history. Responsibility must be sought in the power groups that
controlled it, whether of Spanish, Creole, or North American origin.

As far as ecological damages are concerned, these were not limited to
deforestation, contamination of rivers, and habitat destruction. Everyone
knows that there is a close relationship between nature and culture. In
black Africa, the forest and the river have the highest significance imagin-
able. To start with, the forest is the repository of all knowledge, something like an enormous multidisciplinary library. Furthermore, there live
within it the animist powers as well as the different pantheons of deities
that populate the African cosmogonies. Something similar occurs with
the river, associated with the mysteries of the rainbow, the serpent, the
fish, and the woman. The conservation in Cuba of many African beliefs
and traditions that the slaves brought with them was possible thanks to
the connections that they made between their forests and those of the
islands (Cabrera 13–20). Nevertheless, in the concrete case of the Yoruba
religion, there can be seen in Cuba a notable diminution in the number of
orishas, or deities. Furthermore, the languages of Yoruba, Bantu, Ewe Fon,
and Efik peoples, once spoken fluently by Cuban blacks, are no longer in
use, with the exception of some popular words like *chévere,* and ceremonial chants, invocations, and spells. Why not think this phenomenon is
related to the impoverishment of the Cuban forest?

But the existence of a body of traditional knowledge on the island is
not owing to African cultures alone. Cuba's patron saint is the Virgen de
la Caridad del Cobre, whose syncretic cult includes Atabey's (a Taino
goddess) and Oshun's (a Yoruba *orisha*) under the image of Our Lady

(Benítez-Rojo 13–15). In the earliest years of colonization there arrived great contingents of peasants from the Canary Islands who, within their Christianity, kept alive their forest-related traditions (Cabrera 23–24). Furthermore, in the second half of the nineteenth century, 150,000 South Chinese peasants disembarked on the island. They worked in the sugar-cane fields and fought for Cuba's independence, as African slaves did. Their contact with Cuba's forests is represented in Sanfancon, a Chinese deity adored in Santería (Cabrera 23). His syncretic cult brings in Shango's, a Yoruba god, and Saint Barbara's. To the conjunction of these groups is owed the rich herbal medicine that exists today as an alternative to the scientific pharmacopoeia (Cabrera 289–564).[2] I ask again: how many natural laboratories must have been lost forever in the deforestation? Wouldn't "green medicine" have been even richer without their loss? How many opportunities at cultural syncretism, or rather at multisyncretism, were tossed away? How many traditions disappeared when the small rural property-holder became a sugar-making proletarian?

The Socialist Machine

The socialist machines built by Stalin and Mao belong to the past. For our purposes, they can be defined in a few lines: they were gigantic state machines, directed by one person or by a small team through a single polit-ical party, whose gears were set to conquer nature and private property over the entire globe, toward the goal of raising, in an egalitarian way, the collective standard of living. Given that the ideology that justified their functioning had been announced as the only one capable of saving human-ity from poverty and from other social inequalities, the conquest of nature was to be achieved at the quickest possible pace and at any cost, so much more so when said ideology was competing at a disadvantage with others of the world's modes of thinking. This strategy was followed by the Soviet Union, China, and other countries in Europe and Asia, where it became a common practice to sacrifice the environment in favor of greater agricul-tural, mining, industrial, and energy production. After the disintegration of the Communist bloc in Europe and of the Soviet Union itself, it could be verified that the levels of degradation of air, water, and earth, along with the quality of life in human settlements, greatly exceeded that in the West, not corresponding with the supposed "humanistic" economic develop-ment that these machines' propaganda apparatuses had been hawking.

Cuba, for thirty years, shared the destructive strategy that was followed in Eastern Europe. The collectivization of the greater part of the earth and its reorganization in big state farms and cooperatives with the purpose of adopting an extensive agriculture resulted in the trees and shrubs that were growing within the new boundaries set by the state bureaucracy being cut down. The idea was to level the earth as much as possible. To leave it naked and open to the caterpillar treads of tractors and combines, to fertilizers and pesticides, to leave it without the protecting shade of the Judas tree and the rows of green sentinels that until then had lined the roads and river banks or marked the boundaries of the old landholdings (Dumont 123–27). In this battle against nature, carried out all over the island by the weighty teams of the "Che Guevara columns," which included bulldozers, battle tanks, and explosives, there fell thousands and thousands of royal palms, the most symbolic Cuban tree, and with them all sorts of fruit trees (Díaz-Brisquet and Pérez López 155). Many tilled fields disappeared, and soon there were no fruits or vegetables available, that is, guava, *mammee,* soursop, medlar, tamarind, cherimoya, banana, lemon, lime, orange, grapefruit, papaya, sapodilla, *caimito, marañón, mamoncillo, anón, canistel,* plantain, avocado, cantaloupe, watermelon, pineapple, chickpeas, all types of beans, lentil, potato, sweet potato, yam, rice, yucca, green and red peppers, okra, chayote, watercress, spinach, lettuce, cabbage, radish, red beet, green bean, turnip, carrot, squash, pumpkin, tomato, onion, garlic, oregano, bay leaf, black pepper, cumin . . . Is this paragraph too detailed? Maybe so. I'm trying to be an echo of the dreams of millions of Cubans who for decades could consume only a very limited quantity of those products through the system of rationing. The government's dreams were very different from the people's. They were to supply the European socialist bloc's demand for sugar in order to earn economic aid from the Soviet Union. So almost all of the new areas to be cultivated were dedicated to sugarcane, and the work in the cane fields was mechanized to the maximum; at the same time, new mills and reservoirs were created to guarantee the needed irrigation (Dumont 39). The government made use of every means at its disposal to have the sugar harvest of 1969–70 reach 10 million tons. Almost all of the island's labor, fuel, and transport resources were directed to the sugar industry, to the point that the country was almost paralyzed (Díaz-Brisquet and Pérez-López 155). But although the goal was not met, the government would continue the old policy of monoculture, producing an average of 7 million tons of sugar on the basis of an extensive agriculture that demanded deforestation, the use of enormous quantities of chemical pesticides and fertilizers, and the implacable pumping of underground and surface waters. Soon the unthinkable occurred: after a surprisingly short agony, Communist power died in Europe.

The Transition Machine

The collapse of the Soviet Union brought as a consequence not only the suspension of the economic aid that it was sending to Cuba but also serious problems with the structures of agricultural and industrial production, export and import trade, and investments in both the productive and service sectors. This critical situation forced the government to follow, in 1990, the policy called "special period in peacetime," a policy of hard austerity that brought a maximum restriction of imports. Facing this reality, the government found itself forced to adopt a series of survival measures such as the introduction of foreign investments; the legalization of the dollar; the accelerated development of tourism; the partial abandonment of the Soviet agricultural and industrial models; the creation of free markets and shops, of self-employment, and of new forms of property and land use; and the reorganization of public administration, state enterprises, and industries under economic criteria, including the sugar complex.

Between 1959 and 1990, the government hardly worried about environmental problems. Law No. 33 of 1981, called "On the Protection of the Environment and the Rational Use of Natural Resources," never came to be implemented (Díaz-Brisquet and Pérez-López 57). However, after 1990, environmental issues began to play an important role in Cuba's economy. Because of its inefficiency, Cuba had to dismantle many old industries that were sources of contamination. Further, the drastic diminution of imports of fertilizers, pesticides, petroleum, tractors, combines, and trucks made it advisable that the agricultural system be examined with an eye toward using old and less aggressive methods to exploit the land, for example, a return of the draft animal and organic agriculture. Díaz-Brisquet and Pérez-López conclude that "these changes, at least over the short term, will have beneficial environmental impacts since they have forced the reversal of many development policies that have had, or could potentially have had, adverse environmental impacts" (Díaz-Brisquet and Pérez-López 22). This forced self-examination revealed serious ecological problems, unrecognized until then, and caught the government's attention. By accelerating the reforestation rate and managing annual cutting rates, Cuba was able to reverse its secular deforestation trend. In 1992, according to official estimates, 18.2 percent was covered by forests (Díaz-Brisquet and Pérez-López 145).

Cuba participated actively in the so-called Earth Summit, held in Rio de Janeiro (1992), and commenced to ratify most of the accords and international instrumentations regarding the environment, some of which were offering monetary and technical assistance. Between 1993 and 1994, a legislative package was approved and implemented regarding environmental protection, and the Environmental Agency was created, composed of several centers and research institutes, as a part of the new Ministry of Science, Technology, and the Environment (CITMA). In 1997, Law No. 81, the "Law on the Environment," was passed, and CITMA's provincial offices identified the most serious problems in their respective territories at the same time that they recommended short- and long-term solutions. The results of this investigation must have made the Havana bureaucrats' hair stand on end. The situation was terribly critical from one end of the island to the other: the watersheds were deforested, and their waters—contaminated by human, animal, and industrial waste—were spilling out into the bays and the coastal areas; the soils had been compressed, desertified, and salinated; garbage dumps proliferated, septic tanks overflowed permanently for lack of cleanup teams, and the sewage systems were insufficient or deteriorated; water treatment plants were lacking or ill-functioning, and the industrial use of beach sand and deforestation of the coastal mangrove swamps were eroding the littoral; biodiversity was disappearing and gastrointestinal illnesses had multiplied because of water and vegetable contamination.[3]

In 1997, when Cuba ratified the United Nations Covenant to Combat Desertification and Drought, the summary stated:

> Desertification affects 14% (1,580,996 ha.) of the country's territory. Soil degradation resulting from land mismanagement and land misuse by man in the course of time is the main cause for the emergence of marked signs of desertification . . . The fact that 76.8% of Cuban soils account for the lowest crop yields does not allow deriving more than 30% of the production potential from the cultivable species planted there. This situation indicates that one of the direct effects of desertification is the reduction of soil capacity to produce food and thereby meet the most pressing needs of the population.[4]

On 5 June 2001, with the intention of celebrating International Environment Day, the head of the agency declared that after more than twenty years of work Cuba had not only halted deforestation but had generated new wooded areas, particularly in the mountains, which, when added to the already-existing ones, amounted to 27 percent of the island's territory.[5] This figure seems to be the product of a statistical error, since the provincial CITMA offices complained in their reports of problems ranging from the illegal cutting of trees to the feeble yields from seeds and plantings, this without considering that the demand for wood has grown considerably due to the absence of domestic fuel and the construction of new tourist installations. But even if the official estimate of reforestation is a true figure, original biodiversity can't be restored. One of the most thorough books on the country's birds, *Field Guide to the Birds of Cuba,* written by eminent scientists working inside Cuba, lists thirty threatened species. On habitat destruction, the authors write:

> There has been extensive land alteration due to agriculture, cattle ranching, urban development and lumber production. Logging is common, even within protected areas, to provide firewood and charcoal. Intervals between cuts usually range in the decades, but it is often too short a time to allow adequate regeneration. At present, the northern cays (Coco, Romano, Cruz and Paredón Grande) are among the most disturbed areas, mainly as a result of development for tourism . . . Until the late 1980s, industries in Cuba were developing at a considerable rate. Not surprisingly, sugar refineries and electrical generating plants released a wide range of pollutants . . . Landscapes downstream from the larger sugar mills are usually bleak . . . We believe, however, that the most serious pollution has occurred through excessive use of pesticides, particularly malathion and synthetic pyrethroids . . . The impact of aerially applied pesticides on the bird population in the cays, such as in Cayo Largo, Cayo Coco, and Cayo Guillermo, although never properly assessed, has been great enough to produce visible and widespread avian mortality. (Garrido and Kirkconnell 7–9)

In the excellent photographs of *Natural Cuba,* by Alfonso Silva Lee, one can appreciate the richness of Cuba's endemic fauna. A significant number of its species find themselves in danger of extinction, from the daunting crocodile to the showy snails *Polymita picta.* What's going to be its ultimate destiny? Are existing controls effective? The fact is that Cuba's ecological fate is far from easy to predict. Experience tells us that nobody knows precisely what's happening on the island, so it's not possible to know the true extent of its ecological damage or to what degree the plans of CITMA or, more particularly, the Environmental Agency are being carried out. It's clear that the bad economic situation throughout the island for some years now is an obstacle to the repair of its ruinous infrastructure.

In June 2002, Cuba's official sources announced surprising news: the dismantling of seventy-one obsolete sugar mills—almost half of the country's total—and 60 percent of the lands dedicated to raising sugarcane.[6] How many hectares of forest did those sugar mills swallow during their active life? Nobody knows for certain. Perhaps 20 percent of the original vegetation; perhaps more. To what extent did they negatively impact the island's wildlife and folk culture? It can't be calculated.

However, if it's true that the demolition of much of the sugar-making complex will reduce deforestation and contamination, tens of thousands of workers are going to have to be shifted to other sectors, with the in-between period bringing an important increase in expenditures for social assistance at the expense of other programs. The maintaining of protected green areas and the cleaning up of bays and groundwater, as well as the building of aqueducts, sewer networks, and treatment systems, entail exorbitant costs. What sources of aid or international lenders are ready to finance them? Or rather, who can be sure that, if an economic improvement should occur, the maladroit actions of the past would not be repeated? Whatever the case, on top of its having put in place a system of environmental protection, Cuba has something else in its favor: population growth has declined considerably (at present less than 1 percent). The economic crisis of the 1990s has contributed to a long-term diminution of the fertility rate. According to recent estimates, within a few years the population will stabilize (or begin to decline), at around 12 million (Díaz-Brisquet and Pérez-López 32–35).

It needn't be said that Cuba's case should not be seen in isolation; Cuba is part of the Caribbean basin, the Gates of Paradise that, moved and marveling, the first European explorers and chroniclers described. Today, nevertheless, the archipelago's ecosystems are fighting for their lives against the threats of desertification and poisoning of the waters, of poverty and unhealthiness, of cheap technology and the requirements of tourism (Barker and McGregor). It is the lamentable payoff left behind by colonialism, economic dependence, and the plantation system, bequeathed to an island world already geographically subject to hurricanes, coastal floods, droughts, earthquakes, and volcanic eruptions. In scarcely two centuries, the Antilles have seen the extermination of thirty-four mammal, ten reptile, and six bird species, for a total of fifty species. In contrast, during the same period North America has lost only eight species of vertebrates (Cunningham 32). If we take the five-century period between 1500 and 2000 as a framework, it turns out that one-quarter of all the mammalian extinctions have occurred in the West Indies. In proportion to their size, they have suffered greater losses in their biodiversity than anywhere else on the planet.

In the environmental summit meetings, there is heartening talk about the possibility of sustainable economic development in the poor countries. I'm not one to venture an opinion in that forum; I lack credentials. But among the laments and the protests and the good intentions and solemn hypocrisies of those who make pronouncements there, I ask myself: Perhaps a clean, green development is a possibility in Cuba's future, but is it probable?

Notes

1. Sergio Díaz-Brisquet and Jorge Pérez-López's *Conquering Nature: The Environmental Legacy of Socialism in Cuba,* published in 2000, is by far the most documented and objective work on Cuba's environmental problems.

2. Lydia Cabrera lists over five hundred medicinal species.

3. For official data on Cuba's environmental situation, see www.medioambiente .cu. For 1997 provincial environmental figures, see www.medioambiente.cv/ downloads.asp?cat=4.

4. See the whole document at www.unccp.int/cop/reports/lac/national/2000/ cuba-summary-eng.pdf.

5. See *Granma Internacional,* digital edition, www.granma.cu/ingles/junio1/ 23medio-i.html.

6. See www.miami.com/mld/elnuevo/3400346.html.

Isla Incognita

Derek Walcott

ERASE EVERYTHING, even the name of this island, if it is to be rediscovered. It is the only way to begin. We will try to pretend that we have seen none of it before. It will be impossible, of course, for how can we tell whether our feeling on seeing that rock and its bay, is nostalgia or revelation? Well, combine both, and the illumination made by their igniting would be discovery. One thing is half-true, and that is that the island is little known, that there are several other islands with its name, given either in the monotony of faith or from a tired imagination. Other islands, nearing landfall, are easy metaphors, this one the Needle, this one humped and feeding, the tortoise, and so on and on, until the bored recourse is to the inexhaustible litany of saints. Blue-hazed rocks in apostolic succession, beads loosed from the rosary cord of the horizon. No name, then—otherwise they will all resemble one another. An unknown island, not important.

So where to approach it? A deserted beach that already has a fisherman's bathhouse and fish-cleaning shed? Above it, telephone poles and the litter of vacation people. That's good enough, for the beach has that thick and sultry anonymity of all the beaches in the archipelago. And very few beaches' names are known, far more remembered. No, turn and see where you have come from instead, so you'll know where you are. You look at the ocean behind you and accept that you are nowhere.

But you have a name. And a job or a calling, are clothed, are of a precise, piercing age, and have responsibilities and fear. You are not actually beginning. This is not prehistory, but somehow, as each word progresses, neither nouns nor dates will do.

The weird, raggedly inaccurate, infantile maps of the old explorers, in school, were more fearful than comic. The wrongly real outlines were perhaps more terrifying than their blank confession "Terra Incognita." If what they knew was so inaccurate, how accurate was what they did not? Not Atlantis and all that, or leviathans and sea serpents, but a world without edges, a flat world without edges, giving us two unappeasable concepts—Terra Incognita and Space. Savages have no such edges, no urgency about topography. Short on such ego, they do not try to contain a detailed world whole in their heads, except as a metaphor, except as the word "world."

So the edge of this beach can follow its own course now without obeying its own image, regulating its subtlest curve to copy its representation on charts or on the map; its sinuosity is not predetermined, but as dim as the guessing wrist of the old mapmaker. The island can shape itself in the direction I know and that sensation subconsciously records, and the outline behind me, petulant, ignored can run out of ink and stay unknown. For I don't know where that village is exactly any more than I know the tide gauges. And all can bulk behind me if it wishes: the mountain and the almond trees and the old road, clouds and all, not necessarily to be discovered. There will be none of that impatience, vast, cynical that awaits the real explorer, his every step a noun, a town, a spring, a milestone. As a matter of truth, I'm not moving until I know why I have chosen to sit down on this page of a beach—as a matter of fact, I may not move at all.

Of course, the idea of an "unknown island" is a contradiction, because either it is unknown or it is an island, meaning a bulk with an at least approximated shape, something coherent and separate. I mean "unknown," too, in its use or importance. Unknown means without its own legends. Unknown also its inhabitants, their use, or importance. What does this island produce? Unknowns. For what is it famous? Nothing.

There was a phrase from a Latin text at school. Quales est natura insulae? What is the nature of the island? It has stuck in here for over thirty-five years. I do not know if I am ready to answer it.

Except by hints. Contradictions. Terrors. The opposite method to the explorer's. Not by botany or by the journal that names today's discoveries, today's repetitions. Not by the dial or the pen or the compass. By a method not yet known to itself, appropriately. By a great deal of principled doubt, for this is not undertaken with any great spirit of faith. We lie—we know the island is known.

Yet I must have that humility that knows that unless I triangulate my travels, my self as a poet, both I and the island are lost. It was not originally my island, but I came upon it and had to claim it by necessity, desperation even, and I'm webbed in its design. Who shakes it, however subtly, shakes me.

My favorite stretch of beach shudders to the open Atlantic: a steeply sloping beach with a stand of rusted almonds between the road to Cumana village and the ocean. Continual spume and a fine spray. It doesn't give a damn at evening. Well, at morning either.

Unnecessary idyll, shared by everyone. A frame for the tourist. Such an obvious spot! The negligible revolutions of the "Third World" are even stranger here, because there seems to be nothing to complain about. This is utter desolation or simple geography, and just as the geography is changeless, it also suggests, no, it thunders, that the human condition here is also unchanging. The villages will always be poor. The sand will remain, and the bent, rusted trees. And the spume that, if you want a change now, can become snow and whiten this next page to a snowdrift.

If the reader concentrates, says Pasternak, about here, a snowstorm should begin. Let it begin!

SNOWFIELDS OF OHIO. Foreign domesticity and the barns, and these too possessed by an absent, or invisible race, white hidden within white. How deep is this ancient fear of cold, bite of the dog on the bone itself, shaking it off like the wind? Who teaches the elements hostility and possession that not only barn but the last knife-cold stubble bristles with "no, not here"? The long-frozen sea of humps crested with trees unrolls toward the carfront, the snow flurries whirl in surprise, with "ain't you a little bit out of your ambience, nigger?" And all week long, in cars, in motels, in bland, fake oak, fake Spanish luncheon rooms, the talk of poetry turned into meringue.

The sadness of occupation, poetry, is connection with these fields, its tone is the ground-level whine of a crippled wind through stubble, the noise of snow tires and the soundless white of wires. All the poets who move me from one college to the next have this somber, early-afternoon dark fear or exhaustion within them, or in the broken, hesitating meter of their pamphlets, their desolation of not being published, because their manuscripts are with this or that press, men, like me, into early middle age or in the now forgotten terror of becoming forty. We talk a lot too of the fatality list of the occupation in America, Mr. Alvarez's catalogue, Crane, Schwartz, (in a way, Jarrell, possibly), Berryman, Plath, others whose names I had never heard, and if one name is forgotten it may spring to mouth with an excited morbidity. There is no such tradition of self-murder, degeneration, or madness back there at home, because there is no tradition, and the poetic impulse, however banal as in the calypso, is public. Here, the poet shrinks into his anonymity or his fame. Yet I serenely try to enjoy the sense of Ohio wastes and its highways, since it is overpoweringly strange. The best is that by coming spring the company may go on a tour of this country, and possibly through Ohio too, but one should be less forbidding. Then with spring, we should be nearer the feel of our own country, and I would like to see it break into something else, if only for the old cynical optimism of weather and the race. The isolation of poetry will pass into the vociferous, warm, vulgar communality of the theater back home. Here some have never seen the sea. Can't imagine the islands.

DESPITE THE NOSTALGIA, do we outgrow islands? Are they for children and immature races? And if we do not, is it because we pityingly confine the limits of our ambition, our sensibilities to their known boundaries? Archipelagoes have been known to breed the gigantic. Some warp or flow in time has left us the Galapagos turtle and the lizard, but can islands produce men of giant imagination, heroes of legendary size? Was it that sense of limits that produced the massive heads of Easter Island? Well, there are pygmies in the rain forests of Africa, and if they are stunted because their tribal imagination would not dare farther than the next tree, if a lack of nourishing sunlight kept them to that stature, . . . if, if. All contradictions. In the rarely freckled damps of our own rain forests, the ferns grow to grotesque size. Ferns whose design is that of our spinal cord. These theories lead to the prejudices of anthropology. From that, the decline into history is easy.

Besides none of the inhabitant races here is indigenous, so the pursuit of that idea runs down rapidly. They have come from all over, every continent, even Asia. I was making a wider, illogical loop and was diverted into my usual ignorance of science. I meant to ask whether living on islands means a surrender to their size. And whether that resignation would not produce its consolation of fantasy, just as the prisoner teaches himself to manage his dreams, or, at its worst, as the claustrophobe winds up to delirium. An easy psychology would use this to explain Carnival, but Carnival works for everything. This again is too simple.

Tropical islands, of course, have one climate and should produce a common temperament in their people. Heat and rain, drought and storms, if men's temperaments match their environment, should find their equivalent in passions. Metaphors of temper. The rain laughs and nourishes, storm days cloud rapidly, explode, and shine afterward with an exhilarating serenity. But I can force no comparison about drought, except we go into further absurdities. Except we indulge such large abstractions as periods of spiritual barrenness and call that season a thirst for grace, a drying up of wellsprings. No. Our religions, based on desert endurance and on the cycles of four seasons are not rooted in that direct, dualistic force of drought and rain, of dry season that is not wholly round enough to form a cycle. If we went by those sharp contrasts, dryness then abundance to drowning, the graph would be manic-depressive. It is too simple, true, but weather sticks to the skin here, and our moods are as barometric as those of temperate men. When curtains of rain close off the ocean and we look out of windows on interminable grayness, the leaves' heads beaten down, something heavy and cold as a frog sits on the heart, and if it goes on long enough we doubt the return of the sun, just for longer periods men begin to doubt the fact of spring. The extension of time doesn't matter so much as its intensity. Novembers in this island bring this feeling. Then somewhere between now and Christmas, I think, there is the intensely serene dry spell of Petit Careme, cool winds and bright trees, the little Lent that prologues our dry April. Then there is visible exhilaration in the mood of the race, even if it is only one person who acknowledges it. There's also a naturally sharper edge to what was called Vent Noel, the Christmas breeze, because of the winter up north's horning the trade winds. Maybe there's a kind of angling in the fan of the ocean wind, or something happens to the sun.

These subtle few distinctions are all we have to go by in terms of change, and maybe because they are so imperceptible to strangers or transients, they make landscape and people seem monotonous. They require a different analysis to the boredom of cities, the industrial miasma, the locked-in and lunging despairs of city winters. In London recently, a friend told me that the incidence of suicide rises not in midwinter but at the approach of spring, because the suicide cannot bear another delusion of hope. Our rains may seep into the bone and depress, but I doubt that our weather drives anyone to the act of despair.

But our contemners who see this climate as seasonless and without subtlety also see us as a race without temperament, therefore without any possibility of art. The subtler races are given to the slow colorings of autumn, the sparkle of the first frost, the gentle despairs of fall, the sweet mulch of leaf decay, and all the tribal rituals of contemplative hibernation, spring cleaning, and the slaying of the crop gods, the span of life divided obviously into four seasons, and while we can see all this in a single tree, the earth here is almost illiterate, water and sun refuse to repeat the pathetic fallacy we studied at school. How dumb our nature is then. It hasn't studied Jonson and Wordsworth; it remains monosyllabic, one-dimensional, a child's, a pygmy's drawing. It defeats our artists quickly. It makes bores of our poets.

"I miss the changes," the tourist says. "Snow was my element," says the character in a West Indian novel. That yearlong sun, that either bright blue or slate-colored sea, that idiot green of everything can produce only heraldic, totemic art, art with hard bright edges. No philosophy. No complexity. No matching apprehension of the process of thought with the progress of the seasons.

The answer is not to boast, "We could be as subtle as you"; we have a kind of autumn in the coloring of the sea almond; we have mists too, and sometimes clouds stuck like lint to the edges of the mountains look just like snow, but if you were brought up on Odes to the Season, recited ballads about ships lost in the North Sea fog, about maidens lost in marshes and icicle-bearded February, if your childhood imagination went by the Shepherd's Calendar, and if as an apprentice you were taught that the most graceful and subtlest technique of painting was the English watercolor with its framed climate of evanescence, dissolution, the melting line, it is still hard not to fear that your own hard-edged vision isn't barbarous, that the world of your island isn't as primal and basic and barbarous as ABC and the three primary colors. This affects speech, syntax, customs, politics as well as the attempts at an indigenous art. To the extent where the self-assertion does become barbarous and aggressive, to the self-pity of the new nationalism. In those, to some extent, we represent our two seasons. Darkly impulsive and violent, then stretches of dry desolation. Gusts of enthusiasm. A longing for more variety. An affection for tempestuous, self-contradicting men. Rhetoric, flamboyance. Blazing trees like torches and crowds sounding like rain. Colorful and volatile. Picturesque. Not all of us. though. Not all islanders are fond of "romance."

ALL RIGHT, SHIFT. Here is an unknown plant. Take the arrogance of an Old World botanist naming this plant then, this one on the grass verge of the beach that I do not even have a name for, and I now believe that my ignorance is more correct than his knowledge, that my privilege makes it correct as quietly as Adam's, or Crusoe's, and that what it reminds me of, its metaphor, is more important than the family it springs from. A whole method of our learning has been founded on this acceptance, but eventually the botanically correct and Latin-tagged label or, even worse, the tag with the name of the "discoverer," disappears; it keeps its creole or country name according to its properties, and without properties, medicinal, magical, or edible, without use it remains anonymous, always to be rediscovered, to remain looking like something else. But in our literature it assumes a dead life, a glassed-in imitation of its superiors, and is proud to be a second-rate marigold, or daisy, or crocus. Around it, the anonymous vines and thick-eared vegetation look illiterate. That is not botany, it is society; it is our opinion of refinement.

"The natural graces of life do not show themselves under such conditions." This is Froude, of course, but there are moments when every islander believes it. As the moment of naming by that botanist is the beginning of that specimen's official history; we have accepted our history as a succession of such moments. Columbus kneels on the sand of San Salvador. That is a moment. Bilbao, Keats's "Cortez," looks on the Pacific. That is another moment. Lewis and Clark behold the West, and that is another moment. What do they behold? They behold the images of themselves beholding. They are looking into the "mirror of the sea" (Conrad), or the mirror of the plain, the desert, the sky. We in the Americas are taught this as a succession of illuminations, lightning moments that must crystallize and irradiate memory if we are to believe in a chain of such illuminations known as history. The root of evil may come from the wrong or casual naming of things; for the poor, money is not the root of evil, but history, and perhaps even that word now needs a different name. It has taken me over thirty years, and my race hundreds, to feel the fibers spread from the splayed toes and grip this earth, the arms knot into boles and put out leaves. When that begins, this is the beginning of season, cycle time. The noise my leaves make is my language. In it is tunneled the roar of seas of a lost ocean. It is a fresh sound. Let me not be ashamed to write like this, because it supports this thesis, that our only true apprehensions are through metaphor, that the old botanical names, the old processes cannot work for us. Let's walk.

Note

Written in 1973, this essay has remained among the author's papers at the University of the West Indies, St. Augustine. With the author's permission, it is here published for the first time.

Shaping the Environment

Sugar Plantation, or Life after Indentured Labor

Cyril Dabydeen

RESONANCES, not unlike residues of memory, as I conjure up cane ash like tarantulas floating in the air, then slowly coming down on us standing on the balcony of our house in the village. Everything relived, perhaps not unlike being reborn: such was plantation life and its ambience as cane harvesting came upon us; and it seemed excitement was always in the air, akin to frisson. As children how we tried catching the strands of ash coming down, almost in arrested time. Then the ash disintegrated, became sheer dust! But fires kept emblazoning, in our minds and consciousness, maybe in mine most of all, with the sky always lit up, picturesque, yet also frightening. And indeed the sugar plantation was all for us in Guyana's coastline (we called it the *coastland*)—as if it were all the landscape of the country situated a few feet below sea level: a place we knew intimately with ubiquitous palm trees and other lush flora, interminably variegated; and the rest of the country was the interior, or hinterland, like unknown territory (though this gradually began changing). And a seawall was built to protect the coastland—especially around Georgetown—from the Atlantic Ocean at high tide. And hadn't the Dutch when they occupied the region also built canals, kokers, forts—the most famous being Kyk-over-al—not unlike what occurred in Holland itself? Dutch emblems, colonial residues as they were, combined with other European legacies that helped forge a place, a country, even a people's memory: all I would dwell on and write about in my growing up. The spirit of the place it was, always forming, became ingrained in us: everything intertwining, more than just geography of the imagination, or what destiny had in store for us.

Adelphi, our village: situated in the Canje district—the same district where the Rose Hall sugar plantation is located in the county of Berbice; and the plantation indeed, now thriving under "different" ownership, was where I established, seminally, my own indelible sense of the environment; and Rose Hall is still one of the largest sugar plantations in the country, perhaps emblematic or symbolic of the life lived in other areas of the coastland also. And for one like myself the name "Rose Hall" began to gradually have its own resonance, being more than English since everything was located in the so-called "ancient county" of Berbice, one indeed founded by the Dutchman Abraham van Pere in 1600. The county's main town, New Amsterdam, would have as its principal novelist Edgar Mittelholzer, who wrote of the place's unique lore with his own sense of history and drama: all in his Kaywana series, which I would regularly read, as "things moved among them." Make-believe it all was, too, stirring the fervid imagination, if Mittelholzer's only. Not much later, it was Wilson Harris I also read to help form the spirit of the place: he too was born in New Amsterdam, but the locus of his imagination was the interior, the same elusive or mysterious Guyana hinterland. The polarities of place: always coastland and hinterland, with other juxtapositions of feelings, sensibility, indeed kept shaping the environment as it also seemed like hallowed time itself in us, with us. Would I deny it? Would I want it any other way?

The sugar plantation often carried the sense of an overwhelming empire, as the local place-names suggested diverse origins, influences, always combining European and English; later would come distinctive African and Asian elements, and all other influences too because of who we were becoming as "a people," all of which permeated my consciousness with the sense of otherness, maybe; and other landscapes, environments, as everything kept coming closer in a genuine potpourri world of races, creeds, transforming or reshaping in odd or mysterious ways. Beings, presences, all here in the outpost of empire; and this coastal ground was now all as the ocean's waves lashed, with mangrove and courida spread out along the Corentyne coast—not a seawall—in the same Berbice county.

Maybe it seemed like prehistory itself, everything being imprinted on us in continually remarkable ways. And the Corentyne was not far from the Canje: the former where my father was born and raised, an environment itself always suggestive of the sea: it was my time spent there as a child, a place etched in my memory and redolent of seaweed, mollusk, mullet, shrimp, crab; and seabirds hovering: all with the sense of an extended family, if only my father's; and insects, sand flies mainly, hurling themselves at us at night even as we burned coconut husks, shells, to generate smoke in the air to thwart the pesky flies and mosquitoes from attacking us, like the Eumenides (in my creative writing I sometimes alluded to this). While living in the Canje, we indeed kept visiting my father's district, like compelling ground, as a way to escape the sugar plantation's hold on us. Underlying too was the sense of salt water and freshwater merging in more immediate ways. A riverine territory it was on this coastal belt, as Guyana is indeed known by its indigenous name, "the land of many waters." It was for me literally, but metaphorically no less.

It was the fifties and sixties, you see; and my own particular village, Adelphi, formed part of the Rose Hall sugar plantation—the village's name hinting at what was classical (note the Greek, Delphi), and somewhere was a hidden oracle? The adjacent villages like Goed Bananen Land, with Dutch echoes, as the name Canje itself suggested, and then the town of New Amsterdam also. But Rose Hall carried the sense of the metropolitan world because the plantation's representatives—managers, overseers from the Bookers-McConnell Co., of the U.K.—all lived in palatial homes with well-manicured lawns displaying abundant flowers, choice vegetation: everything almost picturesque, idyllic, far removed from the gritty life we lived in the villages. Our houses were built on stilts, and tenements too they were, all here on the coastland. When the rains came, inevitably, it was like a further assault on the senses, reminding us always that we were in a region known for equatorial downpours: all being part of the wider Amazon basin, didn't we know?

And the plantation world with its physical and social structure wasn't unlike an apartheid system—the way it was all formed or arranged, though we never thought of it as such, never consciously. And our lives, with the customs circumscribing language: speech patterns deriving from Scotland, Ireland, Wales, England, West Africa, India, and elsewhere: everything associated with lore, as if from long ago; and dialectal formations as if stemming from the soil itself, integrated and simultaneously demarcated our spaces.

Language: the verbs, nouns—of doing, naming things, working-peoples' expressions, sprung rhythms, with no abstract phrase, but metaphors rife in everyday expressions, poetic use at best with unforgettable or rhythmic cadences everywhere along coastal Guyana; and it seemed that our Indian ancestry was yet intact the more I intuited it. Feelings seesawed, as I felt fated to be here in this "outpost." A creole—sustaining time too it was, as cultures intermingled. Our being *Guyanese* with a nascent nationhood forming here in South America—far from Africa or India. Yet surprisingly it was also an India inspiring images of Kipling, as I conjured up Mowgli riding an elephant, and my being a mahout, then being with a Bengal tiger—though Guyana is more amenable to the jaguar—untamed, even chthonic, the mysterious Amazon jungle inspiring myths reflective of Amerindian beliefs that Claude Lévi-Strauss would write about.[1] And cosmologically, the jaguar represented the forested middle ground; the anaconda, the watery world below; the eagle soaring the world above the forest canopy—all according to lore, as I conceived it in my imagining.

Time and place were all, with more myths forming, or juxtaposed with the sense of an ancestral past and present time, but invariably associated with the spirit of the place and environment, being immanent the more I thought about it, the indelible imprint of the land no less. And my own family's sense of place, if only a faraway one, was somehow associated with a religious sensibility: my grandmother's Hinduism and lore drawn from the *Bhagavada Gita:* Ram and Sita, and the monkey-god Hanuman, or a distant Lanka, sometimes gripping us. And who was the fierce figure of Rawana, the evildoer? Everything still indelibly linked, inescapably with cane fires, didn't I know? Didn't I think too as I watched the sky light up once more of a dragon spitting fire, and it was St. George with a long-bladed sword engaged in an epic battle, everything active in the febrile imagination? The coastland somehow engendered it all.

In the Canje, far down the river by the same name, at a place called Magdalenenburg—there where the region's first slave rebellion (called a revolution) occurred—I also reflected on, if only subliminally, Cuffy and Akara: slave figures–turned heroes. All that riveted my consciousness, as if the environment itself had spawned the uprising; this was what I grew up with, as I re-created or experienced lurid dreams: palpable images of slaves actually struggling with irons or against whiplash; and their own deep longings for Africa as they dwelled in dark hovels—the ordeal of plantation life. But counterpoint: there were smells, aromas, cane blossoms amidst other flora forming an ambience while the sugar factory kept grinding, and heady molasses smells rose in the air. All I breathed in, inhaled.

But a different reality returned. The adults, villagers—including some who were relatives—would again go out in the fields to harvest the cane, backbreaking work that had to be done: their wielding the machetes—literally cutlasses—across whole fields of cane in the searing tropical heat. In the afternoon I watched the workers coming home, faces blackened with ash, unrecognizable as they seemed. Next punts—long narrow iron barges really—filled with neatly tied bundles of cane clanged thunderously as they snaked along in the network of canals, taking the harvest to the giant factory. King Sugar was lord and master: its economic impact was worldwide—with its own particular social and political consequences or resonance, always shaping the environment, if only ours; and maybe in faraway England, as well.

All the while I was increasingly imbued with the self: in the new place, with a new identity forming, including reflecting on current or past anxieties as Guyana's lurid world also spawned fears of the ole higue, jumbie, backoo, massacouraman, moongazer. All echoic, evil spirits haunting with shadows—indeed moving among us. Past and present seemed one in the village in backwater South America, adding to the fears growing in us as children. Sinews of body and mind too, the more I contemplated it, as I again watched the workers wending their way home, their faces veritable masks . . . far more than idylls one read about in poems by Cowper and Wordsworth. This was no romantic setting, but inescapable reality. And maybe we hoped that the socioeconomic order would change, far more than simply expressing romanticism of "ownership" of the sugar plantation with Guyana becoming independent in the mid-sixties, and not long after to assume a dubious socialist republican status; and would democracy be all, we hoped, as the races, cultures, creeds coexisted, or simply clashed? Upheavals in the new place, after "empire."

The throes of labor strikes followed, and political rivalry with change-over. Corruption, acrimony. Everything festered. Mistrust, tinged with a deterministic Marxism, and then Guyana seemed to be an almost ungovernable land despite the vast potential around: the environment itself seeming to take its toll, because of the vexed or troubled human spirit in a postindependent land. Crime inexorably reared its ugly head: all despite the promises of the vast hinterland resources (as part of the greater Amazon, with untapped forestry and mineral wealth), which we often extolled, or lamented.

For me during this period it was yet primarily the apprehension of a coastal life, coastal memories—as if I wanted it to always remain that way—the sugar plantation being supremely all. And the coastland wasn't yet swallowed up by the vortex of waves as the mangrove provided a barricade. All the while the two main races—Africans and Indians—competed or integrated with more than symbolic expressions of holi, phagwah, Eid, festivals all; and Christmastime as masquerade too, and Easter's kite-flying celebrating Jesus's ascension to heaven. Indian weddings welcomed entire villages, as pujas with the pundit's nasal chants rose in the puri-filled air in the tropical "paradise"—in the land once thought to contain El Dorado, as Walter Raleigh would have it.

Que-que, too: such distinctive African outpourings, as everything appeared immediate or authentic, as expressions of who we were indeed becoming. Underneath it all was the quest to survive as more cane fields were set ablaze, fires burned. And there was the *logie,* like the village's own: this makeshift narrow wooden building, not unlike a stable, where workers were "housed" during the cane-cutting season; and twenty or thirty men would cook, sleep together: blacks and browns, a veritable creole gang; and there seemed to be no sense of racial difference or animosity in congested space with the legacy of a slave past or indentured-labor angst; maybe it was only what was in the imagination, in the spirit's quest to survive above all else.

In odd ways I interacted with these workers in the desultory setting of a grandmother's cakeshop. I contemplated faces with more longings: these same workers, with families left behind—as everyone seemed bent on eking out a living doing truly mind- and spirit-numbing work in then British Guiana. Overhead cirrus clouds drifted by, and coastal birds like the kiskadee, robin redbreast, and blue-sackie skirted the air, or flitted about on the ground, especially during the rice-cutting season. This other form of subsistence, in sparse lands, or swamps adjoining the sugar estate—the villagers with a determined instinct to survive forging on with a memory of continents far away or close up. This I also cogitated on, and made my own experience and intimation over time.

SPACES IMBEDDED in us are often tied to family: in my case a grandfather, who was a "driver"—someone perhaps unique. He was called "Albion Driver": Albion being synonymous with a romantic England I conjured up, but ironic in the sense of outpost and empire. He was tasked with getting the able-bodied locals to go with him to set the cane fields ablaze, whole acres at a time in order to eliminate the hazardous cane thrash, insects, and rodents, all of which impeded the harvesting of the cane as the workers wielded their machetes against cane bark. (I sometimes imagined him in other sugar plantations everywhere across Guyana.) It was also rumored that the fire's intense heat actually improved the sucrose content of the cane's yield; but this was never proven. Looking back, I wondered if my grandfather had a particular management zeal in marshalling the most dependable villagers to go with him to strategically set these fires; and how quickly the flames rose up as I yet stood on the balcony of our house, like recurrent time, and watching it all imagined an apocalypse— the entire world ablaze, including England, Africa, and India. Heraclitan!

The term "driver" derived from the time of slavery—an overseer who "drove" the workers with a whip into spirited action. But did my grandfather really have such a status, illusory as it was? Six or seven I might have been when he was struck down with a stroke in our bottom-house, and he would die after a long and debilitating illness, leaving my grandmother to assume a matriarchal role. She now had to raise us, children and grand-children alike, such being her "lot," or fate, as she lamented: all according to customary Indian belief; and her sense of grief seemed mixed with a willful forbearance. And when the Driver was alive, wasn't she called a "maharagin," the female counterpart of a "maharajah" (of sorts): all that the environment spawned with ongoing mimicry, in the time of empire with the Raj appearing to somehow pantomime us in South America. Never mind Mahatma Gandhi and other Indian freedom fighters agitating for India's independence, and their also wanting to dispense with a caste system. For us, tradition and the indentured life were mixed with pain and penury.

My grandfather's presumed maharajah status was role-playing at best, I knew, a way for him to find refuge or solace from the hard life we lived. Imagine the heroes of Magdalenenburg also mimicking: seeing themselves as Dahomey kings as they rebelled . . . and longed for freedom, not unlike what would later occur in Hispaniola. Toussaint, Dessalines, Henri Christophe: Look out!

Our village cakeshop was where the workers often congregated after the day's work was done: their bodies sore, and I'd sense that they simply wanted to sustain their beings, in a manner of speaking. Our place was like a community center fostering a camaraderie of spirit among people mostly of Indian heritage (though there were also some of African backgrounds), all who desultorily discussed religion and politics, mixing Kalidas with Savaji and Gandhi, everything being interchangeable because of the mood they were in; and their awkward references to Aesop also, or legends invented by Homer. African Anancy stories too I listened to, as east and west, north and south, coalesced, or past and present came together. Everything ubiquitous, or a seeming mélange. Mantras also recited, though without sustained piety, yet with incorrigible ethnicity. A growing confidence, no less.

One or two villagers asserted themselves with intellectual finesse, I remembered, or it was just their pretension as they quoted the German scholar Max Müller on Indian thought and philosophy, or the sage Ramakrishna. And did Müller really say, "If I am asked under what sky the human mind has most fully developed some of its choicest gifts, has most deeply pondered on the greatest problems of life and has found solution of some of them . . . I shall point to India"? Inherent paradoxes, as seen in Warren Hastings's foreword to the East India Company's English rendering of the *Bhagavada Gita*. Did Hastings actually say that the "writings of the inhabitants of India will survive when the British dominion in India shall have long ceased to exist, and when the sources which it once yielded of wealth and power are lost to remembrance?"

Fate's hand at work, or life's inevitability: the same that brought the indentured workers, my ancestors, to these distant shores of the Caribbean and the Amazon. And wasn't sugar first crystallized in India long before the West knew about it . . . long before Columbus came to the so-called New World? Economic circumstances underpinned it all, in extolling King Sugar; and no one in this faraway land, especially those who toiled long in the fields, would ever forget their origins: with the Ganges or Ghana somewhere in the air. Later in Trinidad I would listen to novelist George Lamming concede that "we are endowed with a racial consciousness": this too an undeniable or ineluctable reality. Lamming would describe fears held by some, mostly Africans, as "a strategy for conquest," and that "Indian" is not a monolithic word; that the two major races, East Indians and Africans, come from a "common history of exploitation."

Always recall in me, as I pondered the image of that first ship that came to British Guiana in 1838 bringing my ancestors after the abolition of slavery, and the last such ship that came in 1917, the *jahagis,* as the ships' occupants called themselves, which I dwelled on particularly, since my maternal grandfather, whom I didn't know well at all, might have been on it: he was a boy when he arrived; and then a great-grandmother whom I indeed knew—she, as a woman, had crossed the dreaded *kala pani*!

My memory of this great-grandmother was of a bundle of a woman, without knowledge of English, who irascibly rebuked us with Hindi words—she seemed caught in the umbilicus of time, and was now forever removed from Bombay or Uttar Pradesh where she might have come from. And the environment inflicted itself on her senses. Her great-grand-children would now be also separated from Bharat—the land of her birth—even as we innocently or willfully mocked her in her dotage, because we were becoming "British" in a way. In her kernel of silence she might have re-created a whole tradition as she literally talked to herself, deep in her veins. I would observe her, like a relic; and later when I went to India—something she might never have imagined—and saw a bunch of old women in a side street in Bombay nattering together, their faces creased or corrugated-looking, yet distinctly lively or animated as they seemed, I immediately re-created my great-grandmother.

Vestiges all, the environment's grip always—the same sugar plantation life, as I relived it; and such a great fear was experienced in coming to Guyana and the Caribbean as Atlantic waves rose over a hundred feet high, I conjured; and my young grandfather's own pulverizing fear as a boy, and the lifelong insecurity it engendered because of that first traumatic experience—the same insecurity in us all, subsequently, a perpetual anxiety about survival. Would there be another time or another place for us?

A new mythos also appeared, in our mixing with other races and cultures, and not without the sense of serendipity: this interacting mostly with the descendants of African slaves leading to a creolization that seemed unrecognizable, unplanned or unrehearsed, as time went on; and dialectal impulses sometimes tinged with the rhythms of calypso (later reggae), which we would accept or simply deny because of almost different lifestyles we manifested. Zeitgeist, all. And were there different values associated with work and play too, and sentimental attitudes to family stemming not least from religious customs and beliefs? Committed politicians would berate us about our common social status and working-class background, and how to forge unity, despite distinctive racial consciousness, which the Europeans never had a stomach for anyway: this divide no less; and it always came down to how best to wrest better living conditions from the sugar plantation's powers that be. The struggle was on, integrally associated with the spirit of the environment.

And who were the oppressors, colonizers: all visions we carried with us, and in us? In awkward or amorphous ways I yet remained in the cake-shop in my personal reverie and watched the workers sometimes expressing themselves with bawdy laughter, or observed their frustration and frenzy giving way to rum-shop indulgences, or their idling time away by playing card games mostly, even as some surprisingly argued the poetics of religion: again the *Bhagavada Gita* or *Gitanjali* (Tagore), or formulated associations with the Prophet Mohammad and Christian ideals. Judaic, if also with a touch of the Hellenic. Didn't they also quote Aesop, willy-nilly? Wayside evangelists—hot gospelers—came too, and the children of the same sugarcane workers huddled under a "bottom-house" and lustily sang hymns led by a zealous grandmotherly African type eager to make "converts." How we looked forward to receiving a pristine religious card with a picture of Jesus on it, or one with an image of the Garden of Eden—my own favorite—because it seemed immediate to our environment.

Unconsciously I began cherishing my own sense of faith and belief, as if the environment was dictated by destiny itself and was making it all happen, as I also longed for an immediate salvation, like time to come. Did I just then again contemplate the cane fires? Our district with sluices, canals, kokers, the way irrigation itself circumscribed us: this too like a miracle because of man's will to dominate his place, the alluvium and clayey ground. And more of the individual spirit came into us as the mammoth cane factory hummed, throbbed: like a giant heart beating.

Like my very own.

HIBISCUS, SUNFLOWERS, lily, and bougainvillea: these were always in the air, in the hedges around the village houses; and how our minds worked ceaselessly in such arresting surroundings, the environment's almost romantic or idyllic appeal, yet with an unmistakable sugar-plantation air as cane fields wavered their tassel-like tops in the trade winds blowing. I kept looking out from the balcony of our house, in Adelphi village, or settlement (as it was also called); and maybe in a daydreaming cocoon I found myself in, I waited for an oracle of sorts to appear, not unlike how Wilson Harris evoked a classical Hellenic world with Agamemnon and Hector in his early poems as he saw correspondences while exploring the hinterland, as I'd begun reading about, numinously experiencing it all. I'd also begun listening to drama serialized by BBC on our KB radio, and re-created Victorian worlds, or just Jane Austen's. Opera also came over the radio, and other forms of classical music, such renditions, while those congregating at the shop scoffed, their being unaware of my own changing self. Maybe it was their own sense of an uncompromising identity, or will not to succumb to European culture.

The cane workers preferred Bollywood music as simple recreation for their minds too tired to think of anything else. Occasionally more classical Indian tunes stirred them to deeper thought: deeper longings, not without nostalgia or forlornness upon hearing the nightingale-like voice of Lata Mangeshkar over the radio. Jukebox time too it was with calypso, everything seemingly juxtaposed. But bhajans—such religious songs—with *Bhagavada Gita* appeals often transported them to a far time, a far place. Distant horizons, or new shores yet in the making, rivers or seas crossed, not far unlike the Arabian Sea. A fleeting sense always. Cirrus clouds kept moving overhead. A spectacular sunset also, more than cane fires ever created. Auguries, only.

Then the cane fields for a while disappeared altogether with a further blaze of fire. Tarantulas no longer floated down like ash, and maybe other worlds converged as I was growing up, my own feelings and emotions being on a tightrope. And did I begin to express concerns about saving the pristine, yet unspoiled environment because of the factory's potential for causing pollution? No determined ecological sense was in me, then—only later this was formed, as my awareness and consciousness grew. Then a sense of solitariness or solitude prevailed in me, and in others too. I recall one African villager, an old man, who brought his guitar to the cakeshop and plucked out a few recognizable tunes. His blues, you bet; and he and my grandmother conversed in a strange, mute rhythm. Voices of ancestry, lore, with other indwelling spirits stemming from the immediacy of plantation life, including a semblance of backoo, ole higue, and other jumbie spirits, as the environment itself inspired—all new fears. And then the moongazer, or the massacouraman—this latter a malignant water-spirit, which I would write about in my short novel *Dark Swirl*. Water indeed being everywhere, in our "land of many waters" with creeks, canals, rivers. Torrential rains poured down once more, everything appearing as an elemental onslaught, adding to the sense of forlornness and lore.

I yet mingled with everyone, watched and listened to their incessant jabber, being immersed in their body talk, laughter, the pain and still penury of daily living all around, our always trying to make ends meet because of paltry wages. More twisted, bent bodies: the human environment no less. But underneath it all there was also a zest for life, as seasons changed, or manifested as life's grinding monotony. Visions yet in me, as I imagined more places far away. And sugar was indeed the lifeblood, akin to my own beating spirit. Sugarcane, and rice-paddy fields, all around; and a heartbeat became more emblematic of where I now was, even in my vicarious return to the place of origins, and felt I'd never left. Left where?

The Canje district or the village and country as a whole with the sense of empire never truly disappeared, I figured, because of who lived here first a long time ago, and those who never wanted to be here in the first place but who finally inhabited the land and occupied spaces interpreted as authentic belief.

More waves rising up: a young boy, the same grandfather as he turned out to be, in dire fear, as the ships kept crossing the "dark water," rocking in midocean, but now for the last time. It was 1917. And that old woman, still the bundle, vicariously began returning to India in my imagination and being in a side street in Mumbai, as she cast a wayward glance at me, like an evil eye. Recognition it was; and did I now perhaps come from a new place called Canada with its own Great Spirit, or wherever else I happened to be?

Everything akin to the transmigration of souls, in the old woman's wavering consciousness no doubt due to what was believed by the ancient Greeks being subliminally in her, or what she might have conceived of Alexander the Great's designs on more than northern India (Punjab), but also on the whole wide world. Adelphi, like all other villages on the coastland Guyana not without oracular echoes, I also conceived, and with

Dutch, French, and English legacies, or what else I also vicariously coped with, but tried to deny because of my individual spirit forming.

Ships in all the world's oceans, in all corners of the globe too, more than Walter Raleigh or Francis Drake ever dreamed about. And Alexander the Great's ancestor Heracles, being at it, with the sense of simply being re-incarnated, not just transmigrated. Ashes floating down the Ganges, the wheel of fate or destiny turning because of the flame of fire in a coastland sugar plantation—and who first lived here, or the last, in spaces carved out of real memory, all working together to shape the land—a new environment palpably in the making.

Note

1. This I later tried to capture in my collection of poems *Born in Amazonia.*

Coffee and Colonialism in Julia Alvarez's *A Cafecito Story*

Trenton Hickman

In *A Cafecito Story,* renowned Dominican-American writer Julia Alvarez adventures into the world of progressive coffee cooperatives bent on "environmental, social, economic, and educational sustainability" by telling the story of an American named Joe who successfully aids a Dominican shade-coffee grower named Miguel in his quest to farm coffee in "the old way." The story's afterword, written by Julia Alvarez's husband, Bill Eichner, details the couple's real-life forays into the coffee business and their own dedication to environmentally friendly coffee cooperatives in the Dominican Republic. Certainly, Alvarez's *A Cafecito Story* merits a long list of praise from those concerned about the degradation of the Caribbean landscape by unwise farming practices and the exploitation of its family farmers. The text itself is published by Chelsea Green, an ecologically friendly press that has lavished all the right sort of attention on Alvarez's eco-parable and that makes clear that Alvarez's narrative, though fictional in one regard, is based on Alvarez's real-life coffee cooperative in the Dominican Republic. The book's attractive woodcut illustrations have been commissioned to a Dominican artist, Belkis Ramírez; it includes an appendix, "A Better Coffee: Devloping Economic Fairness," which advocates principles of fair trade, environmental sustainability, and the economic independence of less-privileged nations as well as includes a long list of resources and websites committed to such causes; and the final pages of the book promote the sale of other Chelsea Green books, recordings, and products committed to "sustainable living."

Even as I acknowledge these merits, I contend that although Alvarez's narrative ostensibly clears space for a new future for Dominican coffee growers, it also reinscribes the U.S. expansionist project of Manifest Destiny as a white Nebraskan farmer, filled with a yearning to carve his own homestead out of the "frontier," does so by seizing control of what Alvarez genders as "female" coffee and land as part of a new paternalism. In this manner, the exoticism of coffee grown in forests "filled with songbirds" actually renews age-old market paradigms first deployed in the old imperial centers of Europe and then in the United States. In the end, readers of Alvarez's book must ask themselves to what degree environmentally friendly farming practices in the Dominican Republic can shed their colonialist roots if the tropology to make such practices attractive to U.S. readers merely reiterates stereotypes about the land and resources of the Caribbean. As long as these "new" paradigms merely content themselves with renewing the old colonial relationships of paternalist, Euroamerican whites overseeing subservient filiations of mixed-race people of color, has much changed in the way the Caribbean is perceived? Also, I argue that close study of *A Cafecito Story* foregrounds for its readers the difficulty for writers to "see" the land of the Caribbean on its own merits and not simply as a site to superimpose their own desires onto the landscape through the telling of another unfortunate spatial story.

Coffee Cultivation in the Dominican Republic

Frequently in its narrative, Alvarez's *A Cafecito Story* mentions a return to "the old way" of coffee cultivation, invoking the superiority of shade-coffee cultivation (that is, the cultivation of full-grown coffee trees underneath an "overstory" of other tropical foliage) to the "new" farming of what has been termed "sun-grown coffee" (the growth of coffee "bushes" in full sunlight with heavy doses of artificial fertilizers and pesticides, which generates weak plants but larger, more quickly grown harvests). But when Alvarez's text tells us that Miguel "planted with coffee the old way," or when the narrative's white U.S. protagonist, Joe, passionately argues to the impoverished mestizo farmers that they "need to keep planting coffee your old way," the narrative also invokes a nostalgia for that which is "original," "foundational," or "natural" in the island of Hispaniola, a pseudo-Edenic revisiting of island ways whose historical presence has only recently been displaced by the machinations of corporate greed (15, 22). Hasn't the cultivation of coffee in the Dominican Republic always existed, Alvarez's text seems to ask? Can the cultivation of coffee be separated from the "ways" of the islanders that farm it?

At a fundamental level, Alvarez's nostalgia for the "original" points to an age-old history that never existed, for coffee cultivation in the Caribbean is relatively new, historically speaking, having arrived as part of the European colonial project and finally cultivated as an extension of capitalist development in the region.[1] That the introduction of *coffea arabica* was seen as an unnatural, even violent change for the Caribbean can be seen in the words of none other than Karl Marx, who as part of a critique of free trade noted: "You believe, perhaps, gentlemen, that the production of coffee and sugar is the natural destiny of the West Indies. Two centuries ago, nature, which does not trouble itself about commerce, had planted neither sugar-cane nor coffee trees there. And it may be that in less than half a century you will find there neither coffee nor sugar, for the East Indies, by means of cheaper production, have already successfully broken down this so-called natural destiny of the West Indies" (205).

It is true that Marx's conflation of the cultivation of coffee and sugar betrays his ignorance of the differences between the production and culti- vation of the two crops, and his forecast of the disappearance of both cash crops from the Caribbean by the end of the nineteenth century proved dead wrong. Still, his perception that a discourse already existed that would "naturalize" the history of both crops in the Caribbean imbricates coffee cultivation and the presence of European capital in the region, explaining the ideological investment in portraying coffee as an "original" part of the landscape.

While it is true that the French employed slave labor to grow and har- vest coffee during their dominance of Saint Domingue in the seventeenth and eighteenth centuries (Randall and Mount 16), the majority of coffee cultivation in the Dominican Republic occurred in *minifundias*—small, peasant-owned parcels of land where coffee was initially grown more for local consumption than for export—rather than on the large *latifundia* plantations (Topik 242). In the last half of the nineteenth century, the cul- tivation of coffee in the Dominican Republic "expanded enormously," becoming more widespread along with the farming of cotton, cocoa, and tobacco, and in the coffee-growing north a "decentralized peasant society evolved whose products were exported by a class of urban merchants" (Baud 135–36). Randall and Mount point out that until 1912, "the Dominican Republic's exports were overwhelmingly cocoa and sugar, with coffee consistently a very distant third," but when General Rafael Trujillo assumed dictatorial control of the Dominican Republic in 1930, he realized the attractiveness of coffee as one of the premier cash crops of the country (51). By 1955, Trujillo had created the "Café Dominicano" Company, an enterprise controlled by investment from Trujillista cronies that dominated the coffee revenues of the country.[2] Even though the small coffee grower suffered from the unfair competition generated by Trujillo's consolidation of coffee production and distribution and his preferential taxation of large-scale coffee growers allied to his cause, over half of the coffee production in the Dominican Republic in 1960 came from farms smaller than 100 acres.[3]

The most serious challenge to the small coffee grower in the Dominican Republic came not at the hands of Trujillo, however, but from those who seized control of the coffee industry in the wake of Trujillo's assassination and the abolition of his coffee enterprise. Adriano Sánchez Roa demonstrates that between 1967 and 1988, eight families created a de facto cartel that controlled 66 percent of the coffee production in the Dominican Republic (Sánchez Roa 9). These families, whose power enabled them to broker the price for Dominican coffee on the international market and that dictated the legislation of laws regarding coffee production and sales for all the producers in the Dominican Republic, are most likely the "*compañía*" that Miguel alludes to in *A Cafecito Story*.

The Coffee, The Land, and Alvarez's Songbirds

The development of high-yield varieties of coffee during the so-called "green revolution" of the 1970s increased the number of coffee trees that could be commercially cultivated "from 1,100–1,500 to 4,000–7,000 trees per hectare" (Waridel 34). These new, sun-resistant varieties of coffee encouraged many growers to bulldoze their shade-coffee crops in hopes of increased revenue and at the behest of the large coffee brokers. The resultant monocropping devastated the habitats that had existed in the shade-coffee plantations, which had depended on an overstory canopy of shade trees in order for their crop to grow and which had supported a dramatic biodiversity of insects, animals, and plants (Waridel 34–35). Once the sun-grown coffee filled the fields and this biodiversity largely vanished, other environmental problems occurred, including agrochemical pollution from fertilizers and pesticides and pronounced soil erosion (Waridel 35). In *A Cafecito Story*, Alvarez dramatizes Joe's first exposure to these degraded environmental conditions:

> As the truck heads up the narrow, curving road, Joe notices the brown mountainsides, ravaged and deforested, riddled with gullies. The road is made even more narrow by huge boulders. They must roll down during rainstorms. No trees to hold back the eroding soil. Suddenly, the hillsides turn a crisp, metallic green. A new variety of coffee grown under full sun, the old man beside him explains. A young man with a kerchief over his mouth his spraying the leaves. ¿Qué es? Joe asks the old man. Veneno, he answers, clutching his throat. A word Joe doesn't have to look up in his dictionary. Poison. (12–13)[4]

In fact, Alvarez echoes the words of earlier scholars about the ecological disaster that these coffee fields represent. Eduardo Galeano refers to "the story of coffee" in *Open Veins of Latin America* as that "which advances, leaving deserts behind it" (73); earlier in the century, Fernando Ortiz had labeled coffee one of the "four devils" of colonialist agriculture in the Caribbean (209).

In producing her account of the environmental impact of the coffee fields, Alvarez employs "songbirds" as special symbols to be metonymous for all that will be lost if the sun-grown coffee producers triumph. But Alvarez's prose, which has elsewhere condensed the data of complex environmentalist critiques into terse, gritty glances at the landscape, suddenly veers toward the romantic and the exotic when speaking of these birds. "In the midst of the green desert," she writes, "Miguel's land is filled with trees. Tall ones tower over a spreading canopy of smaller ones. Everywhere there are bromeliads and birdsong. A soft light falls on the thriving coffee plants. Perched on a branch, a small thrush says its name over and over again, chinchilín-chinchilín. A flock of wild parrots wheel in the sky as if they are flying in formation, greeting him" (13). Not only does Alvarez stage this scene to be lush and comfortable in contrast to the harsh "green deserts"—"bromeliad" flowers are in the trees, the lighting is "soft," the plants "full" and "thriving"—but the birds are made to be exotic and inviting, even "greeting" Joe's foreign gaze. Alvarez makes her thrush sound as if it speaks some tropical variant of Spanish, and her "wild parrots" invoke whole generations of literary texts that mark tropical exoticism with a similar plumage. Alvarez continues this pattern of exoticism as the narrative progresses, as the birds "sing to the cherries" to help ripen them (15). Finally, when Joe succeeds in luring the woman who becomes his wife to join him on the cooperative in the Dominican Republic, Alvarez extends an invitation to readers of *A Cafecito Story* that seems intended to ripen their own favorable reading and interpretation of the text: "Read this book while sipping a cup of coffee grown under birdsong. Then, close your eyes and listen for your own song" (37).

In reality, Alvarez's exoticism of the birds and their song depicts only a portion of the birds actually populating the shade-coffee forests of the Dominican Republic. Joseph Wunderle, the ornithologist who has carried out the most extensive recent research on avian distribution in the shade-coffee plantations of the Dominican Republic, reports that "a variety of resident and migrant bird species occupy these [coffee] plantations" and demonstrates that many of these "songbirds" are "Nearctic migrants" to the area; simply put, many of the birds that inhabit the groves that Alvarez details in *A Cafecito Story* are actually birds from North America that winter in the warm overstory of the shade-coffee plantations.[5] Nowhere in the ornithology research on the avian inhabitants of Dominican shade-coffee groves do we read of "wild parrots" populating these plantations, though birds that would be unfamiliar to Alvarez's U.S. readers (the lizard cuckoo, the Hispaniolan emerald, and local varieties of woodpecker, tody, tanager, and oriole) are mentioned in the study, and resident varieties of the "thrush" that Alvarez names do appear in the scientific data (Wunderle 64). Interestingly, Wunderle's research as well as the research of other ornithologists also deflates Alvarez's notion that these birds are drawn to the coffee plants themselves.[6]

Exoticism, Desire, and Nostalgia in Alvarez's Text

Why would Alvarez stay faithful to many of the small details of environmentalists' critique of sun-grown coffee fields and to their corresponding campaign to energize the shade-coffee industry but not accurately portray the songbirds around which she spins the more romanticized aspects of her narrative? I contend that Alvarez's text wants to reinscribe a very traditional set of historical desires and nostalgias onto the Dominican landscape, using the exotic romance of the songbirds as part of a larger strategy to feminize the coffee production that she chronicles and to accentuate the sexualized desire with which she colors the consumption of the shade coffee in her narrative (and, by extension, the land). By feminizing the coffee, its production, and its consumption, Alvarez's text clears a space for Joe, her nostalgic Nebraskan narrator, to reclaim the family farm he lost to agribusiness in Nebraska by means of a "new" homestead in the Dominican Republic. Joe sees his gesture, itself a smaller version of the same Manifest Destiny of which his ancestors were a part, as a "masculine" means to oppose the forces of globalization.

Unlike many of the writers who have composed narratives in the wake of the colonial encounter in the Caribbean, it is true that Alvarez is at one level sensitive to the colonial discourse about the Dominican Republic that she's inherited. She notes, for instance, how the advertisements that hawk their fun-in-the-sun vacations in the Dominican Republic to Joe speak of "the land Columbus loved the best," and she registers the tendency of these same advertisements to paint their tourism in terms of "barely clad beauties tossing beach balls with waves sounding in the background" (6). When Joe arrives at the beach resort, he is dismayed to see that "no natives are allowed on the grounds except the service people who wear Aunt Jemima kerchiefs and faux-Caribbean costumes and perpetual, desperate smiles of welcome" and that, what's more, "the barely clad beauties come with men already attached to their arms" (9).

Indeed, it is Joe's disenchantment with commerce in these worn-out exoticisms that initially compels him to visit Miguel's *minifundio* in the mountains. But Alvarez's postcolonial critique of the Dominican Republic as a simulacrum of post-Columbian sex-and-sun ends when Joe drinks his mystical first cup of shade coffee. Suddenly, Joe, the white divorcé who came to the Dominican Republic seeking an exotic, dark-skinned woman's love, finds himself seduced not by a half-naked, dark-skinned Dominican "beauty" but by a similarly exoticized cup of coffee. "Coffee comes in one denomination," Alvarez writes, "a dollhouse-sized cup filled with a delicious, dark brew that leaves stains on the cup. Joe closes his eyes and concentrates on the rich taste of the beans. He hears the same faint whistle he heard on the plane, getting closer" (10). This "whistle," which we've been told sounds like "a faint whistling of birdsong" that Joe imagines he can hear on the flight south while dreaming of the "barely clad beauty" he'll surely claim on the island, ties the coffee to the very exoticism that Alvarez seemed to critique earlier in the narrative, and the fact that this coffee comes in a "dollhouse-sized cup" only heightens the uncomfortable connection between the "dolls" of the Dominican Republic that Joe thought he would seek out upon his arrival and the exoticized Dominican coffee. When Joe arrives at Miguel's coffee farm and Miguel instructs him in the nuances of shade-coffee production, Alvarez extends the connection between coffee and the exoticized female even further as Miguel explains: "When a bird sings to the cherries as they are ripening, it is like a mother singing to her child in the womb. The baby is born with a happy soul" (15). Miguel goes on to explain: "The wet granos [coffee beans] we take to the river for washing. They must be bathed with running water for eight or so hours—a watchful process, as we have to get the bean to just that moment when the grains are washed but no fermentation has begun. It is not unlike that moment with a woman—Miguel smiles, looking off toward the mountains—when love sets in" (19).

By helping her readers understand that processing coffee beans to have a full-bodied flavor is like coaxing "love" out of "that moment with a woman," Alvarez sexualizes the coffee in a way that reinvokes the heterosexual colonial stereotypes about the exotic female nature of the Caribbean that she seemed to have dismissed earlier in the narrative. Alvarez reminds us of this link between coffee and a sort of exotic sensual pleasure once again as Miguel informs Joe that the "coffee tastes better than anything" because Joe, as "a farmer's son," can "taste with [his] whole body and soul" (20). Only a few pages later, when Joe's sister invites him to a visit in Nebraska and asks if he'll stay, Joe replies, "I have a family," and Alvarez's narration explains, "Although he has never married, he has become a husband to the land," and we also learn that the progeny of Joe's marriage to the Dominican landscape is "his large campesino [peasant] familia, all of whom he has taught to read and write" (26).

Through these associations, Alvarez renews the paternalism that had existed for centuries between plantation owners and their "family" of workers in Caribbean societies and allows a white male to figuratively "inseminate" himself into the "colored," "feminine" land of the Dominican Republic. By tasting the coffee, Joe tastes and ultimately possesses the feminine in the Dominican Republic's exoticized landscape—if he comes to the Dominican Republic looking for a romance, he gets it. Once wedded to the female body of the Dominican coffee plantation, Joe "fathers" the awakening of his Dominican "child" workers into literacy and modernity.[7]

In this way, Joe enables himself to achieve a new sort of masculinity, one rooted in his identification with his Nebraskan farmer father. At the beginning of *A Cafecito Story,* Joe has failed to be a man like his father, who once successfully maintained a large farm in the Nebraskan prairie, where "gulls," "swallows," and "sparrows" enriched the land with their own birdsong before he was forced out by big agribusiness (3–4). This loss of a chance to be a farmer like his father emasculates Joe; Alvarez writes that "something seemed to be missing from [Joe's] life" and credits Joe's divorce to his first wife, a "city girl," in part to the fact that Joe felt "adrift, a little lost" (4–5).

At least part of Joe's characterization as a male-made-man-through-farming likely derives from Julia Alvarez's awareness of her husband Bill Eichner's own attitudes toward the land of the Dominican Republic. Although Eichner makes a specific point of informing his reader that "my wife Julia and I are not the man and the woman of the parable," he concedes that "our story is related to this parable" and goes on to state that he is "from farm stock in Nebraska" and that he had not "realized that the same kind of technification that had eliminated sea gulls and family farms in Nebraska was now doing a job on traditional shade-coffee farms in the tropics" (Eichner 39–40). Eichner concludes, "Julia and I saw first-hand how globalization was changing the *campo,* or countryside, that we had both known as youngsters" (40).

If Alvarez's and Eichner's texts want us to understand Joe's fight against the "globalization" of agribusiness as a worthy cause on the environmental and social levels, the texts' tropes also necessitate that we see their story as the ideologically problematic struggle of a Nebraskan family farmer to carry on a masculine Manifest Destiny on a new female "frontier" found in the Dominican shade-coffee plantation. In this manner, the unfortunately familiar hue of European-American paternalism over the "mismanaged," "exotic" land of the Caribbean emerges anew in Alvarez's narrative.

Spatial Stories and the Land of the Dominican Republic

Michel de Certeau has argued that when an individual or social entity needs to exert its authority over a certain physical space but worries that the legitimacy of the authority over that space will be questioned, a "spatial story" is invented that enables the corresponding appropriation of that space.[8] In Julia Alvarez's *A Cafecito Story,* we encounter a spatial story that seeks to rewrite the economic and social history of Dominican shade-coffee farming by giving us what it calls a "parable" to illustrate the environmental and social woes that are the fruit of a long history of abuse culminating in the latest exploitation of the Caribbean by the multinational capital of agribusiness. The other part of the spatial story that Alvarez tells wants readers to see the coffee and island of the Dominican Republic as one more "colored" female landscape in which a white male presence can figuratively inseminate itself; the "love" of this land is meant to be the love of the supervisory gaze of man for the woman of the landscape. Will this combination of spatial stories enable its readers to escape the abusive paradigms of the past, as Alvarez's text ostensibly aims to facilitate? In raising this question, I do not suggest that Alvarez's text is guilty of a unique or unusual problem; indeed, I argue that because *A Cafecito Story*—a narrative composed by an admirable, engaging writer who has proven herself sensitive to many aspects of the diasporic Caribbean and to its history—perpetuates colonialist views of the Caribbean, its people, and its environment, we should reassess the contributions of all narratives, fictional or otherwise, in their contributions to how one perceives the "nature" and the "natural" history of the Caribbean and its islands.

For if we continue to think of the land, in the Caribbean or otherwise, as female and of the modification of that land in the name of "progress" as male, then we will not be able to conceive of a progressive economics and environmentalism that doesn't first involve the "seduction" and "impregnation" of the land, first metaphorically and then literally by the violent introduction of alien crops, settlements, and societies. In making this point, I would suggest that writers like Alvarez who, like many of us, wish to write about the land in progressive terms don't *intend* to perpetuate these patterns of thinking. But because these writers perhaps wish to honor and conserve a land's "beauty" and have understood the "beautiful" to be equated with the feminine, pejorative male associations with the handling of the land inevitably insinuate themselves into their texts. It is ironic but true that the act of embracing the best qualities of the land through the use of female-associated language simultaneously enables the language of rape and despoilment that cages our view of the land as a victimized, passive entity in the clutches of a malignant male embrace.

As it tells its spatial story, Alvarez's *A Cafecito Story* also relegates the voice of the Dominican shade-coffee farmer to second-tier status, asking a character like Miguel to function as a mere enabler for Joe's Manifest Destiny in the tropics. Miguel knows much about coffee cultivation but is portrayed as one almost completely disconnected from a knowledge of the flow of multinational capital. This, too, is part of Alvarez's spatial story, one that would validate a Dominican-American writer returning to the island of her childhood as a more benevolent, environmentally progressive colonizer of the land, "civilizing" the undereducated coffee farmers through ambitious literacy projects. But as Édouard Glissant has argued on behalf of the so-called "peasantry" of the Caribbean: "It is certainly true that we . . . are no longer the country people we used to be, with our same old instinctive patience. Too many international parameters come into this relationship. A man involved in agriculture is inevitably a man involved in culture: he can no longer produce innocently" (*Poetics* 149). The "innocence" and naiveté that Alvarez ascribes to Miguel and his compatriots would, against the reality that Glissant presents, credit the Dominicans with little more than a vague awareness of the "international parameters" of their situation, and in doing so would absolve Alvarez's spatial story of its obligation to present or represent the ideological commitments of the community in more than a passing, romanticized manner. For Alvarez's spatial story wants to convert Miguel and his family into something not unlike the exotic songbirds that flutter through *A Cafecito Story*: quaint, simple, and unproblematically beautiful in their ties to the earth and in their eroticizing role in the shade coffee's production and consumption.

There would appear to be much more work to be done before we really hear the "birdsong" and "see" the plantations of the Dominican Republic. Glissant has suggested that embracing "an aesthetics of the earth" rather than thinking of the earth as "territory" would offer the possibility of this peeling away of dated spatial imaginations of the Caribbean. He argues: "Territory is the basis for conquest. Territory requires that filiation be planted and legitimated. Territory is defined by its limits, and they must be expanded. A land henceforth has no limits. That is the reason it is worth defending against every form of alienation" (*Poetics* 151). Glissant understands that abandoning an "aesthetic of the earth" for genealogies of economic, historical, and cultural affiliations only inscribes extra-environmental ideologies on the land. The earth, as Glissant apprehends it, could conceivably be loved on its own merits: not on its ability to produce crops, not on a vision of its personification as a feminized Other, and not as a site to enact policies of hopeful postmodern social programs pre-viewed as counterbalances to the heartlessness of globalization.

If this revisioning of the earth is to be realized, it will require that the dualities inherent in spatial stories like Alvarez's (narratives of self/Other, the banal/the exotic, civilized/uncivilized, male occupier and cultivator of the land/female landscape) be collapsed. As Ben Heller has noted, this rhizomatic and "relational" model that Glissant proposes "is not a rejection or abandonment of the self, but an errancy that finds/founds the self through relation with the Other" (405). The "errancy" to which Heller alludes speaks to Foucault's argument that the "see/being seen dyad" is what must be eliminated in order to frustrate the supervisory gazes that warp fundamental perceptions of power distribution in society;[9] if we want to be able to find an "aesthetic of the earth," perhaps for the first time, we must always understand the "errancies" of our gaze of that earth and how the "errant" gazes of the Other are, in turn, supervising and constructing us in their own errant ontological strategies.[10]

In the case of Alvarez's story, a refusal to make the earth of the Dominican Republic metonymous for desires that at a basic level have nothing to do with the tropical landscape itself would seem to be the first step in being able to see the earth and its "aesthetic" for the first time. This would create a rupture of perception that would direct the reader's gaze not toward territorial definition and inevitable "conquest" of the land but toward the earth as an entity worthy of independent consideration. For Alvarez, a writer who wishes to connect herself to new goals for the land of the Dominican Republic, such a consideration would offer the possibility of entirely new solutions—not ones that seek to "impregnate" the "female" coffee plantations of the Dominican Republic with a slightly more beneficent deployment of U.S. capital, but ones that understand how the future of the shade-coffee groves and its songbirds has more to do with the earth, its flora and fauna, and the fluvial movements of its wildlife from one ecosystem to another outside of the recent advent of colonialism, capitalism, and the United States' infatuation with the elusive cup of perfectly flavored coffee.

Notes

1. This is especially true with the "heirloom" coffees cultivated on the real-life cooperative owned by Alvarez and Eichner and detailed in the afterword to *A Cafecito Story,* which descend from *coffea arabica* beans brought from the Middle East in the years following Columbus's "discovery" of Hispaniola and during the epoch in which European states saw in coffee a new mercantilist opportunity. See Topik 229.

2. Of the million pesos invested in the enterprise, around half came from Trujillo's personal coffers, though it was invested by his friends Tirso Rivera, Féderico García Godoy, and Manuel de Moya Alonso. See Sánchez Roa 15.

3. Sánchez Roa 17. It would make sense to see the narrative of *A Cafecito Story* indirectly attack Trujillo's legacy, since two of Alvarez's earlier novels, *How the García Girls Lost Their Accents* and *In The Time of the Butterflies,* critique the abuses of Trujillo's regime. Alvarez's critique of Trujillo, however, seems less a critique of the United States' involvement in the economic practices of the Trujillo regime. In fact, Trujillo's economic commitments consistently played to U.S. desires for regional economic "stability," which meant that *Trujillista* economics were, at an important level, U.S. economic policies for the island.

4. Alvarez's description, which would seem to collapse the entirety of the environmental stress that these new coffee fields place on the Dominican ecosystem into one glance, accords with Eichner's account in the book's afterword, where he notes: "While there [in the mountains of the Dominican Republic where the bulk of the coffee is grown], we were shocked by the "green desert" of the surrounding modern coffee farms. By the uniformity of the monoculture—hillside after hillside without a single fruit or shade tree. No sign of life except coffee plants and a single masked worker walking down the rows in a cloud of chemicals he was spraying on the coffee." See Eichner 39–40.

5. See Wunderle 59; and Wunderle and Latta, "Winter Site" 596–614.

6. See Wunderle 65–68; Wunderle and Latta, "Avian Resource Use" 273–80. Similar findings can also be seen in Perfecto et al. 601. In fact, a study published in the American Ornithologists' Union's quarterly journal points out that the American redstarts, perhaps one of the best examples of a bird that actively forages in the coffee plants by eating the coffee berry borer (its larva destroys the coffee cherries themselves), aren't exclusive to the shade-coffee plantations that Alvarez would champion but also can be found preying on the insects in sun-grown coffee fields that Alvarez condemns. See Sherry 563–66.

7. That Joe returns to the United States to bring back an actual woman to be his literal wife is but an afterthought in the narrative, a way during the narrative's denouement to have the would-be-writer wife give birth to Joe's narrative of how he has placed seed in the Dominican Republic.

8. See de Certeau 115–30.

9. See Foucault, *Discipline and Punish* 202.

10. In other words, the propensity of individuals to think of the Caribbean in terms of "filiation" instead of "relation" means that the landscapes of the Caribbean don't have an existence outside of the colonial genealogies that have overdetermined our perceptions since Columbus. We can't see the Caribbean as a site where different groups have creolized relationships; we only see the Caribbean as a family tree instigated by the colonial project, peppered with the race-mixing of colonial desire (Glissant, "Creolization" 269–75).

PART 2

Myths of Origins

Subjection and Resistance in the Transformation of Guyana's Mytho-Colonial Landscape

Shona N. Jackson

IN HIS SEMINAL work on Caribbean cultural production, Antonio Benítez-Rojo has written, "the search for El Dorado continues . . . carried out by present-day Guyanese beneath the slogan of 'repossessing the interior'" (189). Today, the Guyanese interior is a place of mineral excavation and tourist excursion. It holds a place of both cultural significance and material promise in the postindependence national imagination. The socialist program enacted by the Burnham government in 1969 sought to achieve agrarian reform in the hinterland through the redistribution of land and the vocational training of its Amerindian inhabitants. Essential to this physical reform was the recapture of the landscape, particularly the interior, for the Guyanese cultural imagination. This shift in cultural thought about the landscape was achieved by the Forbes Burnham/Peoples National Congress articulation of anticolonial, black nationalist discourse with the discursive structures of the myth of El Dorado, the existing narrative of domination for the region. Consequently, despite its shift from being re-presented in white-settler, colonialist narratives to postcolonial, nationalist narratives, Guyana's interior continued to be endlessly yielding for both material and cultural production.

At independence, the myth of El Dorado was incorporated into nationalist discourse, its generative capacity transformed. It became central in facilitating a transition from colonial narratives of exploitation and domination to one of a national destiny. The myth continued, in the hands of Guyana's new nation builders, to produce the landscape as a postcolonial, national space. It also continued to produce the raced and gendered subjects that simultaneously try to rewrite their roles in this shifting narrative. Today, the myth of El Dorado codes colonial exploitation of the land as postcolonial development and facilitates Amerindian subjection as a people who are both literally and figuratively "bound" to the hinterland.[1]

This paper elaborates on Benítez-Rojo's claim by arguing that it is not just the "search" that has continued but the historical subjection of the land and people wrought by the El Dorado myth, as it was manipulated by the Burnham regime to create an image of Guyana for consumption in the postindependence national imagination.[2] It further argues that the unevenly subjugated bodies of the land and the people, particularly the image of the Amerindian woman, have always retained recalcitrant elements that constitute a historical resistance to domination.

Guyana's uneven landscape, with its flat, densely populated coastal areas and the variegated landscape of the interior savannahs and tropical forests, is not just the ground on which the drama of Creole culture is played out. It has been the single constitutive element of Guyanese cultural reality and politics, from its objection in colonial discourse as the "land" of El Dorado to its retelling in Wilson Harris's work and his attempt to intervene in the constitutive power of the myth. From politics to literary aesthetics, there has been a ceaseless effort to control and possess the land, one of the most striking images of which lies in early description of the tons of polder moved by slaves to create the coast as it stands today (Rodney 1981). In the struggle to possess the land, both literally and figuratively, one sees the pattern of resistance that it forms within the discourses of power. The inability to contain the land as a singular object of desire inside any colonial or postcolonial discourse is its most consistent feature.

Myth, Treasure, and Transformation

In his essay "The History That Literature Makes," Richard Waswo writes of the significance of the meeting of myth and history. Waswo argues that "the founding legend of Western civilization—the descent from Troy—in its literary retellings from Virgil to the sixteenth century shaped the actual behavior of Europeans and Americans in their subsequent contact with other, newly 'discovered' cultures" (541). In identifying the role of this origin narrative for Western civilization, he writes that over centuries, the myth has had literary and scientific reenactments that validate or reify its telling. Waswo attributes this to the "constitutive power of any discourse." He argues that, as such, history is determined by myth and that literature, like myth, is an integral functioning part of entire cultural systems; these are the discourses that shape "our" world (542). While Waswo is concerned with the enabling myth of European exploration and colonization, he does provide a way of viewing the El Dorado myth and its function in Guyana and Latin America. The El Dorado myth, which led to the sustained exploration of the New World, served the same function as the one through which its discovery and development could be understood. While the myth functioned as a narrative of conquest and right for Europeans, by allowing the West to live out its manifest destiny (its own narrative of origin with relation to its Others), it became a narrative of origin for those already in the New World and all subsequent groups who entered. Following Waswo, the myth of El Dorado can be viewed as the founding myth of the South American continent.[3] The myth has remained integral to the South American region's historical development because of the function myths have served throughout history as narratives of origin or genesis.

The myth became *the* origin narrative for the entire region and as such the region continues to struggle with it because of its capacity to articulate imperial, colonial, and postcolonial discourses of power. It has remained integral to the region's cultural discourse as evidenced by the works of Cuban writer Alejo Carpentier and Guyanese writer Wilson Harris. According to historians, the myth "took shape" in the accounts of Fray Pedro Simón and began to evolve in the work of subsequent writers and explorers (Hemming 1978). While the mythical El Dorado that explorers like Domingo de Veras, Jimenez de Quesada, and others sought after was thought to be in today's Colombia and Ecuador, explorer Antonio de Berrio located it in the region of today's Guyana, and it was this account that Sir Walter Raleigh believed, leading him to Trinidad and then Guyana in search of what has been called a "personal and national El Dorado" (166). In Guyana, the myth heralded the development of the region, the displacement of its original inhabitants, and its eventual transformation into what Percy Hintzen calls a "colony of exploitation."[4] The problem for Guyana is that, following Waswo, the myth of El Dorado continues to be "elaborated as history" (544). With its attendant displacing and de-historicizing effect, the myth is an integral part of the country's national history and destiny as successive generations interpret and continue to live out its promise. As with the "legend of descent from Troy," the El Dorado myth continues to produce not only economic reality but political and social reality as well. Given its onto-historical significance, the myth, therefore, must be considered alongside the plantation system, which it also "produced," as a composite part of the "Caribbean machine."[5]

In his interpretation of the genesis and development of Caribbean culture as a uniquely postmodern one, Antonio Benítez-Rojo, in *The Repeating Island,* has written that "the Antilles are an island bridge connecting, 'in a certain way,' South and North America, that is, a machine of spume that links the narrative of the search for El Dorado with the narrative of the finding of El Dorado; or . . . the discourse of myth with the discourse of history; or . . . the discourse of resistance with the language of power" (4). His work suggests that the myth has made the Caribbean region; it is a key part in its historical narrative. While this claim comments more on the contemporary relationship of North to South America, one that did not begin to emerge until centuries after both were "discovered," it emphasizes the endlessly generative capacity of the myth. Like Benítez-Rojo's Caribbean "womb" that continually births supplies for metropolitan centers, the myth is a generative space that has produced the racialized and feminized space of the Guyanese hinterland landscape. It is a space that no one can reach, except through the language of desire on the symbolic road to wealth, but one that must continually be lived out. However, in living it out, the possibility of transformation emerged and the old fiction became the truth of a new nation in 1966. At Guyana's independence, the myth, reduced to the gold it promised and captured symbolically in a national commitment to progress and development by the yellow on the Guyana's flag, was transformed. After being tied to a Western colonial narrative of being that can be traced back to the fourteenth-century Italian humanists, it became the founding myth of what was no longer a colony, but a new nation, creating a unique historical and political problem. Blacks and East Indians who were formerly integral to the myth's enactment as colonial subjects, as laborers, suddenly inherited the myth as their own narrative of progress at the same time that Amerindians sought to challenge it through a discourse of "prior rights" that, to date, only the United Nations has *fully* acknowledged.[6]

There are several colonial histories and postcolonial cultural and historical works that treat the myth. The narratives include tourist propaganda, autobiography, fiction, and historical works.[7] One text by Mathew French Young, entitled *Guyana, the Lost El Dorado: A Report on My Work and Life Experiences in Guyana, 1925–1980,* deserves mentioning here because of what it suggests about the myth's potential to be articulated with new national narratives of progress and development.[8] It is in Young's autobiography that we witness the new transformation of the initial treasure occurring, as the gold of the El Dorado myth and of Young's own search gives place to the "land" itself.

Young, a white colonial born in Guyana, narrates his life in the interior, chronicling everything from historic events like the Jonestown massacre to the East Indian girl he "ruined" and the stillborn child that resulted. According to Young, he was called out of retirement in 1970 by the new cooperative government of Guyana to build roads in the interior from

Mahdia-Potaro to the Brazil border since he had originally carved a trail along this route in his various explorations of the interior. Young's autobiography, endorsed by government officials, is a key moment where the myth can be taken out of the hands of British explorers and Spanish conquistadors by a native, white colonial and handed intact, with minor changes—such as *you* must now think differently of this treasure than *we* did—to a brown, postcolonial, governing elite.[9]

The road project that Young worked on and that served to connect and open up parts of the interior for subsequent development schemes by the Burnham government is a metaphor for the transfer of power at independence. The "road" is a symbolic bridge of two historical narratives (colonial and postcolonial) that shows how the colonial source of wealth can become the postcolonial "source of power" for a new nation that needs to make its own claims on history. It is a bridge that can only be built or crossed with the service of his skin color, which can move between colonial and postcolonial status with relative ease, unlike those who now employ him and who have on occasion paid with their lives to bring the shift into being.[10] Young is literally helping to build the road to El Dorado. His autobiography is about the continuity of *the* narrative of the search for wealth. It demonstrates how the myth was kept current and how it serves as a discursive mechanism for the production of the Guyanese landscape as the new treasure. The interior remains the last ground onto which the narrative of civilization as it comes out of the West can be enacted for Guyana. Ultimately, the narrative currency for the myth's continual function lies with Amerindian subjugation and subjection, which facilitates the land's identity as the new treasure.

Becoming a Co-operative Republic

In *Stains on My Name, War in My Veins,* Brackette F. Williams has written of the nation-building Guyanese of the 1980s. In the 1970s, then Prime Minister Forbes Burnham was creating the "construct." *Co-operative Republic, Guyana 1970: A Study of Aspects of Our Way of Life* is a collection of essays edited by Lloyd Searwar about Guyanese culture and economics. Sponsored by the Guyanese government and endorsed by businesses, it identifies the sources of culture for Guyanese and shows them how the cooperative is integral to Guyana's economic growth and to its cultural expression as an independent nation. The inside flap informs Guyanese that they need to "reach back beyond the origins of Fort Zeelandia to begin the *urgent* task of hinterland development"[11] (my emphasis). As one writer in the volume puts it: "if we are to extend our vision beyond the coast and if we are to utilize the country's potential to its fullest, we must study the resources available in the interior . . . A knowledge of the land and its resources is therefore a pre-requisite to any program of development" (Poonai 162). It is this "knowledge" that *Co-operative Republic* tries to produce and cement in the national conscience.

The Guyanese interior is the last space undeveloped by white colonials onto which blacks in the Burnham/PNC administration can shift the narrative of civilization. However, bringing the hinterland into the mainstream of the national economy and cultural consciousness cannot occur simply by rewriting the myth. It cannot occur without "the necessary assimilation of the Amerindian into a modern scientific and socio-economic system" (Payne 248). This last measure is what achieves the transformation and rewriting of the narrative of the El Dorado myth, allowing it to be newly productive in a postcolonial setting. The land, with its human and cultural surplus, is now the real treasure for this regime, one on which it can build an economic and cultural base that can sustain a program of economic egalitarianism. The whole of Guyanese history has been a struggle for "possession," and the push into the interior under the cooperative program allows blacks to finally inhabit a conquering position in that narrative.

Co-operative Republic 1970 is part of a propaganda campaign designed to consolidate all areas of society, from economics to ethnic diversity, into one narrative that the regime could essentially manipulate in a kind of economic egalitarianism that would engender loyalty to the state.[12] A central part of this was the rearticulation of the El Dorado myth inside the narrative of cooperative development. However, in spite of the ability of the myth to be represented in postcolonial cultural-nationalist and political discourse, a critical intervention precedes this representation. It exists in the form of Wilson Harris's *The Palace of the Peacock* (1960), and his concern, unlike that of previous narratives, not with the life of the myth but with its subjects. Harris's work, however, demonstrates that even literary retellings must confront the ongoing articulation of the myth inside contemporary political discourse, a reality that, ironically, poses problems for Harris's interpretation. Further, Harris's work has become part of the discourse of a new nationalism, and it is this nationalism that haunts his fictional intervention.[13]

The Recalcitrant Muse

In his preface to Wilson Harris's *The Palace of the Peacock,* literary critic Kenneth Ramchand writes, "the novel arises from an almost literal-minded obsession with expressing intuition about 'the person'" and "the structure of societies men have built for themselves" (3). Harris's intent, a reimagination of the sixteenth- and seventeenth-century search for El Dorado in South America, is to deny that any society has "an inevitable existence." Moreover, Ramchand suggests that what concerns Harris is "a series of subtle links" that compose and are natural to the West Indian (3). Harris himself has said that his task is to "visualize a fulfillment, a reconciliation in the person and through society, of the parts of a heritage of broken cultures" (3).

Broadly, the novel is about seven ill-fated explorers in the region of today's Guyana (formerly British Guiana), traveling to the interior settlement of Amerindian peoples ("the folk") called Mariella. With the novel, Harris recovers the founding myth of the region, the myth of El Dorado, from Western imperial and colonial narratives of exploration and belonging to challenge prevailing ideas about Guyana's interior landscape. He uses this moment of contact as the ground on which a reconciliatory origin for the Creole person in the Caribbean can be imagined. As critics have argued, Harris ultimately narrativizes the "quintessential" myth of pre-Columbian exploration of Guiana in order to reinscribe a "Caribbean psyche." He achieves this through experimentation with West Indian and European cultural and narrative forms, which allows him to write a Caribbean psyche into a discovery myth that has operated in Euro-western historical narratives through the denial of that very subjectivity. As numerous literary scholars have noted, a major strategy of Harris's in positing an "integrated" psychic subjectivity is the consistent blurring of geographic and historical boundaries between the *self* and the *other* until the narrative's close, when the characters come to recognize themselves in and as the other they have externalized and objectified.

Writing about the novel, literary critic Michael Gilkes focuses on Harris's relationships with the land. In keeping with Hena Maes-Jelinek's claims, Gilkes has said that the novel is an attempt to reintegrate this psyche through "an interior journey." In achieving this, Gilkes further claims that Harris necessarily erases the historical and geographical boundaries that would have existed at the time expeditions to El Dorado occurred. The novel, he suggests, involves not only a re-creation of an "innocent" preconquest exploration of the region but also "the *modern* Guyanese dream of 'repossessing the interior': a phrase which can be taken to mean both the developing of an extensive ... hinterland, and the establishment of a genuine sense of cultural and psychological roots" (*Caribbean Novel* 24; my emphasis).[14] At points in Gilkes's reading of the novel, the land

and the people are collapsed and naturalized through spatial othering and through gender when he begins to analyze the relationships among Mariella (as woman and place), the folk, and the land. Gilkes's articulation of these relationships is problematic and suggests limitations in Harris's representations. Gilkes references the sexual metaphors that proliferate in the novel, suggesting that they "relate to Donne's rape of Mariella (like his rape of the land) and serve as a reminder that the capacity for joy is also the capacity for pain" (29). Gilkes continues, "the dreamer is in this way made aware of his own lack of wholeness" in reference to "the dreamers own imperfect manhood and self-knowledge" (30). He then contrasts the dreamer's imperfection with the land and forest and the people in harmony with it. While Gilkes foregrounds this subjection of the land and of the Amerindian woman, he does not complicate the relationship that is established in the novel. Gilkes naturalizes a series of positions or acts without querying what, for example, it means to establish a metaphoric link between two substantively different types of "rapes." In *The Palace of the Peacock,* the land, or its subjection, is feminized through the Amerindian woman, and this feminization becomes a *pre*condition of its own subjection or rape. I suggest that to identify woman with land so entirely, at *particular* historical moments, regardless of cultural belief, is to instantiate a relational subjection where each referent's place validates, explains, or codifies the other's.

One important passage in Harris's work where his narrative style and method are most clearly revealed has been the focus of much critical attention. It is a passage where Harris's technique is elaborated through Mariella's figure. The passage reads: "her crumpled bosom and river grew agitated with desire, bottling and shaking every fear and inhibition and outcry. The ruffles in the water were her dress rolling and rising to embrace the crew" (Harris 73). In interpreting this passage, Gilkes writes, "the old Amerindian woman becomes, in the men's eyes, a seductive siren—their longing for the Folk and the security of the land—whose disturbing presence encloses them all, like the rapids . . . but also guides them to safety" (31). The passage, and Gilkes's reading of it, demonstrates the close relationship of woman to land and the alienated position the men hold. They also reveal the language of desire in which Mariella is caught and through which she must emerge. The old woman that the crew captures and who serves as their guide, identified with the land, must be the object of both longing and comfort. Additionally, the recognition of the latter in Harris's work is what becomes the initial ground for psychic integration.

Through the contraction of Mariella's character into an ambiguous muse, she becomes a multiple signifier that can only be read or understood through these relationships. Even her own relationship to the folk must be expressed in terms of her ambiguous function as a narrative sign of desire, difference, and belonging. Mariella is woman and land (and to some extent "folk" through reference to her as "buck") and also the sign of these things. However, we have no sense of her own subjectivity because, as a sign, she is mediated by a series of oppositional relationships and naturalizing gestures. Maes-Jelinek has interpreted the above passage, arguing, "the word 'embroideries' refers at once to the waves of the river, the design of the Arawak woman's kerchief, and the 'wrinkles on her brow'" (Maes-Jelinek, *Naked Design* 13–14). She further holds that the passage is part of the "creation of a 'native consciousness,'" which Harris ultimately achieves through the union of crew and folk (14). What Maes-Jelinek describes is the link, established by Harris, and elaborated by Gilkes, of Mariella's subjection to the land as facilitator of the social network formed by them all and the space that is consequently reflected in their interactions as they move, psychically, to its perfection or embodied wholeness. This moment in the novel and critical attention to it demonstrate how land, history, and woman are unalterably troubled.

Gilkes's and Maes-Jelinek's interpretations can also be read against Harris's own claims about the novel. In the "New Preface to *The Palace of the Peacock,*" Harris describes Mariella, saying that she "embodies a plurality of woman" and that she is "an embodiment of women and a womb of potentialities" (Harris 56). Further, Gilkes sees Mariella as a "regenerative womb," an "artifice rooted in nature." In her capacity as a sign, Mariella's identification is collapsed with the land, but her subjectivity, or how she experiences herself as a woman, is not represented and cannot be, through her representation as a productive element of the land. In Harris's rationalization of her appearance in the text as a pre-Colombian figure, he does not detail how the myth he utilizes relates to women and necessitates this position via the land. He describes parts of the body as they are important in legend, but not how he moves from that to women. This is not to suggest that pre-Colombian myth cannot identify woman with land, but that the recuperation of that "myth" here leaves Mariella subject to a number of cultural and textual traditions that, placed side by side in this manner, only compromise the identification. Harris does not account for Mariella's own desire or any desire on her part that does not ultimately lead to the fulfillment of the reconciliatory dream he holds for his male characters. Therefore, her position (via the land) at the critical moment Harris recaptures radically alters (through representation) that original position.

The novel and critical interpretation of it restrict Mariella to dualistic representations, but her function as a multiple sign complicates this subject-object dichotomy. Her figure, which is both Amerindian and woman, cannot be fully elaborated in this because she exists as both. Yet, when these identities are articulated together, she is the "buck woman" whose raped position is fixed in the land. Her representation as a muse makes her a recalcitrant figure because it compounds the sign (the different tensions surrounding her), making her resistant to the kind of psychic wholeness Harris posits. As a generative sign (womb) whose meaning is not fixed, her figure continuously embodies and produces her own difference.[15] She therefore has significance or meaning beyond Harris's constructs and for critical interpretation that works through the terms or relationships already set up in the novel.[16]

Mariella can be read as the critical instrument for Harris's transformation of the El Dorado myth. She is also, however, the figure *that extends beyond the space of the text* to reveal the tensions surrounding the folk, her, and the land because of how the intersection of race and sex at different historical junctures objectively positions figures like hers. In continuing to use "woman" as a site for the "imaginary of culture"—especially since the "rape" of Mariella and of the land mimics the relationships of woman and land in male-centered nationalist discourse—Harris does not transform the structures of meaning at the base of cultural thought about the myth, in spite of the image of an unconquered landscape that he offers Caribbean cultural discourse.

Symbolic of woman and land, Mariella, as a *recalcitrant* figure, resists the historical confusion Harris uses as a narrative method to create a wholeness. This suggests two things: that the (Caribbean) woman is an insufficiently elaborated historical figure in these kinds of narratives, still caught in a discourse of signs and images maintained in textual moments like Benítez-Rojo's Caribbean "vagina" or "womb of darkness," and that neither woman, nor land, nor Amerindian subjection can be the ultimate ground on which the reconciliation of culture can occur in literature or in development discourse.[17] The ground for "repossession" in Guyana's historical and development discourse has been the ability to contract the dynamism of the landscape, mining its creative potential, like a muse, for use in various narratives. In his exploration of the symbolic potential of the land, Wilson Harris's work reveals that, as a symbolic structure, the land will always exceed discursive attempts to represent it. Despite attempts to represent it as a space to be contained within some form of cultural discourse, as a space that bears the projection of man's desires, like the woman's body, the land will always retain a plural significance outside the bounds of literal representation.

Conclusion

The Burnham/PNC policies of the 1960s set the tone for the new post-independence relationship between the coast and interior by suggesting that the interior should remain the "domain of the imagination" for post-colonial culture. In doing this, Burnham laid one narrative of inheritance over another. The most striking feature of Burnham's cooperative socialism was its inability to maintain within it the oppositional elements of antico-lonialist discourse it shared with other non-Western territories struggling for independence at the time. Consequently, although one can read in his early speeches a desire to establish a new cultural and political legacy for Guyana that would reflect its shift in political status, the new development discourse of the administration continued to be made in terms set during the colonial period and through the mytho-discursive structure of El Dorado. This was a result of the myth's function as a narrative of origin that had legitimated colonial occupation and could at independence and with the initiation of the Co-operative Republic, guarantee blacks the right to rule; the right to realize the transfer of power as a historical, political, and cultural inheritance long overdue.

This essay focused on the mytho-historical dimension of the nationalist discourse that accompanied the Burnham regime's program of develop-ment, to argue that the mutual subjection and exploitation of the Amerin-dian peoples and the interior landscape today occurs because of how the myth as an exploitative discourse continued to be enacted in order to secure positions of power. Burnham's cooperative nationalism could not be separated from the historical forces—economic, political, and cultural—that preceded it.

Like "race," the myth of El Dorado is an inherited structure of colonial discourse. The discourse of cooperative development that Burnham utilized was one of possession and cultural reclamation that rested on, among other things, (Pan-African) anticolonial discourse, the multiculturalist rhetoric embedded in classical modernist debate on nation formation, and the mytho-historical narrative of the El Dorado legend.[18] It is one of exploitative resource development that strategically incorporates and facilitates the subjugation of peoples and cultures by declaring cultural difference a productive resource of the state.

While the failure of the Burnham/PNC is the larger failure of postcolonial discourse in the region, it does suggest that a vision of ecological sustainability in the Caribbean cannot come from political discourse. Such a relation to the land and how we must inhabit it has so far only begun to emerge in Caribbean literary discourse, which seeks to push forth an idea of humanity as coextensive with nature like Wilson Harris's vision of the interior.[19] Caribbean literature challenges the representation of the land in Western historical and anthropological discourses, both of which have traditionally maintained a hostility to a landscape that is continually exploited in neocolonial capitalist economies. Caribbean literary rethinking of this historical relationship engages the idea that a new imaginative and real relationship with the land is possible, one that can replace the onto-historical drive of possession and exploitation. However, even literature must confront the fact that the land, as it continues to be struggled over as the generative source for identity discourses in the Caribbean, whether they are political, cultural, or both, will always be a shifting symbol in this work.

Notes

1. In Caribbean studies, there is the concern that the myth has "overdetermined" Caribbean reality in historical writing and literary criticism. In positing this argument, I am aware of this "potential" in viewing the myth. However, in saying that the myth is a "constant discursive reality," I do not explore the myth as though it continues to be told, unimpeded, in an unbroken line from the past to the present. There have been shifts in the discourse as the myth was made to articulate "new" cultural and political ideologies. However, it would be inaccurate to say that there has been some fundamental rupture. While overdetermination is a real problem, the significance of the myth for the formation of postindependence national identity must still be evaluated.

2. Since Amerindians historically have been linked with the Guyanese interior in the British colonial and now postcolonial Guyanese cultural imagination, any attempt to engage discourse surrounding the "hinterland" must also deal with the dual and uneven subjection of the land and people in both discourses.

3. I owe this argument about the myth in part to Sylvia Wynter. Although she does not discuss the myth of El Dorado, she uses Waswo to argue the link between the legend of descent from Troy that Waswo speaks of and the "narrative of Christian Providential destiny central to Columbus's reconception of the earth" (152). (See Sylvia Wynter, "Columbus, the Ocean Blue, and Fables That Stir the Mind.") In "1492: A New World View," Wynter argues that with the "discovery," America was brought into the a new worldview that had been emerging with the Italian humanists of the fourteenth century and was marked by a shift from

Judeo-Christianity to secular humanism based on a concept of "rational man" and his relationship not to the church but to the state, of which the church became the "spiritual arm." Wynter is ultimately concerned with the possibility of being truly "human" that exists in premodern and contemporary cultural discourse from the "old" and "new" worlds.

4. This term is taken from Percy Hintzen's *The Costs of Regime Survival.*

5. Antonio Benítez-Rojo's term.

6. "Prior rights" is the name given to Amerindian claims to land based on "historical and ancestral occupation."

7. For an example of contemporary historical work, see David Hollett's *Passage from India to El Dorado: Guyana and the Great Migration.*

8. Several texts emerged after the 1950s to market the Caribbean as a site for neocolonial tourist economies. One of the best examples of how the myth of El Dorado was used to facilitate the marketing of the Caribbean is John Crocker's *The Centaur Guide to the Caribbean and El Dorado* (1968).

9. I italicize the *you* and *we* here to signal the fact that Brown's own subjectivity is shifting.

10. Ethno-political violence in Guyana has resulted in the deaths of hundreds of Guyanese.

11. The inside jacket flap of *Co-operative Republic* states that the erection of a fort on Fort Island (before Zeelandia) by the Dutch "changed the course of Guyanese history." It led to the transfer of the then colony's capitol to Fort Island and to settlement of Demerara by the Dutch.

12. Through the economic and ideological apparatus of the Co-operative, all Guyanese were brought into a new structure of belonging and participation in the state. In *Co-operative Republic,* we see Burnham building on the racial structure that emerged out of plantation-era society in creating "the small man" as a racial/ethnic hybrid to inherit the narrative of progress and development bequeathed to the nation by British colonialism. Burnham built the state through an economic policy of dependence and the uneven distribution of rights through a strategy that fostered both economic and cultural dependence on the state as a prerequisite for national identity and citizenship.

13. This is obvious in a special issue of the journal *New World* that marks Guyana's independence.

14. I begin with Gilkes's reading to introduce the problem of history. Gilkes's almost casual characterization of the "modern" Guyanese dream fails to address how the dream, as a "modern" one, functions in Harris's recasting of it.

15. Maes-Jelinek has also written that "Mariella is also the spirit of the place: not only is the territory of the mission called Mariella but through most of the narrative the imagery coalesces into one reality the woman (and by implication her people) with the country into which they penetrate" (34). She later notes, "the end of the novel confirms that it has been a search for an 'other' which is part of oneself" (*Naked Design* 57). In this passage, there is a complex link among the

land, woman (as Amerindian), and family being established. Maes-Jelinek illustrates precisely my point about Mariella's position but does not question the ways in which this positioning problematizes Harris's narrative, which is what this paper seeks to do.

16. One of these relationships is Maes-Jelinek's claim that Mariella is the "persecuted and vengeful mistress of Donne." I do not agree with Sandra Drake that this position in Maes-Jelinek's work is wholly reductive or that it misses Harris's larger aim to represent Mariella's creative potential. It is simply not elaborated in her text. See Sandra Drake's *Wilson Harris and the Modern Tradition*.

17. For more on gender, representation, and the female figures in Harris's works, see Adler, "The Evolution of Female Figures and Imagery in Wilson Harris's Novels"; and Johnson, "Vulnerable Figures," and "Translations of Gender, Pain, and Space: Wilson Harris's The Carnival Trilogy."

18. Political sociologist Percy Hintzen writes on the development of Afro-Creole nationalism in the Caribbean. See "Reproducing Domination Identity and Legitimacy Constructs in the West Indies."

19. Other examples include Pauline Melville's *The Ventriloquist's Tale* (1997), Paule Marshall's *The Chosen Place, The Timeless People* (1969), and Michele Cliff's *No Telephone to Heaven* (1987).

A Long Bilingual Conversation Concerning Paradise Lost

Landscapes in Haitian Art

LeGrace Benson

THE PARADISE landscape of Wilson Bigaud marks a convergence of languages, of literal and figurative points of view, of habits of attention. At this nexus he created a new moment, a new standpoint, and added a new topic to the Long Conversations that had been taking place in Haiti for over two hundred years. So strong was his graphic voice that after his *Paradis Terrestre (Earthly Paradise)* there would appear thousands of painted Edens, variations on a luxuriant landscape theme ironically produced in an expiring ecology.

The Long Conversations bruited across the years and territory of Haiti were formed through word-of-mouth and texts, certainly, but also through apprenticeships, tools, and implements, everyday gear, ritual, talismanic and sacred objects. In these conversations, telling and showing meld together, rising out of and returning to an environment that also has its histories and geographies. The Long Conversations are the communications aspect of an elaborate ecosystem, always in process, where giver and recipient constantly modify and modulate. Out of these manifold interactions, an artist like Bigaud, receptively attuned, makes works that partake of a complex continuing story, yielding up marvels of revelation. The environment and the Long Conversations afforded Bigaud material for his creations. These were available to all in the same "landscape," but Bigaud made a unique selection. Each aspect of the ecology of Haiti, including its two languages, is directly relevant to the production of and the fate of *Paradis Terrestre* and the youth who created it.

Bigaud's earthly paradise both adumbrates and disguises the tragic actuality of a paradise lost thrice over. The first European reports concerning the island its inhabitants called Kiskeya or Ayiti described a verdant landscape. A century later, they told of continuing depredations. Charles de Rochefort, visiting in the 1650s, wrote, "The greater part of all the isles is covered with beautiful woods, that are green in every season, making an agreeable perspective and representing a perpetual summer." Freshwater abounded in "fountains, lakes, streams, wells and cisterns" (de Rochefort 5). In February 1790, Alexandre-Stanislas de Wimpffen wrote that coffee plantations initiated "the destruction of the cacao trees" (de Wimpffen 151). Moreover, "here as all over [St.-Domingue] the work of men, in despoiling the land of trees that cover it and thus provoking an extraordinary evaporation . . . has produced a notable revolution in the climate . . . fatal to the fertility of the fields" (155). A decade later, Moreau de Saint-Méry related: "The droughts are becoming longer and more frequent. This arises from a greediness which counts the future for nothing . . . People have cut down the trees which covered the higher points and which summoned the life-giving rains and held on to the abundant dews" (Moreau de Saint-Méry 15). M. E. Descourtilz visited Haiti in the years immediately after Moreau de Saint-Méry. His first view of St.-Domingue was of the mountains "covered with the most beautiful verdure" (4). On closer inspection, he saw plantations falling into ruin, deforestations due to agricultural practices, and a reversion to wildness on formerly cultivated tracts. In hunting forays he made with planter friends the prey was European animals, once domesticated, now become feral—pigs, cattle, goats as much in marronage as rebelling slaves. "The habitat . . . is already degraded, and birds and humans together are suffering" (103). By 1923, Haitian forest cover, significantly reduced from the original, was still 60 percent, but by 1982 it had shrunk to only 3 percent (Woods and Ottenwalder 21). The fabric of Haitian history from 1492 to the present moment is one of being-with-the-world in such a way that "the future counts for nothing."

Landscape paintings come about as a result of a mode of individual behavior within a society living in a certain place and time, moments framed out of an unbounded participation. The enframement that results in the creation of a communicative object entails a highly complex individual and social operation with particular modes of attention—an attentive reciprocal and iterative gathering and sharing of perceptions and memories. The work itself becomes a new part of the environment to be experienced.

Haitian landscape paintings can be observed as an artist's selection of certain beauties to enframe. Beyond the paintings and beyond the designated ("framed") national parks, there spreads a jumble of erosion, rain forest, desiccated savannas, sacred waterfalls tumbling down ravines thick with trees and lianes, conservation districts and poisonous landfills: Eden and Gehenna laced together. The genre is itself an example of the bilingual Long Conversation of the country, with sensibilities preserved and cherished over centuries of physical separation from the two foreign motherlands, Africa and Europe. An ecological approach allows us to observe the use of a European, dramatic, and romantic art form in a country where the great majority of people were African, and where the flora, fauna, and weather systems were new and strange to both Africans and Europeans. Bigaud's paradise can be seen as a conjunction of their conversations.

Bigaud created his complex revelation of the material and social history of Haiti when he was only twenty. *Paradis Terrestre* is now one of the chief treasures of the College St. Pierre Musée d'Art, Port-au-Prince. Within months of its creation, both Bigaud and the painting were famous at home and in the international art world. How this came about, and the consequences still apparent half a century later, is a story that reveals many of the significant factors that arise out of Haiti or come to bear on it from overseas. The main actor in the narrative, the artist, is the node where the heterogeneous liens of information converge. Bigaud's experiences connected the ways of being of the rural people with those of the city and beyond to the international art world.

The work, about 36 inches high by 48 inches wide, depicts Eve and Adam about to eat the forbidden apple. The serpent coils down the Tree of the Knowledge of Good and Evil, while Eve stretches on tiptoe to receive the fruit. Adam sits at the base, reaching to receive an apple, past the single-stemmed rosebush that grows between him and Eve. Spider-webbed branches arch over the entire scene, and under its shelter grow varieties of other trees and vegetation common to Haiti. A stream cascades from the left to form a pool beside Eve's feet. A small donkey, chickens, dogs, a black kreyol pig, cows, and colorful birds of the countryside animate this lush landscape. Curiously, a pair of giraffes and a hippopotamus disport in the jungle beyond. This is Eden at the moment of the Fall. It is Haiti. It is Africa.

There was landscape painting in Haiti/St.-Domingue from colonial times. While most of the earlier works are lost, a few remain. A view of La Fossette, probably done before the insurrections of 1791, shows a French planter and his family under trees at the tranquil shoreline of his property near Cap Haitien. The same view today includes the expanse of water. The shoreline is a crowded jumble of houses. There are no trees.

Paintings of the heroes of the revolution, newly become rulers, show their domain as the background of their portraits. General Toussaint-Louverture stands before the bay at Cap Haitien (Lerebours, *Haïti* 1:52). In his portrait, Monsieur de Berau points to his cane fields (46–47).

Numa Desroches, a student in King Henry Christophe's art academy, depicted the king's Palais San Souci with the mountains protecting the Citadel beyond. British artist Richard Evans portrayed Christophe standing before a view of the Plaine du Nord stretching to the Atlantic Ocean. Haitian artists of that time typically depicted the key revolutionary events in the landscape of place and time, all done in the mode promulgated by the French Academy.

Serment des Ancêtres by Guillaume Guillon Lethière (1822), now in the National Palace in Port-au-Prince, is the artist's admiring allegory of the victory against the French, "a gift of the painter in homage to the Republic of Haiti the Black race" (Corvington, quoted in Lerebours, "Les premières" 67). Behind the heroes Alexandre Pétion and Jean-Jacques Dessalines, the broad Plaine du Cul-de-Sac with its population of victorious regiments and cheering freed slaves sweeps to the bay of Port-au-Prince. In the sky above, God Himself extends his hands to bless the new liberty (G. Alexis 17). The view is from the heights where the new landholders spoke French. The medium was the easel oil painting of the French Academy, of which Lethière was a member. The lay of the land was Haitian, and skin color crucial to the meaning. Mulatto Pétion and black Dessalines signal the joining of forces of two distinct social aggregates to free the land from the colonials. The Kreyol conversations the generals would have had with their companions at arms are silent here.

As with European and North American portraits of planters, the landscapes behind the revolutionary events and heroes pronounced the fact of ownership. It was ownership of place understood as a thing separate and separable from the owner, a concept derived from that of the French with their measured land plots and state documents, their inventories of goods, men, women, children, and livestock. For both artists and their patrons of the new nation, ownership of the land signified ownership of themselves. This was the priceless fruit of sacrificial battles. "This is ours. We are proprietors."

Between Lethière's triumphal proclamation of Haitian seizure of ownership and the years just prior to Wilson Bigaud's *Paradis Terrestre,* landscape painting goes into shadow. Under the presidency of Jean-Pierre Boyer, 1818–43, the state coffers, emptied to pay France for reparations, were devoid of resources to support portraits and historical scenes (Lerebours, "Les premières" 61–62). It was a time of earthquakes, hurricanes, conflagrations, and equally destructive political and military storms and tremors. Of land and landscape painting much is lost. However, in old archives and books one occasionally encounters landscapes. An anonymous and ambiguously datable painting shows Cap Haitien before the earthquake and ensuing fires of 1842 (Daniel 91). A peasant with his donkey stops to chat on the high road overlooking the town. It is simply a "scene," of the sort done all over Europe and the Americas during the nineteenth century. The peasants of Cap chatted in Kreyol and painted no landscapes. Boyer's Code Rural consigned peasants to the land, thus imposing a new marronage. The cultural life of these rural people would develop in ways "sometimes archaic but in complete liberty, . . . thus furnishing the first explanation of the tendency of Haitian painting to evolve according to two sets of entirely different esthetic principles" (Lerebours, "Les premières" 63).

The scarcity of surviving paintings from the nineteenth century leaves open the question of what the few Haitian artists may have held in attention. For a view of the land as experienced by Haitians or as the backdrop upon which to spell out an interior and personal geography, we must turn to certain writers. A little book of Haitian poems—a rare set of translations into English by a U.S. author—includes the poets that educated Haitians held in regard (Underwood 1934). Completed the year President Roosevelt withdrew the American Occupation, it provides a brief overview of themes selected by poets from Isaac Toussaint-Louverture before 1800 to those writing at the time of publication. The woodcut illustrations are by the twentieth-century artist Pétion Savain, a noted landscape painter still active at the time of Wilson Bigaud's achievement in 1951.

Just under half the poems are descriptive of land- or seascapes, sometimes melancholy, always romantic. Alexander MacDonald relates: "The wife waits at the door. The children have come with their baskets upheaped— / Fruit tempting and yellow as on evenings before, / Blond ananas and figs gold-steeped" (122). Victor Mangonès's view of Port-au-Prince from the heights where the elite live "flings forth far [a] fine profile, / Steel-bright the Sea preens itself in the sun" (83). These are sentimental scenes observed at an aesthetic distance. The landscape of poverty and the speech of rural people are absent from this book as they were and would be in Haitian painting until 1950. The poets collected here were all educated in the finest private schools in Haiti and France. Their modes were French, even when written in Kreyol, and even when the subject was Haitian.

Artist Savain and his colleagues were members of the group of intellectuals calling themselves *Indigènists,* promoting a distinctively Haitian culture in response to what they perceived as racist indignities suffered from the occupying forces from the United States. They reported the landscape they saw from their privileged points of view, unencumbered by actual experience of life in the cramped little houses of their servants. For them, cane fields were luxuriant green waves in the breezes observed from the verandah, a "view," a "landscape." For the peasants, cane fields were personal intimates, face-to-face, breathing the same air. Cane was refractory stalks and knife-edged leaves resisting muscle and machete.

Pétion Savain would by 1930 begin to paint ordinary Kreyol life. His background was in agronomy and law, professions that brought him into daily contact with soil and water, plants and storms, and the perennial contentions over plots of land that mark Haitian lives from 1804 to the present. He would, like his Indigènist poet friends, re-create the beauties to be extracted from the landscape and the market life: not its pains, not the dirt and misery. Yet, to open a window on that panorama was to render it visible. The romanticized portrayals of rural scenes and people were in fact a first step in the direction of a radical revalorization of Haitian ordinary life. Moreover, Savain and at least one other artist of the urban elite, Albert Mangonès, would champion ecosystem restoration and make personal commitments of time and financial support. Thus, they would bring into Haiti the European Romantics' and nineteenth-century naturalists' Long Conversations that were the precursors of today's ecological sensibilities.

In the economic distress of Haiti in 1944, Savain's work, like that of most artists, would not sell. When the burst of government-sponsored tourism and subventions from the United States began to turn the economy around, it was rural "naives" whose work would come to the forefront. There, in the countryside where people spoke Kreyol, the land was a being to be worked on and wrestled with. There was no leisure to write paeans to the moon or to a beloved. The Long Conversations that continued in vigor echoed Africa. There were the old tales, proverbs, and riddles revised to fit the present landscape. There were the instructions for using a hoe or weaving a sleeping mat. There were songs set to music of the drums and voices of the Vodou ceremonies. They sang of love, death, anger, pleadings and placations to the divinities moving in the sacred trees and cascades, in the ocean and the fields. For the rural people and those recently moved into the towns and cities—*Aiti Toma*—their experience of the land was at once instrumental and religious participation, preserving African heritages. Their visual articles made for religious purposes were, like many of the African works from the times before and after the Middle Passage, aggregations collected out of the quotidian world and arranged upon a sacred table, the *badagri*. As much as they may have drawn upon techniques of the sacred recalled from Africa, the *badagri* were also reminiscent of European altars encrusted with *ex votos,* paintings of the saints, sculptures of cherubim, and offerings of fresh flowers. Out of daily experience with the things and conditions of local world they created a sacred place—a sacred landscape, centered on the wooden *poto mitan,* a symbolic tree down through which the *lwas* would descend into the congregation. Ethnographers of the Indigènist or Négritude conversations were the first to recognize the sacred objects and space as "artistic" and "expressive." Later international collectors would follow suit.

The relationship of the Vodou congregation to the space and activities of the ceremony is one of engagement of the whole person. In this respect it contrasts with the way the many Catholic Christians *observe* the Mass. The contrast of these two ways of being-there in a religious ceremony parallels the two attitudes toward land. Naturalists and planters look *at* it with an eye toward its exact description and useful potential. Western landscape painting portrays it as a source of beauty to be enjoyed. The peasants and the painters who came from the rural milieu understood the land as means for production of life necessities. They went at the tasks with hoe and machete, in collaboration with the visible and invisible material and spiritual forces. The Long Conversations on the little farms centered on this spirited showing and telling. The peasants painted no landscapes. Instead, there was a web of material connections and of nonmaterial but perceivable relationships regarding the land—the "spiritual."

That term, used by anthropologists or ethnographers more than by peasants themselves, is too general and probably misleading as it suggests some immaterial "substance"—a kind of community "ether"—or "collective unconscious or conscious" unavailable for examination. The peasant reality was the thoroughly observable phenomena of Long Conversations: telling and writing the stories, poems and songs, playing music and dancing, making the ordinary exchange of words, gestures and postures of lived lives; apprenticeships too dense and too subtle in their sensual and imagistic texture to be verbalized. They have to be felt in the bone, "caught" from a master by a pupil. Objects in a Vodou houmfo sacred landscape are its products; fruit of religious instrumental relationships.

When Bigaud chose to accept a suggestion from Centre d'Art director Dewitt Peters, that he create a scene like the Adam and Eve in Paradise paintings of the late Renaissance and Baroque art world, it was to join European and African Long Conversations in the spiritual sensibility of one artist. After perusing the Renaissance fabulations, he chose to create brown-skinned Adam and Eve in an Eden so infused with the *lwas* and African animals that it became the Lan Giné of Kreyol Vodou sensibilities. The Tree of the Knowledge of Good and Evil is the *poto-mitan* route from *lwa* above to the couple below. Emblematic of the conjunctive processes at work is the spider and web joining the many branches of the tree. The spider is the *lwa* Anansi, spinning a web from Ghana to Haiti. The geometry of his Haitian landscape is congruent with the architecture of Vodou sacred space.

Bigaud's complex addition to the conversations became the commercially viable prototype of a burgeoning art market. Within weeks of the news that the work had won an international prize, there was an efflorescence of painted Edens that continues in bloom to this day.

In *Ainsi parla l'oncle* of 1928, Jean Price-Mars entreated the descendants in denial about their African past to cherish and celebrate it. The book was an immediate sensation; outrage to some, battle cry to others. In 1944, his younger collaborator, Jacques Roumain, wrote the novel *Gouverneurs de la Rosée,* describing heroic peasants in a landscape at once actual and mystical. Roumain's descriptions of the land Manuel tries to restore from its dry dying are sometimes almost photographic in their precise detail. Manuel contemplates an "emaciated mountain, ravaged by wide, blanched gullies, there where erosion had stripped its flanks nude to the rock" (27). Evoking an actual landscape, Roumain decries the flames that had reduced the oak and mahogany trees, the fields of peas whispering in the wind, and the gardens of sweet potatoes. Manuel lives with a nature under cultivation that is brother and sister, parent and lover. Every leaf and stone is animated. At the end of this tragic yet deeply optimistic story, Manuel dies. But he has found at the foot of the mapou tree the spring of water that will restore the barren fields and slopes. This is close to the long-repeated and honored peasant awareness of the fact of life dwelling in the waters: call out by name Danballah; the life in crops growing: call out Azaka. It was "in the air." Roumain returned it back to the air, sound wave pursuing sound wave, until everybody heard it.

Bigaud and Roumain probably never met each other face to face. There was instead *teledjol,* the old word-of-mouth they both had listened to since birth, bandied down the street from the Bureau of Ethnography to Champ de Mars, to the university and the Centre d'Art at some *vernissage* for one of the artists who had studied in France. By the time Bigaud arrived to study at the Centre, Roumain had died, at only thirty-eight, but he had opened major channels whereby the communications of the bilingual Long Conversation flowed.

Roumain and Price-Mars were joined by other voices. The brothers Philippe Thoby-Marcelin and Pierre Marcelin were associates of Roumain at the *Revue Indigène* and aware of the tenets of Jean Price-Mars. In their series of novels, they created a multidimensional view of the Haitian condition. The creature of their novel *The Beast of the Haitian Hills* is the Cigouave, often discussed by the country people. *Teledjol* suggested that it was Cigouave who stole the local chickens and corn. The brothers turned this rustic entertainment into a novel in which a city grocer, or food entrepreneur, becomes a planter, or food producer, in the country. Morin Dutilleul, idealistic about rural life, looked forward to bucolic contentments. But "since he had come into contact with the peasants, he now found them, on close inspection too uncouth and poverty-stricken" (12). He becomes arrogant toward them, eventually even cruel. Outraged by the Vodou practices at the foot of the mapou on his property, he has it chopped down. It is a murder. Finally, "the Cigouave was standing there beside the bed, close to him, . . . panting like a dog." Morin leaps up and runs into the night . . . but the Cigouave pursued him without flagging. "It became a terrifying chase, frantic, silent, for the monster did not howl and no sound could issue from the throat of Morin Dutilleul. Without knowing it, he finally reached Petionville highway, rushed straight ahead, ran against the guard-rail and [the last words of the novel] tumbled into the ravine" (171).

Landscape here is rutted with difficult paths, clotted with unwonted vegetation, and barren where crops should have been. The population uneasily moves about in a lay of the land where a lane becomes a ditch and passage means a chancy ford across a torrent. The Marcelin brothers re-create a terrain as experienced by the impoverished, the fearful, and the arrogant chased by their own guilt.

A third major work, *Les arbres musiciens,* the 1948 novel by Jacques Stephen Alexis, appeared in the same era. It begins and ends with landscape. Magisterially, Alexis takes on the whole panoply of Haitian life. His three protagonists are brothers: a Catholic priest, an army officer, and an intellectual. Other actors in his grand scheme are the half-wild and precocious youngster with the Taìno name, Gonaïbo, and the Vodou *houngan* Bois-d'Orme ("Elmwood") Lètiro. Alexis, like Price-Mars, Roumain, and the Marcelin brothers, was dedicated to combating the moral, material, environmental, and religious depredations he saw visited upon Haitian land and people by the Occupation and Catholic authorities conducting the antisuperstition campaign that destroyed so many material religious objects. In his marvelous landscape live the great pines and mapous, mahogany and breadfruit trees of Haiti. The woodcutters would hack them down to grow an invasive foreign plant to yield rubber for the United States. The trees sing.

"The land of Aiti Toma sparkles with such marvels that no one in passing can know that misery and distress could take root in such a décor"
(J. Alexis 10). In the face of the antisuperstition campaign, the Vodou
houngans and *manbos* gather with their faithful to determine what is to
be done. The sage Bois-d'Orme Létiro stands. All fall silent. He takes up a
priceless ceremonial mace brought to St.-Domingue in a slave ship and
preserved to that moment. In a long invocation of the oldest of the *lwas,*
Aizan, Bois-d'Orme tells that the ancient spirits are, like the grass, burned
to fertilize the next crop rising from destruction. "Misfortune to those who
challenge the only Grand Personage, God the Father [Papa-Bon-Dieu] . . .
Ayizan says . . . the lwas live as long as hunger endures, and long as misery
endures, that maladies endure, and long as blood is shed around . . .
Enough of crimes! Enough of blood! Save the sacred [Taìno] stones!"
(179). Létiro intones in *langage Arada,* the antique speech of his West
Africa ancestors. The music from the landscape sounds again. "A robust
hope navigates across the black nights, across the tempests, to the new
mornings of life" (180). The living trees, the birds, the water coursing over
the stones reassure the people that the strong will survive though apparently destroyed. At the final coda the "entire forest is a great organ that
modulates with a multiple voice. Each one of the colossal music shafts
with its own timbre, each pine a pipe of this extraordinary instrument"
(385). "The musician-trees collapse from time to time, but the voice of
the forest is always as powerful as ever. Life begins" (392).

This extended metaphor Alexis uses is no intellectual conceit. It is a
finely textured means by which to reveal the truth of the marvelous reality
of this world. It is the means by which to confront the degradation of land
and people—the entire ecology—by those who conduct their existence
outside that ecosystem. Like Roumain and the Marcelins, he raises his
voice to reiterate the old outcry sounded against the devastation of Eden.

Bigaud surely presents another instance of the reality of marvels. Like
the novelists, he lived in the miscible languages and cultures of Haiti. He
shared with the writers a knowledge of all the old stories, both secular
and sacred; the religions Christian and Vodou; experiences of countryside
and city; and the awareness that seems to be part of the vocabulary of
every Haitian—freedom wrested and the expulsion of the planters from
what had been their Eden. In Bigaud's African, Haitian, Christian, and
Vodou garden, Eve is about to fall. The trees in his Eden, already wounded,
will fall. Paradise lost. But the trickster spider escaping the fallen branches
will weave another web. Life begins. The pink rose in the center of his
paradise is a symbol for the Virgin Mary and homage to Ezuli, whose

flower sign is a pink rose. The serpent is the clever animal of Genesis and also Danballah, the African *lwa* of the trees that bring the rains. The giraffes and hippopotamus evoke a return to Lan Giné. Beyond the imminent fall from grace and the subsequent condemnation to gain one's bread by laboriously wresting it from the earth is Africa. The spider high in the branches is *lwa* Anansi, who crossed over on the Middle Passage with the ancestors. Anansi of the myriad disguises and dissimulations spins over Paradise about to be lost.

The *Paradis Terrestre* may seem to be rendered voiceless in its dignified museum silence. The novels may appear to be as unregarded as the numerous Policy Reports and White Papers filed soundlessly away in some bureau. In the art galleries are hundreds of lush Edens uprooted from the ecosystem. Outside, the charcoal incense of the poor sends up its sacrifice of the last 3 percent of pines and palms and mangoes and mapous. May the trickster spider escaping the fallen branches weave another web. May the trees sing. Life begins.

"Caribbean Genesis"

Language, Gardens, Worlds (Jamaica Kincaid, Derek Walcott, Édouard Glissant)

Jana Evans Braziel

> . . . All history
> in a dusty Beefeater's gin. We helped ourselves
> to these green islands like olives from a saucer,
> . . . their green pith sucked dry.
> —Derek Walcott, *Omeros*

MAJOR DENNIS PLUNKETT, a wounded and retired soldier in the Queen's Army, settles in the Caribbean island of St. Lucia and spends his days pig-farming and ruminating on the lost Empire. So his narrative unfolds in Derek Walcott's *Omeros,* but his is only one of myriad tales to be told in this sprawling epic poem.[1] I open with an epigraphic quotation from *Omeros* in order to foreground Walcott's "martini" metaphor and its mixing of an analytical problematic that is political and ecological, post-colonial and ecocritical in nature. In the passage, we see a waning era through Plunkett's mind's eye as he sips dry gin and reflects on colonies and empires. Drinking a "Beefeater's gin," the major sardonically notes that "history" can be read in stiff cocktails, where British colonials con-quered territory, dominated nature, and subdued natives. "We helped ourselves," Plunkett says, "to these green islands like olives from a saucer," and when they had consumed the natural resources, the colonials "spat their sucked stones on a plate" (30). I foreground this passage for two reasons: first, it reveals that environmental damage and colonialism are interlocking systems of domination in the Caribbean; and second, it under-scores the imbrications of colonialism and consumption that marked the expansion of the British colonial empire in the region. Mimi Sheller has persuasively argued that representations of nature in the Caribbean histor-ically have been tied to economies of consumption and colonization. She contends that "the invention of Caribbean nature has in turn been read onto the bodies of Caribbean peoples, implicating them in a sexualized scenic economy in which their bodies are objectified, commodified, and dehumanized" ("Natural Hedonism," par. 28).[2] From Sheller's incisive comments about natural subjugation and racial dehumanization as interlocking forces, I return to the epigraphic quotation from *Omeros* and ask: Who and what are consumed, even subsumed? How can we locate the Caribbean between the poles of creation and consumption?

Caribbean writers—notably Édouard Glissant, Derek Walcott, and Jamaica Kincaid—creatively return to genesis myths to redress historical forms of violent consumption of people, resources, and ecological terrains in the region. Analyzing literary ecocritical resistance by Kincaid, Walcott, and Glissant, this paper theorizes new eco-relations between humans and their animal, botanical, and mineral others, positioning these relations as symbiotic or rhizomic. I hope, thus, to make a critical intervention in the theoretical impasse between deep and social ecology, between eco- and ego-centric positions,[3] between the human and the green in lived terrains.[4] Ecocriticism must not ignore the human, material consequences of environmental degradation by blindly or absolutely valorizing eco- over ego-centrism as if all human beings were equally situated in relation to power, history, and domination: to do so is to ignore the ways in which history and colonial power have denied large segments of humanity its subjectivity and its ego and to perpetuate the deleterious distinction between "Man" and "Nature." Not all men, or women,[5] have had the privileged position of "Man"; some, rather, have been defined as and immersed with "Nature," hence the coevolution of dominating nature *and* human beings through racially hierarchized "Natural Histories" of the colonial era. What would it mean for those historically denied their humanity (denigrated to "savages" or livestock) to be called upon by posthumanist ecocritics to renounce the ego- for eco-, when such a call merely reiterates historical locations of erasure (and collapses them into a dominated nature)? That which is antinature is also frequently antipeople. The impasse between social and deep ecology needs to be renegotiated at the intersections of ecological and human colonization, or through an eco-postcolonialist lens, which would resituate the human in a positively revalued, autonomous nature, and not exclusively within the realm of culture. In this paper, I strive toward those aims. First, I examine the tourism industry in the Caribbean in relation to environmental degradation in the region, trace the emergence of Caribbean ecotourism over the last decade, and demonstrate how Kincaid, Walcott, and Glissant offer ecocritical resistance to the industry in their writings.

Second, I suggest new ecocritical ways of understanding the human in relation to the natural. Caribbean theorists and writers open this rhizomic path (to echo Glissant). For rethinking ecocritical relations—of nature and culture; land and sea; and between mineral, vegetal, animal, and human—I suggest a "poetics of (eco-)relation."[6] To conceptualize Caribbean ecocritical alternatives to ones dominant in current (U.S.) academic discourse, I use Glissant's theorizations of rhizomes and roots as a way of negotiating the seemingly oppositional concerns of deep and social ecology. I demonstrate how these Caribbean writers reveal the importance of thinking of the material, political consequences of colonialism in relation to the vital critiques of natural spoilage offered by ecocriticism; these writers see the conquest of land, domination of nature, and political subordination of marginalized human beings as bound together in a powerful matrix predicated on historical notions of "Man" (along the privileged vectors of whiteness, Europeanness, and being propertied). Specifically, I examine how these writers position the violence of genocide and ecocide as intertwined. They thus unravel the interwoven genres of marked bodies and marked territories, rethinking the conquest of land as imbricated in the colonization of people and refiguring new genres, subjectivities, and conceptions of nature as rhizomic. I also examine how these Caribbean writers alternatively conceive of nature—particularly "uninhabitable" lands and roaring seas—as resistant to domination. They thus envisage new ways of relating across terrains: human to natural; land to sea.

To close, I show the relevance of this transplanted or diasporized ecocritical paradigm for understanding Caribbean returns to myths of genesis (not as origin but as problematic and process) in their writings. These Caribbean writers return to genesis as if returning to the site of an originary crime—not in order to envision nature as a static Eden but rather to reimagine it as a dynamic process of becomings and beginnings. In the Caribbean imaginary, nature itself enters into and enacts the processes of genesis as creation. Kincaid, Walcott, and Glissant also suggest that realist nonfictional forms—those typically privileged by many ecocritics, notably Lawrence Buell—may actually, and ironically, reproduce sterile notions of the world as passive, while experimental literary forms evoke the dynamism of worlds in motion that resist and evade absolute domination.[7] As Glissant intimates, "realism—that is, the logical and rational attitude toward the visible world— . . . betray[s] the true meaning of things" (*Caribbean Discourse* 145).[8]

Caribbean (Literature) and the Environment

Following the 1992 United Nations Conference on Environment and Development (UNCED), held on 14 June 1992 in Rio de Janeiro, the General Assembly adopted Agenda 21 to require the "full integration of sustainable development in the tourism industry" and to ensure that "travel and tourism contribute to the conservation, protection and restoration of the Earth's ecosystem."[9] Secretary-General Kofi Annan, in his 1997 address to the Twelfth Assembly of the World Tourism Organization in Istanbul, noted that "a well-developed tourism industry" could ensure that small island states are "not marginalized by the process of globalization" by serving as a "magnet for international investment." According to Secretary-General Annan: "In welcoming tourists from other regions, countries seek to present the 'best' of themselves, to show all that is unique in their societies, while maintaining the dignity of their traditions, respect for cultural heritage and antiquities, and preservation of the ecology, wildlife and natural treasures—forests, rivers, lakes, mountains. This is crucial not only to the economic and social development of the country itself, but also to ensure visits by tourists in the future."[10] In 1998, the General Assembly voted, honoring the recommendation of the World Tourism Organization, to proclaim "2002 as International Year of Ecotourism."[11] The lures and allures of "island" tourism, however, are not always so neatly aligned with the principles of sustainable development or environmental protection, as many Caribbean scholars, activists, and even prime ministers note. Edison C. James, prime minister of Dominica, who has promoted his country as the quintessential Caribbean site for ecotourism, has also warned, "pollution of the seas, destruction of marine life by waste from ocean liners, and transshipment of drugs and arms posed serious threats to the development of the Caribbean region."[12]

Despite the hype of international ecotourism, in 2002, ten years after the 1992 Rio Conference, the Caribbean continues to be advertised and marketed in North American venues as local "paradise"—near, yet remote; familiar, but exotic; luxurious and green.[13] Notably, the *Lonely Planet* travel guides have taken the plunge into ecotourism, describing St. Lucia as "markedly rural in nature: a mix of small fishing villages, secluded coves, sprawling banana plantations and mountainous jungle." However, the writer unabashedly converts St. Lucia's *eco*-green value into an *econo*-green value: "A spate of resort developments on St. Lucia has made this *high green* island one of the Caribbean's trendy package-tour destinations" (my emphasis).[14] This rural St. Lucia, Walcott reminds us in *Omeros,* is an ecologically threatened world where men and animals, flora and fauna are all endangered:

> . . . Seven Seas would talk
> bewilderingly that man was an endangered
>
> species now, a spectre, just like the Aruac
> or the egret, or parrots screaming in terror
> when men approached, and that once men were satisfied
>
> with destroying men they would move on to Nature. (300)

Kincaid draws similar parallels between human and natural degradation, between genocide and ecocide, writing, "The Carib people had been defeated and then exterminated, thrown away like the weeds in a garden" (*Autobiography* 17). Where Walcott and Kincaid lament losses, travel writers and tourists celebrate nature commodified. Just as in its writings on St. Lucia, the *Lonely Planet* guides ambiguously position Antigua in terms of tourism, ecotourism, and environmental protection. While noting that "Antigua has some excellent diving, with coral canyons, wall drops and sea caves . . . turtles, sharks, barracuda and reef fish," the *Lonely Planet* writers also lament Prime Minister Lester Bird's 1997 decision to sell Guiana Island (located off the northeastern shore of Antigua), which is "one of the country's last remaining tracts of forest," the "sole habitat for the tropical mockingbird," and a refuge for "nesting seabirds, including tropicbirds, roseate terns, brown noddies and endangered whistling ducks."[15] Purchased for $5 million U.S. dollars by Dato Tan Kay Hock, a Malaysian developer, Guiana Island and its wildlife were threatened; initial development plans for Guiana Island included transforming the nature enclave into an Asian Village resort with over one thousand hotel rooms and an eighteen-hole golf course, although plans, fortunately, have been stalled (but not aborted) by legal battles, political activism, and the Asian market crisis.

These glossy, brochure-ready portraits of "small paradises" for the taking curiously echo, yet repackage, historical conceptions of the Caribbean islands as wild, "natural Edens" in the nineteenth century, as Sheller cogently demonstrates ("Natural Hedonism," par. 23), and these portraits are markedly different from those offered by Kincaid and Walcott. "How is it," Sheller asks, "that the massive introduction of alien species, forest clearance, stripping of plant cover, soil erosion, and reef destruction in the Caribbean remain invisible in the global tourist economy where the Caribbean is packaged and sold as 'pristine' beaches and verdant rainforest?"

(par. 26). Kincaid and Walcott propose an answer to this vexing question. "The thing you have always suspected about yourself the minute you become a tourist," Kincaid writes in *A Small Place*, "is true: A tourist is an ugly human being" (14). In Kincaid's framing, the environmental and human degradation of tourism are linked to the earlier historical violence of the Atlantic slave trade and slavery in the region: "You must not wonder what happened when you brushed your teeth. Oh, it might all end up in the water you are thinking of taking a swim in; the contents of your lavatory might, just might, graze gently against your ankle as you wade carefree in the water, for you see, in Antigua, there is no proper sewage-disposal system. But the Caribbean Sea is very big and the Atlantic Ocean is even bigger; it would amaze even you to know the number of black slaves this ocean has swallowed up" (*A Small Place* 14). Walcott similarly reflects on the environmental and human degradation of tourism in the Caribbean, calling the industry a "benign blight" that can nonetheless "infect all of those island nations, not gradually but with imperceptible speed, until each rock is whitened by the guano of white-winged hotels, the arc and descent of progress" ("The Antilles" 82).

Like Kincaid, whose diatribe against the tourism industry in *A Small Place* also indicts North American travelers and corporate investors, Walcott specifically criticizes the imperialist, capitalist appropriation of the region by its more dominant neighbor to the north, the United States, suggesting that the tourist industry (driven by U.S. capital) and tourist brochures envision the Caribbean Sea as a "blue pool into which the republic dangles the extended foot of Florida as inflated rubber islands bob and drinks with umbrellas float toward her on a raft" ("The Antilles" 81). In this passage from his 1992 Nobel Laureate lecture, Walcott echoes an earlier comment that "The Caribbean Sea is not an American lake," from Glissant's 1981 *Le discours antillais* (translated as *Caribbean Discourse* in 1989); Glissant aesthetically and politically resituates the Caribbean archipelago as "the estuary of the Americas" (139). These writers, though, also refuse false boundaries between land and sea. Sea touches land, and land sea, as waves break along the coastline of the small island-states within the Caribbean archipelago, recreating rhizomic or interrelated spaces for eco-becomings.[16]

Also like Kincaid, Walcott accuses the corrupt government and business leaders in the small island-states of complicity in this tourist degradation: "This is how the islands from shame of necessity sell themselves; this is the seasonal erosion of their identity, that high-pitched repetition of the same images of service that cannot distinguish one island from the other, with a future of polluted marinas, land deals negotiated by ministers, and all of this conducted to the music of Happy Hour and the rictus of a smile" ("The Antilles" 81). Walcott, like Kincaid and Glissant, laments this reduction of the islands to "happy hour" calypsos for vacationing tourists, or even to "beautiful beaches," warm breezes, and turquoise waters.

One must, they warn, refuse the seductions and traps of beauty, which may spawn the desire to possess, a caution Kincaid also sounds in *A Small Place*: "Antigua is beautiful. Antigua is too beautiful" (77). Beauty may be precarious, imprisoning. "It is as if, then," Kincaid writes, "the beauty of the sea, the land, the air, the trees, the market, the people, the sounds they make—were a prison, and as if everything and everybody inside it were locked in and everything and everybody that is not inside it were locked out" (*A Small Place* 79).

Kincaid links colonial violence and slavery to neocolonial and capitalist, tourist exploitation: those inside and outside have double resonances—masters and slaves, white tourists and black natives; those who owned the plantation, those who tilled its fields; those "checked in" to luxurious resorts (such as the Mill Reef Club in Antigua in *A Small Place*), those denied entry. The *Lonely Planet*'s online guide to Antigua states equivocally, "Antigua's many beaches, with their white or light golden sands, are protected by coral reefs, and all are officially public."[17] The adverb "officially" casts doubt on the very idea that it intends to affirm. Kincaid counters, "Even though all the beaches in Antigua are by law public beaches, Antiguans are not allowed on the beaches of this hotel [unnamed]; they are stopped at the gate by guards; and soon the best beaches in Antigua will be closed to Antiguans" (*A Small Place* 57–58). Beauty possessed; beaches territorialized.

In "The Burning Beach," Glissant theorizes sulfurous, volatile landscapes as necessary natural antidotes to commodified postcard visions of Caribbean paradises. For Glissant, the "beautiful" but "burning" beach cannot hide the "hills that stand ragged" or the "devastated mangrove" (*Poetics* 205); however, the worlds portrayed in Glissant's texts are not passive receptacles but vibrant and autonomous beings; and the "mangrove swamp," despite zoning for "industry or for major centers of consumption," resists its own destruction (*Poetics* 205). Kincaid, Walcott, and Glissant do not, however, merely lament this phenomenon; they also envision alternatives. In the next section, I theorize a Caribbean *poetics of (eco-)relation* (à la Glissant) to address and redress these historical, colonial, and contemporary neocolonial forms of human and environmental degradation rather than insisting (as do some critics, such as Love) on a radical shift from *ego-* to *eco*-politics.

Poetics of (Eco-)Relation: Antillean Soil, Sea Routes, Rhizomed Lands

In "Distancing, Determining," Glissant distinguishes between two contemporary forms of ecology: ecology "as mysticism" and ecology "as politics." For Glissant, ecology "as mysticism" privileges indigeneity, purity, and notions of the earth as rooted in sacrosanct ideas about "Territory" and belonging or rootedness (*Poetics* 146); in contrast, ecology "as politics" germinates critiques of sacred territoriality and exclusivist, purist links between people and land. Glissant emphasizes the need for ecological visions of "Relation" that underscore the interrelationality and interdependence of "all lands, of the whole Earth" (146). According to Glissant, the unique history of the Caribbean (colonization, genocide, slavery, and diaspora) makes the first ecological form—ecology "as mysticism" with its grounding in the "sacred intolerance of the root" (147)—untenable in the Caribbean. Rife with damaging ideas about territory, belonging, and roots, the issue of land "ownership" also obscures vexing questions about dwelling and indigeneity: "the only 'possessors' of the Archipelago," Glissant writes, "would be the Caribs or their predecessors, who have been exterminated. The restrictive force of the sacred always tends to seek out the first occupants of a territory (those closest to an original 'creation'). In the Caribbean would this be Caribs and Arawaks or other older and, consequently, more legitimate and 'determining' populations?" (146).

Glissant argues that the "sacred" relation between nature and "natives," or territory and indigenous people, was abruptly severed by violent and devastating, if not total, decimation. This passage also pointedly reveals that the first act of ecocide in the Caribbean archipelago was genocide, and the first victims were the Tainos, Aruacs, and Caribs. The entangled histories of genocide and ecocide destroy the possibility for genealogical and arboreal continuity of roots and absolute rootedness. For this reason, a new relationship between people and place must be theorized.

Kincaid also stages this impossible (genealogical and geographical) return in her 1996 novel *The Autobiography of My Mother*, a fictional autobiography about Xuela Claudette Richardson, who at the age of seventy retrospectively recounts the events of her life as they have unfolded in Dominica. She begins by telling her readers that her mother (a beautiful Carib woman named Xuela who was herself orphaned as an infant) died "at the moment that she was born," and this loss is the central preoccupation of the novel. Xuela's personal loss is exponentially compounded by the historical loss of Caribs in their old world that historically and violently became "new" in more dominant eyes, the tragic fate that results from the worst form of cultural contact. Xuela's Carib ancestry is, as she sadly notes, one of the world's "crumbling ancestral lines" (*Autobiography* 200). Xuela's desire for a genealogical return to her Carib mother and a geographical return to the land of her mother's people—or to a pure origin—is complicated by and ultimately fails because of the horrific and irreversible reality of genocide. And the historical legacy of genocide haunts the entire Caribbean.[18]

"The massacre of the Indians, uprooting the sacred," Glissant writes, "has already invalidated this futile search. Once that had happened, Antillean soil could not become a territory but, rather, a rhizomed land" (*Poetics* 146). The indigenous "roots" to territory are impossible for the descendants of enslaved African Caribbean individuals, as for the colonial "békés," and the "Hindus" who arrived during the Other Middle Passage.[19] Glissant thus renounces notions of territory, sacred possession, and roots (as ones forever tainted by genocide and ecocide), for the "complicity of relation" found in rhizomes and rhizomic relations;[20] instead, Glissant theorizes an "aesthetics of the earth," but a poetics that is rhizomic, not rooted: an aesthetics of "disruption and intrusion," of "rupture and connection" (151). Suggesting direct affiliation between territory and territorialization,[21] Glissant refuses a Caribbean "territory," which is the "basis for conquest" and which "requires that filiation be planted and legitimated" (151). Rather than an impossible return to indigenous territory, Glissant detours through the distances of diaspora, intimating that "distancings are necessary to Relation" (157).[22]

The sentiment that distance is necessary for autonomy and alterity recurs in a scene from *The Autobiography* in which Xuela watches her father, Alfred Richardson, as he observes the sea; though her father is a descendant of an African mother, Mary, and a Scotsman, John Richardson—a meeting of the "vanquished" and the "victor," as Kincaid imagines him—Alfred renounces the humility of the former, claiming the mantle of power of the latter. He sees the world through the lens of the colonialist gaze, which closes the distance between self and environ and subsumes all within the self. Alfred Richardson conquers and territorializes the world within his view; he does not allow the world distance and thus does not allow it autonomy or alterity. Xuela sees differently from her father—she feels her father's alterity and stretches her thoughts toward his without collapsing the distance between the two. She imagines his conquistadorial gaze, abstractly and dangerously "Human": "A human being, a person, many people, a people, will say that their surroundings, their physical surroundings, form their consciousness, their very being; they will get up every morning and look at green hills, white cliffs, silver mountains, fields of golden grain, rivers of blue-glinting water, and in the beauty of this— and *it is beautiful,* they cannot help but find it beautiful—they invisibly, magically, *conquer the distance* that is between them and the beauty they are beholding, and they feel themselves *become one with it*" (*Autobiography* 191; my emphasis). Like Glissant, Kincaid suggests that distance is required in order to break with destructive patterns of human domination over nature; and necessary for creating respectful and rhizomic relations between the land, sea, and its creatures.

In a chapter that opens with the abstract, universal question, "What makes the world turn?" (*Autobiography* 131), Xuela imagines a "man" from the British Isles, perhaps a mirror of her paternal grandfather, John Richardson. She imagines a wintry setting where, in the man's eyes, "the grass is alive but not actively growing (dormant), the trees are alive but not actively growing (dormant)," and the "light is pale and weak" (136). Revealing a colonialist regard for nature, the man surveys the land, transforming the "dormant field outside his window" into oceanic vastness to navigate: "in his mind the still earth becomes a blue sea, a gray ocean, and on the blue sea and on the gray ocean are ships, and the ships are filled with people" (136). The dormant grass, trees, fields fuel conquering desires to navigate unknown oceans, accumulate wealth, "explore" worlds. In this memory, the man's desires exemplify an "arrowlike nomadism" driven by the "expansion of territory," which Glissant distinguishes from the impulse of a "circular nomadism" that is a "search for the Other" (*Poetics* 18). For the colonialist man, as Xuela imagines, the "dormant fields" are impartial, but cultivable; in his mind, the field can be cultivated, "carved up" (*Autobiography* 137) and dominated. Xuela muses, "The impartiality of the blue sea, the gray ocean, is well known to him also, but these cold, vast vaults of water cannot be carved up and no season can influence them in his favor" (137). If, for the colonialist man, the field is arable and seemingly conquerable, the sea remains indomitable. But it also served as trans-Atlantic routes for piracy, conquest, and inhuman and inhumane trade—and thus, like land, may be navigated, even "territorialized," or regulated. Kincaid and Glissant remind us of the human consequences of trans-Atlantic routes, where bones are scattered on ocean floors, "huge cemeteries / of bone and the huge crossbows of the rusted anchors" in which "water recorded three centuries / of the submerged archipelago" (*Omeros* 142, 155). Rhizomic or diasporic distance allows one to chart alternative paths for retracing these routes and their detrimental histories without remaining perennially rooted in those paths/pasts. This rhizomic distance—as Kincaid, Walcott, and Glissant all differently reveal—allows us to reconceive nature and human interrelations in more positive ways and to reexperience the world itself as creative, not created.

For example, in *Poetics of Relation,* Glissant reverses the packaged and commodified images of the Caribbean (tropical paradise, wild Eden, and white sand beaches with cool oceanic breezes): these beaches are black, burning, volcanic, sulfurous, boiling, roiling; he scatters over the sands looking for *points chauds* (hotspots) where the beach is orange, earthy, alive. These hotspots on the beach signal its life, its vitality, its volcanic possibilities. He also sees the salty waves that lap these black shores, imagining cavernous underground paths where rivers flow and connect these islands, conjoining ocean (Atlantic) to sea (Caribbean), a rhizomic route from a hotspot on La Diamante beach in Martinique and the volcanic town of La Soufrière in St. Lucia and its twin Pitons. And he even writes, "I recognize myself in Derek Walcott" (*Poetics* 71–72), seeing self in other, not subsuming other into self. In *Omeros,* Walcott similarly imagines a "burning beach," seared with the memory of genocide. As Achille rakes the leaves of a pomme-Arac tree, he reflects on loss and extinction:

A beach burns their memory. Copper almond leaves
cracking like Caribs in a pepper smoke, the blue
entering God's eye and nothing raked from their lives

except one elegy from Aruac to Sioux. (*Omeros* 164)

Shabine, in Walcott's "*The Schooner* Flight," similarly recalls the smoldering memories of genocide and how he "ran like a Carib through Dominica / . . . nose holes choked with memory of smoke," hearing the "screams of my burning children" (*Collected Poems* 356).

Carib genocide was the first act of ecocide in the "New World," and yet it was not total or absolute. And Caribbean writers like Walcott, Glissant, and Kincaid create rhizomic lines of "eco-poetic" relations between Carib ancestors, Carib survivors, and African and Asian diasporics in the Caribbean. Walcott and Glissant thus imagine Caribbean relations: between Martinique and St. Lucia; between self and other; between the extinct and the survived; between ocean and sea. They imagine rhizomes of shared becoming, not commodified tourist destinations.

In book 7, Omeros guides the narrator across an Antillean Styx and through the underworld, "up heights the Plunketts loved, from Soufrière upwards / past that ruined scheme which hawsers of lianas / had anchored in bush . . ." (*Omeros* 289). La Soufrière is riddled with "holes of boiling lava / bubbl[ing] in the Malebolge" (59), and in his journey guided by Omeros (as Dante is guided through inferno by Virgil in the *Inferno*), the narrator hears

> . . . the boiling engines
>
> of steam in its fissures, the deep indignation
> of Hephaestus or Ogun grumbling at the sins
> of souls who had sold out their race, . . .
>
> . . . .
> . . . These were the traitors
>
> who, in elected office, saw the land as views
> for hotels and elevated into waiters
> the sons of others, while their own learnt something else. (289)

For Walcott, they are infernal traitors who with "sucking faces that argued Necessity / in rapid zeroes which no one else understood / for the island's profit" (290). St. Lucia and Soufrière are paradise and inferno, original sin and light of the Caribbean, as the name of the island suggests. The Caribbean—heir to histories of diaspora, slavery, and dispossession— is the legatee to other violations: imperialist intervention, governmental corruption, treachery, tourist exploitation, and environmental degradation. Walcott especially scorns the national "traitors" who "saw the land as views for hotels." These violations resonate in the human and the natural dimensions; this passage from *Omeros* moves in two directions at once, allowing the natural world to be read through a historical frame and history to be read through an ecocritical one. Soufrière holds eruptive potentials for resisting its destruction and for creating or spawning new worlds. Who has forgotten Montserrat?[23] In the final section, then, I explore Caribbean returns to myths of genesis in order to understand the ecocritical interventions such returns offer.

Caribbean Genesis and Ecocritical Resistance

Kincaid, Walcott, and Glissant share a sense of genesis in writing, of creating and re-creating worlds in words, of worlds that create and recreate autonomously. For these writers, poetic creation involves the translation of the natural world into language, as much as it does a making of worlds from words. Glissant disrupts Western genesis mythologies that are grounded in notions of filiation, genealogy, and legitimacy through his theorizations of creolized or composite cultures that are "digenetic" rather than genetic.[24] Walcott's embrace of the "second Adam" as the spirit of poetic creation in the Caribbean interestingly parallels Kincaid's textual and philosophical tilling of the garden as a metaphor for historical forms of colonial violence in the region.

Their textual returns to genesis or creation disrupt, rather than affirm, myths of origin, revealing the entanglement of history and memory in the Caribbean. Historical memory suffuses past, present, and future, reflecting on past historical violence, even as it projects future hopes and dreams. History and memory are indeed entangled ideas here, not separate ones with the first belonging ostensibly to public culture and the second to individual psyche; however, both are interwoven in the Caribbean imagination as it reflects on nature and remembers subterranean and submarine histories. This interweaving is a genesis of future spaces and times, as well as the creative remembrance of past spaces and times. As Glissant theorizes, memory must not be conceptualized temporally or even historically by the "rhythms of month and year alone"; rather, memory is provoked by the abyssal confrontation with the "final sentence" of plantations (*Poetics* 72). But this touching upon the void, this experience of the abyss that is the inheritance of the Middle Passage is also genesis, creation—"the infinite abyss, in the end became knowledge" (8); for Glissant, land and sea touch upon one another in infinite renewal, "one vast becoming, but a beginning whose time is marked by these balls and chains gone green" (6).[25] To counter the erasures of History (with a capital *H*), it is necessary to unravel other submerged histories through an imaginative, if not literal, "effort of memory." As Walcott eloquently notes, "If there was nothing, there is everything to be made" ("Twilight" 4).

These Caribbean returns to genesis, to myth, also stage cultural contestations of Western ways of knowing; and these writers' preoccupations with "Caribbean genesis" also reveal a profound suspicion toward myth and how it is entangled with power. For these writers, genesis myths— particularly Western creation myths that are centered on hierarchical notions of Man and Being and that impose rational order on the natural world, subjecting it to anthropocentric domination—are deeply embedded within Eurocentric knowledges based on dualistic notions of nature and culture, self and other, man and beast, white and black. As Glissant notes in *Caribbean Discourse,* "The control of nature, and of one's nature, by culture was the ideal of the Western mind" (73). This way of knowing is powerful and embedded in political, social, cultural, and historical power structures; knowledge, self-knowledge, and knowledge of other "objects" was the historical apex of Man's Being. "Man, the chosen one, knows himself and knows the world, not because he is part of it, but because he establishes a sequence and measures it according to his own time scale, which is determined by his affiliation" (73).

Kincaid's, Glissant's, and Walcott's visions of nature are, as Dash writes in his introduction to *Caribbean Dicourse,* "the direct opposite of 'the Eternal Garden.' Here no Creator provides the text that makes this world intelligible, and perhaps there is no Creator for Adam to ape. The problem for the New World Adam is how to inhabit such a world, which in the past has defeated all who tried to possess it" (xxxvi). Dash speaks of a "New World Adam," which echoes Walcott's "second Adam"; Glissant imagines an errant beachcomber, circularly nomadic, as the one who dwells and moves without possessing or dominating ("The Black Beach," in *Poetics* 121–27). Echoing Walcott's call for a "second Adam," Glissant welcomes "the appearance of a new man . . . able to live the relative after having suffered the absolute" (*Caribbean Discourse* 147); and Kincaid creatively refigures the diasporic as the diabolic, even as she positively infuses it with creativity. These models all diverge from privileged or powerful notions of Man. We need to part with "Humanism (the notion of man as privileged)" (74), as Glissant urges, and replace this corrosive, tragically destructive belief with one of "planetary consciousness" (see *Poetics* 164–65).

These writers return to genesis as if to the site of an originary crime, a place of an infraction against the natural world in order to unearth the idea of a beginning that is intrinsically tainted and marred. Their notions of Caribbean genesis refuse a static Eden, a fixed Paradise; rather, their Caribbean geneses are plural, becoming, autonomously flowing, and above all, dynamic. They acknowledge, as Wilson Harris writes, that "the life of the earth is not fixed, it is not a description of fixed mountains or valleys divorced from the characters that move on it . . . so that we may speak of a humanity whose feet are made of mud or land or water" (263–64). Their revisions of genesis, spiraling infinitely toward chaosmos, depart from an ordered cosmos; they move us from a static Eden to dynamic, myriad becomings. Their critiques of genesis myths are also critiques of worldviews that subordinate nature to cultural domination: their ideas are directed not only toward an inherited past but also toward future horizons of becoming. Their Caribbean returns participate in what Bindé calls an environmental "ethics of the future." By so doing, they move ecocriticism beyond nature writing,[26] investing it with an ethical, future-oriented imagination that is necessary to envision and create future alternatives to ecological disaster or environmental catastrophe.

Creative (In) Conclusions

So why do these Caribbean writers return to myths of genesis in their writings? What ecocritical interventions are made by their textual returns to genesis? Through their textual revisions of genesis, Caribbean writers offer ecocritical resistance to deleterious models that subordinated nature to culture, beasts to Man, creation to God. Kincaid's interest in gardening and botany, Glissant's investment in a "poetics of landscape" (*Caribbean* 110–50), and Walcott's "fragments of epic memory" all powerfully articulate modes of ecocritical resistance to capitalist development and tourist economic structures in the Caribbean. They imagine both alternative environmental futures to ecological disaster and altered relations between humans and the natural world. Their theorizations also initiate a reconsideration of the "natural" in subjectivity—not as a pregiven medium but rather as a created mode of relation in the world. Their ideas also suggest a reconfiguration of landscape in citizenship—not as citizens bound by and inextricable from a fixed territory and not as subjects bound to a *pays natal* but as a land diasporically reconfigured, or as subjects with rhizomic roots that do not exploit the terrains in which they dwell. Caribbean returns to genesis also shift the contemporary ecocritical frame away from ecological disaster/annihilation: in Judeo-Christian terms, Adam subdues, names, and codifies nature, ultimately dominating and destroying it; in Caribbean returns to myths of genesis, humans live in symbiotic relation with nature and are often subdued by it!

Notes

1. For ecocritical analysis of *Omeros,* see Buell, *Writing* 70.
2. See Grove, *Green Imperialism;* and Sheller, *Consuming the Caribbean.*
3. On the distinction between *ego-* and *eco-consciousness,* see Love, "Revaluing Nature." On ecocriticism, see Glotfelty and Fromm, *The Ecocriticism Reader;* Buell, *The Environmental Imagination* and *Writing for an Endangered World;* Hochman, *The Green Cultural Studies Reader;* Kerridge and Sammells, *Writing the Environment;* Gaard and Murphy, *Ecofeminist Literary Criticism;* Coupe, *The*

Green Studies Reader; Armbruster and Wallace, eds., *Beyond Nature Writing;* and Rosendale, *The Greening of Literary Scholarship.*

4. O'Brien analyzes Kincaid's "garden" essays in order to "productively explore the points at which they [environmentalist and social justice agendas] fail to cohere" (181). Ecocritics who attempt to negotiate between environmental and social justice politics include Dodd; Armbruster and Wallace; Bennett; Alaimo; Platt; and Shiva, *Biopiracy, Stolen Harvest, Tomorrow's Biodiversity,* and *Water Wars.*

5. On ecofeminism, see essays in Gaard and Murphy's *Ecofeminist Literary Criticism;* and Armbruster, "Poststructuralist Approach."

6. On the concept of a "poetics of relation" and the distinction between root and rhizomic identities, see Glissant, *Poetics,* especially 143–44.

7. See Buell, *Environmental Imagination* and *Writing for an Endangered World.* For a critique of Buell's privileging of realism, see Phillips, "Ecocriticism, Literary Theory, and the Truth of Ecology."

8. Harris notes that belief in realism "led the rulers of civilization into an 'obliviousness' of the many diverse peoples under the umbrella of empire" ("Theatre" 262). For a discussion of "genesis" in texts by Harris, see Bundy's *Selected Essays.*

9. UN Economic and Social Council Resolution 1998/40.

10. UN Press Release SG/SM/6364.

11. UN Press Release GA/9537.

12. UN Press Release GA/9320.

13. For a critique of ecotourism as *more* business as (*than*) usual, see Giuliano.

14. "Saint Lucia," *The Lonely Planet Online.*

15. "Antigua and Barbuda," *The Lonely Planet Online.*

16. DeLoughrey's "Tidalectics" is particularly important for its theorizations of this Caribbean "dialectic *between* land and sea" (32).

17. "Antigua and Barbuda," *The Lonely Planet Online.*

18. In an interview for *Talk of the Nation,* Ray Suarez asked Kincaid about Caribs and their "absence" or "presence" within history, geography, and culture in the Caribbean. Kincaid replied that "they survive in the way of relics and we needn't pretend." However, Caribs do still live in Dominica (where *Autobiography* is set), in Guyana, and elsewhere.

19. For the history of this term, see Ramdin.

20. Glissant's theorizations of the rhizome are key to his un-rooted "aesthetics of the earth." See *Poetics* 11.

21. This is what Deleuze and Guattari define as a sedimentation of concretization of power, as opposed to deterritorialization, the diffusion or erosion of concentrated power structures.

22. Rhizome addresses forces of cultivation, transplantation, and transculturation, all part of diasporic experiences; and diaspora, like rhizome, is a botanical term, yet one rooted in processes of cultivation. See Braziel and Mannur 1.

23. Kincaid also envisions living, vibrant worlds in *Autobiography* (17). Xuela intuits trees, leaves, rivers, lagoons, birds, frogs alive and spawning life, evoking worlds that are alive, dynamic, generating, creating, creative, not passive, sterile, or created by human subjective or technological intervention. Compare *At the Bottom of the River.*

24. See especially *Faulkner, Mississippi.*

25. Also quoted in DeLoughrey, "Tidalectics" 21.

26. See Armbruster and Wallace, *Beyond Nature.*

"The Argument of the Outboard Motor"

An Interview with Derek Walcott

George B. Handley

BORN IN St. Lucia in 1930, Derek Walcott is well known internationally for his poetry, playwriting, and cultural criticism. He is the recipient of numerous awards including, of course, the Nobel Prize for Literature, which he received in 1992. George Handley conducted this interview in two stages, first in July 2001 at Walcott's residence in St. Lucia and then at his residence in New York City in November 2001.

GH: What was your response to the construction of the Hilton Jalousie Hotel between the Pitons here in St. Lucia?[1]

DW: I didn't go there in a protest. And the people around Soufrière wanted it because it gave them jobs, and that's the usual argument of these hotels that provide employment. And that's true enough, but right now in St. Lucia we have a serious decline in tourism, and it is very perilous and fragile for us to depend completely on tourism. I'm sure experts may have looked at alternatives, but I think that one of the things that may have happened is that we have settled down, or the economy and the economists have settled down into an idea that tourism is the alternative to agriculture. I don't like the dependency of thinking that the generosity of tourism becomes the equivalent of a waiter looking for a big tip, and depending on that big tip for sustenance, for his livelihood. I don't like to see that happening, and I think that we are building more and more hotels. The dangerous thing about it becomes not the fact that another hotel is being built, but where it is being built, so that there is nothing sacred. I mean, you live in Utah—if I said I was going to put a big hotel in any one of those primal sites, turning to spiritual locations for Americans, then that would be a serious thing. But the investor who can come here and think, "Well, it's just a small island. Who is going to care?" and then be supported by politicians, by the government on the pretext that it is very good for the island, he is doing serious damage to the mentality of St. Lucians who say, "Yes, we should do it because it is going to bring employment." If I build a McDonald's on one of the rocks, or bluffs, the sites of all those great Western movies, it is the equivalent of a Jalousie Hotel. I am talking about the direct desecration of a thing. I am not even against hotels, really. I said so. I said build a hotel, but don't build it there. For Christ's sake, leave something that is really spiritual to St. Lucians more than just two big mountains sticking up out of the sea. I mean, would somebody really have the guts to say, "I'm going to build something under one of those two things?" No.

GH: How important is it to defend sacred spaces? Is it more important than defending art?

DW: It is stronger than art. Nobody can go by the Pitons and not be really moved by the power they emanate. The same thing would be true of any other sacred location that has become cherished for some vibration it gives off. I mean, we have a volcano. Once nature starts to act up, then we get very religious. Hurricane season comes, and that's a condition we live with. That's okay, that's natural in a way. I'm talking about someone deciding and ignoring the devotion of people. Well, that has happened to the American Indian, perhaps, the demoralization of violating sacred ground, or a sacred burial ground, for instance. That's the standard crime that is the history of America. So, again, historically, you see the support of people thinking it is a good idea, your own people, your own government thinking, "It's okay, there is nothing wrong with that."

GH: But many people around Soufrière wanted the hotel, didn't they? Is it an economic luxury to defend sacred spaces? How do we balance such a defense against economic need?

DW: You can individualize it; you can make a specific example of it if you say to somebody representing the government that it's not a good idea to build a structure because it violates the feel of the structure and violates it in a very profound way. The people feel an awe that all tribes feel in certain parts of the territory; certain parts are inviolable. So that inviolable part is the feeling of the tribe. If somebody who is more pragmatic says, "Yes, but what does inviolable do for bringing bread on the table or for giving shelter?" Then you have the exact crisis of America encapsulated there, because all you have to say is that it doesn't do anything for the Indian. But that is a blasphemy, really, however strong that word may sound, because these things are sacred.

If someone who is an Indian then says, "Look they're right. Let's do that," then you have a crisis not only in America, but we know that it is now a crisis that is happening with great celerity in the global balance. I mean, people are protesting what is happening to the earth. I don't want to sound like someone preaching ecology, but that's the core of the question, and it's a moral question. And if people ignore immoral questions of landscape and do what they have to do, then ultimately the damage is incalculable. So the person who is protecting the sacred piece of earth is doing more than the person who thinks that right now concrete and steel are going to do more for some other generation coming. That's now a world crisis. It's an emblem that the Pitons are an example of. And I mean more than just to hate the idea of the hotel, or to challenge it, and if possible to have stopped that hotel from being built there, because aesthetically it is like a wound, and if I could look down at that hotel and see what I see, and it looks like any other hotel, then the Pitons will become what? They become prostitutes; you're making them whores. Basically you're saying it's okay to violate the landscape, it's okay to desecrate it, because they're the real thing that's bringing people money. It's very hard to communicate that to people in Soufrière who can't feel some ancestral anything about it, but who know that these are two emblems of something more than, say, another building.

GH: Philosophically speaking, is human activity always, inevitably, using nature in some way that results in a spiritual death of some kind? To what extent can we avoid such death? At what point does our activity move from being an ethical necessity to a violation?

DW: When you say nature, I hear a nineteenth-century echo "nature," meaning a Wordsworthian or even Miltonic feeling. But we have to update nature. A canoe is a beautiful thing in St. Lucia, the object which is hollowed out and has great elegance and speed. So there is the emblem of a canoe going across the sea with a man on it, and it is a great image and something organic, because that tree is like wood and water; it is made out of wood and is now afloat and moving on the sea. So you have two elements in a way there. None of that is thought of by the fisherman apparently, but the relationship of somebody who hammers, or sculpts, a canoe, into a shape that is elegant is really, if you want to put it bluntly, creating a work of art. It is also more than a work of art: it is the thing from which he makes his living. If I put an outboard motor on that canoe, it doesn't lose its elegance and is brought up to the immediacy of the twentieth century today and is an outrigged, outfitted canoe with a powerful engine that does what it does to help the fishing industry and so on. You can even accommodate it into the design of the canoe, but a man rowing on his own sea has something a little more strange, a little more evocative, a little more baffling in terms of what he feels being on the water at sunrise, rowing with wooden oars, as opposed to starting his engine and going out. That subtlety that has been lost between the outboard motor and the oars is the area that we are talking about. One is obviously not saying "don't have an outboard motor because you are violating the symmetry of the canoe, the meaning of the canoe." On the other hand, you are saying, "Okay, have the outboard motor, it's good; you need it for your fishing." But if you let your outboard motor be your equivalent of, say, a hotel, of a skyscraper, of a big building, of another something that paves the ground and pays no attention to the contours of the earth, then you have the architectural question of what you are doing to the landscape. If you magnify the argument that the outboard motor does more for the fisherman than the oars, then you have the argument of people who say, "That is progress," and therefore it is legitimate to transform every little village in the Caribbean to a mini Miami or a small functioning modern outlet. And you can look at the architecture of the Caribbean and see it change. You don't know sometimes whether you are in Puerto Rico or Miami. They are identical. And you can continue on down the archipelago. This is what tragically is going to happen. What does that do in terms of the psyche of the fisherman we are talking about and the fisherman with an outboard motor? The industry is called progress.

What has been lost between the feeling and the pace of a man rowing and an outboard motor is exactly, well, not only poor countries but any country on earth now has to realize that that outboard motor distends its own sense of time. In other words, you row and get your own rhythm and then you fish and that's your industry, that's your feeling, that's your relationship to what you're doing. You get an outboard motor and it's like a third person with you—that's an engine that you use. But the ironic thing about time is that the rhythm of the human body is never satisfied with its own pace. In other words, you get in an outboard motor, and you wish you could go faster, so you build a faster boat, and you discard the canoe, and you build something made out of plastic that goes faster and faster until you get to the point that there's no more canoe; not that you can't have a relationship between sunrise and being in an outboard motor rig craft, but something has gone and what has happened recently with all of these demonstrations and riots in terms of ecology is that people are seriously, really seriously aware of the danger to the planet. This is a very large thing, but you can take a microcosmic thing like that, or like Jalousie, or violating something that should have a certain sanctity for every tribe—once you start to do that, then you start to use that argument in the name of progress. Then you are doing the historical thing. You are saying that if I get twenty-five soldiers and I go into a territory that has Indians, if I shoot the Indians and if I convert them, then I am doing it for their own good. That has always been the argument for the outboard motor.

GH: How would you defend the idea of Adam as creator, not so much for yourself, but as an idea for the Americas? Is it really something transferable to urban areas?

DW: I don't think it can be seen as an industrial concept. I mean it's not going to work to think that in the heart of London somewhere, you are going to get up and get this feeling of the beginning of a new world. If you want to stretch it, you can say you want to treat it metaphorically and say that no matter where you are, you could condition yourself to look at the world, even if you were in an industrialized location. That's very hard to do. It has to relate, not to the inner sense but to the immaculateness of nature. That's what it is. The action of nature is to renew, and that kind of inner sense is possible because of the example in nature. So if you put it down in a ghetto in Chicago, you can ask how you can apply that practically to somebody living there. But I wouldn't say that it applies. I would say that the quest that one would have to have is to find that place in nature and to renew oneself from time to time by that awe and respect that we have in nature outside of cities, in any famous place or cherished locale. I think that's what these things are preserved for. They are preserved for more than the spectacle. They are preserved for something that restores that kind of feeling of a beginning, a reinstituting of Adamic principles. That's why people go hunting or camping or fishing. The Adam idea is not an industrial theory. It won't work in that environment, but what it does do, I think, is it cherishes the environment, and if it's properly cherished, then it gives something to the cherisher. Obviously, to write with that in mind in the Caribbean, where the Caribbean is still preserved, still pristine, still organically spectacular, then that awe that comes with the experience of the sea brings certainly more than a possibility; it brings the concept of a beginning, of another day, the beginning of the possibility of another kind of culture, another kind of civilization.

I think the possibility is continually betrayed, even by island politics and by the repetition of the sea and by a kind of world ambition. But I think that it is still valid in terms of the relationship of what we are to the environment. It's what, in other words, could have been if America had somehow adapted its industry to growth. If the fusion had been possible between industry and, say, the American Indian's idea of nature, then that would have been America. But it's no longer America because that's gone, and it's an elegiac America because what the American Indian could have taught a new culture would have been the cherishing of all those values that are Adamic, that don't want to violate what is pure. And that the struggle is still going on.

GH: Has the destruction of so much Native American culture in the Caribbean facilitated the Adamic idea in some way? Might it be more difficult to defend the idea with a more populous Native American presence to remind you more emphatically of a persistent and prior history and culture?

DW: Well, I think that they are all one tribe, from the Alaskas all the way down to Tierra del Fuego. It's all really one tribe with different branches, so that the Arawak is related to the Sioux. It really is one huge tribe of different families. The same way you might say, I don't know, some other ethnic group, Semitic tribes, for instance, cover a large territory. And there is not much difference really between the Egyptians and the Israelites. They are the same people. Not the Egyptians so much, but, say, other tribes who are in the Mediterranean.

GH: Why do you suppose Whitman's views of Adamic poetry didn't survive, or didn't work as well? What's wrong with his democratic embrace?

DW: I was at Columbia once, a long time ago, and somebody got up from the audience and gave a virulent and vehement attack on Whitman as a racist, and I guess it must have come from his essays and his polemical pieces, because it's not there in *Leaves of Grass*. But what's also not there in *Leaves of Grass* is what happened to the Indian. So *Leaves of Grass,* as great as it is in terms of its vision, does not include the American Indian or whatever happened to the slaves, really. It doesn't include slavery. It doesn't include the decimation of the American Indian. It's too idealistic for me to completely take it in. Had it taken in the guilt and the horror of becoming America, it might have been a greater achievement. It's a splendid achievement, it's immense, magnificent, but it's exclusive, and it does not include American sin.

GH: And yet you still want to preserve that idea of innocence in poetry?

DW: I think that *Leaves of Grass* would have had the stature and depth of *Paradise Lost* or *The Divine Comedy,* because there is sin in there. There is the reality of the cruelty of man, and that is something that Whitman does not take into account. It's very broad-shouldered and very gusty and so on, but it doesn't take in evil like Blake does. I mean, you can't compare the spiritual width of Blake's proverbs or Blake's epic to *Leaves of Grass* because Blake takes in the horror of mankind as much as he takes in the innocence. So it's all innocence, in a way, in Whitman, as great as he is. I can understand the man from Columbia's position because he was saying a Yankee and imperial idea of the vision of the future doesn't include us from Latin America or wherever we are. It was hard to hear that, but the older you get and the more you read, you find works you sort of avoid or don't wish to take on. Then you get a little less, not respectful, but you find that which is missing in a great work like *Leaves of Grass*. It's not there really.

GH: I suspect that's why some have criticized the idea of Adamic poetry.

DW: But the idea of Adam contains original sin. I'm not talking about someone without a spiritual past. I am talking about someone looking at a morning that is unspoiled, not devastated by any means, and the feeling that one can rechristen things, rename things. That's what you are offered if you live in the Caribbean. Every morning you get that. Naming means you can say the same name. You don't have to try to get a new name for something. It's repeating the name, whether it's grass or water, or sea or sky. To say it again is Adamic, it's a rechristening. You are endowing it with a name, you have been given the privilege, by whomever you want, to name these things again. That's what I mean. If a blade of grass is coming out of a ruin, then that's what I'm talking about, no matter where the ruin is or how big. You know, the grass that emerges from the ruins is the grass that says it's a beginning again.

GH: Is the Adamic idea in a way an addiction to newness, to frontiers? Does it justify impatience with the old? Some people argue that the environmental crisis is in part due to this tendency of Western civilization to always want an Eden that it can go into and be the only civilization or the only individual—to be the lone Crusoe figure—and that that's always the precursor to a kind of environmental destruction. It's the idea of land as virgin so that you can be the one to have "her" first.

DW: Well, there are a lot of angles to answer from, but one is particularly a factor when you are talking about the Caribbean mainly, and that experience, as a Caribbean experience, is also an antidote to the idea of a consequential history. So the idea of being in a place that has not got history, that doesn't have ruins and mementos, or promises of civilizations, is in a way a Caribbean experience because the renewal has to happen, particularly in people in a shipwrecked condition (that is the idea of Crusoe). The legacy of the erasure of what was there, say for Robinson Crusoe, what he left behind and what he may miss, is that he has to have another beginning. Now, if you think in terms of Friday, if you think in terms of the slave or the person whom eventually Crusoe is supposed to subjugate and educate, then the issue will not have anything to do with the Adamic experience, but it will have to do with the attitude of Crusoe to Friday. The attitude of Crusoe to Friday in Defoe is still the attitude of the conqueror to the person who is captured, even by kindness.

All right, that's one or two emblematic figures dealing with a landscape that has no memorials and hasn't got any architectural promises in it. In both cases, though, what Robinson Crusoe has to strip himself of is nostalgia, memory, and despair, because he is in another place where he has to create a different kind of Crusoe. It is not quite the same thing as Adam, but it is quite close in the sense that it is a new world, and it requires a certain kind of physical courage and physical adaptability, all of those things that Adam himself as a beginner has to learn to do, including naming things.

Now Crusoe on his island doesn't know the names of the plants that he is living among. He doesn't know the names of the natives that he may find there. So he renames them, probably from what he already knows, so that the naming of America has simply been a repetition of names that come from Europe, like New York or New Brunswick, etc. Generally, the conqueror or the explorer renames something by associating what he is looking at with another image from the old world. I'm not talking about, necessarily, deliberately erasing the idea of history, but not treating it as a consequential thing, a thing that is bound to obey a certain mathematics of one, two, three, four, five, six. So if you think of an Adam who is not compelled by some kind of mathematical destiny that such and such is going to happen, then you are talking about somebody who really has to begin from the immediate surroundings that are there.

Well, I think that that is a condition that the poet gets into before he embarks on a poem, because none of the words that he knows can already express the experience he will create when he writes the words. It is not that he is making a reference to a standardized vocabulary with all of its associations. What has to be undertaken is a vocabulary that may be the same word, or same noun, but in the context of this idea of discovery, and immediacy, and freshness, and exploration, then that noun has to acquire its own identity in the poem. I don't think that's very different from, say, the naming of either the explorer or the naming that is already there in the mind of the native. I think that it's a simultaneous, common experience.

The other idea of longing for an Eden, for isolation or for removal from civilization, is a normal feeling for the essential separation of the soul from what surrounds it and what is too active and too disturbing. That is one attitude of flight, of escape, of trying to rediscover a place where one can begin again and not be persecuted by all the harassments that are there in daily life. But the daily life itself, even in a castaway situation, has to have its own rhythm. In fact you have to eat, bathe, and do whatever, so that diurnal kind of thing happens anyway. I think the simple premise that I am taking is that everything that has to do with the prelude to the creation of anything is an Adamic situation. Now maybe I haven't answered yet very precisely some of the things that you are pointing out related to the idea of Adam. Metaphorically you could say yes, it's a person walking naked, or walking around in an atmosphere that is benign and in which nature is benign and has that kind of bliss of innocence. Well, I don't see anything wrong with that because I think that that is not a physical condition; it can be a condition within a writer or within an artist. In fact, I think that *is* the condition, that one is reduced to that nothingness before one makes something. That wondering and the isolation that is there in the artist trying to make something is an Adamic thing.

Geographically and historically, the Caribbean origin is of slavery and indenture. It is not escape from history to go into a kind of Edenic or blissful geography in which then you don't owe anybody anything and you are not responsible to anyone—that is not the idea of it. The idea of it is what I think has happened to the Caribbean, and that is the degradation, the condition of humiliation that was there when the slave was brought in and the indentured servant. Now I think that that is something we have worked ourselves out of, and I think that it is part of the geography of the place that permits that. I think in a desolate situation there would not be that elation and that pleasure that happens in the Caribbean landscape whether it's from the sea, or from the sky, or whatever it is that is there; and therefore, that renewal that happens daily in terms of what should be the experience of someone living in such a geography would be to rename the objects and plants around that person, and that is really an eradication of the inevitable alphabet, inevitable vocabulary that is there for what precedes the other kind of naming. But that's a condition, I think, for every poet anywhere. So if one is in Ireland or in Montana and you want to write about something you are looking at, you go to that condition, which is exactly that of the, not the noble savage, but of somebody who is trying to relearn the nouns that are around one.

GH: How is it that art escapes tourism, because great nature writing and so many great landscape paintings are converted into, or are used by a touristic mode of logic or power, and it contributes to it in a way, but how is it that you can escape being a tourist in your relationship to your own land?

DW: I think what does it is good art. Real art does it. The first time I went to Spain and every time I go back, maybe particularly at a bullfight or maybe when I have been a little bit out of the low mountains or somewhere not far from the villages, but every experience I had of Spain was a repetition of what I had read in Hemingway. Now technically I am a tourist when I am in Spain. That did not prevent me from enjoying things that are there in Hemingway like, you know, the bulls running, the bullfights, and all the cliché things that are there for one when you go back to Spain. But what has happened because of the art of Hemingway, and because of the thorough sensation of enjoyment that is there when Hemingway writes about Spain and love, if you want to put in another way. But that is communicated through the words, through the writing, through the prose. The same would be true if I went to any other part of the world that I had read about. If I went to the Lake District, maybe, and there was a Wordsworth poem that was in the back of my head—or, for example, I just went and was astounded by the beauty of Monterey [California]. I was knocked out by it, and I remembered as I went around Steinbeck's Cannery Row, and all the buildings there, and everything there was vitalized from what they used to be, and that change came because of the recognition of something that had been illuminated by art, and I think that that is true of whatever a great writer or painter can do to a certain area when it goes past the real and into literature or painting.

The Caribbean is extremely photogenic, but nothing photogenic lasts in the sense of the depth of what is registered. Every Caribbean advertisement has a good-looking girl, generally Caucasian, in front of some view, right? And so there's a combination of that kind of sensuality with the landscape behind it, and so on, or a golf course where people are playing, and all these cut-out things which are common to all advertisements about places, right? But what happens to the landscape that you look at, if you see it through the eyes of someone who has written lovingly about it? It becomes a totally different thing. So that if you are looking at the landscape in Trinidad of the Indian villages and you think of Selvon, then something is illuminated there in the same way that Cannery Row was illuminated by Steinbeck's prose. So everywhere you get those banalities. There are photographs, I imagine, of the Forum; there are photographs of, I don't know, the mountains in Utah, but what makes these mountains more memorable are the films of John Ford. I mean, anytime you see them you think of John Ford, and you think of what he did there. And so there's another dimension that happens because of art, and I don't think it has anything ultimately to do with tourism.

GH: But the great western films have themselves shown how easily art can be adapted for the purposes of tourism. You won't find an advertisement for travel to the American West without some reference to the stereotypes that come from those films. Consequently even those who live in the West often relate to their own landscape as if they weren't really there, loving something that isn't there.

DW: You'd have to specify the kinds of tourists one is talking about and what does that tourist want, and so forth. If somebody went on a quest, a sort of literary tour, which they often do of, say, Joyce's island. I mean that's kind of flattering, in a way, to talk about people doing that, but, I mean, Bloomsday is observed in Ireland, and it's a tourist thing if you want, but it depends on with what reverence you look at the same objects that Joyce looked at. I mean, I went to the tower and I felt the presence of *Ulysses* the book every time I turned. I felt, well, I'm *in Ulysses*. And that's fine. I've been to Spain and looked out on some hills, you know, going outside Madrid and going south, or whatever, and said if it were not for *Don Quixote* these things would just be windmills or they would just be the landscape. But if you have a dramatic echo of something that is associated with that landscape, then some things are being formed in the landscape.

What's your main point? Do you think there is something dangerous in that?

GH: I believe there is a potential danger if we can't pinpoint the distinction between an artistic relationship to landscape and a touristic one.

DW: I think you can't separate the idea of poverty from the whole experience. In other words, people can afford to go to Spain and can afford to go and look at cathedrals or go to bullfights, from America or from wherever they come from. That's part of the luxury of location. People who come to tour the Caribbean are going to tour a lot of poverty, and that's going to be visually and practically there. What is corrupt is if you exploit the picturesqueness of the poverty, and if you say, "Well, the poorer scenes are better than the expensive-looking scenes." Anse La Raye, as you know, is a very poor village, and is a very photogenic village. And therefore, what's photogenic is to have a very poor, young, black kid in front of some terrific-looking shacks in great sunlight. Now that's the kind of whoring that you are talking about.

This is a very profound question in a way because I know, for instance, that when they were building Jalousie, they made sure that the road did not go through any place that had a lot of poverty because they didn't want to upset the tourists. There's that. The obvious thing to do is not to avoid the poverty that is there but to do something about it, right? Even if it doesn't look as picturesque to do some concrete houses or houses in the places you are trying to avoid, that would be better than saying that I am saving the tourists from being exposed to the horror of poverty. But it is also true of the politicians and the people who have the money and may be able to do something about it who retain that attitude of a kind of happy poverty that may be presented to the Caribbean. That is horrendous. But what is the other reality? The other reality is that these places *are* picturesque, that they do look a particular way. I think that it is what illuminates them; when an artist illuminates them, then it becomes a different thing. Because now what you're looking at is not only the reality of poverty but something beyond it that the artist finds worth illuminating.

GH: You said in *Tiepolo's Hound* that you can't paint overseas, meaning, I suppose, that the physical and intimate immediacy of the environment is very crucial to your conception of painting. How is that different from your conception of poetry? Is less immediacy necessary to create poetry?

DW: When I say things like that I try to mean them from the very depth of what they could really mean, and even if I paint or draw or do something while I am away somewhere, it's not really where my work really belongs. In other words, if I were doing a landscape in France or Italy, and I did my best to do it, it would not be the same to me as a landscape that hadn't already been painted. The whole excitement of painting in the Caribbean is the newness of painting in the Caribbean, not the idea of going to Provence and trying to paint like Cézanne, which is like going to Italy and the next thing you find yourself doing is something really Italian-looking—the Tuscan landscape or something.

I was amazed when I went to Monterey. I was so startled by the beauty of the landscape, seascape, and everything there that I thought that nothing had ever really been written that had done justice to that, that I know of. I mean, Robinson Jeffers is kind of a morose for whom everything is going to pot, and everything is doomed, which is very stoic Greek stuff, which is not the feel of the landscape to me. That is his hang-out, that is his anguish, if he wants to call it that. But the exultation of the landscape is not there, and no one has done justice to it. Not in poetry and not in painting. So this is strange, because what I saw was more beautiful than what I had seen in Europe. It's incredible. It's staggering. I mean, I'd go down to the car and I was shaken. Okay, what does that mean? This landscape is waiting to be described, waiting to be heard, waiting to be painted. I think someday somebody is going to write about it or paint it. In some way there is going to be memory of it. And, would I paint it? I don't know if I would, because it is not mine, in a way; as beautiful as it is, it is not mine, and what I would have achieved would have been a translation of what I felt, in a way. Now that may be nonsense. I am talking really radically about feeling, in terms of relating to a landscape.

I think the same is true of poetry. If you took poets out of their locale, if you uprooted them, it would be pointless; then you would be deracinating them from something very profound in their spirit. If you took Hardy out of his countryside and Faulkner out of his, then you would have a different person. So the growth that happens in terms of a poet and a place (not quite the same as a painter and a place, but it's close)—it's not likely that you would have as severe a detachment if one was a painter only. Or that even as a poet you might feel that if I lived somewhere else I don't have to remember the landscape or even the streets I walked in when I was younger. Ultimately, as with everything that is provincial, the area that is around an artist is really a very small area; although he can have a huge vision, a world vision of things, the ultimate experience remains very strict and very provincial.

Note

1. Hilton built the Jalousie Hilton Resort and Spa in the early 1990s between St. Lucia's Piton peaks, the island's most recognizable natural attraction. The property was previously privately owned, sold to the government, and then, after some debate, sold to Hilton. Today only patrons of the resort are allowed behind the peaks, where some of the island's most attractive hiking areas and vistas can be enjoyed.

PART 3

Hybridity and Creolization

Cultural and Environmental Assimilation in Martinique

An Interview with Raphaël Confiant

Renée K. Gosson

AN ASSISTANT PROFESSOR of regional language and culture in the Department of Applied Multi-Disciplinary Studies at the Université des Antilles et de la Guyane in Martinique, Raphaël Confiant is one of the most recognized French West Indian writers. He is cofounder of the most recent identity theory to emerge from the French-speaking Caribbean, Créolité. In addition to teaching and writing (in French and in Creole), Professor Confiant is a member of several ecological associations on the island of Martinique. An ardent defender of Creole culture and the environment, he voices his opposition to the threat of French assimilation in both his writing and his action.

This interview took place at the Université des Antilles-Guyane in Schoelcher, Martinique, on 15 March 2001. At the time, Eric Faden, my film studies colleague at Bucknell University, and I were collaborating on a film that investigates France's continued colonial and cultural presence on the island. Parts of this interview were integrated into the narration of this film, *Landscape and Memory: Martinican Land-People-History.* For this volume, I have translated the interview into English.

RG: The project we're working on at the moment involves examining the dangers caused by industrialization and overdevelopment, not only to the Martinican environment but also to a Martinican collective cultural past. First, I'd like to ask you in what way one could consider the Martinican landscape as a space of memory?

RC: Well, first I have to say that, for me, industrialization is not a danger for Martinique, because Martinique used to be an industrialized country. When I was a kid, I saw factories everywhere. At the entrance to each town, there was a factory. Today, it's a ruin. There were distilleries. There were trains that transported the sugarcane. There was an entire industrial activity. And when the sugarcane industry was ruined at the end of the 1960s, Martinique became de-industrialized. You see, sugarcane is an industry because you can't transform it without a factory. To make sugar or rum, you have to have factories. On the other hand, the banana, which replaced sugarcane, is just a fruit. You don't need to transform it. You cut it, put it in a box, and send it to Europe. So, in reality, we've gone from being an industrialized country to being a de-industrialized country, which is a garden that produces a fruit called a banana. For me, paradoxically, our *lieux de mémoire* are the ruins of our factories. All these abandoned distilleries and factories that are everywhere in Martinique, plus the train rails that you see in the countryside preserve the memory of industrial activity. They prove that during three centuries, our country was productive, even if there was slavery and all that. We were a country that produced something—a country albeit dependent on the exterior for its food because all the land was being used for sugarcane and so we had to import all the food, but it was a productive country. After the fall of the sugar industry, the banana was not capable of replacing sugarcane, and this is why Édouard Glissant says that we went from being a society with an economy to an "Économie-Prétexte." This means that we would have businesses, but in reality they only existed because the French state gives money so that they can subsist. If they'd been based on a real economy, they would have collapsed. This is why Glissant calls this an "Économie-Prétexte": A pretense to give the appearance of an economy, that there are people who go to work, etc., but in reality, our country has been, and is, economically ruined.

As for overdevelopment, *bétonisation* [cementing over the landscape] comes from the disappearance of an economic system because why work the land when you can put up a gas station, a hotel, or a supermarket that will bring in much more? Even the people who own banana plantations would rather sell their land or transform it into something else, but they're prevented from doing so by law. These are agricultural lands, and you can't touch them because there's a classification of lands in "France." There's agricultural land, forests, and then designated construction land. Recently, there's been an increase in the declassification of agricultural lands, which are transformed into construction sites. Over a period of thirty years, all the big plantations were transformed into supermarkets, gas stations, hotels, etc. And this is a serious danger because it threatens our economic survival and, what's more, our very food autonomy is endangered. This means that if there were a world war, or if Martinique were blockaded for any reason, our supplies would last about a week, whereas in Europe, it's three months. When the Arabs shut off the petroleum supply in 1973, the Europeans had enough stock for three months. But us, on the other hand, when there was the revolution of 1968 in France and no products were arriving—because there were no boats or planes coming in—there was panic. More recently, during the Gulf War, people thought that the war would last a long time. They descended upon the supermarkets and they bought all the supplies and, at one moment, there weren't any matches because people bought ten to twenty boxes. So some people couldn't buy any, and they had to return to the ancient system of charcoal burning and having a fire that is constantly lit. This is serious: a country that has one week of food self-sufficiency. That means that at the end of one week, the supermarkets are empty because 98 percent of the products on our supermarket shelves come from Europe and not even from the Caribbean or the U.S. At least we could face a world war if we could receive products from the Caribbean, South America, or the States. But no. Ninety-eight percent of the products are from Europe and only 2 percent from Martinique.

People are not aware of this, or they prefer not to be conscious of it. They prefer to live in a sort of dream. They don't realize that their country is being cemented over, that their food survival is threatened, and that there are too many cars on this island. There are more cars per person in Martinique than in France, proportionally speaking. Each family here has at least three or four cars because there's no public transportation or none that works. So even very poor people have cars, whereas when you go to other countries comparable to Martinique, when you're poor, you don't have a car. In Venezuela, which is a large country where there's petroleum, poor people don't have cars. But in Martinique, all the poor have cars because they must—otherwise they couldn't go anywhere. But look around. Have you seen the traffic in Martinique? And all that carbon dioxide? Fortunately, we're small so the wind takes it elsewhere [*laughs*]! And to think that Martinique's largest economic product isn't the banana. It isn't rum or pineapple either. It's its own trash. We produce 250,000 tons of garbage per year.

RG: What's done with it?

RC: Oh, we're in the process of constructing a factory to burn it, but it's a dangerous process. I'm a member of an ecological association, and we fought against this factory because it releases dioxin. Even today the exhaust is released into the open air near Fort-de-France, and of course it smells with the rain, and it pollutes the entire bay of Fort-de-France. This is why they wanted to construct a factory to burn the trash. But the procedure they've chosen is not an ecological one because an ecological process would have been biomass. But they preferred a factory that transforms the trash more rapidly, but which produces dioxin. How sad that the largest product of this country is its trash. This is serious.

RG: Could you say a bit more about this ecological association? Is it ASSAUPAMAR [Association pour la Sauvegarde du Patrimoine Martiniquais]?

RC: Yes, that's right, but now I'm in another association called "Urban Ecology" that focuses more exclusively on Fort-de-France, Lamentin, and other cities. ASSAUPAMAR is concerned with the entire island and especially with agriculture. Since I live in Fort-de-France now, I got involved with Urban Ecology, and we're working on public transportation and on the pollution of the bay of Fort-de-France. You see, people don't know what pollution is. They see the clear blue water, for example near the Fort Saint Louis. There are a lot of people who go swimming there, but it should be forbidden because there are metals, lead, in the water, all kinds of products that you can't see with the naked eye. There are no fish in the bay. They're all dead. The bay is dead or dying. Political figures talk about it all the time, but nobody does anything.

RG: Speaking of politics, I've noticed a lot of slogans during this election period that refer at the same time to the safeguard of Martinican landscape and patrimony. Would you say that there is a link between independence and ecology?

RC: I make a distinction between *indépendantistes* and *nationalistes*. You can be *indépendantiste* without being *nationaliste*. Nationalists are those who think that their country is the best and who want to live closed off from outsiders, whereas there are *indépendantistes* who are *internationalistes,* like me. I am a Caribbean internationalist, which means that I am for a federation of the Caribbean islands. I don't want there to be a Martinican government, like in Saint Lucia, for example. That's ridiculous. There should be one government for an entire Federation of the West Indies, for example. Being an ecologist precludes being nationalist because when there's an ecological problem, it doesn't respect boundaries. When the factory in Chernobyl released its toxic cloud, it didn't stay in Russia. It crossed the Ukraine and Poland and went to France. So even if you're nationalist, you can't be nationalist because ecological problems are not national problems. They are international problems, like global warming. So you could even go as far as to say that there's a contradiction between nationalism and ecology, which is why I say that I am *indépendantiste*. I want Martinique to govern itself and to unite with other countries around, but I am not a closed-minded nationalist. For me, independence is not nationalism. This doesn't mean that I don't love my country. I love my language. I defend Creole and I've even written books in Creole. But I don't think that Creole is better than English or that Spanish is better than French. It doesn't bother me that foreigners come here. There are a lot of immigrants, from Haiti and elsewhere. That doesn't cause any problem for me. But it's true that there are nationalists in this country that are not ecologists. On the contrary, these are people who only want one thing: That Martinique becomes independent so that they can put a little dictatorship at the head of the country that will then sell all the beaches to hotels for a little money that will permit them to live like the bourgeoisie. Too bad for the people! This is why I'm suspicious of these nationalists. In general, they are not ecologists. Ecology doesn't interest them. [Alfred] Marie-Jeanne, the president of the Regional Council, which is the strongest nationalist movement, speaks of course about ecology, but they don't do much. Ecology doesn't interest them that much. What they want is power, and I'm sure that when they have it, they will say that for economic reasons, they're obligated to put up hotels everywhere like in Barbados or Hawaii. *Indépendantistes* don't share the same nationalist perspective because an ecologist can't be nationalist. It's not possible. Because when an oil tanker releases a black oil slick, it doesn't stay in one country. The only way to resolve ecological problems is internationally, not nationally, even when you live on an island. Because even the American oil tankers empty their tanks, when they're almost empty and there's just a little left, they release that in the Caribbean Sea—far from Louisiana or Florida. But can a little country like Martinique confront the United States? No, because the U.S. says that it is in international waters and that it's not releasing the oil anywhere near Martinique. But the currents bring the oil to our shores. When you go swimming off the so-called beautiful beaches of Martinique, take a good look at the white sand. You'll see bits of black tar. They were released by oil tankers, most often American. The Caribbean has to unite in order to say to the U.S.: "Stop! The Caribbean is not a trash can. If you're going to empty your tanks, go do that near Louisiana or Florida, not in the south part of the Caribbean."

RG: In addition, an island represents an especially vulnerable space because it's small, with limited resources.

RC: Yes, but people here don't see that their resources are limited because they're living a dream. Because France gives a lot of money, people don't think of limited resources because there's no misery like in Haiti or Santo Domingo. Martinique's standard of living is almost as high as that of Puerto Rico. The workers are immigrants. The sugarcane and bananas are cut by Haitians, Saint-Luciens, Dominicans—not Martinicans. All the banana fields that you see—those aren't Martinicans working there. Sugarcane? Not Martinicans, ever. And what's more, the prostitutes that you see in Fort-de-France at night come from Santo Domingo or Haiti. So, thanks to France, Martinicans have a certain quality of life so they don't give a thought to limited resources. Not their problem. Just to give you an example, when there's a cyclone—and there are usually a lot of them in September—on an independent island, the next day, everyone spontaneously goes out to lift trees that are blocking roads, to repair electric wires, to clean up, etc. But not in Martinique. We wait for the French army to take care of everything. One day, there was a very violent cyclone here that destroyed houses, and the next day I went out to see if I could do something, you know, help out in some way. And not far from here there are tennis courts. It was around seven or eight in the morning, and I saw people playing tennis. I said: "These damn tourists. They don't care that the island is totally destroyed. They're playing tennis." And as I got closer to them, I realized that these were Martinicans playing tennis, the day after a cyclone, because for them, they are French, and the French army was on its way and so there was no need for them to lift a finger. That's the mentality occasioned by assimilation.

In 1946, Martinicans were people who took responsibility for things. At that time, we weren't a department yet, and so we didn't receive any help from France. Martinique was a colony, and colonies serve to nourish the *métropole*. Then, people produced something, and their products went to France. But as of 1946, when we became an overseas department of France, people decided: "This is great. We want the same rights as the French. We want the same salaries. We want it all: roads, highways, supermarkets" . . . and France gives it all because it absolutely wants to keep its territories in the Americas, even if it's expensive, but at least it can say "I have territories in the Americas." And the only European country that still has territory in the Americas is France. Spain, Portugal, and England have left. France is the only one left. But it's because France sees itself as a large power, a big country, which is in the four corners of the world, in the Americas, Europe, Africa, the Indian Ocean, Tahiti. France is everywhere, so they maintain General de Gaulle's dream of grandeur, even if it costs them a fortune.

In reality, our country is completely turned toward Europe. If you ask a Martinican, "Who is the president of Venezuela?" he wouldn't know. "Where's Costa Rica or Guatemala?" No idea. "Who's Colin Powell?"

Who knows who he is? Martinicans only know Clinton because of Monica, because everyone's talking about the Monica Affair down here. It makes everyone laugh. I'm not speaking about the intellectuals, of course, but of the everyday people, the majority of the population. They know nothing of the U.S. They think that it's a place where blacks are placed in ghettos and beaten every day.

You can't believe everything that the French tell you. We're really "brainwashed" by the French. They tell us: "If you become independent, you're going to end up like Haiti. You'll die of hunger. You'll have boat people like Cuba. The Americans are going to take over." So how can you expect these people to say that they want independence when the television belongs to France? *France-Antilles,* the local newspaper, is a French newspaper, which is why it's called *France-Antilles.* The schools, university, programs, books are all in French. The exams are the same exams that they have in France. How can these people not be completely brainwashed? Of course, some intellectuals have criticized this, but it's hard, very hard. We're in a sort of European ghetto here. The people we see on TV are Tony Blair, Putin, etc. We don't know anything of the U.S. We don't know what's going on in Canada. In fact, I can't even remember the name of the prime minister. That's how cut off we are. People don't even know that Quebec wants to become independent.

RG: But I thought that there was an effort to put more Creole programs on TV and the radio and in the classrooms—that in the high schools, for example, students were beginning to read literature from their own country?

RC: Sure, but that's just 2 percent of the school population. Here, at the Université des Antilles-Guyane at Schoelcher, for example, we have a B.A. and a master's in Creole, but only 30 students out of 12,000 on campus study it. Don't be deluded. Of course there's a Creole news program that lasts thirty minutes, but the TV functions nonstop, and for the rest of the day and night, it's French—French programs or American movies translated into French. So, of course, in comparison with where things were twenty years ago, there's been a small amount of progress, but I call that "cosmetic progress." It's just a façade. The French government gives us just enough to keep us quiet: "You want a little Creole, we'll give you a little Creole." But, fundamentally, the French will never leave Martinique, except in the event of a colonial war because, historically, France has never left a colonial territory of its own will. England left its West Indian territories, with ten years of warning and preparation for autonomy and self-government. But unless you're willing to fight, and even then! Look at New Caledonia, next to New Zealand. France went to war in order to remain there! France never leaves a country where it is, even if it's expensive, because we're talking about French pride, the French flag. Whatever the cost, it stays.

RG: Given this permanent presence, what can one do to preserve Creole culture?

RC: Creole culture does not have a lot of future. I'm obliged to say it because for my own children, Creole has become their second language and French their first. Why? Because my kids are in front of the TV all the time, and the TV speaks constant French. Their models are French, or American. My kids say that at least they are black Americans. But I disagree. In the 1970s, there was John Wayne, Marilyn Monroe, Elvis Presley, and today it's Michael Jordan, Whitney Houston, but it's all the same. It's the same culture.

Our culture has no place on TV. There are Caribbean films, but they're on the TV once per year. There's Caribbean theater. They could film that and put that on TV from time to time. Now, a Caribbean child in front of the TV will only see French programs or American ones that have been translated. How can this child preserve his Creole culture? Of course I read Creole folktales to my sons when they were little, and I spoke to them in Creole, but it was ridiculous because they'd tell me: "Your stories bore us. We'd rather watch *Pocahontas* on TV or Japanese cartoons. It's better." So Creole culture has no means of expression. So much so that it is receding. The force of French assimilation is very strong. To give another example, when I was my students' age, around eighteen, I didn't know a word of French slang because in those days, there was no TV. TV arrived when I was fifteen or sixteen, but we didn't watch it that often. But the young students today grow up on French TV, from the day they're born. They know French slang as if they were living in Paris. I hear them and I am stupefied. These are people who have never gone to France, but who listen to rap—which is not our music at all—and appropriate that language.

We don't have the means to fight against French TV. It's ridiculous. We can't. It's too powerful. The French state is too powerful. I'm pessimistic. I doubt that Creole language will survive, and Creole culture may last a bit longer, but it won't survive either. No. The only identity that we'll have in fifty years will be a racial identity, like the African Americans. It's unfortunate, pessimistic, perhaps, but history has shown me that I'm right.

We're becoming a people for whom identity is not cultural but racial because there isn't any cultural difference any more. People of my generation didn't have to defend a racial identity because we have a cultural one: our Creole language and heritage. So I don't care about race. But when you have a people without a cultural identity, the only thing left to hold onto is race.

I refuse to go from a cultural identity to a racial one. When one has a racial identity, this means that that's all you have left. What does one defend? Color? But that makes no sense. It's culture that you have to defend. I don't care about color. That has no meaning for me. But, unfortunately, because we are losing our culture, people find refuge in racial identity and are becoming like the African Americans. We don't live on the same territory, but that's exactly what's happening in the States. We'll have sports champions, which we already have, "Marie-Jo Perecs" and entertainers. I think that there are two really bad things for the black community in the U.S.: to invest exclusively in sports and music. When I buy a magazine like *Ebony*, which I read from time to time so as not to lose my English, what do I see on the cover? Always a singer or a basketball player. Do they ever put a scientist? A philosopher? A writer? Never. Well, the black Caribbeans are doing the same thing. They're following the same process. My son says that if he becomes a professor, he'll look ridiculous, whereas if he becomes a professional basketball player, he'll earn ten times more. He's right. But I tell him that it's not for sure that he'll become a great basketball player or a great musician. So there's the problem of money as well.

People don't want to pursue long degrees anymore, like doctorates. We don't have a lot of doctorates here. At one point, we had a very strong intellectual elite. The majority of our professors were West Indian, with 10 percent or 20 percent French. Today, 50 percent are French because there are no young West Indians with doctorates who teach at the university. They are practicing sports or fashion or music. They sing or are disc jockeys. I find this to be a lamentable evolution but against which I cannot fight because France is too powerful. It's the fourth-largest world power, after all. It has a lot of money, and we're very small. France asks us: "What do you want? You want cars, highways, supermarkets? You even have Saint-Luciens and Haitians to cut the sugarcane for you. What else do you want? Independence? But the U.S. will come colonize you, so stay with us."

Sometimes I get discouraged, and I say: "Oh well. Forget it! I'm going to be just like everybody else and just not care. I'll buy a big car and go to the beach on Sunday and forget it." I often have this feeling because it's ridiculous to fight against such a powerful enemy. Maybe I'm pessimistic, but when you see the disproportion of power. If we had our own TV, we could show our films, our plays, etc. But even to make our own films, it's very hard because there's a French organization that gives money to make French films, but these have to be French films because of the famous quota system in France. They don't want there to be too many films in English, for example. Well, our films are considered foreign films because they're in Creole, and so they won't give any money. To make a West Indian film, you have to do so in French.

RG: It's true, there are not a lot of French-Caribbean films out there.

RC: But there are other Caribbean films. Each week, they could have put one on. Cuba, for example, has a lot of films. But when do they show a Cuban film? Maybe once per year. Same thing for a Haitian film or a film from Venezuela. And it's not expensive. It's more expensive to buy *Pocahontas* than a film from Venezuela, because in Venezuela it costs nothing. In Brazil, telenovelas don't cost anything near what an American film costs. Okay, they have made *some* progress. I saw that they did buy some telenovelas. And since Brazil looks a little like Martinican society, they saw that people like it, so they put more telenovelas on than American sitcoms. They tried to put on black American shows but it didn't have any success. On the other hand, when they put on Brazilian shows where there are whites, people liked those because they see that even if they are physically different from the whites, culturally these are not whites, you see? And this is great because it challenges the racial perception. Whereas the *Cosby Show* is perceived by us as white, a Brazilian film with whites is perceived as Caribbean. What interests us is not race-based solidarity, but cultural solidarity.

And that's what Créolité is: the promotion of ideas that go beyond ethnic identity, firm nationalism, and the diabolicization of other peoples. And this is the most difficult path. It's so easy to close oneself off in one's culture, race, or religion and to say that the others are no good. The path we've chosen is the most difficult one. It takes a lot of intellectual courage to defend what I've just described to you in the United States and in an amphitheatre of two hundred black American students because it can provoke some violent reactions. For us, cultural identity is predominant.

I don't have a dichotomous vision of our reality. I believe that slavery is part of our history. Colonization is part of our history, and we can't deny that. We are the product of slavery and of the mixture of whites and blacks. First of all, for us, race isn't important. And second, we refuse to choose among our ancestors. Maybe the blacks are in the majority, but we also have Amerindian ancestors, white ancestors, Hindu ancestors. We have a Creole identity, an identity which allows us to reconcile all our ancestors.

This is why we say that Créolité is something that started three centuries ago in the Caribbean and that is spreading in the entire world. For a Caribbean person, multiple identity does not pose any problem on a religious front. Whether one believes in Jesus Christ or practices Hindu or black witchcraft, for example. If he has cancer or another illness, he can pray to Jesus Christ at the church, go to a Hindu ceremony, or go see the African witch doctor and not see any contradiction with having three religions. This is not a problem for him, even though usually if you're Christian, you can't be Muslim, and if you're Muslim, you can't be a Buddhist . . . Why not?

For us, Créolité is the acceptance of a multiple identity, the recognition of this multiplicity and openness. Not striving for cultural purity and not remaining closed upon oneself.

I'm sure that the racial principle will change. I'm sure because you can't always categorize people. When you have a Korean-American child or a child of a Native American and an Indian, how are you going to categorize him? And the U.S. accepts more immigrants than any other country in the world. These immigrants settle and marry but not always within their community, which makes for an interracial community. And in fifty years, things will absolutely go toward a multiple identity.

That's Créolité. It's a little utopist, of course, but intellectuals are there to produce utopia, right?

Moving the Caribbean Landscape

Cereus Blooms at Night as a Re-imagination of the Caribbean Environment

Isabel Hoving

With its yard-long, bean-like purple pods, the mudra had taken over the side of the yard, completely blocking out the road beyond and glimpses of the town. It took generations for a mudra tree to grow so large. The peekoplats hopped to the edges of the branches and their whistling subsided as though in curious and worried anticipation . . . He suddenly felt himself a trespasser, an awkward voyeur . . . It was as though he had stumbled unexpectedly on a lost jungle, and except for the odours he would have sworn he was in a paradise.

—Shani Mootoo, *Cereus Blooms at Night*

THIS AMBIGUOUS yard plays a central role in the much-praised 1996 novel *Cereus Blooms at Night,* by Caribbean-Canadian writer Shani Mootoo. At first sight, the yard recalls the image of the lost Garden of Eden, which European explorers wanted to recognize in the lush Caribbean islands they visited for the first time. At second sight, however, there is something seriously wrong with this lost jungle paradise. It surrounds a house in a relatively ordinary village called Paradise, on the imaginary Caribbean island of Lantanacamara. Despite its unexceptional setting, this garden contains exceptional plant and animal life, life that is only found in the heart of a primeval tropical rain forest. There is something very eerie about the garden, a feeling enhanced by the abhorrent smells that offend the visitor. In this ambiguous paradise, delicious odors mingle with the abhorrent stench of decay; the awed visitor is both repulsed and delighted.

This exceptional garden is presented as the counterpart to another garden in the novel, the professionally maintained institutional garden in the yard of the almshouse, where much of the action takes place. The contrast between the two gardens emphasizes the eerie wildness of the jungle garden, in which the trees, we are told, "had sprung wherever birds and insects dropped their seeds" (124). This uncultivated Caribbean yard echoes an ambiguity found in present-day Caribbean women's writing about nature. In this paper, I argue that this ambiguity is part of a productive effort by Caribbean women writers to radically redefine nature and create a new understanding of the natural. I will test an even bolder thesis: could this imagining of Caribbean nature be useful in developing a new ecological approach to the vulnerable island ecosystems, in which many of the endemic species have been destroyed? Could such a literary redefinition of nature serve as a welcome alternative to the destruction of colonialism? Mootoo's novel *Cereus* will allow me to show that it does— but in unexpected ways.

Repulsion and Delight: Evaluating Hybridity

"[T]he world seemed quieter, as though time had slowed down. The soil smelled damp and rich with earthworms . . . there was the buzzing of insects, the flutter of wings and the sounds of a breeze circulating earthy odours" (161). The preceding quote shows how a young man, a protagonist of Mootoo's novel, reacts with contradictory feelings when he enters the mysterious garden in Paradise for the first time. The garden is a smelly, tactile universe swarming with insects, reptiles, and unruly, creeping, rampant weeds. Remarkably, the most delightful sensual element in the yard—the cereus blossoms with their unearthly scent—is also the site of the yard's horror. The night-blooming cereus in itself is already an ambiguous plant: it is an invasive cactus, ugly in its bareness, and its blossoms seem to have been soaked in blood. But its smell evokes sensual bliss, and it will become the symbol of transgressive passion and indeterminacy. "A ghost of scent hovered close to the blossoms, remnants of last night's fullness now souring in the heat. Replacing the perfume was an even more startling one that seemed to emanate from the wall behind the blossoms. The smell . . . quickly grew nauseating" (165–66).

The story behind this repulsive smell is revealed when the reader learns about the cruel history of the dysfunctional family who once lived within these walls. As a boy, the father (Chandin Ramchandin) was adopted by the British Reverend Thoroughly and his family, becoming a successful mimic man until his foster father refused to let him marry his daughter. Stating that the boy's love was in fact the incestuous love for a sister, the Reverend prevented their interracial love affair. The frustrated Chandin marries the daughter's (East) Indian girlfriend instead. This undesired wife, however, later leaves her husband to elope with the white daughter, whose lover she had become. Chandin begins to sexually abuse his daughter Mala, until, after many years, he dies during a violent quarrel with her. The daughter conceals his decaying body in the basement, shuts herself off from village life, and passes most of her years in the yard that grows around the father's corpse. The yard's intoxicating scents now intermingle with the stench of the father's corpse, which is in a state of incessant decay.

This excessive garden is not just a literary medium for conveying the traumatized condition of its heroes. Images of gardens are closely linked to a wealth of cultural narratives, ranging from the Garden of Eden, sought by European seafarers in the American tropics, to the secluded garden, a site of intimacy and eroticism. As Sarah Casteel has shown, the garden can be used to articulate a critique of the New World pastoral. Gardens have also been used to evoke an alternative, often feminist experience of nature, as I will now explore.

As the quote that opens this section suggests, Mootoo's yard exists outside of normative linear time; it is a place of decay and decomposition as much as of regeneration (123). Witness Mala's manipulation of time: "Every few days, a smell of decay permeated the house. It was the smell of time itself passing but lest she was overcome by it, Mala brewed an odour of her own design . . . The aroma obliterated, reclaimed and gave the impression of reversing decay . . . The odour hung, rejuvenating the air for days" (123). In resistance to decay, linear time is stopped. By reversing the decay before it reinstalls itself again, the natural cycle of endings and beginnings is interrupted and deferred.[1] In this strange timelessness, processes of growth and rotting are extended infinitely. This explains why a body may rot for decades here without turning into a dry skeleton, and why the yard can harbor a mudra of such a size. Since the yard is thus turned into a space where nature takes on the form of a timeless primeval forest that exceeds the normal social order, one could indeed interpret it as the ideological, utopian image of an asocial feminine Nature. This image could then be understood as a woman's safe space, outside of the violent patriarchal sphere.[2] An argument in favor of this interpretation might be found in Mala's retreat from verbal and literary signifiers, until she "all but rid herself of words. The wings of a gull flapping through the air titillated her soul and awakened her toes and knobby knees, the palms of her withered hands, deep inside her womb, her vagina, lungs, stomach and heart . . . every fibre was sensitized in a way that words were unable to match or enhance" (136).

At the very moment that the Law breaks into this wordless universe, the most traumatized part of Mala (personified in the thin girl she once was) tears itself away and literally flies away. But to interpret this vision of nature as the desire for a woman's safe space misses the point. First, this space represents more of a pathological retreat from traumatic reality. Second, the novel is not structured around the binary opposition between pure, exalted nature versus soiled, perverted culture, and it does not oppose the yard's paradisiacal nature to the horrors of the house. As I have shown, the yard itself is a place where life and death intermingle; where the abundant insect life, smells of rot and decay, and traces of dead animals combine to unsettle the squeamish visitor. The house itself is as full of spiders and insects as the yard, and the swarms of moths that are attracted by the cereus blossoms in the yard also cloak the incestuous father's body. Remarkably, the crawling insects have even found their way into the pages of the novel itself. The many sketches of insects in the novel seem as indispensable to understanding the narrative as the words themselves, and in this way the binary between the natural world and the cultural one is again subverted. Readers are warned that words alone cannot tell this story since it exceeds the boundaries of the cultural.

The narrative structure of the novel will not offer its readers a comforting retreat from ambiguities. For example, the primary narrator, a male nurse who cares for the aged Mala Ramchandin, introduces himself as Tyler, "neither properly man nor woman but some in-between, unnamed thing" (76). His endeavors to narrate Mala's story are disturbed by his desire to tell his own story, and as we learn about Mala's trauma, we also learn about Tyler's cross-dressing, recognized and encouraged by the old lady Ramchandin herself. Thus, the story is not just refusing a strict separation between nature/culture, but it is also narrated from the perspective of a border-crosser par excellence.

A second reason why the novel cannot be said to celebrate a utopian feminine natural space, as opposed to a patriarchal, perhaps colonial space,[3] is that it does not associate nature with femininity in any traditional way. The conflation of woman and nature has a long history; ecologists such as Carolyn Merchant have critiqued the gendered binary between woman/nature and man/culture. By redefining people as "relational and ecological selves" (Warren 2), ecological feminism has attempted to overcome the notion that human beings (and especially men) somehow stand outside of nature. Merchant has emphasized reciprocity when she pleads for a partnership ethic in the interaction between humans and the nonhuman (*Earthcare* 56), an approach echoed in Mootoo's work. Jim Cheney, who formulates this reciprocal view of environmentalist ethics, helps to highlight the parallels between *Cereus* and ecofeminism: "For a genuinely contextualist ethic to include the land, the land must *speak* to us; we must stand in *relation* to it; it must *define* us, and we it" (174–75). On first sight, this is precisely what seems to happen in the Paradise yard: "Mala's companions were the garden's birds, insects, snails and reptiles. She and they and the abundant foliage gossiped among themselves. She listened intently . . . She did not intervene in nature's business" (137).

If this passage seems to express Merchant's and Cheney's ethics of reciprocity, Mala's decision not to intervene in the natural process suggests that the text is not really about a productive harmony between a woman and her nonhuman surroundings; the novel puts too much emphasis on the yard's excessiveness. Far from being a representation of a utopian reciprocal relation between woman and nature, Mootoo's novel is an example of a more general distrust among women writers of utopian perceptions of Caribbean landscape.[4] Nevertheless, Mootoo's work is different because of the excessiveness of its representation.

I see the excessiveness of this yard—in which both nature *and* the character Mala are represented as wholly other to the patriarchal, colonial social and symbolic order of the Caribbean island of Lantanacamara— as an expression of the unspeakable excess of the border-crossing that victimized Mala. The strongest element in the representation of the yard in this novel seems to be the *intensity* of its evocation of ambiguity. I want to argue that, because of this intensity, the image of the yard not only is different from feminist utopias but is also more than an assessment of the creolized nature of the Caribbean landscape or a critique of pastoral nostalgia, even as it signifies both. If the yard is evoked as highly repulsive, seductive, unspeakable, and at the same time as the inescapable truth at the heart of a shared Caribbean reality, it is because it signifies the unspeakability of the Caribbean condition. This great anxiety is of course a response to a personal trauma, as Vera Kutzinski explains in detail, but it can also be understood as a response to the general Caribbean condition of ambiguity and hybridity, which forms the context of the individual trauma. To understand this anxiety, it is necessary to examine the ongoing debates about what can and cannot be considered natural. As Nancy Stepan and others have shown, these debates have already played a vital role in colonialism, particularly in the tropical environments of the Americas.

Hybridity and the Order of Nature

"Over the years I pondered the gender and sex roles that seemed available to people, and the rules that went with them . . . I was preoccupied with trying to understand what was natural and what perverse, and who said so and why. Chandin Ramchandin played a part in confusing me about these roles, for it was a long time before I could differentiate between his perversion and what others called mine" (51). As this quote from *Cereus*'s narrator suggests, definitions of what can be termed natural have a special urgency when it comes to issues of sexuality and race. The sexual and the racial are intimately intertwined: Chandin is constructed as racially other in terms of the Reverend's refusal of marriage to his white daughter at the same time that sexual desires are labeled incestuous.

Cereus can be read as a radical intervention in these debates about the natural, especially those that uphold the essential purity and stability of a nature that opposes hybridity. As Nancy Stepan and Robert Young have explained, the ideologeme of racial purity has been central to Western debates on hybridity and race, making a tremendous impact on ideas (and legislature) about the social and cultural position of people of African, Asian, indigenous, or "mixed" descent. Young argues that colonial discourse constituted intertwining debates about race and sexuality. Nineteenth-century racial theories were derived from an emergent taxonomy of normative sexuality and naturalized desire. As Young explains, racial taxonomies arose out of a new science of colonial plant propagation and animal breeding. By 1840, European scholars began to defend the view that there were different human species and that the hybrid offspring of parents of different species would prove to be infertile; "a degradation of humanity [that] was rejected by nature" (R. Young 15). In this example, nature is constructed as pure and inimical to hybridization; sexual relations between people of different "races" were defined as contrary to nature's order.

When Chandin's white foster father exclaims: "You cannot, you must not have desire for your sister Lavinia. That is surely against God's will" (40), we can recognize this as a symptom of the anxiety with which Europeans often reacted to hybridization. Like many of his British compatriots, the Reverend rationalizes his anxiety in terms of a "natural" abhorrence of the unnatural, coded as a divine, God-willed order. Seen in the larger historical context, claims to the superiority of undiluted European culture justified colonialism and the slave trade, much as they constituted the Reverend's self-congratulatory missionary project in the Caribbean; "racial" intermingling would mean a serious threat to this claim. The European obsession with Caribbean hybridity and degeneration can also be understood as a displacement of its fears of its own degradation and decline as a result of hybridization; a process observed in other empires as Europe extended its colonial reach (Edmond 42–43). These intense political and cultural fears were partly displaced through an obsession with health, sexuality, and ideologies of the natural. Thus the naturalization of "Nature" results in assumptions of purity, stability, boundedness, femininity—the opposites to hybridization.

Yet within environmental theories about "Nature," hybridization and instability appear as essential processes. Recent scholarship has shown that ecosystems are dynamic, unstable, and open systems, in which new species are incessantly settling, intermingling, and crossing with earlier species (see, for example, Botkin). This approach has a counterpart in theories of culture. Caribbeanists have examined the age-old processes of creolization through which the plurality and diversity of the dynamic, open space of the region has been formed.[5] Decades after Edward Brathwaite's and Édouard Glissant's influential works, it is almost commonplace to consider Caribbean cultural identities as creolized. Nevertheless, David Watt's observation in the 1980s that creolization did not serve as a sound foundation for "a regional cultural identity common to all inhabitants" (xviii) still applies at the beginning of the twenty-first century. For some it is a challenge to embrace and celebrate a creolized identity, either as an individual, or as a nation or region; and it is certainly hard to take pride in the hybrid character of the landscape. The colonial denigration of interracial marriage and hybridization maintains its influence.

Instead of arguing that an uneasy reaction to hybridization and creolization is misplaced, *Cereus* takes a closer look at the challenges to embracing hybridity. Similar to other gothic novels, which evoke a European anxiety about the degradation of its culture, the text *deepens* the association between sexual and racial border-crossing and hybridity on the one hand, and madness and decay on the other. Simultaneously, the novel plays on the association between border-crossing and ambiguous beauty.

Responding to nineteenth-century racial theorists who held that degraded hybrids could be very beautiful but that their beauty was treacherous and unnatural, *Cereus* takes these two aspects as its narrative foundation. Through the image of the yard, the text explores precisely those sensations —repulsion and delight—instead of merely criticizing anxieties about racial and sexual border-crossing. Rather than celebrating nonviolent forms of border-crossing (such as the interracial love affair between two women), readers are invited to reflect on the nature of border-crossing itself.

To convey the ambiguity of this border-crossing, Mootoo's novel addresses sexuality head-on, because it lies at the heart of debates about Caribbean nationalism, nature, and hybridization. National discourses on the preferred forms of sexual relationships and family life are strongly prescriptive, taking recourse to traditional notions of the natural. But how does acknowledging the dynamism and creolization of all natural

environments and the history of enforced hybridization change our understanding of border-crossing? Mootoo's novel raises questions about which
forms of racial and sexual border-crossing will be acceptable and productive, and which forms will be seen as perverse and degrading. In what follows, I will show that *Cereus* proposes a very specific definition of both
the natural and unnatural as an answer to these questions.

A Queer Way to Go "Back to Nature"

Ideas about natural sexuality have been shaped by a host of historical discourses, particularly natural history. Londa Schiebinger has pointed out
that in the eighteenth century, Linnaeus's (hetero)sexualization of plants,
which became the basis of his botanical taxonomy, "came to recapitulate
the sexual hierarchy of Western Europe" (4). If one turns to nature for
models of a natural sexuality, one will often find oneself peering into a
reflection of *social* ideas about sexuality. The reconstruction of nature as
a racial, sexual, and gendered hierarchy was motivated by the desire to
find an authorization of social ideas: "Nature and its laws spoke loudly in
this age of Enlightenment, where philosophers attempted to set social
convention on a natural basis . . . Scientists . . . took up the task of uncov-
ering differences imagined as natural to bodies and hence foundational to
societies based on natural law" (9). Eighteenth-century botanists "gave
undue primacy to sexual reproduction and heterosexuality" (22), down-
playing the fact that most plants are hermaphroditic, and not "male" or
"female."

Theories about nature and what is natural are integral to colonial discourse, where they are employed to build authoritative arguments about
the organization of society. A century and more after the work of the botanists mentioned above, "(b)iological theories of decline were becoming
the dominant form of social critique" (44), and worries about social and
political stability were expressed as an anxiety about the condition of the
"national body" (45). But we can also note opposite strategies: arguments
about nature can be used to create a critical argument against present-day
dominant discourses about sexuality and race.

Taking recourse to a habit that was also used by the modernists,[6]
Mootoo questions these naturalist discourses in their own terms. Instead
of referring to nature in order to picture the degradation and decline of
hybrid cultures and persons, *Cereus* can be read as a plea to acknowledge
the inevitability of sexual and racial border-crossing and the resulting
intermediateness and hybridity, however ambiguous and uncanny they
may seem. It is also a plea to differentiate between the ambiguous and the

violently perverse. To make its point, the novel focuses on a specific flower, that part of the plant favored by eighteenth-century botanists to make *their* point about natural sexuality.[7] To create a different discourse about sexuality and hybridity, the novel takes the night-blooming cereus as its central image—an ugly cactus with beautiful flowers that only bloom during one or two midsummer nights each year, and that exude an overwhelming scent.

The cereus, like all cactus plants, is a hermaphrodite; it can boast of both a stamen and an ovary, parts usually designated as respectively male and female. In the novel, it also becomes the central token of border-crossing.[8] The first cereus clipping we hear about is brought to the aged Mala Ramchandin in the almshouse by her visitors Otoh Mohanty and his father, Ambrose. Father and son form a curious pair, and they embody the novel's most remarkable instances of border-crossing and mirroring. Ambrose is a former suitor of Mala, but he proved unable to save her from trauma and he has slept away most of his life ever since. Otoh is his remarkable son: he is a transgender boy who succeeded in letting even his parents forget that he was born a girl. But Otoh is crossing not just the border between genders but also that between generations: he takes over his father's place by bringing Mala food, sometimes even dressed like his father, in an effort to make amends for his father's betrayal. The cereus is therefore a gift from two people who cross borders between genders and generations, past and present, sleep and waking life. Earlier, the cereus was used as a gift from the woman lover of Mala's mother, who wished to delight her and her sister. The cereus clipping plays a role in a significant exchange between the almshouse gardener and Tyler, who begin to reach a mutual understanding when the gardener tells Tyler about his gay brother. The cereus both covers and points at the incestuous father's body behind the wall against which it has grown, linking the decay and delight of Mala's space (the yard) to the unspeakable horror of the father's space. Finally, the cereus is the plant that regulates the blossoming love affair between the transgender boy Otoh and the homosexual transvestite Tyler —they promise each other to hold off the consummation of their love until the cereus blooms. In this way, the cereus marks and mediates many transgressive relations, linking peoples and spaces that are not considered naturally related. Apart from its great ambiguity (as both excessively repulsive and delightful), the cereus itself is not a hybrid plant. Not a hybrid or an "alien" border-crosser itself, as it is native to the West Indies, the cereus still functions as the inspiration for the novel's many border-crossers. In Piercean semiotic terms: the cereus is not an *icon* of the hybrid, but it is an *index* of border-crossing (as it is all but touching the evidence of that transgression—the father's corpse). As an ambiguous night flower, it is a *symbol* of the hidden and the transgressive.

The fact that the cereus is indigenous to this part of the world suggests that ambiguousness is at the heart of the Caribbean. And, indeed, Mootoo's Caribbean world abounds with queer, hybrid border-crossers par excellence. The novel is a dizzying game of endlessly crossing sexual boundaries, boundaries of gender, and even the boundary between human and nonhuman life, where characters are likened to plants or animals. As a result, ambiguities and mistaken identities abound: a man (Chandin Ramchandin) "mistakes" his daughter for his wife; a mother (Chandin's wife) "mistakes" a woman from another race for her husband; the parents of the transgender boy "mistake" their daughter for a son; the son is mistaken for his father; there is the transvestite male nurse; and finally the abused daughter herself, Mala, takes on birdlike qualities, and at times even seems to become one with a tree. But this is not all. For these characters also identify with each other: Tyler, the nurse, finds in Mala Ramchandin a "shared queerness" (51), and Otoh too states: "I felt as though she and I had things in common. She had secrets and I had secrets" (133). Indeed, these three characters, recognizing in each other different forms of in-betweenness, different kinds of becoming ("becoming-animal" and "becoming-plant," "becoming-woman" and "becoming-man"),[9] are in comparable positions, though they are not equally traumatized. But the novel suggests, through Otoh's mother, that many more citizens may share that condition. She addresses Otoh: "You grow up here and you don't realize almost everybody in this place wish they could be somebody or something else? That is the story of life here in Lantanacamara" (258).

In other words, in Mootoo's Caribbean, border-crossings are inevitable. Natural and social life are represented as an interconnected web in which intimate contact constantly leads to disguises, transformations, hybridizations, and border-crossings. Since many of these borders were imposed by colonial administrations and ideologies, Mootoo's novel creates a different context for the evaluation of these sexual and other border-crossings. She represents a return to nature—but an unexpected, unconventional, queer return, which brings with it a completely different notion of the natural from colonial or nationalist views. In *Cereus,* sexuality takes on diverse forms (between people of different "races," of the same sex, between a boy-who-has-been-a-girl and a transvestite, between night-blooming cereus and the night-flying insects that pollinate it), that it becomes impossible to point out one normative sexuality. These diverse expressions of sexuality all appear to be in agreement with what happens in nature. The novel suggests that the only perverse forms of border-crossing are produced by the violence of colonial sexual and racial laws. Consequently, the refusal of hybridity, and thus a denial of exogamy, as in the Reverend's refusal to let the East Indian Chandin marry his white British daughter, leads to the ultimate form of endogamy: incest.[10] This is a cynical comment on the violent consequences of the colonial fear of border-crossing.

Cereus shows how the painful hybridity and ambiguity of nature cannot be healed, for they are the result of the history in which the Caribbean has been violently interpellated. Instead of trying to return to an organicist and harmonious sense of nature, *Cereus* works through the pain caused by colonial destruction and transformation, subtly differentiating the queer from the violence of the perverse. Its exploration ends up suggesting a productive way to cross borders: with great care, and always open to the reactions of others involved. The two hybrid heroes of the novel can become lovers only by means of an interactive and tentative transgression. And, in the midst of that process, the novel suggests that a happy end could be possible—though it is not a return to authenticity and purity. It is here that *Cereus* shows its modest, critical utopian dimension.

If I were to sum up the approach to nature most clearly articulated in Mootoo's novel, but also suggested in other women's texts (for example, Roemer, Kincaid) in ecological terms, I would argue that nature is not presented as an essence from which one could deduce norms about what is natural but as hybrid interrelatedness; an unstable, inharmonious, damaging and damaged, productive, vital interrelatedness, in which hybridity is the norm.

These last questions remain: In what way does *Cereus*'s imagination of nature help to come to terms with the environment that has been damaged by globalization? Is it possible to relate this poetic representation of nature to environmental discourses of the Caribbean? And if so, what is the role of literature in debates about the environment?

Conclusion: New Plots for Living with Environmental Chaos?

Like Mootoo, feminist ecologist Carolyn Merchant is driven by the wish to develop an intimate interaction with the unpredictably interrelated world. In her eyes, chaos theory has put an end to a simplistic linear understanding of nature. It "fundamentally destabilizes the very concept of nature as a standard or referent. It disrupts the idea of the 'balance of nature,' of nature as resilient actor or mother who will repair the errors of human actors and continue as fecund garden" (*Earthcare* 54). As in Mootoo's novel, there can be no question of recovery; a "recovery-plot" is unthinkable—a happy return to authenticity is impossible. What other plot might then be appropriate? "What would a chaotic, nonlinear, non-gendered history with a different plot look like?" Merchant asks (55). She muses that such a plot can "only be acted and lived, not written at all" (55). But does that mean that there is no use for literature—that source of new, written plots—within environmental debate?

Perhaps there is. Merchant's ethical reflection on the way to relate to a chaotic, interrelated world ties in, for example, with Édouard Glissant's poetics of Relation. The importance of Glissant's poetics, which is based on his analysis of Caribbean creolization and of globalization, lies not so much in its emphasis on the world's interrelatedness itself, as that notion has been developed in many environmental discourses, though often in problematic ways. The significance of Glissant's poetics is rather located in its complex, critical approach to the notion. In his evaluation of the philosophical debates around environmentalist discourses from the 1970s onward (most explicitly Arne Naess's "Deep Ecology") that assume a "fundamental connectedness/relatedness in the natural world that encompasses Homo Sapiens" (Kirkman 4), science philosopher Robert Kirkman also notes that a model of unified totality is destined to remain out of reach (152), in spite of the hopes of many environmentalists. This conclusion is nothing new for the Caribbean theorists of creolization and interrelatedness, for whom "ambiguity" and "multiplicity" have been key words. Glissant theorizes the world as unknowable because it is chaotic, unpredictable, and contradictory. This does not mean that Glissant gives up on the attempt to grasp this totality. Quite the contrary, in an exploratory essay on different efforts to create a new, nontotalizing, nonrepressive, nonexclusive discourse on the universal, Natalie Melas explains that such discourses are needed as much as ever, for "the notion of the degeneralized universal" can be seen "as one aspect of contemporary globalization's cultural potential" (135). Giving up the desire to speak about the world-totality would amount to giving up on working toward a nonconservative, nonimperialist theory of the transnational world. However, it is open to debate to what extent Glissant's poetics of the world-totality is able to do just that.[11]

Glissant's poetics is, nevertheless, relevant to my discussion about the role of literature in environmentalism, as it argues that the interrelated world can never be completely known; Glissant's insistence on the opacity of space captures that insight very well. This is also one of the main insights in Mootoo's novel: the world can never be known by watching, naming, and classifying it. The words of Otoh's mother quoted above underline that insight, as do the images of insects on the novel's pages, as does Tyler's hesitant style of narrating the story. In other words, the privileged way of knowing is not visual.[12] But that does not mean that one cannot interact with the world. If Glissant calls for the incessant *imagination* of the world, then Mootoo, in line with Merchant, calls for an ongoing, subtle *interaction* with the world—an interaction subtle as the insect touch, open to the other's response.

Cereus is close to ecological feminism in the subtlety with which it unravels the intertwining ideas about nature and social issues (gender inequality, sexuality, race, colonialism). But the question that seems to drive the novel is not how it might imagine the world truthfully but rather which poetics is most helpful in *relating* to the often painful, hybridizing, globalized world—to find ways to *live* in it. Through the narrative of an abused daughter who tries not to intervene in nature's business, Mootoo's novel depicts a pathological attitude to nature, an attitude dictated by trauma, resulting in the inability to interact with one's surroundings and in the creation of the ambiguous yard. Thus the work as a whole insists on the imperative in order to interact with one's environment and to engage with historical truth.

This novel, then, takes as its point of departure the assumption that interaction is the key to a productive lifestyle in a damaged postcolonial world. This interaction inevitably implies border-crossing and will lead to hybridization. The novel shares many of the assumptions of ecological feminism, even if it is critical of the ecofeminist belief in a harmonious, reciprocal relation with nature. Instead of endorsing the tenets of system ecology, in which the natural environment is seen as ultimately autonomous and best left alone to develop its own stable ecological system, *Cereus* shows an affinity with an evolutionary ecological approach, where the environment is seen as always unstable, always changing, in response to social and environmental events (Keulartz). *Cereus* offers neither the plot Merchant desires nor a vision of a definitive return to an undamaged, original environment. It does offer the inspiration to think through the complicated global and local contexts of environmental sustainability. More strikingly, perhaps, than its capacity to critique colonial and national narratives of nature, is the powerful way in which it helps to uncover the very real deep-seated anxieties and interests that shape society's attitudes to hybridity, and its desires for certain landscapes. The most valuable aspect that this novel submits is its ability to let us *feel* that, ultimately, nature always exceeds social discourse. These accomplishments may well be the greatest gift that literature has to offer to the debate about the environment. By means of this complex and wayward writing, the Caribbean landscape is moved—moved out of narrow colonial and nationalist discourses, out of all idealistic ecological discourses, and into a new, as yet undefined, interrelated global imaginative space, where it receives new meanings and a new vitality.

Notes

I am grateful to Elizabeth DeLoughrey for her invaluable criticism and editorial comments. I also thank Sean de Koekkoek and Saskia Lourens for their patience in correcting my English.

1. See Kutzinski for an incisive analysis of the psychological reasons behind this manipulation of time, and of the role of repetition in Mala's way of dealing with her trauma.

2. In this respect, Mootoo's imagination could be related to other efforts of Caribbean writers to create a woman's space within hostile surroundings, such as Marlene Nourbese Philip's writings, and especially her brilliant and complex essays on what she terms "Dis Place." To grasp the complexity of these efforts, see Heather Smyth, who concludes her analysis of Caribbean women writers in Canada by highlighting the insight (strongest in Dionne Brand) that a home can be created only by shared political activism. Philip's and Smyth's analyses suggest that such projects are complex and multidimensional and should not be interpreted as merely the utopian imaginations of a woman's sphere. Thus, they offer an argument against this interpretation.

3. This is symbolized in the almshouse yard, the Thoroughlys' well-ordered garden, and the Royal Botanical Gardens. See also Casteel.

4. Jamaica Kincaid, for example, in *A Small Place,* suggests that the excessive beauty of the Antiguan landscape is related to its exclusion from world history; Surinamese-Dutch writer Astrid Roemer shows that corruption is part of Caribbean nature. If women writers are unwilling to accept utopian imaginations of Caribbean landscape, it is often because they know all too well where these images come from.

5. Although hybridization and creolization are both concepts referring to processes of mixing and merging, they cannot be considered as synonyms. See, for example, Purdom; and Hoving, "Hybridity," for evaluations of the concept of hybridity, and see Shepherd and Richards for a discussion of creolization.

6. An essay by Samuel Beckett states that in Proust "[h]omosexuality is never called a vice: it is as devoid of moral implications as the mode of fecundation of the *Primula veris* or the *Lythrum salicora*" (89–90). I would like to thank Dirk van Hulle for presenting me with this example. Bauer offers a more elaborate analysis

of plant metaphors in male French literary writing about homosexuality. A comparable use can be found in Caribbean gay writing, such as Lawrence Scott's beautiful *Aelred's Sin* (1998).

7. Flowers are apt images to explore issues of sexuality. The work of other Caribbean writers shows that images of flowers, plants, but especially trees, can be used to question colonial assumptions, such as those about identity as autonomous. See Licops and Mitsch for analyses of tree metaphors in Caribbean writing.

8. As Casteel has argued, the novel also relates how the cereus was transplanted from one garden to many other gardens.

9. This remark does not imply that the novel shares a Deleuzean aesthetic. Its love of horizontality, thematized in the dwelling on surfaces and indexicality, is balanced by its insistence on secrets that must be acknowledged before life becomes possible.

10. A big thank-you to Elizabeth DeLoughrey for suggesting this conclusion to me.

11. Peter Hallward suggests that Glissant's later work increasingly represents a so-called "singular" approach to the world, in which he (like Deleuze) assumes that reality is the expression of one self-actualizing principle. As this principle realizes itself independently from any ethical of political context, it is hard to see how a singular approach would help in analyzing specific political conditions.

12. Kutzinski discusses the novel's representation of spaces in which "existing does not mean being visible to someone else, as it does in Hegelian paradigms of selfhood" (179).

"Rosebud is my mama, stanfaste is my papa"

Hybrid Landscapes and Sexualities in Surinamese Oral Literature

Natasha Tinsley

SODOMITES, Jamaican dub poet Cherry Natural claimed in a piece performed in Kingston in 1995, are antinature. *No natural black woman,* she insisted, could be a lesbian. But what *is* natural to the Caribbean? "Nature" itself is not. The Caribbean botanical landscape was aggressively colonized by arriving Europeans who imported sugarcane, coffee, mangoes, breadfruit, flamboyant, and bougainvillea—a very few of the agricultural and decorative species transplanted here—in order to systematically re*plant* these newly claimed territories as *plant*ations. Neither is "black" or "woman." Racial "Others" were invented to turn the colonial sugarcane machine: Natives, Africans, Asians, and various taxonomies of *métis* were legally distinguished from whites for the purpose of securing European land rights and providing labor for the cane harvest. Racialized gender roles, from plantation mistress to coerced slave *misi* (concubine), were consolidated in order to populate house and field: these multiple models of "woman" conscripted black, brown, and white female bodies to perform different types of reproductive/productive labor necessary to perpetuate the plantation system. Calling on the naturalness of heterosexual black womanhood, then, denies a history that maps how and where Caribbean landscape, race, gender and compulsory heterosexuality were constructed as interlocking topoi, delimited to serve imperial economic systems.

Understanding the parallel construction of *landscape* and *black women's sexuality* provides powerful conceptual tools for rethinking environmentalism, feminism, and queer theory. Recognizing nature, sex, and sexuality as constructs need not invalidate discussions of material conditions of Caribbean peoples and landscapes, as Northern feminists' attempts to divorce woman from nature often seek to do. Instead, it can become a point of departure for strategic transformations of both *nature* and *female sexuality* that transculturates these concepts to serve *Caribbean* cultural and economic interests. Queering nature becomes a poetics and politics that radically revisions environmentalism and gender/sexuality in the Caribbean context. This essay traces an example of such revisions in performance poetry composed by Afro-Surinamese Creole women at the turn of the twentieth century. Beginning with a sketch of the histories of the environment and of working-class women in this Dutch colony, I read landscape imagery in Creole women's poetry as a critical response to both situations. Refusing the binaries natural/unnatural, heterosexual/homosexual, and passive flora/active humanity, these texts demonstrate how dynamic, complex understandings of relationships between nature and sexualized femininity have been and can become a powerful politics of decolonization.

Creole Ecologies: *Dyari, Mati,* and the Capital of Women

Traveling in "Netherlands America" in the early twentieth century, Philip Hanson Hiss described the street scene in Paramaribo as a male homosocial space "recognizably Dutch in its character" (27). Along with canals, he cited as evidence of Dutchness well-ordered flowering trees lining the streets and landscaped public squares that government officials enjoyed on the way to their offices, "always at the same hour . . . their white suits freshly starched and gleaming in the sunlight." These were spaces where the colonial government had visibly rationalized nature's excess: tropical trees manicured out of improper fullness, time consistently measured, clothing untouched by the dirt underfoot, even the sun "gleaming" rather than blazing. This rationalization, he suggests, reflects and enables the success of Dutch imperial capitalism, the productivity of its white (suited) officials. But Melville and Frances Herskovits, doing fieldwork in Paramaribo some years before, colored and gendered the urban landscape differently. Their 1936 *Suriname Folk-lore* records a recognizably *Afro-American* city and locates the center of Creole culture in the yards of its working-class, colorfully kerchiefed Afro-Surinamese *women*. There, they explain, urban Africanisms were passed on behind Paramaribo's "recognizably Dutch" streets, where eighteenth-century slaves and free people of color began grouping their houses to open into common *dyari* (yards). By 1821, the number of yard dwellings was three times that of Dutch-style houses; after the 1863 abolition of slavery, these numbers increased dramatically as Afro-Surinamese migrated to Paramaribo, quickly becoming four-fifths of the city population (Hoefte 11).

When Melville and Frances Herskovits arrived in 1928, *dyari* typically included several female-headed households where mothers raised biological and adopted children. These yards were built around an environmental ethic that contested colonial rationalization of nature. Their ecologies worked not to discipline or exploit natural resources but to safeguard these resources, so protecting the households' welfare. In working-class neighborhoods without government-financed landscaping or sanitation, compounds set their own environmental standards through the *kina* (taboos against polluting communal spaces, usually with feces, urine, or menstrual blood) that each yard established. *Kina* communicated respect for *doti,* the earth mother of each plot, whom inhabitants believed vital to the yard's well-being. While government buildings showed authority through carefully manicured gardens, yards manifested *doti's* favor through naturally occurring flora and fauna whose value was based on a *lack* of human intervention. Lucky *dyari* were marked by the unsolicited presence of a friendly snake representing *doti* and a flowering tree that "chose" to grow there alongside medicinal herbs and decorative flowers (Stephen 25). The luck of the yard, the ecology of the communal garden, and the survival of *dyari* families were conceived as interlocking propositions and collective responsibilities: everyone must make sure *gron mama* and her tree are fed, just as everyone must make sure each human inhabitant is fed.

In view of this tree, inhabitants gathered to cook, gossip, tell stories, sing, and hold religious ceremonies and wakes. Also in view of the tree, *dyari* women engaged in the sexual and social praxis *matiwroko (mati* work). Well before 1900, a sociocentric tradition of women's relationships had developed and been given language in Suriname. In her exhaustive research on Creole working-class women, anthropologist Gloria Wekker studies this tradition as a *dual sexual system.* While Creole women often have relationships with men, they simultaneously engage in socially recognized partnerships with women. The goal of the former may be to ease physical hunger by gaining a second wage earner, and the goal of the latter to meet both material and emotional needs. *Mati* ensure companionship, attention, moral support, and help with yard management that men are not expected to provide (Wekker, *Subjektiviteit* 165–66).

While *mati* work involves relationships of mutuality and exchange, the word *mati* also references a very specific and still present history of environmental and human violence in the Caribbean: the Middle Passage. Sally and Richard Price document *mati* as "a highly charged volitional relationship . . . that dates back to the Middle Passage—matis were originally

'shipmates,' those who had survived the journey out from Africa together
. . . those who had experienced the trauma of enslavement and transport
together" (396, 207). As the Prices record them, women's relationships
arrived on American shores as resistance to conditions of enslavement: an
eroticism asserting the sentience of bodies that Dutch slavers attempted to
forcibly transform into brute matter. In addition to Africans of various
nations, slave ships carried fruit trees and seeds to feed their human cargo
in the Americas. Ships' tight packing of human and botanical cargo sys-
tematized the reification and brutalization of African floral *and* human
ecologies. People, like plants, were turned into profitable objects of exchange. But kidnapped Africans resisted this commodification by *feeling
for* the other occupants of the sex-segregated holds. Wekker notes the
importance that bonds between shipmates acquire throughout the Afro-
Atlantic: "In different parts of the Diaspora the relationship between people
who came to the 'New' World on the same ship remains a peculiarity of
this experience. The Brazilian *malungo,* Trinidadian *malongue,* Haitian
batiment and Surinamese *sippi* and *mati* are all examples of this special,
non-biological bond between two people of the same sex" (*Subjektiviteit*
145).[1] Formation of these bonds may have been facilitated by the existence
of socially legitimated same-sex erotic practices among precolonial Africans including Akan, Dahomeans, Yoruba, Azande, Ashanti, and Naman
(Connor, Sparks, and Sparks 1–3). But the emergence of *mati* in slave
holds created an Afro-Caribbean same-sex eroticism that transculturated
African ideas of gender and sexuality to serve as topoi of resistance in the
violent "New" World. Even as European colonists invented spatial and
economic bonds between slaves and the nonhuman botanical cargo imported alongside them, *captive African women created erotic bonds with
other captive Africans,* formulating an Afro-Caribbean model of relation
that refused European symbolic and economic systems' violent reification
of "tropical life" by introducing eroticism where shipowners assumed it
could have no place. These kidnapped women never accepted that to be
"floralized" meant to abdicate sentience.

Botanical Studies and Colonial Reports:
Taming Landscapes, Disciplining Sexuality

Despite its long history, colonial accounts did not register *mati* as a social
"problem" until after the turn of the twentieth century. In 1900, Paramaribo
police temporarily stopped all *lobisinghi*—performances in which women
sang songs to their *mati* in public squares—citing them as neighborhood
disruptions (Comvalius 358). Soon after, *mati* work entered colonial

records as a social ill needing immediate redress in A. J. Schimmelpennick van den Oye's memorandum to his 1912 report on urban poverty. Deploring working-class conditions, he listed as causes of local women's physical weakness unhealthy food (disapproving *dyari* ecologies' foodstuffs) and "geslachtelijke gemeenschap tusschen vrouwen onderling (het matispelen)" (sexual communion between women [mati play]) (quoted in Wekker, *Sub-jektiviteit* 146). Schimmelpennick explains *matisma*'s prevalence by the predominance of women in Paramaribo. Beginning in 1890, exploitation of balata and gold drew Paramaribo's Afro-Surinamese men to the interior to bleed trees and mine, leaving women the overwhelming majority of the black population of Paramaribo. Paramaribo suddenly was, as Melville and Frances Herskovits noted, a city of women.

Although *mati* work was not established in response to the balata/gold exodus, these demographic and economic circumstances help explain why it came to Dutch attention around 1900. The turn of the twentieth century witnessed a crisis in Suriname's colonial machine. While declines in sugar and cocoa markets rapidly sapped the plantocracy's economic base, discovery of balata and gold attracted continental Dutch, German, and North American investors. These investors manifested a keen aware-ness of the need to "tame" Suriname's *oerwoud,* or "virgin" forests. This domesticization took the form of new legal ownership, as the colonial gov-ernment prodigally bestowed gold concessions and let the balata industry take possession of forests with no intervention. It also took the form of new scientific ownership, as botanical and zoological studies undertook to document the "contents" of this previously undervalued Caribbean colony. The principal achievement of these new studies of flora, fauna, and mineral resources, as Stuart McCook writes, "was, for better or worse, a physical and cognitive reorganization of tropical nature . . . on the basis of modern scientific principles—the commodification of nature" (McCook 139–40). New investors also showed keen awareness of the need to conscript the evasive Creole male workforce—reluctant to work outside Paramaribo since emancipation—in order to assemble workers to tap the trees and mine the gold of this newly commodified landscape. Creole women were deemed crucial to meeting this second need. Schim-melpennick deplored that *matisma* existed not only among "unattached women" who might live together out of poverty but among women with male partners to support them, labeling this threat to heterosexual nuclear families "immorality" (quoted in Wekker, *Subjektiviteit* 146). His judg-ment may be colored by the fact that like later colonial observers, he mis-understood the dual sexual system and assumed that sharing partners with women would nullify men's patriarchal and "moral" obligation to earn the higher wages that mining companies promised. His consistent translation of *matiwroko* as *matispelen*—unproductive "play"—underscores that the impact of this "weakness" on the labor pool was one of his chief concerns.

But the threat that Schimmelpennick sees in *matispelen's* prevalence among women "attached" to men is symbolic as well as economic. Its organization of gender and sexuality denaturalizes an imperial socioeconomic organization erected to fulfill investors' first need, to "rightfully" claim and exploit "virgin" lands. The dual sexual system established a complex system of *kamra prekti,* or "bedroom obligations," communally recognized codes of behavior understood to be *eerlijk* (fair or honest) in sexual partnerships. These codes diverged widely from the duties of husband and wife propounded by the contemporary Dutch household manuals distributed to European colonists. Instead, the cooperative ecology of erotic relationships paralleled the cooperative ecology of the *dyari.* Whether relationships are between a man and woman or two women, partners are expected to bring equal resources to the association. Sex, housework, and money all count toward fulfilling *kamra prekti.* "Ef o tel' a sensi, dan ab'verplicting, dan na wan *wroko*" (If you take money, then you take on obligations, then you have to work): whenever a woman takes money from a sexual partner she understands that she is not his/her dependent but a worker in an equal partnership, and must match the monetary contribution with equally valued contributions of sex, domestic labor, and money she earns herself (Wekker, *Subjektiviteit* 127–28). The more money she brings in, the less she performs sexually only to please her partner; the more often a partner cannot please her in return, the less housework she does. At any time she can choose to take other work or lovers to fulfill unmet needs, as *eerlijkheid* is understood not as sexual exclusivity but as a woman's ensuring that she gives what she can and receives what she needs in any partnership. Men's acceptance of female lovers' *mati* expresses recognition that the economically, socially dominant partner in a relationship is *not* entitled to exclusive possession of the "natural" physical and emotional resources of significant others.

The Dutch government, in turn, maintained a system of "colonial obligations" that were neither mutual nor egalitarian. Suriname itself never profited significantly from the gold or rubber industries. Its environment was rapidly depleted: land stripped for mines, balata trees bled dry by 1917, deforestation a growing problem. While individual Surinamese obtained jobs as miners and bleeders, profits produced by these industries went entirely to their Dutch, British, or North American owners, and the Hague never required them to make financial or environmental contributions (such as reforestation) to local governments. Instead, the Dutch forced local government to pay for a railroad initiated to facilitate mining even after the gold industry folded. The logic of Creole bedroom obligations and that of Dutch colonial obligations were in fundamental opposition. Suriname was providing overseas companies with natural resources—unregulated amounts of raw materials—and getting no money and little else in exchange. Applying the guidelines of *kamra prekti* to the colonial relationship, Suriname had neither the obligations of political and economic linkage nor, in fact, the subordination that the Dutch government insisted was its due. No money, no obligations, no work. As it involved both men and women, *mati* was not only a non-European sexual configuration but an anticolonial model of societal (*maatschappelijk*) ecology—one calling for an environmental and economic responsibility that Dutch colonists had no interest in accepting. Schimmelpennick's description of *mati* as "gemeenschap," which evokes economic as well as sexual commerce and indicates a relation to "gemeente" (the local political unit), suggests that he perceived potential symbolic—and potentially threatening—linkages between alternative sexual, economic, and environmental systems of community established in Paramaribo's *dyari*.

Creole women continued to speak in defiance of Dutch policing, carrying on *lobisinghi* without the written permission the government called for. "Law!" (craziness!), contemporary *mati* worker Misi Juliette exclaimed when told of the 1912 report (quoted in Wekker, *Subjektiviteit* 146). I now go on to begin a reading of a traditional *mati* performance text, a song in the genre *lobisinghi*. *Lobisinghi* literally translates as "love song" but, like Paramaribo's Dutch-style streets, contains something not immediately expected. These musical compositions act as social criticism leveled against *mati* who violate *kamra prekti*. Analyzing the women-as-flora metaphors in one text, I argue that the government was not incorrect to judge that *lobisinghi*'s floral images were social criticisms targeted not only at individual *mati* but at colonial imaginations of landscape and woman; and to shut them down as social *disturbances*. In these performances, resistance to colonial control of the woman of color's sexualized body is inseparable from resistance to colonial commodification of landscape. *Mati*'s reinvention of gender and sexuality is environmental criticism—and their environmental criticism, a reinvention of gender and sexuality.

Decolonizing Gardens and Gender:
The Botany of *Lobisinghi*

At the turn of the twentieth century, *lobisinghi* took place on Sunday afternoons at established locations in Paramaribo. The best known was Saramaccastraat: a lot on the Suriname River that trader Abraham de Vries rented to women for three guilders during hours when no ships were loading the balata and gold extracted from the interior. Performances began with the gathering of a mostly female crowd that walked to the lot in a musical procession. There performers traditionally opened with *langasinghi*, improvised lyrics composed of three-line verses. But after 1900, *langasinghi* began to be omitted because, as original compositions, they might bring slander charges if police arrived. Many *lobisinghi*, then, consisted entirely of *kot'singhi*: shorter, more fixed texts whose words the lead singer would alter slightly between choruses to speak to a wronged lover's situation. Songs were performed as a call and response whose chorus remained set and ended with a series of dance steps, dancers lifting their skirts in back to shout "Ha! Ha!"

Dutch musicologist Th.A.C. Comvalius cited the heavy use of imagistic language in these texts as a distinctively African element of their composition (Comvalius 355). The recurring *lobisinghi* imagery that he notes includes various metaphoric conventions linking women's sexuality to landscape. One of the oldest examples comes in the following *kot'singhi*:

> Fa yu kan taki mi no moy? (x 3)
> Na tu bromtji meki mi.
> Rosekunop na mi mama,
> Stanfaste na mi papa.
> Fa yu kan taki mi no moy, no moy?
> Na tu bromtji meki mi.
>
> [How can you say I'm not pretty? (x 3)
> It's two flowers that made me.
> Rosebud is my mother,
> Everlasting is my father.
> How can you say I'm not pretty, not pretty?
> It's two flowers that made me.] (Wekker, "Re: Mati and Literature")

In what follows, I focus on providing an interpretation of the two terms key to the natural and sexual ecologies of this song: *bromtji* (flowers) and *uma* (woman).

The word *bromtji* draws immediate attention by its position in the middle of the song's first trochaic line, a moment of accelerating rhythm; by its appearance directly following the metrically free and repeated first line; and by its inclusion in a series of alliterations in which [m] occurs in a stressed syllable. This meter and alliteration link *bromtji* rhythmically and phonetically, as well as semantically, to the stressed *mi* ending the line: the strong relationship between woman and flower is inscribed not only in the meaning of the song's words but in their form. In fact, all the last words of the song's lines—the most powerful position in a line—refer to the speaker and her kin, while two of the lines' beginnings—the second-most powerful position—speak the name of flowers, metrically balancing the power of woman and her mother/father flowers. These overlapping connections serve to introduce a flora-woman metaphor that images how Creole epistemologies conceive both natural ecologies, and ecologies of gender and sexuality.

In fact, this song builds on a complex environmental history of various decorative flora imported to Suriname. The rose—many varieties of which were imported to Europe from Africa and China during the Renaissance—became in turn one of the flowers most frequently transplanted to the Americas. Letters from British settlers requested specific varieties of roses from England, while French colonists brought seedlings to imitate Josephine's famed rose gardens. *Stanfaste* (*Gomphrena globosa*), however, was imported directly from Southeast Asia, not to imitate traditional European landscapes but to flush out the borders of exotic gardens with multicolored blossoms in brilliant purples, pinks, blues, oranges, and yellows. They were especially valued for the heads of the flowers, which, if dried early, could be displayed for many years.

Imported for different purposes, rose and *stanfaste* image two models of womanhood—and two models of relating to the environment—negotiated in *dyari*. Wekker notes: "Many ambiguities of Surinamese gender relations can be understood as tension existing between male-dominated gender ideology and praxis in society's dominant strata, and a more egalitarian gender ideology and to a certain extent praxis that continues in the traditional Surinamese working class" (*Subjektiviteit* 62). "Rose," chosen for its visual impact, refers to a pretty woman possessing qualities of physical attractiveness that *mati* understand to be valuable in the dominant gender ideology. These include attributes such as paleness (pink, white, and yellow rose—relatively subdued colors in the tropics) and softness (of petals/protected bodies) of skin, both associated with upper-class privilege. Wekker details as a central feature of this upper-class model the colonial institution of "Surinamese marriage." In this "marriage," upper-class white men have access to two or more "vrouwen" (women/wives), one *getrouwde vrouw* (legal wife, necessarily white) and one or more *buitenvrouwen* ("outside women"/concubines, usually light-skinned Afro-Creoles) (Wekker, "Of Mimic Men" 181–83).

Surinamese marriage formalizes white men's prerogative to collect women as objects, accumulated for display value: multiple women in multiple houses serve as important signifiers of social prestige. This ruling class use of women—a Surinamese "cult of true womanhood"—parallels the ruling class model for use of the environment: the search for true wealth. In the Dutch colonial economy of the turn of the twentieth century, women are like flora in that they are commodities whose accumulation and exploitation secure European men's dominant positions in an imperial capitalist system in crisis; women are like flora in that they are passive *things* that first-world, first-sex owners desire to keep in their possession. However: when *mati* sing of the *mama rosekunop* in Saramaccastraat, they disrupt the power dynamics of the floral metaphors that operate in elite living rooms. The rose—the hegemonic model of ideal woman and flora—is recast by becoming a prized possession that Creole "women keep for each other," subverting the ownership paradigm of the dominant system (Adisa 29). The natural "commodity" of feminized (*mama*) decorativeness (*moy*) is not surrendered to an upper-class patriarch but stays metrically, phonetically, and semantically linked to the woman speaker and to another flower, *stanfaste.*

Stanfaste, on the other hand—chosen not only for its physical properties but for associations tied to its name (staying together, not falling apart)—speaks to Afro-Surinamese gender ideology and represents qualities that Creole women value in themselves: self-sufficiency, emotional strength, knowledge of yard ecologies, and community loyalty. These flowers come in deeper colors and sturdy textures, suggesting physical qualities—dark skin, endurance, vitality—associated with black working-class women. In Creole yards, the valued model of womanhood is the *dyadya uma* (upright woman), who is "a woman who knows how to take care of business, is a psychological and economical broker; she has a network that importantly includes female relatives, but also her lovers, male and female; she has command of spiritual and cultural knowledge, including the use of *odo* (proverbs)" (Wekker, "Of Mimic Men" 188). Once again, this model of Creole womanhood parallels a model of Creole environmentalism. Flora and women are alike in the *dyari* because neither can be exclusively possessed; both must be engaged as upright (*dyadya/stanfaste*) living forces to interact with horizontally—at eye level—and responsibly. Like *stanfaste,* the *dyadya uma* and *doti* are feminized presences that yard dwellers respect for their abilities to act and react even in situations of hardship, so contributing to the yard's survival and well-being. The insufficiency of ruling-class models of botany and sexuality to explain Creole landscapes and womanhood appears thematically in a number of sayings and *lobisinghi,* imaged as the weakness of the rose without the support of the *stanfaste.* "Roos e flaw a de fadon," remarks one *kot'singhi,* "ma stanfaste dat e tan sidon" (The rose is weak, it falls down, but stanfaste stays upright) (quoted in Wekker, *Subjektiviteit* 62).

What does it mean to Creole ecology and gender ideology for rose and *stanfaste* to be metaphorized as the mother and father of this *lobisinghi*'s singer? Certainly it means *mati* act like no kind of flower or woman recorded by colonists. The song's imagery contests both foreign investors' botanical studies and government public health studies. The pseudoscientific rhetoric justifying the taming of tropical nature relies on metaphors of the hypersexuality of uncontrolled West Indian flora. Caribbean botanical studies researching the decline of sugar yields cited cane's noncompliance with "natural" heterosexual reproduction as one cause of its decreased productivity: "According to the planters, the degeneration of a variety [of cane] was the logical consequence of asexual reproduction," McCook writes (81). Balata and gold industries, however, by bringing "virgin" forests into compliance with colonial penetration, would suitably heterosexualize the feminized landscape and so restore productivity. *Lobisinghi,* elements of cultural knowledge by which *dyadya uma* evaluated the world, countered these studies with an anticolonial, feminist reading of the feminized sexuality of nature. In these texts, flora refuse to stay in the places assigned in European botanies. Not only do flowers of a different genus crossbreed, but two flowers consistently feminized in *lobisinghi* imagery reproduce nondegenerate, "moy" offspring. Flora is imagined not as a commodity that produces capital for investors when properly sold/married off but as an actor that produces a sentient, erotic being who will not enter into the economy of European-style trade or marriage. Namely, it produces the nonheterosexual *mati* singer with whom *roos* and *stanfaste* have family, not business, relationships. The natural world of *lobisinghi* is not the dead, exploitable territory inscribed on Dutch maps. These *bromtji* exist *somewhere else,* in a decolonized landscape ordered by a horizontal Creole environmental epistemology, one where flowers and people interbreed.

Schimmelpennick's study echoes botanists' in its move to blame the sexuality of the object of study—here working-class women—for its own material decline. Refusal to comply with compulsory heterosexuality—rather than the economic slump caused by the resource drain of balata and gold industries—appears as the cause of ill-health and poverty; exclusive heterosexual partnering, the solution. This hegemonic model of heterosexual womanhood, which mandates that Creole women choose heterosexuality to reproduce a population of gold and balata workers, also explodes in the chorus of the *lobisinghi*. "Tu bromtji meki mi": the singer will "meki" her identity through a floral metaphor that humanizes the feminized natural world rather than through one that botanizes or pathologizes Creole women's world. *Roos* and *stanfaste* here image Creole women's identity conceived beyond the possibilities of slave/wife/colonized territory. Though both flower and woman are entities falsely naturalized to the region, the choice to negotiate identity via the former rather than the latter defiantly proclaims that hegemonic constructions of these "natures" have *not* left *mati* without options for self-construction—and construction of their physical and social environments. Poor, black and female, they do not have to navigate their gender, race, or economic status in the ways Schimmelpennick imagined for them (better food and men with better mining jobs). *Tu bromtji meki mi:* two women/flowers can create economic and kinship ties that refuse to reproduce patriarchal colonial orders yet birth a "moy" Surinamese landscape and population. Not only is the *dyari* not recognizably Dutch in its character, but its flora cease to be botanically recognizable, unable to be claimed as exploitable commodities. Not only are *mati* not born women, but they are not of woman born, socialized in sexual systems that defy dominant gender ideologies.

"Nature Is a Cultural Construction."

So writes Rosa Braidotti in *Patterns of Dissonance* (129). But what are our tools for understanding this construction outside a European or North American context? Environmentalism, feminism, gay rights: these neologisms and phrases are all products of Euro-American political discourses, and their dominance in international activist rhetoric bespeaks a Eurocentric balance of power in framing terms of worldwide debates. Groups looking to build coalitions with Caribbean and Third World activists often assume that because these words came from Europe, opposition to hegemonic constructions of nature, woman, and sexuality are also Northern inventions to be shipped to those backward postcolonials who, in Aimé Césaire's words, "have not invented" (44). This essay examines marginalized Surinamese women's texts to disprove this assumption. Undercutting the image of the Caribbean as intellectual importer, *lobisinghi* enunciate indigenous strategies of resistance that pre-date global export of liberal Northern politics. Their *roos* and *stanfaste* image the development of Creole women's overlapping, resistant constructions of nature, gender, and sexuality that refuse to make commodification and subjection "organic" to sexualized Surinamese landscapes and women. Listening to these voices as Third World theorizing on the "natures" of environment, gender, and sexuality provides a critical space from which to begin decolonizing international political discourses not only of environmentalism and feminism but also of gay and/as human rights. It introduces ground (*doti*) from which to interrogate and shift when and how natural resources, women of color, and sexual minorities are taken into account. In Suriname, *mati* insist, a rose is not always a rose; and it behooves not only local intellectuals but also international environmental and queer activists to listen to what else it can be.

Note

1. All translations from Wekker's Dutch original are mine.

"He of the Trees"

Nature, Environment, and Creole Religiosities in Caribbean Literature

Lizabeth Paravisini-Gebert

All misfortune comes from the cut trees, they have cut them down, even the calabash trees, even the trees of Ogou.

—Marie Chauvet, *Fonds des négres*

IN HAITIAN VODOU, the *lwa,* or spirit known as Loco, the chief of Legba's
escort, is known as "he of the trees." He governs the tree or temple center-
post that serves as channel for the *lwa,* the divine life forces of Vodou, to
enter into communion with their human *serviteurs* through the phenomenon of possession. Loco and his consort, Ayizan, are, as Maya Deren
describes them in *Divine Horsemen: The Living Gods of Haiti,* the moral
parents of the race, the first *houngan* and *manbo* (priest and priestess of
Vodou), whose chief responsibility is that of imparting to humans the
knowledge of *konnesans* on which the future of the race depends. They are
also Vodou's first healers, as it was Loco "who discovered how to draw
their properties from the trees and to make the best herbal charms against
disease" and Ayizan who protects against malevolent magic (Deren 148).
Together they represent the belief in Vodou that spiritual maturity rests
on the understanding of the necessary balance between cosmic forces and
the natural world.

Loco and Ayizan, together with Osain, their orisha counterpart in
Cuba's Regla de Ocha, and Palo Monte (the practices commonly known
as Santería), offer a path to an ecocritical reading of the relationship
between the Caribbean folk and nature, and of the representation of this
relationship in Caribbean literature. Osain, the patron of *curanderos*
(folk or herbalist healers), is the master of the healing secrets of plants, the
deity of *el monte*—the Cuban forest or bush: "All the *ewe* [plants or
herbs] is the property of Osain, and without enlisting his aid beforehand,
it is not possible to do any work in Santería" (González-Wippler 55).
Osain defines the parameters of the bond between man and his natural

environment—the most crucial relationship in African-derived religions—as Santería, like Vodou and Rastafarianism, is a religion that integrates human concerns with spiritual forces. It has been described as an "earth religion, a magico-religious system that has its roots in nature and natural forces . . . a system that seeks to find the divine in the most common, ordinary things . . . All that Santería wants to do is to embrace nature, but in so doing it embraces the soul of all things" (González-Wippler 4, 23).

My primary concern in this essay is to trace how some salient works of Caribbean literature have articulated the relationship between Caribbean peoples and their environment, as seen through the prism of African-derived Caribbean religiosities. It uses the figure of the *houngan,* the priest and healer, as the focus of an ecocritical reading of several examples of the twentieth-century Caribbean novel, such as Alejo Carpentier's *The Kingdom of This World,* Marie Chauvet's *Fond des nègres,* and Mayra Montero's *In the Palm of Darkness.* My main focus in these readings is that of addressing the articulation of an environmentalist thought linked to religiosity in the Caribbean novel as revealed through the examination of the role of the *houngan* (or related figures) as protector of the balance between nature, the spirits, and man—as chief conservator, so to speak. A secondary concern is that of how these novels interpret the threat to the Caribbean environment posed by increased pollution and development as a menace to Creole religiosities themselves, whose connection to nature is transformed as landscapes change and the "trees" that are fundamental to Loco's role as healer disappear.

In the Caribbean region, the relationship between man and nature was determined early in postencounter history by the ecological trauma represented by the establishment of the sugar plantation. Pre-plantation Arawak culture—as described in Spanish chronicles and most vividly in Friar Ramón Pané's *Relación acerca de las antigüedades de los indios (An Account of the Antiquities of the Indians,* 1571)—was dependent on a simple economy of subsistence agriculture and fishing centered on "a harmonious relationship between religion, culture, politics, and patterns of work and exchange" (Paravisini-Gebert, "Caribbean Literature" 670). Pané's collection of Arawak myths and legends articulates poignantly the symbiotic relationship between man, nature, and the gods that was the foundation of pre-Columbian Caribbean cultures: man worked along with nature to produce the crops and claim the fish needed for the welfare of the community, and this labor was accepted as a pleasing offering by their principal deity, Yocahú, provider of yucca and fish.

Although devastated by warfare and the virgin soil epidemics that dec-imated the aboriginal population, the Arawak worldview survived the wreckage and environmental assault of European conquest and coloniza-tion to eventually lay the foundation for traditions of resistance that would serve as a counterworld to the economy of the plantation. In early colonial texts, such as Friar Bartolomé de las Casas's *Brevísima relación acerca de la destrucción de las Indias* (*A Brief Account of the Devastation of the Indies*, 1522), the Arawak native emerges as a noble savage living in harmony with the environment—the Indian as classic hero—an image to which Caribbean writers will return again and again in search of symbols of preconquest, preslavery cultural wholeness. Las Casas's concern with the question of how to incorporate the Arawaks into the Spanish nation as subjects with rights and prerogatives—the central focus of both the *Brevísima* and his *Apologética historia sumaria* (General Apologetic History, 1575)—brought him to an early understanding of how, from its inception, Spanish expansion in the Caribbean region was dependent on the eco-nomic, political, and cultural exploitation of the native populations and new environments (Paravisini-Gebert, "Caribbean Literature" 671–72).

Throughout the Caribbean, this exploitative expansion found its most efficient form in the economy of the plantation. Caribbean societies, Eric Williams has argued, "were both cause and effect of the emergence of the market economy; an emergence which marked a change of such world historical magnitude, that we all are, without exception still 'enchanted' imprisoned, deformed and schizophrenic in its bewitched reality" (quoted in Wynter 95). This change was both demographic and ecological. Thou-sands of African slaves were brought to the new world with the sole aim of making it possible to produce a luxury crop for the international market in plantations that required the complete transformation of the Caribbean's tropical landscape. The Caribbean sugar plantation grew at the expense of the dense and moist tropical forests that needed to be cleared to make way for the new profitable crop. This rapid deforestation led to soil deple-tion, landslides, erosion, and climatic changes that included significant decreases in levels of moisture and rainfall (Grove 64–70). The resulting environmental degradation was exacerbated in many areas of the Carib-bean by ungulate irruptions—the introduction of domestic grazing animals alien to the pre-encounter Caribbean environment—that transformed the cultural and social landscape. Together, these rapid environmental changes brought about an ecological revolution, "an abrupt and qualitative break with the process of environmental and social change that had developed in situ" (E. Melville 12).

Sylvia Wynter has argued, however, that despite the seemingly irrevo-cable consequences of this ecological revolution—despite the apparent victory of the forces of the plantation and the *emporium*—there remains a tension in Caribbean history and culture between the forces of the plantation and an equally powerful cultural and environmental drive to return to the plot system of subsistence agriculture—"the indigenous, autochthonous system"—that characterized the cultures of both the original Arawak and Carib inhabitants of the region and of the African slaves brought forcefully to provide labor in the plantations. She bases her theories on the work of Guatemalan novelist Miguel Angel Asturias, who defined this clash as one between "the indigenous peasant who accepts that corn should be sown only as food, and the *Creole* who sows it as a business, burning down forests of precious trees, impoverishing the earth in order to enrich him-self" (Wynter 96). Wynter, in her turn, saw the plot system—which in the Caribbean was reinforced by the planters' practice of giving the slaves plot of lands on which to grow food to feed themselves—as "the focus of resistance to the market system and market values" (99). Holger Henke has argued, following Wynter, that these provision grounds—to be found most commonly on the edge of the remaining forests—became "the living proof to the enslaved African of wo/man's ability and vocation to live in natural harmony and in harmony with nature" (63). The plot system may thus be read—although this is a point that neither Wynter nor Henke develops—as the foundation of a specific approach to nature and envi-ronmental conservation in the Caribbean that would allow the return to a pre-encounter ecological balance.

Wynter contends that the articulation of this tension between plot and plantation—with its environmental implications—is at the core of the development of Caribbean literatures. Her reading of Victor Reid's *New Day* and Herbert De Lisser's *Revenge: A Tale of Old Jamaica*—tales that address the 1865 Morant Bay rebellion in Jamaica—underscores historical and textual anxieties that are closely tied to the environment and religion, and to the possibility of recovering the roots of history in the oral tradi-tion of the plot-oriented folk. Reid's novel, in a pivotal scene centering on a Kumina ceremony, portrays Bogle, the rebellion's leader, as an ancestor-god who conveys the peasantry's desire for the recovery of their connec-tion to the land; De Lisser, in his turn, as a defender of the colonial class, demonizes the peasantry's aspirations by embodying them in the figure of the "voodoo" priest as false revolutionary leader, both in *Revenge* and in his better-known novel *The White Witch of Rose Hall* (Paravisini-Gebert, "*White Witch*"). In both cases, however, the link between Creole religiosity and the plot is manifest. Henke underscores this connection in his study of the provision grounds as places where "all elements of a free wo/man's life came together in a condensed form," especially those religious rites "abhorred by the Caribbean plantocracy" that played such an important function "for the stabilization of internal social order among the slave population" (63).

Wynter's essay predates the development of ecocritical approaches to the reading of literature, but she nonetheless pinpoints the basic dichotomy that underlies pan-Caribbean approaches to writing about nature and environmental conservation: that the political, economic, racial, and religious elements associated with the development of the plantation economy (and the tourism that follows in its wake) will be most fundamentally at war with their counterparts on the side of the plot system of agriculture. It suggests an ecocritical stance that pits colonialism versus independence; an international market economy versus a locally driven subsistence economy; European culture versus Creole culture; the anthropocentricism of Christianity versus the man/nature symbiosis of autochthonous Caribbean and African-derived religious practices; the land cleared for either plantation or golf course versus the forest. Questions such as the role of the physical setting in the plot of a novel; the consistency of the values expressed in the text with ecological wisdom; how the metaphors of the land influence the way it is treated; how the text articulates the people's relationship to the natural world, among others, have been addressed in the Caribbean from one or the other of the positions suggested by Wynter (Glotfelty, "Literary Studies" xix). Caribbean writing has always been deeply engaged with the landscape, with the creation of geographically rooted narratives where the environment takes a central role in determining the possible ideologies available to a character (Poirier 15–16).

Take, for example, the various characters in *Hamel, the Obeah Man,* a little-known two-volume work published in 1827 (see Paravisini-Gebert, "Colonial and Post-Colonial Gothic"). Set in Jamaica, the novel traces the career of Roland, a white preacher whose teachings about the equality of man and attempts to lead a slave rebellion (elements that place him on the side of the plot system) are corrupted by his underlying desire to forcibly marry the daughter of a local planter and side with the supporters of the plantation system. The novel's unknown author, unambiguously pro-plantation, denounces Roland's unnatural desire to overthrow the planters' legitimate social order by turning him into a "villain of Gothic dimensions" whose "fevered mind twists increasingly towards violence as the tale progresses," culminating in "nightmare desperation" (Lalla 10). A Eurocentric narrative haunted by the then recent memory of the Haitian Revolution, the novel finds a somewhat implausible hero in the black Obeah man, Hamel, who is made to move from an early enthusiastic revolutionary fervor to the denunciation of the cause of revolutionary freedom. Hamel, a black man linked to his ancestral culture through the practice of Obeah, ultimately turns his back on "civilization" and sets out on a solitary journey to Guinea, leaving behind the plot/plantation dichotomy. In this ability to retreat to a mythical (and still forested) African homeland, he is luckier than his fellow characters, the "Gothic unnaturals" who must remain in the contradictory space between "loyal subject and vengeful rebel," the tainted product of "the undisciplined sexual passions of their white fathers" and the "savage inheritance of their non-white mothers," literally stranded between the plantation and the plot (Lorimer 681–84).

Hamel, the Obeah Man is of interest in our context because of the ways in which the text makes clear the almost deterministic connections between geography, race, class, and ideology in writing about the Caribbean, and because of the ways in which it equates ideology with specific religious practices and stances concerning the land and its forests. In the geographical space of Caribbean literature, where characters must choose allegiances to either the plot or the plantation or remain stranded in a contradictory, ambiguous no-man's land, the religious leader emerges as the troubled articulator of environmental ideology. Roland, a white man and a Christian priest, is torn between his impulse to help the enslaved population regain its connection to the land and his will to wed the plantation heiress, and is consequently demonized. Hamel, an Obeah man and therefore the focus of the planters' fears of slave insurrection, is made to disavow his "natural" allegiances to the plantation workers and their dream of a plot of land and flee to Guinea. They are both in a way defined by their relation to the land—to the plantation, the plot, or the mythical geography of the ultimate provision ground, Lan Guinée.

Hamel's flight to Guinea allows the text's anonymous author to sidestep the novel's most problematic issue: that of the implausibility of making a practitioner of Obeah, by definition a subversive figure, the spokesman for the defense of the plantation system. The practice of Obeah, seen by British colonial authorities as a threat to the stability of the plantation and the health of colonial institutions, had been outlawed in most British Caribbean islands early in the eighteenth century, after being perceived as one of the few means of retaliation open to the slave population. Obeah men such as Hamel, moreover, were seen as potential leaders who could use their influence over the slaves to incite them into rebellion, as had been the case in the Jamaican rebellion of 1760. Edward Long, as Alan Richardson underscores, had discussed the role of a "famous obeiah man or priest in the Tacky Rebellion in his *History of Jamaica* (1774), a work notorious for its virulent racism, and stated that among the 'Coromantyns' (slaves shipped from the Gold Coast) the '*obeiah-men*' were the 'chief oracles' behind conspiracies and would bind the conspirators with the 'fetish or oath'" (Long 2:451–52, 473).

The history of slave rebellions in the Caribbean can be read as the artic-ulation of the tensions between plot and plantation that Wynter describes. Slave rebellions—like the establishment of maroon communities by run-away slaves that functioned as spaces to preserve cultural and religious practices—had as their goal the return to familiar patterns of interactions between the transplanted Africans and the land inhabited by the spirits. Like Obeah, the practices of Haitian Vodou—the array of practices that Michel Laguerre has called "the collective memory of the [African] slaves brought to the sugar plantations of Haiti" (3)—grew in intensity as the colony's accelerated rate of production during the mid- to late eighteenth century redoubled the massive migration of thousands of men and women to a new and unfamiliar world marked by their brutal exploitation and early deaths in the plantations of Saint Domingue.

Like the Obeah-inspired rebellions in the British West Indies, the Haitian Revolution (1791–1804) would be rooted in the commonality of religious and cultural practices centered on Vodou, and its beginnings would be marked by a pact between the revolutionary leaders and the Vodou *lwa* or spirits. The links between religion and the uprising were established early through the slaves' belief in the powers of their legendary leader Makandal to predict the future and transform himself into various ani-mals—attributes conferred by the lwa, or spirits, which served him well in his clandestine war against the French colonists. The connection between religion, the uprising, and the environment emerged out of Makandal's identification with the forest and its vegetation, which yielded to him the secrets of the poisons that constituted his chief weapon against French planters. His reputation as a *houngan*, or Vodou priest, therefore, grew in proportion to the fear he instilled in the French settlers that his knowledge of the poisons, spells, and other subtle weapons he deployed against the white population had its source in magical powers linked to mysterious African practices and a supernatural symbiosis with the forest.

Makandal's link to the forest and the *lwa* is central to Alejo Carpentier's fictionalized rendition of the history of the Haitian Revolution, *The King-dom of This World* (1949), where he is portrayed as an *houngan* of the

Rada rite, the Lord of Poison, "invested with superhuman powers as the result of his possession by the major gods" (Kingdom 36). He is simultaneously endowed with "the supreme authority by the Rulers of the Other Shore" to exterminate the whites and create a great empire of free blacks in Saint Domingue and with the power of Loco and Osain, having mastered the herbs and fungi of the forest—"the secret life of strange species given to disguise, confusion, and camouflage, protectors of the little armored beings that avoid the pathways of the ants" (23). In this portrayal, knowledge of the powers hidden in nature is bestowed on Makandal as a sign of his blessing by the gods of Africa who have followed those who serve them across the waters to a new land.

Carpentier's reading of this pivotal moment in Caribbean history is complex and ultimately flawed (see Paravisini-Gebert, "Haitian Revolution"). His reading of the ecological implications of French colonialism and of the failure of the environmental project behind the Haitian Revolution, however, is of profound interest in our context. Carpentier's descriptions of the Haitian landscape in *The Kingdom of This World* underscore the ecological wreckage the plantation and the Revolution have left in their wake:

> But around the turn in the road, plants and trees seemed to have dried up, to have become skeletons of plants and trees in earth which was no longer red and glossy, but had taken on the look of dust in a cellar. There were no bright cemeteries with little tombs of white plaster like classic temples the size of doghouses. Here the dead were buried by the side of the road on a grim, silent plain invaded by cactus and brush. At times an abandoned roof on four poles told of the flight of its inhabitants from malignant miasmas. Everything that grew here had sharp edges, thorns, briers, evil saps. (108)

Carpentier's despoiled earth is a crucial element in a meditation on Haitian history that has as its focal point the failure of the Revolution's leaders to imagine a landscape without the plantation. If indeed, as Wynter's work suggests, the slave leader's natural role would be that of leading his or her people away from the structures of the plantation and into the "natural" order of the provision ground at the edge of a protective forest, then Carpentier's text, resting as it does on Spenglerian notions of ever-repeating cycles of freedom and tyranny in history, leaves little hope that the land of Haiti can recover from the devastation of the plantation. His Mackandal, the *houngan* who called for battle in the name of the *lwa*, dies leaving the Revolution in the hands of leaders incapable of redressing the natural balance that would have returned the land to the people and their gods. Boukman, who early in the novel had "stated that a pact had been sealed between the initiated on this side of the water and the great Loas of Africa to begin the war" (66), disappears from the text, dismissed in two lines that speak of how his corpse was left to rot and feed the crows. Toussaint never emerges from the shadows. The magnificent but weak Christophe is the only one to get his full due in the text, where he is depicted as a mimic man, striving to become an ersatz French aristocrat, a parody of a French king who has learned too well how exploitation and forced labor are the paths to power and glory. The Cristophe of *The Kingdom of This World* is a cardboard figure who denies his people the pleasures of the communal labor of the *coumbite* by returning them to the pre-Revolutionary patterns of forced labor they had experienced in the plantation.

It is in the treatment of Dessalines, however, that Carpentier's hopelessness concerning the Haitian land and its people surfaces most startlingly. The one page dedicated to the most "uncompromisingly ferocious" of the leaders of the Revolution (Dayan 21) stresses his connection to the African gods,[1] but it fails to address the efforts he made to redefine land ownership in Haiti, a project that most probably led to his death (Dayan 26). Carpentier does not address either Dessalines' "attempt to destroy 'false property titles,'" or "the violence with which he tried to carry out what has been called 'an impossible reform of the mentality of the ruling classes, and perhaps his own mentality'" (Dayan 27).

Dessalines' efforts at legislating the redistribution of land were central to the project of restoration of the Haitian landscape to a harmonious balance with its people. His decrees sought both to validate the former slaves' claim to property and to give them access to the land inhabited by their gods—an undertaking that was at once political, religious, and ecological. Carpentier's text underscores the connection between Dessalines' ferocity and adherence to the *lwa* but erases the other aspect of this communion with the gods—his role in trying to assure Haiti's would-be peasantry access to a family plot of land, an *heritage*—that could serve as a foundation for a new society and offer a home for the familial *lwa*.

In Haitian literature, as in the country's history, the environmental crossroads that the Revolution failed to negotiate successfully—and that has become since then the burden of the people, their *lwa*, and their *houngans*—has become a central leitmotif. This is hardly surprising, as the devastation brought upon the Haitian landscape by continued deforestation has become the country's most glaring socioeconomic problem. As Haiti entered the twenty-first century, the country's extreme deforestation, and the concomitant soil erosion, droughts, and disastrous flash floods, have ravaged the countryside and led to its critical environmental condition. Haitian writers, understanding the centrality of the environmental situation, both as a historical reality and as a metaphor for addressing this history in literature, have made it a cornerstone of the development of the national novel. In Jacques Roumain's *Masters of the Dew,* a seminal text in the development of the Haitian novel, the hero, Manuel, returns after years of working on the Cuban sugar plantations to the village of Fonds Rouge only to find it parched and dying from a drought caused by deforestation. Mired in a violent dispute over inheritance of the land, the villagers must come together if they are to find a solution to their ecological crisis. Led by their revered *lwa* Papa Ogoun, who counsels during a Vodou ceremony that the villagers must dig a canal to bring water from the still-forested mountains where "the vein is open, the blood flows," Manuel realizes that a *coumbite,* a bringing together of labor of all the villagers, will be necessary to accomplish the task. Despite Manuel's untimely death, the villagers unite and "a thin thread of water advanced, flowing through the plain, and the peasants went along with it, shouting and singing" (Roumain, *Masters* 190).

The importance of Haiti's deforestation to the development of Caribbean literature in general can only be adumbrated here. In Marie Chauvet's powerful meditation on Haiti's history, *Amour, colère, et folie,* her clear-sighted narrator describes how the devastation caused by deforestation threatens the peasantry's hold on that *heritage* that was Dessalines' legacy:

> It has been raining without check, and what is worse is that the rains came after the intensive clearing of the woods. Monsieur Long's electric saw has been buzzing without interruption for the last fifteen days. A tree falls every five minutes. Yesterday, I took a long walk down the length of the coast to take a look at the damage. I saw huge trees falling to the ground, making the most awful noise, as if they were roaring before letting out their last breath . . . Avalanches of soil stream down the mountains, forming mounds below. There is no longer any coffee, except in our memories. Mr. Long is no longer interested in coffee. He now thinks of nothing but the export of lumber. When the lumber is gone, he'll go after something else. Maybe he'll start exporting men. He can have his pick from among the beggars and easily ship them out. (132; my translation)

Chauvet's condemnation of the neocolonial (American) forces complicit in Haiti's twentieth-century deforestation finds its way into her two most important novels. In *Amour,* she dissects the forces that led to the ecological revolution produced by deforestation as a factor in Haiti's internal politics and international economic relationships. In *Fonds des nègres,* on

the other hand, she turns her gaze to the peasantry itself and its relationship to the land and to the *lwa* who inhabit it.

This relationship, as Joan Dayan has brilliantly analyzed in *Haiti, History,
and the Gods,* is mediated by an *houngan,* Papa Beauville, who has himself been complicit in the deforestation of Haiti through selling his own
land, bringing upon himself "the vengeance of the vodou gods" (Chauvet
quoted in Dayan 93). His path to redemption—partly spearheaded by his
efforts to bring a young newcomer from the city into the path of the gods—
effortlessly weaves together religious (Papa Beauville), political (Facius),
gender (Marie-Ange), and environmental concerns in a progression toward
the restoration of the land to the peasantry. As Dayan argues:

> Though Marie-Ange wonders if such belief brings resignation, Facius assures her
> that his struggle to help the poor people in the countryside to reclaim their land
> from the thieving urban bourgeois by forming a cooperative is not inconsistent
> with serving the gods. Far from weakening the will or inhibiting successful rebel-
> lion, vodou remains the necessary basis for political action. (92)

Haiti's environmental dilemma—in which history, ecology, religion,
literature, and politics intersect—speaks eloquently to writers across the
Caribbean. Haiti's symbolic position as the region's first republic and as a
land whose history has been emblematic of the economic and political
vicissitudes that have plagued other islands in the area gives the embattled
nation a central position in Caribbean discourse. It's ecological conun-
drum, in the hands of Caribbean writers, becomes, as we have seen in
Carpentier, the focal point for meditations on the region's environmental
quandary, such as we find in Mayra Montero's 1995 novel, *Tú, la oscuridad (In the Palm of Darkness).*

In the Palm of Darkness is an avowedly environmentalist novel—the
region's first. It narrates the tale of American herpetologist Victor Grigg,
who, with the aid of his Haitian guide, the devoutly Vodouist Thierry
Adrien, is on a quest for an elusive and threatened blood frog, extinct
everywhere but on a dangerous, eerie mountain near Port-au-Prince. In
the volatile and bloody setting of the Haitian mountains, controlled by
violent thugs, Montero uncovers a haunted postcolonial space built upon
the interstices between Grigg's scientific perspective and Adrien's animistic
Vodou-inspired worldview. Montero uses this dichotomy to unveil how
the extinction of species is the direct outcome of an environmental collapse
as the forests that were the frogs' habitat disappear. She shows, concomitantly, how the troubled landscape of Haiti—and the very environment
on which the Haitian people depend for survival—peopled with zombies

and other frightening, otherworldly creatures who have escaped the control of the *houngans,* has decayed precipitously due to political corruption, violence, institutional terror, murders, brutality, and religious turmoil.

Using the Vodou principle of an organic relationship between humans and the environment as a point of departure, Montero portrays the frustrating search for the elusive *Eleutherodactylis sanguineus* as a voyage to the center of a Caribbean darkness where corrupt neocolonial forces threaten the very environmental context that makes possible the religiosity of the Haitian people. In her exploration of the propagation and extinction of species in the natural world, paralleled by the narrative of how the mysterious forces of nature govern the fate of all living creatures, Montero extends the link between humanity's spiritual relation to the natural world to human vulnerability in environments that are pushing species to the verge of extinction. The possible existence of the last remaining specimens of the *Eleutherodactylis sanguineus* in Haiti's Mont des Enfants Perdus, the Mountain of Lost Children, points to the lost innocence that the despoiling of nature implies for Caribbean societies.

In her essay "The Great Bonanza of the Antilles," Mayra Montero writes of how she "suspected in some way, even at [an] early age, that there was a philosophy in the [Afro-Caribbean] cults of Ocha, Palo Monte, Vodou, and Espiritismo de Cordón that in one way or another expressed an integral conception of the world—a concept of man and of his organic relationship with the world" (Montero 197). In the magic-religious world of her texts—as in those of many Caribbean writers—the plot often revolves around fundamental ruptures in this relationship between nature and man, the healing of which becomes the task of the *houngan,* Obeah man, *santero,* or similar priestly figure.

In *Divine Horsemen,* Maya Deren identifies the protection of the parameters of the relationship between spirits and humans—the basis of Vodou as a religion—as the fundamental role of the *houngan* or *manbo.* As she explains, writing about the phenomenon of possession:

> Thus the possessed benefits least of all from his own possession. He may even suffer from it in material loss, in the sometimes painful, always exhausted physical aftermath . . . But since the collective consists of ordinary men with a normal interest in their personal welfare, it is dependent upon its ability to induce in them a moment of extra-ordinary dedication if it is to have access to the revitalizing forces that flow from the center . . . In the growing control accomplished by the ordeals and instructions of initiation, and in the prospective vigilance of houngan and societé, he is reassured that the personal price need

not be unpredictable or excessive. In the principle of collective participation is the guarantee that the burden shall, in turn, be distributed and shared. (276)

I cite Deren in some detail here because she articulates a fundamental notion of Haitian Vodou, and by extension of Santería, Obeah, and other creolized religious practices: the idea of the protective function served by the *houngan* as the one who controls the balance in the reciprocal relationship between the spirits and the humans who serve them. This protective relationship, in practice as well as in literature, is projected upon the land and its forests. In Erna Brodber's *Myal* (1988), for example, the devastating extent of the spirit thievery committed against Ella is externalized through a hurricane whose victims are catalogued primarily as trees: tens of thousands of coconut trees and breadfruit trees join the 1,522 fowls, 115 pigs, 116 goats, five donkeys, one cow, and one mule destroyed by the storm. Mass Cyrus, the Myal man whose healing of Ella has unleashed the rage of this storm on the unsuspecting landscape, can only excuse his act by trusting in the regenerative power of nature and pleading his need to protect his grove—his right to protect "his world," which contains his healing plants and trees—against destructive forces brought "from foreign."

Mass Cyrus's faith in the regenerative power of nature reflects Brodber's experience with the seemingly never-ending capacity of the Caribbean's tropical vegetation to renew itself if given half a chance. It provides a stance—simultaneously ecological and political—that provides a context for the representation of the *houngan, santero, quimboiseur,* or Obeah man as a figure that has sought to reconcile the tumult, violence, and destabilization of Caribbean historical experience with the balance, struggle for survival, and the physical and mental health that emerge out of the living contact with the spiritual forces that accompanied African slaves on their Atlantic Passage. The endurance of Loco—"he of the trees," as Maya Deren calls him—exemplifies the indispensable protection of the environment needed to guarantee the survival of principles and practices vital to the continuity of Caribbean cultures.

As the writers discussed in this study—from the anonymous author of *Hamel* to Brodber—make clear, however, the question of environmental preservation in the contemporary Caribbean is ultimately, as it has been since Dessalines failed in his efforts at radically altering patterns of land ownership in Haiti, a political one. The Creole religions of the Caribbean may articulate the environmental tenets of their belief systems—and writers may echo them—in vain until these notions enter the realm of political discourse and lead to concerted conservationist action. Recent events in

Haiti and the Dominican Republic have demonstrated the tragic complexity of the region's ecological quandary.

On 24 May 2004, the Haitian village of Mapou—named after a tree sacred in Vodou practices—was washed away by a deadly torrent produced by two weeks of continued heavy rains. Sweeping through Mapou and other villages and hamlets clinging to the deforested hills near the border between Haiti and the Dominican Republic—among them Fond Verrettes and Jimaní—the floods and mudslides left around three thousand people dead in their wake. More than eleven thousand families were displaced when their homes and shanties were buried under the rushing walls of mud (Weiner and Polgreen). Crops were destroyed, goats and pigs drowned, the water wells contaminated by decomposing bodies, and the villages isolated by the destruction of the roads. Epidemics were expected.

> While roughly five feet of rain fell Sunday and Monday, the water ran down land denuded of trees, over thin soil eroded by decades of slash-and-burn farming. The rain filled rivulets and rivers, running so hard down the steep and treeless slopes, until the raging muddy waters reached the valley that sheltered Mapou and engulfed it. (Weiner, "Floods")

The trees, newspapers around the world reported, had been cut for charcoal in a country that relies on wood for cooking and other activities. The rich topsoil had long since been washed to sea. In Guadalajara for a political summit of European and Latin American leaders, Haitian prime minister Gerard Latortue echoed the international concerns over the connection between the deadly flash floods and his country's massive deforestation: "The deep cause of this situation is the deforestation of Haiti. We have lost more than 80 percent of forest because people like to use wood charcoal as a source of energy" ("Haiti's Deforestation").

"Like to use wood charcoal as a source of energy" is perhaps not the most accurate way of describing a situation in which most of Haiti's 8 million people depend on charcoal to cook because there is no electricity, gas, or kerosene outside major cities and towns. It is a stance that blames a desperate population that has endured two centuries of political corruption, mismanagement, and greed for a process that began long before they found their deaths in the choking mud. "Most people here work the earth, but the most desperate take the trees to make charcoal, which sells for a few pennies a pound at market," Fernando Gueren, a surviving farmer from Mapou, told a *New York Times* reporter. "When they take the trees, there's nothing left to drink up the water. They wreck the land to survive" (Weiner, "Floods").

After the recent floods, however, even the trees are gone from Mapou:

> First villagers chopped down hardwoods like mahogany and cherry. Then they
> went after mango and avocado trees, destroying a food source. The sprawling
> mapou trees were cut as a last resort. Followers of voodoo, Haiti's official reli-
> gion, believe the trees are repositories of a pantheon of spirits and hold cere-
> monies and sacrifices in their shade. And mapous usually indicate the presence
> of spring water. In some dry patches of the country, only legends of the mapou
> remain. (Dodds 11)

"My grandmother used to tell me stories about the mapou trees and
how they should always be respected for the power that they had with the
spirits," Dereston Jean-Louise, a Mapou survivor, told Paisley Dodds, a
reporter from the *Los Angeles Times*, "but that was a different time. People
are poorer now and a lot of us don't have choices" (11). They also don't
have the help and comfort of their *houngan,* who was among the hundreds
buried under the mud. He and his *ounfort,* or temple, made from scrap
wood collected from the felled trees nearby, had been swept away by the
waters. With them, it seemed, went all remaining faith and hope. "My
family's all dead," said Pedro Nisson, a young traditional healer who had
watched his family drown. "When the rains came, the people tried to flee
to the hills, but the water drove them back. It's impossible to see how we
will make it through the days to come" (Weiner. "Floods").

The Haitian government, bankrupt and overwhelmed, had few solutions to offer. "We can't go on like this," Prime Minister LaTortue told
reporters in Guadalajara. "When I return I have plans to speak with the
government to invite students in a re-forestation project" ("Haiti's Deforestation"). He vowed to "create a forest protection unit made up of
former soldiers of the demobilized Haitian Army" (Weiner and Polgreen).

No Haitian leader, however, has ever visited Mapou. "For the poor,
there is no government," said Lilie Jean-Baptiste, a survivor of the floods
in Mapou who used to eke out a living growing cassava and now feels that
the "land is cursed": "The only government of Haiti is God" (Weiner,
"Haitian Village"). Without a concerted government-led effort, the Haitian
people may have to trust to God and their *lwa.*

Note

1. His victory was "the result of a vast coalition entered in by Loco, Petro,
Ogoun Ferraille, Brise-Pimba, Caplaou-Pimba, Marinette Bois-Chèche, and all
the deities of powder and fire" (Carpentier 109).

PART 4

Aesthetics of the Earth

"Man Fitting the Landscape"

Nature, Culture, and Colonialism

Helen Tiffin

WHILE THE ontological existence of nature-in-itself is an indisputable fact,[1] the term "landscape" both denotes and connotes more than simply "land" or "earth." An observer, an attitude to land, a point of view are implied, such that "landscape" is necessarily a product of a combination of relationships between living beings and their surroundings. In the case of human beings, "landscape" becomes a form of interaction between people and their place, in large part a symbolic order expressed through representation.

Theoretically there are as many expressions of this interaction as there are human cultures or individuals, but some important (if broad) distinctions can be drawn between the "landscapes" of indigenous peoples and those of the migrant, that is, the ancestrally or recently translocated. Whether such migration is or was involuntary or voluntary, it inevitably fractures ties with the homeland; while those relations with land that are established in the "new" place are generally assumed to be different from the sense of being-with-the-earth experienced by the "native," whose understanding of both self and culture is as an *intrinsic* part of it.[2] But for the exile or migrant, "landscape" consists in the formation or (re)formation of connections with the adopted place; connections understood as necessarily different from those of the indigene even where settlers and natives occupy coextensive territories. And for colonized peoples who are also ancestrally migrant, any coming to terms with the "new" landscape frequently involves a journey back through the depictions of that land by the imperium whose perceptions and representations of it exert a powerful hegemonic influence on the colonized.

In the Caribbean, with the exception of the Caribs and Arawaks,[3] all present-day populations are to some degree in *ancestral* exile, whether they be descendants of European settlers, Africans kidnapped into slavery, or the Chinese and Indian indentured laborers who followed slavery's abolition in the 1830s. Thus almost all modern West Indian peoples have had to adjust (or are still adjusting) to radical transplantation; and the "landscapes" they thus apprehend are different from, we assume, those of the Caribs or, in fact, those of each other. Unlike indigenous peoples, such relative "newcomers" bring with them the values, cultural memories, knowledge, and traditions of their former environments, a prior "natural" history of being-in-the-world that, consciously or unconsciously, implicitly or explicitly, influences (through expectation, comparison, and contrast) their perceptions of the new. Whether the imported population of the West Indian islands (and their descendants) are aware of this or not, the Caribbean landscape is to some degree always perceived in relation to their earlier homescapes; and second, their relations with the land are, to varying degrees, influenced by both the conditions of their translocation and their lived circumstances in the new locale.

The rigors of diaspora, slavery, and indenture hardly predisposed such "settlers" to their island (or Guyanese mainland) environments. Europeans, however, as planters, overseers, or entrepreneurs, experienced the tropical environment differently. While European whites formed (and still form) only a small minority of Caribbean "migrant" communities, they were historically cast in dominant positions where their attitudes to land and landscape—both that to their homescapes and to the tropics and the Caribbean—necessarily exerted a powerful influence on the majority populations of African and Indian descent. With the institution of colonial education systems[4] and other measures of formal colonization, the hegemonic power of English perceptions of land was vastly exacerbated. For colonized peoples, an English landscape—which most Trinidadians of V. S. Naipaul's generation had never seen—became both normative and ideal, while the Caribbean was regarded as at best exotic, and at worst, aberrant or second-rate.

For Caribbean writers, representation of Caribbean landscapes is thus particularly complicated, imbricated as it is in crucial ways with histories of transplantation, slavery, and colonialism and with imported European traditions of land and landscape perception and representation. In depicting their Caribbean environments, writers are obliged to negotiate historical, cultural, political, climatic, and biological factors, resulting in works that frequently deal with the interplay between historical and current Caribbean and ancestral homescapes, ideal or normative environments, and attitudes to tropical and island flora and fauna imported and imposed through colonial rule.

In this essay, I wish to focus on the ways in which a number of Caribbean writers at the intersection of Caribbean nature and culture are obliged by these tangled imaginative histories to deal with the English landscape and English perceptions of the Caribbean in order to fully encounter and represent their own place. Caribbean tropical landscapes are "always already" imbricated with that normative or temperate ideal, most usually in the hierarchized order that colonial relations imply. Moreover, the Caribbean was often perceived as richly but degeneratively tropical, frightening, fecund, even pathological; and, through colonialist interpellation, it became exoticized for its own inhabitants by the dominant European visions.

Attitudes to landscape are intimately connected to social values and mores. The disturbing fecundity and decay of tropical vegetation, the debilitating effects of non-European climates on Europeans, necessarily involved attitudes to bodies. Maxims for dealing with the vagaries of hot climates were imported from Britain, while the tropics, with their emphasis on the somatic, seemed dangerous to English reason and control, the very basis of imperial rule. Edward Rochester of Charlotte Brontë's nineteenth-century novel *Jane Eyre* is both repelled and frightened by the sensual riot in which, as a younger son, he has been obliged to seek his fortune. Like the Caribbean landscape and climate itself, his Creole first wife, Bertha Mason, had to be redrawn by the Dominican writer Jean Rhys to present the "other" side: a positive picture of both climate and people that addressed earlier English constructions of the Caribbean landscape and Creole character.

Writers from Caribbean island communities—in contrast, for example, to mainland Guyanese writers such as Wilson Harris—refer very little, if at all, to remnant "wilder" landscapes. Instead, the inescapable encounter between English and Caribbean versions of the West Indian environment occurs more often within the liminal zone of the garden, in areas of plantation or cultivated land, and over flowers and floral symbology. Just as the plantation necessarily emphasized an agricultural landscape—negatively for the slaves forced to work it and more positively for the planters who enjoyed the wealth it produced—the psychic "battleground" of representation occurs over a "cultivated" nature and most significantly, almost always involves reentry through English or European perceptions to effect the reexamination and revaluation of the local.

By the twentieth century, West Indian landscapes were necessarily inscribed with highly charged cultural and horticultural histories. As W. J. T. Mitchell notes, imperialism was and is "a complex system of cultural, political and economic expansion and domination that varies with the specificity of places, peoples and historical moments." It is also "a complicated process of exchange, mutual transformation and ambivalence . . . a process conducted simultaneously at concrete levels of violence, expropriation, collaboration and coercion and at a variety of symbolic and representational levels whose relation to the concrete is rarely mimetic or transparent" (9). Representations of crops, flowers, trees, and gardens in contemporary Caribbean writing cannot escape the symbolic freight of their own indigenous heritages and their contrasting associations acquired in the Caribbean, whether they be crops such as sugarcane and breadfruit or ornamentals like the rose and the daffodil.

As well as the connections between particular plants and various West African religions, Europeans brought Christianity to the Caribbean, a religion whose founding myth was that of a garden:

> Catholics and Protestants alike held that the first home of mankind had lain in a garden planted by God, where the climate was always mild, and the trees flowered and bore fruit continuously. Throughout the Middle Ages the Garden was believed, somehow, to have survived the Flood, and in the great age of geographical discoveries in the fifteenth century, navigators and explorers had hopes of finding it. When it turned out that neither East nor West Indies contained the Garden of Eden, men began to think, instead, in terms of bringing the scattered pieces of the creation together into a Botanic Garden, or new Garden of Eden. (Prest 9)

For the West, the botanical garden stands at the crossroads of the beginnings of modern science (in its collection of data and experiments in cultivation) and the older Christian view of botanical gardens as re-creations of an earthly Paradise. "Like an encyclopaedia, [the botanical garden] was a 'book' laid out in pages, which were 'printed' or 'set' for reference" (Prest 9). In the case of the Caribbean, however, this "Paradise" existed from the seventeenth century onward in the context of plantation slavery, and while the Caribbean might seem to offer, for some, an abundant tropical paradise, it was one whose history had necessarily rendered it, as a potential New World Garden of Eden, parodic, ironic, and tragic.

As well as this Western ur-myth of "The Garden" and the records of anticolonial conflict and exchange, other kinds of representational histories are imbricated in the connotative range of Caribbean landscapes, gardens, and floral symbologies. European accounts of the Caribbean (or tropics) from the Renaissance to the twentieth century were frequently reprojected to colonial peoples as the authoritative descriptions of their own local environments. Concomitantly, the second representational archive foundational in the construction of colonial subjectivities consisted in those images of the imperium itself, which presented England as ideal, axiomatic, or static.

Many postcolonial writers, including V. S. Naipaul and Chinua Achebe, have commented on the social and cultural effects of such projected representations of, for instance, Trinidad and tropical Africa against those of England, whereby the local is denigrated in favor of the ideal or normative English landscape and weather. The effect was, as Achebe has noted, to make Nigerian schoolchildren ashamed of their own climate for being aberrant or defective in not having four "proper" seasons;[5] or, as Jamaica Kincaid writes, explaining why she knew nothing of Antiguan flowers and plants while being quite familiar with European ones: "This ignorance of the botany of the place I am from (and am of) really only reflects the fact that when I lived there, I was of the conquered class and living in a conquered place; a principle of this condition is that nothing about you is of any interest unless the conqueror deems it so" ("Flowers of Evil" 156). The plants in the botanical gardens in Antigua, she continues, were named and interesting. None were Antiguan.

While a number of Caribbean writers address different forms of colonialist interpellation and middle-class subjectification more generally, Jamaica Kincaid, Olive Senior, and Lorna Goodison deal directly with the complex cultural and representational histories of agriculture and flowers and the parts these play(ed) in the denigration of the local. Phyllis Shand Allfrey in *The Orchid House* and Jean Rhys in *Wide Sargasso Sea* both employ tropes of the ruined or "parodic" garden to express the impossibility of the retrieval, in the Caribbean, of that "Paradise Garden" European botanists had hoped to find or later sought to create. In all cases, the imported floral symbols and the Ur-Myth (the Garden of Eden) underwent significant alteration as a consequence of the Caribbean environments to which they were "relocated." The "fallen" garden and the rose and the daffodil then became inescapable elements in the Jamaican, Antiguan, Dominican, and Trinidadian imaginaries and thus part of the lived reality of the Caribbean itself; and an apprehension of contemporary island plants and gardens has thus involved a deliberate interrogation and reorientation of these received symbolic complexes.[6]

Literary reconfigurations of traditional English horticulture indicate the degree to which material and symbolic transplantations of plants and gardens are rarely, as Mitchell noted of landscape painting, "mimetic or transparent." Where the myth of the Garden of Eden is transplanted to the Caribbean, it undergoes similar historical and intercultural pressures. As "found" or reassembled in the region, the tropical garden as Paradise was—at least from the seventeenth century onward—rendered an impossibility by its (re)creation on the very grounds of genocide and slavery. Consequently the (fallen) gardens of contemporary Caribbean writers, while sharing a Western foundational biblical basis, have more specific local referents and more ironic and parodic narrative trajectories.

As Carolyn Merchant notes, the Enlightenment idea of progress is rooted in the recovery of the Garden lost in the Fall: "The Lapsarian origin of the story is thus reversed by the grand narrative of the Enlightenment that lies at the very heart of modernism. The controlling image of the Enlightenment is transformation from desert wilderness to cultivated garden" ("Reinventing Eden" 139). Merchant refers specifically to the United States, and to the continental expansion that extended, through Puritan ideology, to the limits of the Frontier. While the Caribbean partakes of both the myth of the Garden of Eden and the Fall and, in spite of its prejudicial history, a potential "recovery," the narrative forms these representations take are different from those of Merchant's model. Instrumental in the Enlightenment "recovery plot," as Merchant notes, is labor: "The recovery plot is a long slow process of returning humans to the Garden of Eden through labor in the Earth—to turn the Earth itself into a vast cultivated garden" (139). But in the Caribbean, the redemption of a postlapsarian world is by contrast thwarted, not facilitated, by its particular form of labor in the earth: plantation slavery. Hence labor itself, in a rewriting of the Enlightenment recovery narrative, becomes the serpent in the postlapsarian garden; and the mood of the Caribbean "recovery" narrative is necessarily one of tragedy or regression,[7] involving a reentry into slave and colonial histories and their interrogation and rewriting.

In Rhys's *Wide Sargasso Sea,* the connection between slavery and the ruined garden is established by Antoinette early in the novel:

> Our garden was large and beautiful as that garden in the Bible—the tree of life grew there. But it had gone wild. The paths were overgrown and the smell of dead flowers mixed with the fresh living smell. Orchids flourished out of reach or for some reason not to be touched. One was snaky looking and another like an octopus with long thick brown tentacles bare of leaves hanging from a twisted root. Twice a year the octopus orchid flowered—then not an inch of tentacle showed. The scent was very sweet and strong. I never went near it. All Coulibri Estate had gone wild like the garden, gone to bush. No more slavery—why should anybody work? (16–17)

Descendants of the white plantocracy like Antoinette had never been expected to work. But the conclusion of *Wide Sargasso Sea* imaginatively "returns" Antoinette to her postlapsarian Caribbean "Eden" where eventually the fundamental division between black and white, planter and slave is resolved through Antoinette's increasing identification with black rather than with white Caribbean history and with collective Caribbean legend: "As soon as I turned the key I saw it hanging, the colour of fire and sunset; the colour of flamboyant flowers. 'If you are buried under a flamboyant tree,' I said, 'Your soul is lifted up when it flowers. Everyone wants that'" (151). The "anybody" of the first passage ("why should anybody work?"), with its mildly ironic invocation of the racially divisive past, becomes at the conclusion of the novel, "everyone," as a fiery tropical flowering is gladly embraced by Antoinette. And Rhys's refraction and inversion of the values of landscape imagery in *Jane Eyre* enables the Caribbean landscape, not the "temperate" English countryside, to be the one accepted. The garden at Coulibri seemed to the child, Antoinette, to be, at times, the abode of evil; but by gladly embracing as her own—not the white plantation garden but the Afro-Caribbean legend of the flamboyant tree—with all its European associations of heat, fire, excess—Antoinette jumps from an imprisonment in the temperate "ideal" to embrace her Caribbean "natural" and cultural world.

In Kincaid's perennial return to the subject of gardens, she too is concerned with issues of labor and the destabilization of the apparently dichotomous "native" and "exotic/immigrant" in terms of both human cultures and horticulture. In her *New Yorker* garden articles, she describes herself not as "Antiguan" or "American" but as "someone from somewhere (the place I am from—Antigua)" in dynamic counterpoint to "the place I live now, Vermont" ("A Fire by Ice" 65). This naturalized "visitor" but never-quite-indigenous position enables Kincaid to investigate the complexities of the concepts of "exotic" and "indigenous"[8] in terms of both plants and people; and as an acceptor of her own intercultural subjectivity, her own activities as a gardener make her a laborer in the earth and, in an inversion of slave-plantation history, an employer of other gardening laborers. Two men come to rebuild her garden wall, and, she writes, "as they worked, I sat on a stone step . . . reveling in my delicious position of living comfortably in a place that I am not from, my position of visitor, of not native, of seeing my orders carried out by two of the men who were stooped over before me" ("A Fire by Ice" 65).

There is a deliberate play here on the word "native" that not only invokes the divisions between natives, visitors, exotics, immigrants (whether

plants or people) but also plays on the derogatory use of "native" by Europeans to conjure an abusive dismissal of the "savage, the uncivilised, the
inferior race or group." "I had to tell one of the men", Kincaid continues,

> to save Mrs. Woodworth's roses, which he had dug up in the process of disman-
> tling the wall. Mrs. Woodworth was the previous owner of my house (she is
> now dead) and her roses had been in that spot for forty years and had come
> from her mother's house in Maine, so I had a sentimental feeling about them, a
> false feeling that no native can afford to have. ("A Fire by Ice" 66)

This time, although both meanings of "native" are involved, the emphasis is on the term's derogatory nineteenth-century connotation. Through
the repeated use of such conceptual entanglements, Kincaid deliberately
destabilizes "belonging" and "non-belonging," "roots," and the preservation of origins and originary mythologies (like the Paradise Garden) to
insist on the inextricably entangled legacy of the movement of plants and
people across the globe over the last four centuries. In such a world, the
native/visitor (Kincaid in Vermont) easily becomes the guardian (through
the resuscitation of the rose bush) of "native" American traditions. The
atrocities and inequalities of the past and present have not been forgotten,
but the inevitable hybridization to which this attests makes any myth of
origins—and the retrieval or re-creation of an "original" unchanging
Paradise—impossible.

V. S. Naipaul's *The Enigma of Arrival* presents its readers not just with
a picture of such entangled imaginative conceptualizations but also with a
meditation on landscape consisting of constant repetitions and rework-
ings; reinscriptions that destabilize the process of landscape perception
and representation in the context of those categories of ancestral homeland, place of birth, and imaginative ideation. Returning imaginatively to
other landscapes of the Caribbean and England from his Wiltshire residence, the narrator stresses the need for a more protean perception and
creation of "place," investigating, through the myth of the garden and a
literal and imaginative return to the landscapes of the English countryside, the "indigenous" conception of "man fitting the landscape."

In *A House for Mr. Biswas* (a narrative based in part on the life of his
father), Naipaul, like Goodison, Kincaid, and Rhys, recognizes the inextricably intertwined relationship to place generated by ancestral exile and
colonial interpellation. The protagonist, Biswas, gradually moves away
from the Tulsi family (who represent the ancestral Indian past, albeit in an
inevitably eroding, Creolizing context) and from the Anglo-based ideal
images of climate, landscape, and society inculcated through a colonialist

education and English reading. The walls of Mohun Biswas's aunt Tara's house are decorated with "photographs of dead friends and relations" and "coloured prints of the English countryside" (32), and it is from these attachments that Biswas moves to acquire his own (imperfect) "ideal" Port of Spain house and garden. His eventual acceptance of his Trinidadian context is symbolized by his move in sign painting from Santa Clauses and "cool ordered forest scenes," to painting the Keskedee and humming-bird for local café proprietors; and his change from assignments for "the ideal school of writing," conducted from Britain and culturally embedded in English landscape and society, to accounts of Port of Spain life.

But in *The Enigma of Arrival,* Naipaul recognizes the necessity of actu-ally reentering English contexts in order to find his own "center." Both *Mr Stone and the Knight's Companion* and *The Enigma of Arrival* have usually been read conservatively as admiration of English society and countryside. But both are more appropriately read, I would suggest, as part of the necessary process of reentry into English subjectivity, English landscape, and its representation to achieve a clearer view of the Caribbean homescape and Caribbean subjectivity.

An essential component of any "ideal" is generally its immutability; changeless and ageless, like the original Garden or indeed any paradisal conception, the ideal exists without erosion or decay; its image fixed, static. *The Enigma of Arrival* destabilizes this fixity in two ways: first, by emphasizing the change and decay of the English countryside and the mutability of the iconic English gardener/countryman, and second, by destabilizing the categories of "native" and immigrant in relation to place. Thus Naipaul returns us to the English countryside—complete with Great House ("the Manor") and planter-overseer (the Landlord)— and to his own imaginings of the Garden of England formed and fixed for him during his Trinidad childhood by literature, painting, and even advertising.

As in Naipaul's earlier *A House for Mr. Biswas,* the relationships be-tween the native or migrant and his or her place and their different con-ceptions of landscape are focal. As the narrator of *The Enigma of Arrival* first walks in the Wiltshire countryside, he is acutely conscious of his own "out-of-placeness" (19) both racially and geographically. A migrant "alien" ("uprooted" from an ancestral India, and from his birthplace of Trinidad), he contrasts himself with the quintessentially English gardener Jack, who is "part of the view. I saw his life as genuine, rooted, fitting: man fitting the landscape" (19). Reflecting on and describing this initial response after finding, later, that Jack and his garden are, in the very "nature" of things, impermanent—Jack's garden is dug up and concreted over after his death—the narrator nevertheless reiterates his long-held understanding of the contrast between his own ancestral past and that of the English peasant farmer: "I had seen Jack as solid, rooted in his earth" (87). For the narrator, doubly colonized, doubly displaced, Jack's condition seems an enviable one; his life "rooted" in a landscape that is also that of his ancestral history and one in which labor, in spite of some loss of autonomy in a machine age, has never been tainted by slavery. And Jack's relationship to his land seems apparently insulated from change; without exile, journey, or readaption, and without the colonialist interpellation that necessarily stood between Trinidadian and the Trinidad earth, making Jack, as the narrator describes him, "an emanation" of the "natural": a man "fitting" his landscape.

Since the narrator writes of his time in the Wiltshire countryside, in his Manor cottage, in the past tense, such a vision of an indissoluble, unselfconscious relationship to place has already been compromised at the time of writing by the knowledge of its own impossibility. This occurs not only because of Jack's death and the eventual disappearance of his garden, but because during his extended meditation on his own alien presence and Jack's indigeneity, the narrator has come to see relationship to place as far more complex than a dichotomy between native and interloper, or even a dialogue between English and Creole imaginaries.

From the moment of his arrival in Wiltshire, the narrator's relationship to the countryside around him is mediated by prior representation; by words and pictures of a rural England imaginatively internalized during his Trinidad childhood, and by his current project of (re)writing the English landscape through these filters. His English environment is one that has been literally learned "by heart" during childhood in Trinidad. The satisfaction of entering this known and cherished "magic land of abroad" (as Naipaul terms it in *The Loss of El Dorado*) is one of imagination and place at last conjoined as a fulfillment of the "promise within the promise." But paradoxically, this long-desired "emplacement" of self and imagination in a thoroughly known, yet never before actually seen Wiltshire, is simultaneously evocative of the Trinidadian childhood in which such images were grafted onto the colonial world and projected into an imagined future where the fairy-tale world of England's climate and landscape would "come true."

The Enigma of Arrival begins with a comment on the Wiltshire weather, followed by a statement that symbolizes the "natural" entanglement of landscape and image, colony and imperial "homeland." "For the first four days it rained. I could hardly see where I was" (11). The phrase "see where I *was*" introduces both the Wiltshire residence of the narrator *and* his Trinidadian past, the two landscapes that will constitute the "novel" he is writing. "Ways of seeing" a land through the reading and absorption of its literature in distant colonial contexts and the impact of this process on one's own attitude to colonial landscapes are crucial to the purpose of the novel, and while remembered images of England are particularly preponderant in the early sections of *The Enigma of Arrival*, they are reiterated throughout. The trees the narrator observes are "bare and brushlike" as in "the water-colours of Rowland Hilder" (11); while an old orchard must, according to expectation, surely be "a forest". Fairy tales and the root meanings of English words provide an intimate "knowledge" of landscapes seen only in representation: The narrator's knowledge that "walden" and "shaw" mean wood, together with "the fairy-tale feel of the snow and the rabbits" (13), convince him of having now "seen" a forest. Salisbury, he notes, was "almost the first English town I had got to know," internalized "from the reproduction of the Constable painting . . . in my third-standard reader. Far away in my tropical island before I was ten. A four-colour reproduction which I had thought the most beautiful picture I had ever seen" (12). Hay bales conjure "the story about spinning straw into gold, and . . . books with European settings of men sleeping on straw in barns" (17). Sheep shearing is "like something out of an old novel, perhaps by Hardy or out of a Victorian country diary" (18); a thatched cottage is "so pretty, so like a postcard . . . so like something one had always known" (55).

Colonial "knowledge" of the Imperial landscape, then, a knowledge that is also a form of love and longing, provokes not just the delight of recognition—place conforming to its representation—but actually ensures that the observed landscape is still read through representation even though these are not actually recalled but rather are created by the narrator himself: Jack is naturalized as "part of the view" (19), while his father-in-law "seemed a figure of literature in that ancient landscape . . . exaggeratedly bent, going gravely about his tasks as if in an immense Lake District solitude" (20). And the narrator returns to his Wordsworthian image of "man-in-landscape-fitting-representation" a few pages later, even giving his idyll a title: "A poem Wordsworth might have called *The Fuel Gatherer*" (26). Here man and landscape "fit" representation so apparently seamlessly that the pleasurable similarity catalyzes a re-cognition of even the Wiltshire landscape as always/already represented in Wordsworth's images of the Lake District, a region "learned by heart" by children across the Empire.

This is more than just a "real" confirmation of what the colonial had "always known." Rather, the pleasure consists in a confirmation of the accuracy *of the representation* absorbed and cherished in the colonial Caribbean environment. The "physical beauty" of the Wiltshire country-side provided the narrator with a world "perfectly suited to [his] temperament and answering . . . every good idea I could have had, as a child, in Trinidad, of the physical aspect of England" (52). The cows on the hillside, in the distance, against the sky, seem to match the Trinidadian child's "fantasy of the beautiful, other place, something which, when I saw it on the Downs was something I had always known" (80). This "fantasy" was initially sparked by "the cows in the drawing on the label of the condensed milk tins I knew in Trinidad," a knowledge confirmed by Gray's "Elegy" and "The Deserted Village." "Pictures of especial beauty at one time, those lines of poetry, matching the idea of the cows on the condensed milk label" (80).

Winter, however, does prove a little disappointing. The "idea" of winter and snow had always excited the narrator, "but in England the word had lost some of its romance for me, because the winters . . . had seldom been as extreme as I had imagined they would be when I was away in my tropical island" (11). The very phrase "my tropical island" itself suggests an English fantasy of exotic landscapes, reinforcing the idea of the impossibility of unitary environmental perception in a world in which the human imagination is constantly at play, and of which the colonial-imperial relation provides an especially forceful example of multiple visioning and the matching and mismatching of imagination and embodied experience. Onto the Trinidad landscapes of his childhood the narrator has projected those of England, as well as imagining their "coming true" after a journey to their source in the future. This projection was possible, indeed necessary, because, for Naipaul an unrepresented landscape does not really "exist."

But in *The Enigma of Arrival,* where the narrator—so often transparently Naipaul himself—details the connections, historical as well as imaginative, that have constituted for him the landscapes of England and Trinidad through a dynamic interplay of representational recollections, presences, and absences, he finds himself, at last, apparently "fitting" a landscape. He writes that the first four days of fog in Wiltshire, when "I could hardly see where I was" (11), were like a rebirth for me . . . After twenty years in England I was to learn about the seasons here at last; that at least (as for a time as a child in Trinidad) I would learn to link . . . natural events . . . to certain months. That in the most unlikely way, at an advanced age, in a foreign country, I was to find myself in tune with a landscape in a way I had never been in Trinidad or India" (157). This is neither the "knowledge" of the English landscape through representation with which he arrived nor the result of the conjunction between representation and the "real" landscape of England. Rather it is a "fit" between man and land conferred by the very process of writing about landscape and about its representation. In writing the Wiltshire countryside and representing it as a product of the many worlds in the mind's eye of the colonial beholder, Naipaul/the narrator bring together Trinidad and the other landscapes of actual journeys in a known and loved place and time; a complex geography of mind and heart in which all are intrinsically interwoven through imagination and representation.

In *A House for Mr. Biswas,* with its (qualified) "progression" from "unaccommodated" man to an identifiably Trinidadian way of being, omniscient narration was clearly an appropriate mode. Critics have suggested that Naipaul's designating his first-person, autobiographical *The Enigma of Arrival* as "a novel" indicates a coy approach to the relationship between the man and the writer. But like the reiterative structure, the split subjectivity hinted at in the sobriquet "a novel" seems entirely appropriate to a work wherein the constitution of human identity in relation to environment is always fractured, unstable; both nomadic and settled, real and imagined, imperial and colonial. By necessity, in *The Enigma of Arrival* the categories of Naipaul and "the narrator," life-writing and fiction, are collapsed. Colonial lives, imbricated with the "fictions" of the imperial center, made the ideal Garden of England an essential part of Trinidadian experience; an indissoluble component of the Caribbean landscape. Between the Wiltshire tenant (Naipaul) and his landlord, "an empire lay [and] this empire at the same time linked us. This Empire explained my birth in the New World, the language I used, the vocation and ambition I had; this empire in the end explained my presence there in the valley, in the cottage, in the grounds of the manor. But we were—or had started—at opposite ends of wealth, privilege and in the hearts of different cultures" (191).

Brought together on English soil, Naipaul and his landlord in the "great house" are moving in different directions. Clinging to the old vision of empire, the landlord is, like his grounds, in a state of inescapable decline, even implosion. For the narrator/Naipaul, this encounter has led to an entire re-cognition of the relationships between imperial and colonial landscapes, "native" and visitor. The ironic re-playing of the colonial "game" in the Wiltshire countryside does not signal a reversal of roles at the end of an era but rather a recognition of the protean nature of all relationships between humans and landscape, wherein the intimate nature of human being in the land is accorded not by ancestry or migrational adaptation but through absorption, interrogation, and rewriting of the human history of its representation.

Caribbean writers of African, Indian, and British descent have all shaped their understanding of their island landscapes—whether of Jamaica, Antigua, Dominica, or Trinidad—through some form of engagement with English representations of the tropics and their particular islands and with the imaginative ideal of the Garden of England. In so doing, they reenter, in a variety of ways, the archive of imperial depictions of landscape, interrogating, rewriting, accepting, or rejecting the entangled apprehension of environment generated by the history of the human occupation of the Caribbean islands.

Notes

My thanks to the volume editors for their assistance with this essay.

1. Hay 24.

2. The assumption of difference in attitudes to and an affection for the land between indigenous peoples and migrants has been a particularly popular one in the West since at least the second half of the nineteenth century. Such an assumption necessarily has major implications for contemporary land rights issues.

3. While people of Amerindian descent are still to be found on the South American mainland, Saliba on Dominica is now the only island on which a small Amerindian population survives.

4. For the precise dates of the institution of colonial schools in the Caribbean (both private and state), see Shirley C. Gordon's comprehensive accounts.

5. Achebe 29–30.

6. See my "'Flowers of Evil,' Flowers of Empire: Roses and Daffodils in the Works of Jamaica Kincaid, Olive Senior, and Lorna Goodison."

7. See, for instance, Allfrey's *The Orchid House.*

8. For a much fuller account of the implications of Kincaid's self-positioning for ecological ideals, cf. Susie O'Brien, "The Garden and the World: Jamaica Kincaid and the Cultural Borders of Ecocriticism."

Flashbacks of an Orchid

Rhizomatic Narration in Patrick Chamoiseau's *Biblique des derniers gestes*

Heidi Bojsen

> When a people's culture conserves ancient dynamics that play "in a certain kind
> of way," these resist being displaced by external territorializing forms and they
> propose to coexist with them through syncretic processes . . . Culture is a discourse,
> a language, and as such it has no beginning or end and is always in transformation,
> since it is always looking for the way to signify what it cannot manage to signify.
> —Antonio Benítez-Rojo, *The Repeating Island*

PATRICK CHAMOISEAU'S latest novel, *Biblique des derniers gestes*,[1] presents several ways of approaching nature that are reminiscent of the French
pre-Romantic and Romantic ideas about landscape and territory. It is my
contention that Chamoiseau, in his re-imagining of place, presents a narrative mode that challenges the Romantic legacy inherent in the terms "territory," "landscape," and "independence." My analysis aims to show how
the novel evokes these concepts only to reveal them as existentially insufficient in the historical and ecological context of Martinique. Martinique's
current status as an "Overseas department" of France (*Département
d'outre-mer*) has been contested by several local politicians and intellectuals whose nationalist argumentation often draws on Romantic-inspired
conceptualizations of nature, landscape, and territory. My sporadic references to the independence debate are, in fact, anticipations of an analysis
that would explore the interrelatedness of Chamoiseau's writing and
nationalist thought.[2]

The novel presents a narrative structure that constantly emphasizes
the importance of the narrator in the process of signifying. Throughout
the text, the narrator explores the gap between his own position and the
determinacy of the subject of enunciation. The signification of the concepts mentioned above is negotiated in the narrative space between the
narrator's imagining and the accounts of the people in the novel.[3] This
"disjuncture" is not represented in any given phrase but refers, according

to Homi Bhabha, to "the acknowledgement of its discursive embeddedness and address, its cultural positionality, its reference to a present time
and a specific space" (*The Location* 36).

The novel *Biblique* opens with a brief introduction that gives the official account of the life of a former "warrior of independence." These
fifteen pages are followed by the almost 750-page-long "Book of Agony,"
which begins with the narrator meeting the independence fighter, Balthazar,
who is dying in his armchair; the two of them are joined by others who
have come to pay their last respects. Drawing on the anecdotes and memories revealed by the people present, the narrator uses his intuitive reading
of their body language, as well as of Balthazar's spasms and silent agony,
to imagine how Balthazar may remember and re-imagine his life through
an incoherent series of flashbacks. It is as part of this specific narrative
mode—which is engineered by the narrator and his subjective desires—
that the orchid acquires totemic signification. The narrator's rapport with
orchids becomes an emblem of coexistence with nature as an Other
whom you may not fathom, but with whom you can still communicate.[4]

Ecology and Other Narrations of "Place"

Even if Chamoiseau wishes independence for Martinique and declares
himself to be an engaged political writer, he has, on several occasions,
kept his distance from mainstream nationalist discourse (Valhodia, "La
guerre"; Bojsen "Entretien"). This break with the traditional nationalist
approach to independence is apparent when one considers his conception
of space. Being highly influenced by the Martinican author and philosopher Édouard Glissant, Chamoiseau uses the notion of "Place" (*Lieu*) to
evoke a conception of placement that aims to create a sense of "homeli-
ness," in the Freudian sense, without relying on rigid distinctions between
the familiar and the foreign (*Écrire* 205–7). *Lieu* in Chamoiseau's texts
often means "locality" as it is constituted through the inscribing of a place
in *Relation* to the surroundings, an inscribing that underlines how different histories and modes of imagining are intertwined and often dependent
on each other. In Glissant's *Poétique de la relation,* the concept of *Relation*
represents dynamic and nonhierarchical modes of interacting with the
Other without necessarily understanding him or her. This approach becomes
a guiding principle in both Glissant's and Chamoiseau's discussions of
cultural identity. In the beginning of this theoretical essay, Glissant refers
to the Deleuzian and Guattarian metaphor of the rhizome, which is vital
for the definition of *Relation,* but he does not draw much on the notion of
the "arborescent." In *Mille plateaux* (*A Thousand Plateaus*), Deleuze and

Guattari present the metaphor "tree-root" (the "arborescent"), which signifies centralized hierarchies and subjections of meaning, whereas the rhizome makes alliances with its surroundings. The rhizome makes "its map of the world" by writing itself onto and into reality without aiming to produce an identical icon. The two intertwined modes prepare the way for agency (25, 32, 36). In Glissant's work, the rhizome is nevertheless diametrically opposed to the concept of "roots." In the same way, he opposes "relation identity" to "root identity"; "place" to "territory"; and atavistic to composite cultures (Glissant, *Poétique* 157–60; *Traité* 194–95).[5] Far from being just the expression of a predilection for a particular philosophical stance, the notion of *Relation* also refers to the specific historical context of the Caribbean where openness and interaction across geographical and political borderlines have been essential in order for small island communities to survive. This may also be why Glissant does not theorize the "arborescent" directly and ascribes roots and affiliation exclusively to the notion of territory. In Chamoiseau's texts, "Place" is never categorized unambiguously as "locality" and "territory" within specific cultural spheres. Instead, it is stressed how territorial aspirations can exist within structures of the locality just as these structures can work within the apparent hegemony of the territory (*Écrire* 206–7).

Glissant has also dealt with the use of ecologist discourse in the narration of land and territory. He detects a double orientation in its representation: ecology is either seen as a product of the sacred, a sort of mysticism, or as having the potential to critique the territorial conception of the sacred and its exclusive character. This is where ecology becomes political, according to Glissant (*Poétique* 160). *Biblique* is set in the chaos of this double orientation of ecological concerns. However, instead of adhering to a representation of ecology as a metaphysical principle, the story of Balthazar conveys how living with the actual components of nature is of existential and material ("earthly") importance in sections of Martinican society.

The close connections between the narration of nature, ecological discourse, and the definition of national and/or cultural localities have been analyzed on several occasions with regard to the Romantic period and in connection with colonialism.[6] This connection is also apparent today in Martinique, where most of the independence movements give high priority to environmental concerns. *Biblique* goes beyond Glissant's observations as it unravels how ecology, also as an emblem of sacredness or mysticism, is always part of a political struggle inasmuch as the narration of land, nature, and identity are highly political "gestures"—hence the title of the novel. The mysticism of the ecological discourses, Glissant says, is based on an intolerant and reactionary mode of thinking about land, a mode that will praise only local tradition and fixed rooting and will resist all changes (*Poétique* 161). Instead of maintaining this dichotomy, which is largely created by the history of European and colonial ecologist conceptualization, Chamoiseau insists on telling a history of Martinican ecological experience where the sacred is not confined to a transcendent level of purity or a nonpolitical and ahistorical essence. The sign of the sacred emerges in a performative narrative struggle that seeks to communicate with both the human and vegetal surroundings.[7]

As the narrator in *Biblique* discloses the numerous possible stories connected with Balthazar's life, he deals with three types of language: written, spoken, and body language. Balthazar's education began in the tropical forest under the care of a female *mentô*,[8] Man L'Oubliée, and is continued in the library of a communist anticolonialist ideologue, Déborah-Nicol. This particular combination has made him sensitive to the three kinds of languages and has had a decisive impact on his life as an independence warrior. Both women help him to escape from the witch Yvonette-Cléoste, who saved his life when he nearly died at birth yet has haunted him jealously ever since, as she had wanted to keep him to herself. In very different ways, he has learned how to survive by entering into *Relation* with both human and vegetal surroundings. These lessons help him survive the most atrocious circumstances as he joins the various wars of independence in India, Indochina, South America, and North Africa.

In Déborah-Nicol's house, Balthazar meets her sister, Sarah, and falls in love with Sarah's daughter, Anaïs-Alicia. However, both Sarah and her daughter seem of another world, and their preoccupation with poetry as well as with ghosts and zombies is far removed from Balthazar's political and revolutionary concerns. Once grown up, Balthazar leaves the house to participate in the colonial wars and also to live in different parts of Martinique in his constant flight from the witch. Through the imagination of the narrator, we learn how his life and journeys appear to have been determined in decisive ways by his early intimacy with the vegetation of the tropical forest and especially with the orchids, whose presence helps him everywhere in the world. The narrator equally emphasizes the significance of the women in Balthazar's life, and in particular the never-yielding power of Man L'Oubliée. Déborah-Nicol has initiated his political commitment, whereas Man L'Oubliée has provided him with an intimate knowledge of nature. It is in the description of this intimacy that the orchid functions as a semiotic "shifter."[9] Not only does it combine the narration of the struggle for independence with environmental concerns and Romantic aspirations to communicate with nature, but, more importantly, this narrative use of the orchid also points toward an enunciative positionality (and thus a cultural and historical embeddedness) where the physiognomy of nature meets human perception and its apparatus of representation and evaluation. The reader is never allowed to forget that "the place of the plot" is more than anywhere else in the imagination of the narrator.

Relation as Interdependency:
Mapping the "Locality-Place"

Cartography as a tool for conceptualizing land as territory predates colonialism but has, along with the disciplines of history and ecology, been appropriated by the colonial "machine" in order to control and organize the new territories as well as subjects.[10] Deleuze and Guattari oppose a rhizomatic mapping (*carte*) to a cartographical tracing (*calque*) of land and populations that claims to genuinely render reality through the logics of genetic filiation (19–21).

In *Biblique,* Balthazar and Déborah-Nicol spend days in her library drawing their world map. Their working process constitutes an elegant *mise en abîme* of how Chamoiseau's "locality-Place" is formed by a rhizomatic, narrative mapping. While Balthazar pinpoints the various places to carry out his anticolonial warfare, his mentor uses the world map as a safe haven, where she finds an answer to the absurdities of life (495–97). The impossibility of this project is what brings Balthazar to the conclusion that they must invent the places of safe haven themselves, turning the world map into a booklet about "the Places in the second world" (530) [Livret des Lieux du deuxième monde]. In other words, they move from the tracing of colonial representation to mapping. They are mapping a "second world," a poem, by means of imagination and poetic language (530–43). Furthermore, in their attempt to move beyond the traditional categories of the colonial predicament, they assume the responsibility of the subjective and creative mode of representation that goes with the writing of history. Balthazar and Déborah-Nicol's drawings on the world map do not erase the tracing as part of their narrative strategy but rather inaugurate a dialogue with its "lines."

The implicit questioning of the mimetic aspect of the tracing has a concrete historical dimension in the Caribbean space and undergirds Chamoiseau's critical distancing from the Martinican "regionalist" authors who dominated the literary scene before the poetry of Aimé Césaire and the blossoming of the Négritude movement (Chamoiseau and Confiant 116–22).[11]

Peder Anker's *Imperial Ecology* and Richard Grove's *Green Imperialism* both give detailed documentation as to how the discipline of ecology originates from an equivalent conceptual approach (that is, that of "territorializing" and "tracing") in the historical context of colonialism and Romantic nationalism. During the colonial period, Romantic and imperial views played important roles in the critique of urban life and culture, and, inspired by the writings of J.-J. Rousseau, certain ecologists would read a sentimental innocence into nature (Anker 197). As Anker points out, lending sacred values to nature or subjecting it to industrial exploitation are, in fact, two sides of the same tale: the history of empowering epistemological languages that both aim to connect nature and human life. He concludes that the success of the discipline of ecology has been dependent on its ability to mesh its concepts, its "ecology of knowledge," with imperial concerns and, as the colonial empires fell apart, with national aims (237).[12]

Chamoiseau may share the attributing of agency or "life" to the objects of nature with the Romantic poets, but his narrating differs significantly through its refusal to penetrate and understand the objects of nature, which is the ambition of Victor Hugo's poet-narrator (*La légende des siècles* 48–49). His narration of interdependence with nature does not arise from the narrator's privileged position from where he or she seeks relief and metaphysical insight through a direct communication with nature. It is rather the various marginalized subjects in the novel, with their blended interpretations of past events, who "give voices" to the narrator's imagination. In this way the subjectivity of narration is spelled out. There is an apparent contrast to the mode of Hugo's poet-narrator, who does not listen to the voices of the people but urges them to admire his genius.[13] Hugo was, along with other French Romantic poets such as Alfred de Musset, influenced by the contemporary pantheist philosophy, and both poets often depicted a nature of animist objects possessing a soul and a secret to be revealed. Starting out with a Rousseauesque contemplation of nature, which could provide comfort through its beauty, peace, and order, the Romantic poets moved on to attribute their own (often religious) thoughts and desires to the objects of nature and made them respond like human beings.[14] However, Chamoiseau's descriptions cherish the opacity that Hugo attempts to dissipate. He does not describe transcendental essences, but the agencies of trees and orchids that act as plants and thus stay beyond the *comprehension* of the protagonist.[15]

The first chapter of *Biblique* presents the reader with several possible openings to the story. One of them starts out as a description of the orchid as an ally to confide in, a parallel to canonized Romantic poetry.[16] Never-theless, the Romantic mastering of nature as an imaginary confidant is disrupted as the perfume of the orchid triggers another memory (40). This other memory is of the women in Balthazar's life, of his dependence on them and his failure to recognize this dependence. The ally acts all of a sudden as an independent subject that delivers an uncomfortable mes-sage, thus forcing Balthazar to rethink his life. This shock is what makes him realize that he is about to die. What is striking about this description is the fact that even if the orchid acts as a subject, exercising a certain power over Balthazar, it is *not* personified in the Romantic sense. It is not endowed with human characteristics. The narrator merely describes its effects on its surroundings while underlining his own subjective interpre-tation of the events. Even if it is possible to enter some kind of *Relation* with the trees and orchids, they are never personified as they are by the Romantics. On the contrary, it is Man L'Oubliée and Balthazar who, under certain circumstances, will undergo a seeming "vegification." Nature and its objects may be mysterious, but their mystery is not transcendent in a metaphysical way. They stay *opaque* according to the principle of *Rela-tion*. The notion of the sacred is detached from its pedagogical status as a religious or transcendent qualifier and is implemented through basic, but significant, everyday rituals. This comes about through Man L'Oubliée's forceful gestures, Anaïs-Alicia's reciting of poetry, as well as through the nar-rator's erratic and iterative account of Balthazar's life. In Chamoiseau's other novels such as *Solibo magnifique* (1988) and *Texaco* (1992), the sacred has mostly been represented as the power of the spoken language (*Parole*).[17] But as the title *Biblique des derniers gestes* suggests, the physical communication with the surroundings has become of vital importance. The sacred is a performative sign whose enacting and significance is his-torically and environmentally determined. Its contesting of the Romantic pedagogical narration of nature is, in fact, a "putting into Relation" (*mise-en-Relation*) at an enunciative level.

Land-Shaping and Narrating

Like the independence movements, Chamoiseau is concerned about the right to make decisions locally in the domains of economics, the environ-ment, and in general in the interaction with other countries and communi-ties. Still, his writing distinguishes itself from several of the formulations in the *Declaration of Cayenne*, whose authors remain within the Romantic framework, expressing the need for "our peoples to master their land with due respect to their identity and culture." In Chamoiseau's texts there is no question of "mastering the land"; rather, one lives with it. *Biblique* describes a dialogue with the constituents of what we call nature without the use of personifying or deifying metaphors and proposes thereby an alternative way of imagining the relationship between individual, collectivity, and the physical environment. "Mastering" the land corresponds more to the colonialist tracing of the new territories than to Chamoiseau's description of the Martinican locality.

Like painting and photography, narrating creates a frame around and a perspective on what is being said or represented. As for the concept of landscape, the word itself refers to a long history of narrating physical surroundings. The Romantic period of colonialism has played an important role in the history of narrating nature as landscape as it had its own particular use of nature (Mitchell 7–13). The description of specific landscapes was, in fact, interwoven with the representation of patrimony, territory, and its people.

In the beginning of *Biblique,* we have one among numerous examples of a Romantic point of view of the landscape. We are introduced to Balthazar's garden and find a somewhat surprising juxtaposition of a scruffy old wooden house, painted in loud, bright colors, and delicate hummingbirds and orchids that thrive on his porch. From the porch, "one [the narrator] discovered the countryside of Saint-Joseph, the floating fogs, its green shadows and the celestial emerging of the peaks of Carbet, which the old man would never grow tired of contemplating" (34). In this panoramic Romantic landscape, the word "celestial" denotes the metaphysical grandeur of the beyond, while the word "discover" plays on the colonial project of inventing new territories and incorporating them into scientific disciplines and terminologies. In this particular discovery, nature and landscape are not objects to be invented but rather witnesses, marked by past events, whose testimony must be taken into account. Balthazar's reflection on the landscape clashes subtly with both the tourist representation of the Caribbean forest as well as the Romantic perception of an "untouched" and sacred nature. Colonial discovery is about putting land into language in "a certain kind of way," but here the discovering "gaze" is directed at the buried knowledge of the country as well as the subjectivity of the narration, at the discursive process of discovery itself. "Celestial" describes not the peaks but their mode of representation, their "emerging."

In *Biblique,* landscape is a conscious putting into perspective. It becomes a verb—*to landscape*—whose meaning must be negotiated and reformulated in *Relation* to the surroundings. When certain independence movements set fire to the courthouse and place bombs in selected administrative buildings, Balthazar is suspected by the police and some poems are confiscated. The narrator does not hesitate to give us his own interpretation of the poem *Oala: Grand forest-silence,* which displays another kind of resistance than the "terrorist codes" (144) sought by the police: In the poem, Balthazar refers to a "de-installed landscape" (144) in and by which he remembers Man L'Oubliée. The poem is written from Balthazar's childhood perspective, and the landscape is seen through its specific elements rather than as a holistic frame. As in a painting, it is through the effects of light and shadow that these elements acquire the active enunciative power to endow Man L'Oubliée with the significance she is to hold for the child (145). The overall setting of a landscape is kept, but its meaning of representation is changed from the static frame of the Romantic painting into a de-installation or de-stratification of what is perceived. Landscape as a symbol is here displaced to the status of a sign that "creates a crisis for any concept of authority based on a system of recognition" (Bhabha 114). The poem refers to the subjective perspective underpinning the concept of "landscape" and to the historical context that determines this perspective. Thereby it performs a maneuver of resistance, not only against the colonial authority itself but also against its discursive mode and its repercussions in traditional nationalism. The way is now open for new narrations of land.

The "land-s(c/h)aping" in the manifestos of independence, on the other hand, does not challenge territorial connotations. *The Martinique Project* expresses an environmental concern closely connected to the management of "territory": agricultural lands are to be preserved through specific legal regulations, which will protect them against the growth of urban tourist areas. A public service regulating access to the land should be put in place. But the text also suggests that areas for tourism and urbanization should benefit from an equivalent protective administration. Even if this is not recognized, the need for regulating the two forms of "lands(c/h)aping" (tourist and agricultural) exemplifies how these landscapes have acted as discursive agents, exercising a certain influence on people's living conditions and ways of conceptualizing their lives. Adding a historical perspective, the "landscaping" of the sugar plantation was inextricably tied up with the market and price development of sugar at an international level. The Code Noir was imposed within the French colonial empire when the triangular trade prospered in the late seventeenth century (1685). This law prohibited sexual relations between people of African and European descent. Not only was it made on ideological racist grounds, it was also an economic measure, an expression of the arborescent genetic logic that ensured the continued existence of "black manpower" for the plantations.

Conclusion

The correlation between the narrations of nature and of cultural setting, which I have sought to place in a literary and historical perspective with reference to Romanticism and to the emergence of ecology as a scientific discipline, is also present in Chamoiseau's work. While some of the current Martinican nationalist arguments for independence present ecological and environmental concerns in a discourse dependent on the arborescent scaffolding of roots and territory, Chamoiseau's novel inscribes its characters in the environment by means of physical gestures and imagination, exploring the dynamics of the rhizomatic mapping. In Chamoiseau's text, the physical environment of Martinique is not confined to a category of "nature" as opposed to human civilization, nor is it isolated as a transcendent realm of sacredness. Recognizing these modes as part of the historical narration of Martinique and its population, Chamoiseau shows their limits by letting his characters deal with the components of nature in a certain kind of way. These components act as *subjects* that are both separate, yet inextricably parts of the *Relation* of everyday life. "Translating" Bhabha into Chamoiseau, I propose that in this process the sign of the sacred is not abolished but inserted into performative narrations, a process that alters its meaning and the impact of this meaning. At first, Balthazar's world mapping is a traditional drawing of territories, but his subsequent redrawing, along with the narrator's re-imagining of the warrior's life, transforms the territorial conceptualization into a conflictual narrative space in which the identity and "cultural embeddedness" of the subject of enunciation is continually contested. The sign of the sacred acquires its meaning from this ongoing battle.

The subjectivity of narrating and representing, and the chaos of multiple voices and conflicting desires are cherished and used to promote a certain effect. This effect conveys something as old-fashioned as the writer's political and social engagement. His objective remains to achieve independence for Martinique but also to avoid traditional nationalist concepts such as "territory." Even as he is dying, Balthazar's memories are narrated as indeterminate flashbacks that come to life through the power of the narrator's imagination. The gestures of the warrior's aching body are transferred into words, and, as in the life of an orchid, another blossoming occurs on the basis of an apparent festering.

Notes

1. Biblical Tales of the Last Gestures. The novel has to my knowledge not yet been translated into English. All translations are therefore my own.

2. My analysis is based on the following texts: (*a*) *The Declaration of Cayenne,* October 18, 1998, signed by nine political parties of independence from Martinique, Guadeloupe, and French Guyana; (*b*) *The Declaration of Basse-Terre,* published in 1999 by the presidents of the regional councils of Martinique, Guadeloupe, and French Guyana; (*c*) *The Martinique Project,* formulated in January 2000 as a concrete plan for the autonomous rule of Martinique by representatives from various parties and movements of independence from all three departments. The manifestos are available online (see bibliography), which is why I give no page references.

3. The narrator's name is also Chamoiseau. As in most of Chamoiseau's novels, the author creates a literary representation (and questioning!) of his own enunciative agency through the figure of the narrator.

4. In order to leave room for detailed discussions, I have chosen to focus on the narration of the tropical forest, leaving aside the role of the sea and the coastal areas, which is not to say that they are not important in the novel.

5. Glissant's somewhat hasty division between seemingly "harmonious" historical developments of the "atavistic" European cultures and the violent history of the "composite cultures" of the Caribbean (*Le discours* 23, 274; *Traité* 194–95) has been contested convincingly by Romuald Fonkoua.

6. Bennahmias and Roche. See also the Marxist readings of André Gorz in *Écologie et politique* (1975) and André Gorz and Michel Bosquet in *Écologie et liberté* (1977).

7. I am suggesting a reading along the lines of Bhabha's distinction between pedagogical and performative discursive agencies (142, 148, 245), similar to my reading of Chamoiseau's novel *Texaco* (1992) (Bojsen, "L'hybridation").

8. A wise person with a talent for physical and mental healing and profound knowledge of local history. Usually only men hold this title.

9. I am referring to Emile Benveniste's reading of Peirce. Throughout his works, Benveniste distinguishes between the act of enunciation and the enounced itself (*l'énoncé*) (see, in particular, 43–50, 80–81). Yet I am proposing to contextualize the enunciative signification, as Bhabha suggests, in its "cultural embeddedness" (36).

10. The word "machine" is used as in Benítez-Rojo's *The Repeating Island,* where he brilliantly translates the Guattarian and Deleuzian "machine" into the Caribbean context.

11. Their analysis deals in particular with the regionalist writers Daniel Thaly, *Le Jardin des Tropiques* (1911), *La Clarté du Sud* (1905); and Victor Duquesnay, *Les Martiniquaises* (1903).

12. See also chapter 6, "Planning a New Human Ecology" (196–236).

13. See Hugo, *Les rayons et les ombres,* 1030–31.

14. One example is Alfred de Musset's "La nuit d'août" 1835–37.

15. See Glissant's reservations regarding the word *comprendre* (understand) (*Poétique* 206).

16. See, in particular, Alphonse de Lamartine and Alfred de Vigny.

17. Chamoiseau uses the capitalized *Parole* not in the Saussurian way but as an emblem of a means to insert oneself as a subject in the world. In Caribbean history, the spoken word was used by slaves to resist the *comprehension* of the slave owners (Ludwig 18–20). The slaves constantly changed the meanings of words and invented new phrases as part of a discursive resistance (Chamoiseau and Confiant 59–61). As for Chamoiseau's exploration of the power of the spoken word, see *Solibo magnifique* (1988), *Texaco* (1992), and *Écrire en pays dominé* (1997).

Landscapes, Narratives, and Tropical Nature

Creole Modernity in Suriname

Ineke Phaf-Rheinberger

THE AIM OF this essay is to trace the conflict between tropical nature and Creole modernity in Suriname as it developed in colonial visual representations and as it has since been reimagined in three contemporary narratives by Cynthia McLeod, Clark Accord, and Astrid Roemer. Critics have typically treated these authors' attitudes toward plantation society and slave labor, but this essay will instead focus on the perception of the hinterland in their work so as to demonstrate how they overturn the colonial legacies of scientific appropriations of the tropics. Collectively, these authors argue that the chief crisis of Creole modernity remains the tenuous relationship between the metropolis and the tropical interior, and that until that relationship is directly confronted, neither the region's rich biodiversity nor its cultural and racial diversity will be adequately represented. The inhabitants of Suriname, Guyana, and French Guiana possess a cultural and ecological heritage shared with the Caribbean but also extending into Brazilian and Venezuelan Amazonian territories. Indeed, while the cities typically are located on the Atlantic or along the rivers that reach the Atlantic from the interior, it is this interior space and not the metropolitan centers of Europe that has historically challenged modernity in the region. In order to develop historical criteria for my argument, I will first present some important points related to a formative period of Dutch modernity in the Americas, specifically the Dutch presence in Brazil from 1630 to 1654. Thereafter, I will focus on the representations of this modernity in Surinamese narratives by McLeod, Accord, and Roemer published on the eve of the twenty-first century.

The Dutch Period in Brazil

The West India Company was founded in the Dutch Republic in 1621 with the explicit goal of gaining a share in the successful Portuguese exploitation of sugar and wood in Brazil. After its failure, Essequibo, Berbice, and

Suriname became the substitutes for the loss of Brazil. The Dutch pursued the alternative of a "New Brazil" with a successful plantation economy. The spirit of those days is particularly well preserved in the collections of natural science and art of the Dutch period in Brazil. These works are the outcome of the humanist court of architects, scientists, and painters in Recife-Mauritia during the eight years of governor John Maurits of Nassau in Pernambuco. One of these painters was Frans Post (1612–80), celebrated in Brazil as the first American landscape painter.

Brazil is central to studies that focus on tropical nature's sensibilities and its cultural stereotypes. Nancy Leys Stepan examines, in her book *Picturing Tropical Nature* (2001), the representations of the tropics in natural history, the new human sciences, and the history of medicine. Claiming that tropical nature lies at the heart of contemporary ecological debates, Stepan elaborates on the "characteristic tropes or modes of representation which were developed in the process of colonial expansion" (35). She insists that "naturalists failed to understand indigenous harvesting techniques and their suitability to the fragile ecological systems of the tropical forests" (54). Consequently, linking the superfertility of nature to the supposed low capacities of tropical peoples became a familiar trope in scientific opinions beginning in the eighteenth century. Only recently, in view of the struggle for survival of fragile ecological systems, have we seen writers and critics begin to question this trope.

The scientific representation of the tropics in many ways merges with Dutch art in the seventeenth century. In *The Art of Describing* (1989), Svetlana Alpers explains the emergence of a specific modernity. In her opinion, optical innovations caused a revolution in the observation of nature, or "looking within." Their impact on mapping, navigation, and architecture brought the work of some painters closer to mathematical constructions or technical designs than to humanist representations that refer to textual sources about human dramas for the logistics of their narratives. I add to Alpers's argument another motif of these abstract calculations, namely the representation of human engineering of untamed nature in the form of hydraulic drainage for agriculture in the polders. In order to illustrate this scientific modernity, it is sufficient to compare the oil canvas *The Fall of Icarus* (ca. 1556, Brussels) by Brueghel the Elder with *The Avenue at Middelharnis* (1689, Amsterdam) by Meindert Hobbema. Brueghel shows a farmer with a simple plough and a fisherman with a hook against the sophisticated background of a prosperous trading town on a bay. Hobbema's painting is different. We see only the silhouette of a city and its harbor against the horizon, whereas in the foreground an almost aristocratic posture is given to a specialist who controls the cultivation of the tree plantations in a polder landscape with a refined instrument.

It was this last type of specialization that came to Brazil in the seventeenth century. In recent debates about the Dutch period, Brazilian historians have outlined that the Dutch implanted a modern urban society but did not successfully take over the plantation economy from the Portuguese. It was precisely this urban modernity that was an important aspect of Post's work. As I have demonstrated elsewhere, in the heyday of his career, Post drew, designed, and elaborated on the creation of an infrastructure of drainage, roads, harbors, and bridges, and the documentary value of this aspect of his oeuvre is outstanding ("La utopía moderna" 12–15).

No personal letters have survived in which Post describes his impressions and feelings about Brazil. Therefore, it is necessary to explore his artwork in relation to a manuscript written in Latin by his contemporary, the famous Dutch philosopher Caspar Barlaeus. Barlaeus published *Rerum per octennium in Brasilia* (1647) in Amsterdam and gave a detailed account of the Dutch occupation in Brazil. He had never been in Brazil himself but obtained his information from personal contacts and abundant archival sources. We know nothing about Barlaeus's contacts with Post, only that his book contains a series of splendid illustrations of that artist. Among the moral values in Barlaeus's approach, apart from his extensive treatises on armed disputes and power relations, I distinguish three different points: (1) Barlaeus admires scientific inventions and thinks more highly of them than of any other possible analytical resource from which to obtain knowledge about nature; (2) he does not value intercultural relationships but is very interested in ethnological information about customs, behavior, and language; (3) he formulates a moral ethical code for transatlantic trade transactions influenced by the Roman idea that non-Roman trade partners—heathens—were capable of ethical and honest behavior. As I have argued elsewhere, Barlaeus thought the Roman code suitable and proper for global trade relationships in his own time ("Caspar Barlaeus y la ética" 132–34).

Barlaeus's confidence in technical innovation is typical of Dutch modernity, and Alpers's observations certainly confirm this spirit. This can also be said of a certain period in Post's work. His city views of Recife-Mauritia celebrate modern Protestant society in America, where it encounters significant differences in vegetation, animals, and people. Post used to place a typical tree of Brazil as a landmark at the left side of his landscapes. These trees represented the frontier between the European observer and tropical nature in the compositions. They also appeared on Post's city views of Olinda, the Portuguese capital of Brazil, with its convents, churches, and big houses in ruins. Otherwise, the administrative and commercial Dutch center of Recife-Mauritia is portrayed as being under construction with dikes, dams, bridges, and polders. In this case, the land-mark of the tropical tree is absent. Instead, nature is pictured as cultivated by specialists. Bruni describes the presence of the botanical garden next to the palace Friburgo as follows: "so we can say that Friburgo gardens were witness to the first botanical collection in Brazil originating from scientific practices and where had been set a perspective of the rational use of nat-ural resources" (Bruni 22).

The abundant documentation of Brazilian biodiversity in the work of Post and his contemporaries is highly esteemed today "at a moment when Brazil is awakening to the immense environmental responsibility of being the principal holder and guardian of its biological diversity, and of the important part of the remaining fragments of the gradually destroyed ecosystem" (Bruni 9). But critical attention also is paid to Post's interpre-tation of African slavery. His documentary precision in this regard is hailed by many critics.

This critical attention to slavery, however, started to manifest itself in art and literature chiefly in the eighteenth century, and therefore it is hard to find in Post's work (Kolfin 30). The differences between his portrayal of slaves and that, say, of John Gabriel Stedman, the author of a late eighteenth-century book on plantation society in Suriname, are more than clear on this point. Post was loyal to Dutch examples of relaxed and joyful people in carefully constructed landscapes, whereas Stedman's illustrations are particularly revealing about the harsh slavery conditions in the Dutch colony (Stedman, plates 4, 11, 22). This difference suggests the challenge that tropical nature presented to the artist's ability to address simultaneously the social ills and environmental features of his time. Once slavery became the focus, the impulse to document nature's particularities was portrayed in a separate view.

Recent Surinamese Narratives

Northeast Brazil, Suriname—the former Dutch Guiana—and also neigh-boring Guyana and French Guiana all have in common that contempo-rary social dynamics are still profoundly marked by the past pattern of plantation society. But given the extent of the natural environment of the interior, the former plantation areas are less relevant. Large parts of the Guianas belong to the rain-forest zone, and Suriname is particularly fascinating in this respect. The country has an undisturbed hinterland and one of the lowest population densities of any tropical country on the globe. Only about 5 percent of Suriname's inhabitants live in the interior, with the rest concentrated in the capital city, Paramaribo, and the small towns of the coastal region. Paramaribo lies inward on the Suriname River, not far from the river delta that borders the Atlantic Ocean and connects with the southern and eastern part of the interior.

The ecosystem of the interior is nowadays seen as relevant for the conservation of biological diversity. This was different in the seventeenth century, when the first plantations were located along the inland riverbanks. Albert Helman (1903–96) identified strongly with European migration to this plantation area in 1686 and paid much attention to the difference between the tropical environment and Europe in two early works. He described the expectations and impressions of a Huguenot family arriving on the ship from Holland to Suriname, when they "saw only trees, so dense that it seemed impossible to pass through them. The dark green wall was almost black." Sailing on the river, they observed the coastal woods, "tall and dense, green in the underbrush, green along the trunks, green right up to the high canopies—a medley altogether that seemed to form one closed roof" (*Silence in Flames* 73–74).

The rain-forest coast and the riverbank are typical landmarks before the arrival in the small town. In *De stille plantage* (The Silent Plantation, 1931), Paramaribo looks similar to Recife-Mauritia with the dikes, bridges, canals, and botanical garden. In Helman's second novel about the same family, *De laaiende stilte* (*Silence in Flames*, 1952), in contrast, it becomes clear that this urban outline was not what he was looking for. He now moves to live far from town in the interior, where his main characters encounter violence, lack of humanity, and the unpredictable power of "nature" on the plantations.

Considering this shift from the city to the hinterland, it might be assumed that Helman intended to stage emancipation from a Eurocentric vision, but, in fact, no such emancipation occurs. His European migrants do not succeed in resisting the violent forces and have to return to Europe. Helman argues that, for them, the gradual appropriation of the tropical surroundings is impossible in the long run. In *Frontier Society: A Social Analysis of the History of Surinam* (1971), the historian Rudolf van Lier goes even further. The country itself is a "frontier society" by virtue of the differences between the cities and people of the coastal zones and riverbanks and the tropical interior with its Amerindians and the Maroons. The urban zone—with the Creoles, East Indians, Indonesians, and Jews—is very much connected with European civilization. Behind this frontier reigns the darkness of nature's unpredictability, and this division enforces the maintenance of a rigid hierarchical system among the different groups, especially the Amerindians and Maroons. Van Lier asserts that when he spent seven months doing research in Paramaribo in 1947 and 1948, he was "struck by the degree to which ideas engendered by past situations still exercise a direct influence on the judgment of present events" (*Frontier Society* 1). He defines the Creoles of African and European descent as the first native group to be involved in the Dutch colonial administration. They were the driving force in the urban social framework characterized by those sharp divisions.

This was the Paramaribo that Helman was familiar with, and whose dynamics were still influential in the 1970s, when van Lier's book came out in English. In this same decade, a group of young Surinamese writers started to publish and began to revise our understanding of the geographical dynamics of Surinamese modernity. These were the days of political awakening. Elections, party propaganda, and national expectations set the tone on the eve of Independence, 25 November 1975. In general terms, this awakening was an urban phenomenon, and Astrid Roemer, one of its most characteristic representatives, has not stopped writing ever since. Roemer focuses on contemporary urban life and published a trilogy (1995–98) about life in Paramaribo since the Second World War. Because of space limitations, I will discuss only the last volume of her trilogy, *Was getekend* (Signed, 1998), which I will compare with two other novels: *De konigin van Paramaribo* (The Queen of Paramaribo, 1999), by Clark Accord, and *De vrije negerin Elisabeth: Gevangene van kleur* (The Free Black Woman Elisabeth: Prisoner of Color, 2000), by Cynthia McLeod. The prolific novelistic production in those years at the turn of the twenty-first century expresses the urge to know more about the cultural history of Suriname. Each of the writers represents a wide palette of orientations. McLeod authored several historical novels, and this book is based on the life story of an exceptional black woman in the eighteenth century, Elisabeth Samson (1715–71). Accord made his debut with *De koningin van Paramaribo,* based on the life story of another exceptional black woman, Wilhelmina Rijburg (1902–81). In contrast to McLeod and Accord, Roemer develops her contemporary characters as purely fictional constructions.

McLeod's research on Elisabeth Samson reveals that Elisabeth was repeatedly mentioned in history books because as a black woman she "succeeded" in marrying a white European man, which was forbidden by law. But no more details were known about her life and motivations.

McLeod has filled this gap and published a historical report as well as a novel about her findings. Elisabeth, the daughter of slaves, was born free and became the richest woman of Paramaribo. Her money bought her entrance into the highest circles of colonial society. However, McLeod does not give her book a happy ending. Elisabeth dies of despair when she suddenly senses the lack of meaning in her life. Always striving to be equal to the whites, she did not develop a strong identity of her own.

Elisabeth Samson lived in Paramaribo, not far from the Waterkant, the avenue with the most impressive buildings on the bank of the Suriname River. The Waterkant is the visual logo of Suriname's capital city: it has symbolic kinship with the presidential palace, the botanical garden, the ministerial buildings, and the lively market scenes on the street. In Accord's *De koningin van Paramaribo,* Wilhelmina Rijburg operated in this area as a prominent prostitute. She was known as Maxi Linder, a person about whom many legends and myths still survive. Besides being most successful in her profession, Maxi Linder was known for her charity. She often financed the education of poor children and supported others through her contacts in the business and political world. However, Accord reveals that, toward the end of her life, Rijburg was treated as an outcast. Her money was gone, and "respectable" inhabitants of Paramaribo no longer wanted to be identified with her in public. In the sense that she was left alone in poverty, Rijburg also died tragically.

The main characters in McLeod's and Accord's novels are of Creole descent. They are citizens of Paramaribo and have regular contact with Holland and with the Dutch administration. Roemer, who shares this same Creole background, carries out a radical change in the stereotypical urban décor. Her Creole community perceives the atmosphere loaded with family and political violence. The city more or less falls apart because its inhabitants are planning to travel to and study and live in the Netherlands. This is not the case with the protagonist, Ilya, whose professional career unfolds in Suriname itself. He leaves his regular profession as a schoolteacher in Paramaribo and goes to live on his own piece of land in the outskirts, where he builds a house and cultivates different products in his garden. In eleven chapters, the history of his life is developed chronologically within the framework of a countdown, from 1:12 a.m. until 10:12 a.m., the length of the nine-hour flight in a DC 10 from Amsterdam to Zanderij, the airport near Paramaribo. This countdown alludes to the fact that Ilya is awaiting the arrival of his wife (from whom he is separated) and two children to join him for his fiftieth birthday. At 10:12 a.m., the countdown stops when the plane crashes just before landing. All of the passengers die in the accident, and Ilya seems to be the only survivor of his family. In the final chapter of the book, however, it is revealed that Ilya's wife and children were not on the plane, but that another woman, Foetida, his first love, was onboard instead, together with his mother.

In all three novels, the characters' ambivalence toward Creole society in Paramaribo is evident. McLeod's Elisabeth seems to be the exponent of successful social mobility in a highly divided plantation society. This pattern is already present in Post's canvasses of urban Brazil, in which he depicts the typical Creole woman of African descent on her way to material success in the city (Phaf-Rheinberger, "'Und Dideldumdei'" and "La utopía moderna"). In McLeod's Paramaribo, Elisabeth Samson is the ultimate personification of this dynamic. She lives in a house with expensive furniture and other objects of value. The writer incorporates the habitual views of plantation houses near the riverbank. The rain forest, meanwhile, is not important for the plot. Moreover, Elisabeth seems to distance herself as much as possible from tropical nature, a typical behavior in the urban society to which she belongs.

Whereas McLeod chose Elisabeth Samson—the black owner and manager of plantations—as the protagonist, Accord prefers a more contemporary black woman. Maxi Linder applies a different strategy for social acceptance, operating as a prostitute who dismisses ethnic or cultural differences. High society, for Maxi Linder, was something she belonged to in an indirect way. She knew intimate details of many families in Paramaribo. Her own family was of modest but respectable descent: her father earned a regular salary with his work in the rain forest. He felt that Wilhelmina had betrayed him by becoming a prostitute. In Accord's novel, therefore, the parents and the interior disappear from Maxi Linder's optic. The author emphasizes the urban setting of his novel by inserting a few photographs of central streets or historical war events in Paramaribo, as well as a photograph of the real Wilhelmina Rijburg on her deathbed in April 1981.

This dramatic end contrasts with the one in Roemer's Paramaribo—the abrupt death of the two women on the plane. Ilya knew Foetida since he was a boy and had always wanted to marry her. But she, unfortunately, was in love with another man, a married diplomat, for whom she moved to Holland and became a Dutch citizen. Ilya's mother was Dutch, and after having lived her married life in Suriname, she returned, after her husband's death, to her native country. Without any doubt, the disappearance of these women at the end of Roemer's book is conceived of as an act of liberation. Ilya finally feels himself free to declare his love to the young woman who lives in his house in the outskirts of Paramaribo without any intention at all of leaving Suriname.

To stress the meaning of this happy ending, Roemer elaborates on the motif of Grimm's fairy tales. She remarks that Grimm did not comment on their local meanings in his collections. The writer herself intends to do the opposite by bringing the legends in her country into the context of her narrative structure. Her characters are familiar with oral traditions, which rituals are performed with the rhythms of the drums and a combination of the Djuka-language, Sranan-tongo, and Surinamese-Dutch. It sounds "Festive. Familiar. Estranging also" (Feestelijk. Eigen. Vervreemdend ook) (212–13; my translation).

Roemer frames this link with the oral and rhythmical performances in a specific narrative device. The plane from Amsterdam crashes against the *kankantri,* the giant of the forest, the typical Surinamese *kapokboom,* a tree of American origin. The tree belongs to the family of the *Bombacaceae,* the *ceiba pentandra,* called *samaúma* in Brazil, *ceiba* in Colombia, Cuba, Peru, Mexico, and Venezuela, and *kapokier* in French Guiana. It is a wild silk cotton tree with hard wood whose cotton is used for pillows and mattresses, for weaving and medical cures. The tree was already described in the earliest Spanish chronicles on America as "trees with cotton, trees with wool, mocarix" (Pardo and Terrada, *Las primeras noticias* 274) and equally documented by Dutch botanists in Brazil in the seventeenth century. Maria Sybille Merian reproduced the tree in her book on metamorphoses at the beginning of the eighteenth century, for which she did the fieldwork in Suriname. Stedman also dedicated a fragment to the *kankantri:*

They also bring their Offerings to the *Wild Cotton tree* which the Negroes Call *Cot-tan teeree* and which they Adore with high Reverence. This Proceeds / said an Old Black Man to Me / from the following Juditious Cause, having no Churches on the Coast of Guinea and this Tree being the largest and most beautiful Growing there. Our People Assembling often under its branches to keep free from the Heavy Show'rs of rain and Schorching Sun Shine, when they Are Going to be instructed; do not You Christians Pay the Same homage to Your bibles &. We well know that our tree is but A Wooden Logg Covered With Leaves of Green. Nor is your book Assuredly any more than a Piece of Lumber Composed of Leaves of Paper.—Under this tree the Gadoman or Priest Delivers his Lectures and for which the Vulgar Negroes have much Veneration, that they Will not Cut it down upon any Consideration Whatever. (*Narrative of a Five Years' Expedition* 520–21)

In contemporary Amerindian and Maroon oral history, the *kankantri* continues to play a crucial role. Albert Helman (1977), for instance, encounters the tree in the legends of the Caribs at the Maroni River, in which they explain the metamorphosis into an animal. Edgar Cairo (1984) places him in the center of a *winti* ceremony, during which a Kromanti spirit possesses people. Albert Mungroo (1986) depicts the lamentation of the *kankantri* to remember the tragedy of the hate between the two brothers Akwawé and Dombé. And Harry Jong Loy (1993) understands the *kankantri* as the mother-tree of the invisible Maroon village in the interior, No-Meri-Mi-Kondre (Don't-bother-me country), without exit to the outside world.

In the painting of Post, as I have mentioned, tropical trees disappeared as landmarks when he portrayed urban modernity with its social hierarchy without critical comment. Obviously, recent Surinamese narratives are completely different in this regard. McLeod and Accord judge the possibilities for social mobility in the hierarchical structures of the past as tragic. Roemer, in contrast, searches for a radical change in this tragic fate and widens the cultural horizon considerably. Doris Hambuch studied the implications of the displacements from Suriname to the Old World in Roemer's work and argues that the author succeeds in representing "all . . . ethnicities, and especially their interactions, throughout her trilogy" ("Displacements" 150). She uses this pattern of interactive cultural dynamics for her portrayal of the pre- and post-independence period: "extensive flashbacks, however, allow the narrated time to cover all of this century's second half" ("Displacements" 153).

In contrast with Barlaeus's and Post's moral code in the seventeenth century, these Creole narratives seem almost exclusively concerned with intercultural relationships. When they do not exist, life is tragic; when they do exist, the *kankantri* intervenes to make an end to violence and drama. In accordance with the philosophy in the essay by Ngũgĩ wa Thiong'o (2002), Roemer's *kankantri*-accident clearly insists on the violence implied in "breaking the mental contract with the colonizer's country" (Thiong'o 141). The community has to develop without the stress from this outside pressure, which produces a blockade for removing the obstacles of social discrimination within.

The *kankantri*, therefore, functions as a landmark between the inside and the outside world in Roemer's novel. He is responsible for the disenchantment of Creole society of Paramaribo and the Surinamese coastal zones, populated by the phantoms of Dutch modernity in past and present. In this sense, these narratives can be understood as making a plea to overcome the scientific view of the seventeenth century. Its hierarchies have caused a lack of balance and a psychological trauma. The arguments for this situation have been explained in several studies. Stepan argues that the inner dynamics of the rain-forest zone (cultivation, strategies of survival, etc.) were systematically disregarded in science and visual art. Alpers theorizes that the Dutch modern viewpoint has introduced an alternative to a humanist reading of landscape and city life. When relating these interpretations to recent Creole literature, it is clear that it conceives the tropical-landscape neurosis as a result of the "objective" conceptualization of their society. Creole modernity, therefore, is still under pressure when negotiating the relationship with the inhabitants of the interior. This point might be clarified by comparing this debate in Suriname with a critical reading of contemporary narratives in French Guiana, Guyana, Venezuela, and Brazil concerning the interpretation of this same traumatic situation against the background of the historical representation of urban modernity in a tropical environment.

The Uses of Landscape

Ecocriticism and Martinican Cultural Theory

Eric Prieto

ECOCRITICISM TENDS to have a strong activist component. Like gender, ethnic, and Marxist modes of criticism, it uses literature to promote a political agenda—in this case an environmental one. This, no doubt, is as it should be. Such politically oriented modes of criticism can play a real role in shaping the values of readers and improving the quality of public debate over important policy issues. Nevertheless, it is essential that activist critics guard against allowing the urgency of their political views to interfere with the slow work of dispassionate exegesis and the patient search for objective truth. Otherwise they risk skewing their results or presenting them in a way that is too easily dismissed by skeptics.

Even more important, perhaps, is the need to avoid merely reiterating the programmatic platitudes of the field. Critics should put their core beliefs to the test as rigorously as possible, refining, revising, and even rejecting them when necessary. For this reason, I believe that it is useful to reread ecologically minded works against the grain, by asking three kinds of questions: First, what are the ideological presuppositions that structure the deployment of environmental themes in a given work? Second, how is the environment being represented, and what does that mode of representation imply about the way it is being used? Third, what, if any, impact will the work have on real attitudes toward the environment? How does it change the way we think about the environment?

These are the kinds of questions I will be asking in this essay. Accordingly, I will make no attempt to argue for the need to preserve, protect, or promote the environment or the values associated with it. (I take this as a given and trust that that argument will be made elsewhere in this volume.) Instead, I will focus on a small set of key works of Martinican literature, attempting to answer the three questions just mentioned with as much accuracy and depth as possible.

Early Problems in the Ecology of Disalienation

Much of the literature and cultural theory of the French West Indies has been devoted to overcoming the alienating cultural and social attitudes fostered during the colonial era. There is a strong sense that the Eurocentric attitudes and assimilationist policies of the colonial period have made it difficult to see the Caribbean world as it actually is, since it is always filtered through the distorting lens of imposed Eurocentric norms. Consequently, we often find that the discourse of nature in Caribbean literature functions as a metaphor for the need to strip away the European spectacles that have been imposed on West Indians over four hundred years of European domination. In this sense, getting back to nature means seeing things as they truly are, developing a specifically Caribbean sensibility attuned to local realities. This is not to say that nature is never an object of representation in its own right, but that postcolonial depictions of the Martinican landscape are consciously inflected by ideological debates to a degree that is unusual outside of the Caribbean. Indeed, one of the most interesting ways to track the evolution of Martinican cultural theory is to follow changes in the way the environment has been represented in its literature.[1]

In Aimé Césaire's *Cahier d'un retour au pays natal,* for example, the ideological determinants of the landscape imagery are perfectly clear. Césaire explicitly identifies Négritude with nature and opposes it to the technological achievements of Europe, identified with the city ("my negritude is neither a tower nor a cathedral . . . It plunges into the red flesh of the soil," *Collected Poetry* 68; my translation). By allying Négritude with nature, Césaire is able to associate it with a moral order superior to the technological imperatives ordering European civilization. It is impossible today to accept this kind of binary distribution of faculties along racial lines, but in the colonial context of the 1940s such imagery had an important role to play in putting to rest the myth of European superiority embodied in such expressions as the "white man's burden" and the *mission civilisatrice.*

From an ecocritical perspective, however, what is most notable about the *Cahier* is its almost complete lack of interest in nature per se. Despite the attention lavished on detailing the flora, fauna, and topography of Martinique, Césaire's poem is not really *about* the Martinican environment at all. On the contrary, all depictions of the local environment are integrated into the allegorical struggle between European and African values. In this sense, Césaire cannot be considered an environmental thinker; he is, rather, a political thinker who uses environmental imagery as a rhetorical tool for advancing a sociopolitical argument about *human* nature. To be sure, Césaire's argument relies on some implicit assumptions about nature as a general category (that is, that Europeans could learn a lot from Africans about the importance of maintaining contact with nature), but his depictions of the environment are entirely subordinated to his argument about social and political justice. It is as if he can only justify using landscape images when they are structured by a sociopolitical logic.

Césaire's attitude is more easily understood if we remember that the thinkers around him at the journal *Tropiques* were equivocal about the positive value of Martinique's natural beauty. There are, to be sure, serious attempts to embrace the environmental specificity of the French Antilles (see, for example, the Nonon and Stehlé pieces listed in the bibliography), but there is also quite a bit of suspicion about succumbing to the island's paradisiacal qualities. Suzanne Césaire's articles in *Tropiques* are of particular interest in this regard. In "Misère d'une poésie" (The Poverty of Our Poetry), she excoriates earlier regional poets for their exoticist tendencies, accusing them of presenting idealized images of the tropical environment beholden to European sensibilities and poetic forms. Similarly, in "Le grand camouflage" (The Great Camouflage), she associates the natural beauty of the islands with camouflage, a veil hiding the economic and social misery of the island's populace. She incites poets to pay attention not to the tropical foliage draped languorously over the mornes, but "to the hungers, fears, hatreds, and ferocity that burn in the valleys" (273).

Equally important from an ecocritical point of view is her "Malaise d'une civilisation" (Malaise of a Civilization), which attempts to diagnose problems in the relationship between Caribbeans and their environment. She seems initially to adopt a position close to the one espoused by her husband in the *Cahier.* Thus she characterizes the prototypical Martinican as "l'homme plante" (vegetal man) and emphasizes his "Ethiopian sensibility," which makes him more inclined to abandon himself to the rhythms of nature (46). Predictably (at least for readers of Aimé Césaire), she argues that the "durable and fertile harmony" between man and nature has been upset by the forced imposition of European values on the African majority and that this oppression must be lifted if the ecological balance is to be restored. But, as Maryse Condé points out in her reading of this article, Suzanne Césaire also makes a much less predictable move, explaining the specificity of Caribbean society with a concept that is totally absent from her husband's thought, that of *métissage:* "The [Martinican] race is the result of continual mixing [*brassage*]" ("Malaise," 48; Condé, "Unheard Voice" 65). She presents this *brassage* as a central feature of Martinican society, suggesting a way to move away from the still essentialist, bipolar vision of her husband and toward the evolutionarily inclined environmental discourse favored by later thinkers such as Édouard Glissant.

Glissant's Dams and Dykes

Glissant is a key figure for any ecocritical study of Caribbean environmental literature, not only because he is one of the giants of West Indian cultural theory in general, and not only because his literary works overflow with environmental imagery, but also because he was able to complement his literary interest in environmental imagery with an ongoing public discourse on real-world environmental concerns. It is important to note, however, that this second environmental vocation seems to have come about rather slowly.

Throughout the early part of his career, Glissant uses the landscape in an allegorical manner very close to that of Césaire. We can see this in *Le discours antillais* (*Caribbean Discourse*), where the landscape becomes legible only once it is read as a function of its historical associations. Thus he writes: "Our landscape is its own monument: the trace that it signifies is visible from below. It's all history" (32; my translation). It is clear here that he is reading the physical attributes of the landscape in purely symbolic terms, subordinating them entirely to the history of its inhabitants: "Our landscape . . . is all history." This impression is confirmed in the passage leading up to this remark, in which he sketches out an allegorical landscape of Martinique and concludes: "There are then periods which are spread out underneath our appearances, from the Heights to the sea, from the North to the South, from the forest to the sands. Flight [*marronnage*] and refusal, anchoredness and endurance, Elsewhere and dreams" (32; my translation). Here, the social and psychological states of the second sentence are mapped onto the geographical points mentioned in the first. Significantly, this is the same set of associations he uses in his first novel, *La Lézarde,* to which I now turn.

Like Césaire's *Cahier, La Lézarde* approaches naïve allegory in the straightforward, one-to-one correspondences it sets up between history and landscape. And like Césaire's, Glissant's depictions of the environment are always overdetermined by his political agenda. What has changed is the vision of history that structures Glissant's environmental imagery. Whereas Césaire had figured Martinican history in Marxist terms, as a cataclysmic conflict between city and country, Glissant envisions it as a progressive hybridization or *métissage* of the two. To Césaire's revolutionary view of history, Glissant responds with a more properly evolutionary one.

Still, despite the tendency toward allegory, *La Lézarde* does display the beginnings of a serious reflection on the natural environment. The novel spells out a set of normative prescriptions about the proper relationship between man and nature and suggests a number of practical recommendations, albeit not necessarily the ones an environmentalist would choose today. Thus the narrator speaks of the necessity for cooperation between man and nature but emphasizes the need to domesticate it, by building dykes and dams, for example, so that the river can be made to nourish the city before being sent on to the sea. The principle of cooperation is paramount here—man must learn to work with the river rather than exploiting its resources ruthlessly—but there is never any question of leaving the river undisturbed. If man must learn to understand his place within the natural order, it is not out of some metaphysical or aesthetic deference to undomesticated nature, but so that he can put its resources to better use.[2]

By the 1990s, when Glissant publishes *Poétique de la relation* and *Traité du tout monde,* his thinking on both the environmental and cultural needs of Martinique will have changed in a number of important ways. Concepts like *Antillanité* and *métissage,* first developed in *Le discours antillais,* give way before more properly dialectical concepts like *tout-monde* and—the master concept of his mature cultural theory—creolization. This evolution in his thought takes place largely in response to the ongoing cultural debates (some would say wars) that have preoccupied Caribbean intellectuals since the 1960s and that reached their peak in Martinique with the emergence of the Créolité movement. Before turning to Glissant's later environmental writings, then, it will be useful to consider the environmental discourse of the Creolists.

Creole Environmentalism in Chamoiseau's *Texaco*

No doubt the most complete exploration of the Creolist attitude toward the environment is given in Patrick Chamoiseau's novel *Texaco.* There we find that nature plays a critical role. Like Glissant and Césaire, Chamoiseau emphasizes the need to live in harmony with nature. He condemns the tendency of city dwellers to forget this need and promotes renewed contact with the island's Creole heritage as a way to restore it. Unlike Césaire's *Cahier* or Glissant's *Lézarde,* then, Chamoiseau's novel explores the relationship between his cultural theory and environmental attitudes in a fairly extensive way. Moreover, those attitudes have far-reaching implications for public policy, especially as concerns the need for an ecologically sound approach to the construction of the urban environment. The framing narrative of the novel, which revolves around the changing attitudes of a character known as the urban planner, makes this environmental message explicit.

The urban planner initially comes to Texaco—a shantytown on the outskirts of Fort-de-France—in order to prepare it for demolition. A civil servant in the mayor's office, he is predisposed to see Texaco as a nuisance: an unsanitary, crime-ridden settlement of squatters living in precarious structures erected illegally on land that is, to top it all off, dangerously close to a petroleum depot. He is eventually convinced, however, that marginal neighborhoods like Texaco must not only be allowed to exist, but must be actively supported by the government. They form what he comes to call an "urban mangrove," a transitional area between city and country that plays an essential role in the ecology of the city.[3]

This "urban mangrove" metaphor, borrowed from the same set of nature metaphors used by Césaire and Glissant, is central to the novel's meaning. Just as the swampy terrain of mangrove forests allows a mutually beneficial exchange of nutrients and waste between land and sea, the ring of shantytowns surrounding Fort-de-France allows an analogous exchange between city and country. It acts, for example, as a kind of staging point for new arrivals from the countryside while also providing a refuge for all those who are unable to find shelter in the city center. In this sense, it provides a vital service for the city: a kind of safety valve that helps to relieve the demographic pressures that might otherwise overwhelm it.

Equally important to the environmental message of the novel is Chamoiseau's belief that this urban mangrove constitutes one of the last remaining reservoirs of Creole culture on the island. From an environmentalist perspective, this is important because one of the primary attributes of Creole culture, at least as Chamoiseau describes it, is its profound understanding of the island's natural environment. Rather than trying to impose their will on the landscape through sheer force—paving over it, as the richer, Europeanized denizens of the *en-ville*, or city center, tend to do—the inhabitants of Creole neighborhoods like Texaco have maintained a more direct, vital link to the natural environment. Signs of this include traditions like the Creole garden. This is a practice born of necessity (subsistence farming), but it is particularly well adapted to the needs of those who live on the periphery of mainstream society and its supply lines. Moreover, it is presented by Chamoiseau as a viable alternative to the destructive monoculture of plantations, which threatens the biodiversity of the islands and leaves crops susceptible to parasites and pests. Thus, although it might appear to an outsider as a particularly humble form of agriculture, Chamoiseau interprets the practice positively, presenting it as a kind of organic gardening *avant la lettre*. He provides a similar defense of Creole herb lore. To an outsider, herb lore might appear to be based on a bundle of superstitions, but Chamoiseau presents it as a homeopathic alternative to modern pharmaceuticals. Endowed with the prestige of a generations-long study of the land, it has the added advantage of being within the financial means of the impoverished, marginal groups that have kept Creole culture alive.

There is, then, a straightforward environmental discourse in *Texaco*, emphasizing two of the vital roles that Creole neighborhoods have played in Martinican history: limiting the damage caused by sudden periods of massive urbanization, and perpetuating the environmentally friendly cultural practices of Martinique's rural past. Still, it is far from clear that the cultural practices of Chamoiseau's Creoles are allied to ecological wisdom in any essential way. It is significant in this regard that the novel's historical narrative, which spans several generations, is organized into "eras," or "ages," each of which is defined by the primary building materials used in the construction of Creole shanties. The first of these materials is natural (straw), and the second is almost natural (crate wood), but the last two are as artificial as they come (asbestos and concrete). What do these materials have in common? Only that they are the ones that were ambiently available at the time. Whether scavenged from other sites or donated by the city government, they all reflect the need to make do with whatever materials are at hand.

It might be thought that these changes in building materials are meant as a sign of degradation and loss, with the progressive shift toward industrial materials transforming Martinique's natural landscape into an urban wasteland. But this is not the conclusion that Chamoiseau draws. He suggests, on the contrary, that the industrial materials used by recent generations have become as much a part of the Creole environment as the natural materials favored by previous generations. In other words, although Creole culture has traditionally seemed to have an aptitude for living in harmony with nature, that aptitude may have been more a product of necessity than of any built-in affinity for the environment. Hunger and scarcity have long been central features of life in poor Creole communities, and they, more than anything else, explain why such practices as subsistence farming, scavenging, squatting, and *bricolage* have become such characteristic features of Creole culture. In this sense, the environmentally friendly features of Creole culture are probably best understood as by-products of the more general struggle to survive in times of scarcity.

For these reasons, I would argue that the concept of nature at work in *Texaco* cannot be defined in opposition to culture or to the built environment of cities; it must be understood, rather, as a process, the process of adaptive evolution. Chamoiseau is ultimately more interested in understanding the adaptive strategies that have enabled Creole culture to survive than in extolling the virtues of the natural environment from an aesthetic or moralistic point of view. This is important for Chamoiseau because it is this process of adaptation to local conditions that enables him to certify Creole culture as authentically Martinican. Although it is not indigenous to the island (only Arawak and Carib cultures could make that claim), it grew up spontaneously in response to local conditions. In this sense, Creole culture is "natural" to Martinique in a way that its African, European, and Asian source cultures are not.[4] We could say, then, that Chamoiseau's defense of Creole culture has a strong evolutionary component bordering on environmental determinism. He defines the legitimacy and authenticity of Creole culture in terms of the progressive adaptation to changing conditions that enabled it to survive in the crucible of colonial history.

This evolutionary bent of Chamoiseau's defense of Creoleness has important implications for the future of Creole culture. It is clear that the nature of the Creole struggle for survival has changed dramatically since the *départementalisation* of Martinique. Thanks to the modern French social security network now in place, adequate nutrition and shelter are no longer the desperately urgent preoccupations they once were. Freed to a great extent from the day-to-day struggle for individual survival, contemporary Martinicans have begun to develop new cultural practices in response to the new challenges and opportunities facing them. For better or worse, many of the most typical features of traditional Creole culture—including the Creole gardens, oral traditions, and shantytown neighborhoods described in such loving detail by Chamoiseau—are mutating into new and often unrecognizable forms, while others have already devolved into folkloric shadows of their former selves. (Witness the madras displays and dance demonstrations featured at the tourist hotels.)

So what does all of this imply for the future of environmental policy in Martinique? The only way to answer this question is to ask what impact these new economic and social realities will have on the cultural values that shape environmental attitudes and practices. I'll conclude this essay, then, by considering some of the ways in which recent developments like *départementalisation* and globalization have influenced contemporary environmental attitudes in Martinique.

Martinique Biologique?

Judging by the recent "Manifeste pour un projet global" (Manifesto for a Global Project), whose signatories include Glissant and Chamoiseau, local environmental issues have caught the attention of Martinique's leading cultural theorists as never before.[5] The central proposal of the "Manifeste" is a project to invest heavily in transforming the entire French-Caribbean region into a green zone, with an economy focused on the production of high-quality organic products aimed at an international luxury market.

In order to understand how this ecological project relates to the cultural concerns of Glissant and Chamoiseau, we'll need first to understand the economic problem the "Manifeste" is trying to address. The French West Indies find themselves today in a Catch-22 situation: *départementalisation* has undeniably raised the standard of living and eased social tensions in the region, but it has also cemented it into a position of perpetual dependence. In a paradox that has become familiar in the neocolonial era, the region's former oppressors have become its benefactors, but their new-found generosity has created new forms of victimhood. The region's industries now depend on French subsidies and protected trade relationships for their survival; much of its populace has learned to depend on French social security allocations; and infrastructural maintenance and development depend on French investment and economic aid. This means that the region can't achieve political and economic independence without making huge, perhaps unbearable, sacrifices. In Martinique, for example, the population has grown to a size well beyond what could be supported by local agricultural production (with almost all necessities being shipped in from France). Meanwhile, high wages (which are protected by French law) make the island's workers uncompetitive with those from other Caribbean islands, while its small size, relative isolation, and tenuous supply lines make economies of scale impossible to realize.

The region's entrenched economic and political dependence on France has in turn created a host of sociocultural problems. They are partially masked by the relatively high standard of living but are no less real for that. Among these, the "Manifeste" emphasizes a kind of generalized infantilization of the populace. Although one-third of the population is unemployed in Martinique, rampant consumerism continues unabated, thanks in large part to generous government assistance and the availability of easy credit. This combination of comfort and a lack of opportunity has fostered widespread political apathy and a resigned acceptance of the status quo. Moreover, the increasing penetration of global markets into

Martinique's economy (and the attendant proliferation of foreign cultural commodities) threatens to further disrupt the society, discouraging local production and destabilizing identities.

The "Manifeste" emphasizes the interrelatedness of the economic and sociocultural problems: since the latter is a consequence of the former, it cannot be addressed in isolation. Any solution to the cultural problem presupposes an economic strategy.

The economic strategy proposed in the "Manifeste" is to mobilize the entire society in an effort to transform each of the Caribbean *Départements* into a "terre biologique" (organic zone). This would require, as a first step, cleaning up the region's environment to the point that its ecological health would attract international attention. That would, in turn, give rise to an attractive brand image that could be used to market its products to the rest of the world. The region would no longer attempt to compete on price, competing instead on quality. It would specialize in "value-added" products with large profit margins like organic produce, ecotourism, and artisanal rum and would target luxury niches in marketplaces around the world. Combined with the sense of shared mission necessary to carry out such a project, this economic strategy would, it is hoped, promote a sense of regional pride while revitalizing local economies, thereby creating the conditions necessary for economic self-sufficiency, administrative auton- omy, and eventually political independence.

It's not at all clear to me how viable this proposal actually is.[6] Nonethe- less, it is notable for its attempt to reconcile the socially progressive poli- tics of its authors with the hard-nosed market-oriented thinking of the neoliberal marketplace. Whatever the weaknesses of this strategy may be, its authors have sought to lend weight to their recommendations by adapting them to the realities of the global marketplace, embracing the challenge of economic competition rather than complaining about it or wishing it away.

Even, then, if this project turns out to be unworkable, it provides at least one important lesson for ecocritics and activists of all stripes: the need to frame our recommendations in relation to the larger context of the polity's overall economic, political, social, and cultural needs. A proposal like the "pays biologique" manifesto is more likely to achieve the political objec- tives of environmentalists than are idealistic appeals to noble sentiments because it shows that environmentally friendly policies can be good for everyone, even those who have no particular interest in ecological issues. It presents investment in the environment as the means to an end, rather than an end in itself, and attempts to show that such investment can benefit the economy rather than burdening it. Ecocriticism, I believe, would do well to follow this lead, promoting environmental values by exploring the interrelation between ecological issues and others that are not immediately recognizable as such. Only in this way—by seeing the big picture—will ecocriticism be able to make real contributions to the complex, multivariabled debates that must take place in the political search for the greatest good.

Notes

1. I have studied this link in two previous articles ("The Poetics of Place" and "Landscaping Identity in Contemporary Caribbean Literature"), so rather than retrace that genealogy here, I will limit my analysis to concerns relating to the ecocritical enterprise.

2. For more complete analyses of the environmental themes in *La Lézarde,* see Michael Dash's introduction to the English translation of the novel; his article "Le cri du morne"; and my discussion of *La Lézarde* in "Landscaping Identity."

3. It is worth noting here that the urban planner is modeled on Serge Letchimy, author of *De l'habitat précaire à la ville: l'exemple martiniquais,* and successor to Aimé Césaire as mayor of Fort-de-France. Chamoiseau clearly took much from Letchimy's account of informal urbanization in writing *Texaco,* including the "urban mangrove" metaphor, which is Letchimy's. As for Texaco, it is a real place, one of the Creole neighborhoods to benefit from Letchimy's more humane approach to the problems of squatting and informal housing.

4. It is on this point that the environmental discourse of *Texaco* meets up with the cultural theory of *Eloge de la créolité.*

5. This piece was first published in the Caribbean weekly *Antilla.* It was subsequently reprinted in *Le monde* (21 January 2000) under the title "Manifeste pour refonder les DOM," and signed by Patrick Chamoiseau, Gérard Delver, Édouard Glissant, and Bertène Juminer. Many of the ideas expressed there had been aired previously, often word for word, in Glissant's essays "Martinique" (in *Traité du tout-monde*) and "Distancing, Determining" (in *Poetics of Relation*).

6. The authors themselves admit the immense obstacles that would face the implementation of such a project, and it seems to have elicited mainly dismissive reactions in the local press. (See, for example, Cabort-Masson.) It's worth noting, in this regard, that Raphaël Confiant was asked to sign the document but refused, on the grounds that it was patently unworkable.

From Living Nature to Borderless Culture in Wilson Harris's Work

Hena Maes-Jelinek

> Many believe that there is a firm and irreconcilable barrier between person and environment. Whereas I see the environment as a measure of reflection in the person, a measure of the cosmos in the person . . . We need . . . to scan with subjective eyes landscapes/oceanscapes/riverscapes and the elements within these for complex reflections or absent/present creatures and beings.
>
> —Wilson Harris, "Age of the Imagination"

THIS EPIGRAPH on the interaction or "mutuality" between the environment and the human person epitomizes Wilson Harris's perception of man's place in the universe as well as the historical and philosophical implications he developed in his fiction after the revelation of "absent/present creatures and beings" he experienced on his expeditions as a surveyor in the heartland of Guyana. In an early essay, he explained how the eruption of a "constellation of images" from the depths of a dangerous river affected his mode of feeling, of thinking, and, most important, of writing: "I felt as if a canvas around my head was crowded with phantoms and figures. I had forgotten my own antecedents—the Amerindian/Arawak ones—but now their faces were on the canvas . . . There was a sudden eruption of consciousness ("A Talk on the Subjective Imagination" 40–41). Harris is clearly saying here that his sudden awareness of his Amerindian ancestry made him also conscious of the historical significance of the pre-Columbian resurrecting, as it were, into the present. In a talk given in 1998, he insisted again on the impact of the living landscape on his perception of an essence, later called "bloodstream of spirit" (interview, D'Aguiar 76), pervading and animating both natural elements and men:

> I became aware of a vibrant, secret life in the arteries or branches or scales in landscapes, riverscapes, oceanscapes, skyscapes. That life differed from the human pulse but it gave range, mystery, cross-culturality, unique music, to the language in which I wrote. From my first expedition into the deep interior, in which I felt I had arrived on a new planet, I was drawn to consider and re-consider the

reality of consciousness, the eruption of the unconscious into the subconscious from the heart of a stone, or a branch, or "a sigh out of the gloom of the trees, unlike any human sound as a mask is unlike flesh and blood." ("Introduction to *Palace of the Peacock*" 1)[1]

This passage makes three important related points about landscape: that it is not passive or mute but alive with a "pulse" and a language of its own; that it is a prime mover to consciousness; and that its secret life underpins Harris's fictional language with cross-culturality and, as he says elsewhere, "wordless music." From his first novel, *Palace of the Peacock* (1960), cross-culturality was not only the major feature in his conception of Caribbean culture—which is obvious enough in the light of the area's history and social formation represented in the narrative—but it was and still is the substance of his universalist apprehension of humanity. It informs his view of the connections between man, nature, and the animal world and his dissent from the dogma of anthropocentrism, and it shapes his original style. Strangely enough, it was Harris's immersion in a nonhuman environment, sparsely peopled by small groups of Amerindian survivors, that made him aware of the deficiencies of Caribbean culture and of cultural patterns generally. The powerful contrasts in a landscape "potently alive, potently still" (interview, D'Aguiar 76), its free movements and constant metamorphoses, its paradoxical unpredictability—like the Atlantic tides pushing upstream and running counter to the normal flow of the river as described in *Genesis of the Clowns* (1977, 115) or the "geological upward displacements of the ocean tides" in *The Four Banks of the River of Space* (1990, 35)—aroused by comparison his perception of the fixed values and hierarchies in Caribbean society and made him reject literary realism and what he called "progressive realism" in technology and politics.

In each novel of *The Guyana Quartet* (1960–63), the multilayered jungle is a place of revelation. From the very beginning of the voyage upriver in *Palace,* the narrator identifies the map of Guyana with his own body and realizes that nature, itself frequently humanized, is pregnant with invisible presences: "Formidable lips breathed in the open running atmosphere . . . [the crew] bowed and steered in the nick of time away from the evasive, faintly discernible unconscious head whose meek moon-patch heralded corrugations and thorns and spears we dimly saw in a volcanic and turbulent bosom of water . . . The silent faces and lips raised out of the heart of the stream glanced at us" (32–33).

Similarly, in the three other novels, the protagonist apprehends a neglected or eclipsed reality, part of the country's historical legacy, buried in a dense environment, and with which the Guyanese must come to terms. The *Quartet* outlines the foundations of a cultural approach that becomes increasingly obvious with each installment of the author's fictional opus.

The density of the jungle as catalytic agent of consciousness is further explored in *Heartland,* which blends with an extraordinary suggestive power the spells of terror of the lonely traveler in the interior, the fear of what this experience might make him discover in his inner self, and the existential anguish that "there might be nothing at all within the store-house of the heartland" (28), and one might get lost in a godless, meaning-less world, though he later discovers that the resources of the heartland are spiritual and intangible. For the first time, moved by the prevailing mysterious atmosphere, Harris's protagonist asks the metaphysical ques-tion of "who" or "what" there might be at the heart of the phenomenal universe. There is no definite answer to that question but rather a twofold intimation that all living beings become "their own shadowy essence" (43) after death and that a "process of relations" (42) informs each per-son's inner life and the course of all existence. These are major elements in a "wholeness" always in the making as, I hope, will become clear below.

Harris's novels so far had evoked latent manifestations of the spirit of place mainly through his characters' reactions to the phenomenal world, their sense of an enigmatic presence in the landscape.[2] In *The Secret Ladder,* it took a human form when Poseidon appeared to Fenwick and addressed him in "the silent accents of an ageless dumb spirit (370–71). In *The Eye of the Scarecrow* (1965), the re-creation of the nameless protagonist's journey into the jungle captures in minute detail the free movements and the obstacles in the flow of life in both outer and inner space, nature and human psyche. For the first time, this self-reflexive narrative identifies Harris's conception of the art of fiction and the regenerative power of the imagination (adumbrated in *Palace*) with the progress of the individual soul toward an open and dynamic condition, or "negative identity" (101), free from the "fixed instincts" (58), or habits of thought and behavior in a static society, which he opposes to a "new map of the fluid role of instinct" (76). Harris's concept of "negative identity"[3] developed from his conviction that the construction of a positive Caribbean social and cultural future first requires a psychological descent into, and digestion of, the traumatic historical dismemberment and negation of the self that most West Indians experienced rather than a politics of protest such as the Guyana strike of 1948 re-created in the novel.[4] Again, nature offers the model and poetic image that stimulate the narrator toward a recognition of ebb and flow in the existential process (life-in-death, death-in-life) and of the eclipsed victims in Caribbean society. "A ripple, a footprint almost, appeared in the middle of the water and vanished . . . *The dazzling sleeper of spirit,* exposed within the close elements . . . awoke all too suddenly and slid, in a flash, like speechless gunfire . . . vanishing into a ripple, a dying footfall again . . . and rising once more, distinct web and trace of animation upon a flank of stone. (48–49; my emphasis)

Raven's Head, the mining ghost town that the nameless narrator and his companion try to reach, is subject to a similar movement, as one of the "mysterious locations [that] had been plumbed to disappear and return once more into the undisclosed astronomical wealth of the jungle" (54). Harris clearly associates here what he calls "spirit" with the "undisclosed astronomical wealth of the jungle" and with all who people the so-called void of Caribbean history, to him an apparent void only.[5] These fluctuations of appearance and disappearance initiate the general structure of Harris's narratives and of his opus as a whole. They develop through movements inspired by the animated configuration of the environment, an alternation of eruption from, and dying again into, apparent nothingness discernible in the interweaving of life and death, of blindness and insight in man's consciousness, in the ebb and flow of emotions. Similarly, in the open-ended canvas of his fiction, characters disappear to reappear in later novels like one of the Da Silva twins, who vanishes from the narrative in *Palace of the Peacock* but turns up again and dies in *Heartland,* then is resurrected in *Da Silva da Silva's Cultivated Wilderness* (1977) and *The Tree of the Sun* (1978).

In his excellent chapter "Wilson Harris and Caribbean Poeticism,"[6] Paget Henry contrasts two cultural traditions in the Caribbean, one poeticist—to which Harris belongs—which, in the construction of a new Caribbean self, focuses on ego/consciousness relations, whereas the historicist tradition favors ego/society relations. Henry locates the difference between the two in "the ontology of character in the novel" (110) and writes that, for Harris, "the transformation of the postcolonial ego is a precondition for postcolonial reconstruction" (110). This is the usual opposition between the philosophical conviction that individual moral progress will eventually bring about social progress and the Marxist/sociological tenet that better institutions will help produce better individuals. Henry is right to argue that "in the case of Harris, the mythopoetics of ego/consciousness relationship replaces a historicized political economy as the grammar of human self-formation" (111). Nevertheless, history is more important in the Harrisian self-formation than Henry makes out; the void in consciousness that, as he rightly points out, precedes self-formation was originally induced by history. This is eclipsed but revived in all the novels, as we see in, among others, *Tumatumari* (1968), *Companions of the Day and Night* (1975), and *Jonestown* (1996), where "history retrieves an emotionality, a passion to unveil the facts" (46). Additionally, Henry makes little or no difference between consciousness and imagination when he writes that "Harris refers to the unity of [the] textuality of consciousness as 'the fabric of the imagination'" (*Caliban* 105) and that "consciousness . . . is immemorial in its temporality and infinite in its creative possibilities" (*Caliban* 96). The two are indeed closely intertwined, and there is no doubt that Harris gives consciousness the paramount role that Henry describes in the ego formation since all his protagonists are involved in a "drama of consciousness" (*Tradition* 55). But consciousness is, I believe, the purpose of their quest spurred on by the imagination, which is both creative capacity and the all-pervasive uniting force that holds the world together. As Harris wrote: "The key word for me as a writer is *imagination*. One is involved in *imagined natures, imagined sciences, imagined arts*" ("Voyaging Imagination").

A major feature in Harris's work is the close link between all aspects of his writing or what is actually a connecting thread running through them. "*Imagined natures . . . imagined arts*" reminds one that the environment is for him a "living text": "The landscape is alive . . . it is a living text. And the question is, how can one find, as an imaginative writer, another kind of living text which corresponds to [it]. There is a dialogue there between one's internal being, one's psyche, and the nature of the place, the landscape" (Gilkes, "Landscape of Dreams" 33). In other words, Harris was urged by the need to find "a new conceptual language"[7] to match his perception of living nature and interpret a culture that should itself be animated by a similar livingness: "How does one combine with, and transfigure, a cultural fixity that passes for action ingrained into one's education? How does one bring into play—through various aspects and layers—a sense of profoundest cross-culturality beyond the immobility of habit or of virtue that exterminates all unlike itself?" (interview, D'Aguiar 76).

Harris's way of "bring[ing] into play . . . a sense of profoundest cross-culturality" is through his concept of the "living text" of nature as a "womb of space." This is his expression for outer landscape, inner multi-layered psyche, the seat of the "non-verbal arts of the imagination"[8] (*Womb of Space* xix) and a metaphor for the expanding consciousness. Just as the environment is pregnant with endless evolutionary possibilities, so is the person's inner being. Both enrich and partake of the "complex reality" (*Carnival* 87) of which the external world offers an endless variety of manifestations. Hence his assertion that "Plural masks imply a living cosmos in all its grain and particularity that may appear to sleep, to be dormant but is susceptible to riddling proportions of eruptive life" ("Quetzalcoatl" 39). Conversely, this subterranean existential flow, or, as he says, "unfathomable wholeness" (interview, Tiffin 24) is continuously nourished by the partial environmental phenomena and existences that merge into it as they die and become "the residue of experience we all share" (*Explorations* 43), the "shadowy essence" mentioned above. This confirms the importance of history, particularly the experience of conquered peoples, as an intrinsic, ineradicable component in the human unconscious.

These formulations of an ontological, philosophical, and moral nature, as well as the concept of a cross-culturality rooted in the "womb of space," were expressed gradually in essays in which Harris retrospectively analyzed his own creative process repeatedly described as intuitive.[9] To take but one example: before he wrote any of his critical comments on Caribbean culture, Carnival—a typical Caribbean event—metaphorically epitomized the "plural masks" of external reality and their connection to an inner source of being from *Palace of the Peacock* to *Tumatumari*. Its accretions of meanings from one novel to another until *The Carnival Trilogy*[10] illustrate a method one could sum up as revision of "intuitive clues" ("Validation of Fiction" 45).

Intuition in Harris's work is not an exclusively human faculty but a "living spark"[11] of creation operating in both the environment and all living creatures, with men, animals, and gods all partaking of the "measureless fluid life of the earth" ("Theatre" 3). This fluid life informs Harris's conception of the arts and of a nonstatic culture. It also generated a style developing through what he later called "convertible imageries" (*Guyana Quartet* 10), protean metaphors also inspired by the language of the landscape. He writes: "Language possesses resources which one has to sense as coming not only from within oneself, but from outside, from the land itself, from the rivers, from the forest. And also from those persons and those cultures that existed in the landscape and have left their trace" (Gilkes, "Landscape of Dreams" 33).

Tumatumari admirably combines the language of the land, the eloquent presence of "persons and . . . cultures" who left their trace in the landscape, and a revision of history issuing into a vision of a more dynamic culture and what Harris calls a "treaty of sensibility" (104, 109) between nature, humanity, and the social fabric. The novel covers the history of one family and of Guyana from the end of World War I to the late 1960s.

Both space and time are fragmented and reassembled in the memory and developing consciousness of the main character, Prudence,[12] who transfigures in retrospect the experience of her family, particularly of her father, Tenby, a historian, and her husband, Roi, an engineer. Both men knew that Guyana's natural environment and a social order born of oppression required a complete change of former policies. Yet out of self-interest and fear, they steeled themselves against their insights and better judgment. The real upsurge of consciousness occurs in both of them as they die— Roi in the waterfall,[13] Tenby on his deathbed when he remembers his guilt for allowing another daughter, Pamela, to act according to the "pattern of conquest, of history as [he] had accepted it, lived it and written it" (60). Culture, then, is predominantly the kind of worldview and behavior that counters "the immobility of habit or of virtue that exterminates all unlike itself" (quoted above). It is an awakening to the mutable realities in both nature and society.

Such an awakening takes place in the novel. Tumatumari means "sleeping rocks," though rocks that prove "convertible" (26), like the "*lapis* of populations" (22, 26) turned to stone after conquest: "Painted figures issuing from a crack in the fastness of an age, the well of time. Sleeping rocks . . . Crying to her to be born again (expelled from the bandage of history towards a spiral of 'vision'" (49).

Space is lacking to develop the multilayered meaning of this dense novel, in which the life and resources of nature generate Prudence's psychical "drama of conception" (41) as she re-lives and envisions the redeeming potential of her father's missed opportunities. There is an interpenetration of character and landscape into which she eventually drowns after achieving, through her re-creation of her family's past, a "[t]*ranslation of the Gorgon of history*" (155):

> The glare of the sky above the river made her partially close her eyes until her long lashes were strokes of colour, green and orange, purple and red—the attenuated branch of a tree whose long exploding arm reached across her. With a slight backward tilt of the head she could discern a dense shoulder of forest approaching her, bones of sunlight. . . . An enormous excitement gripped her— authenticity—in which *her being, the being of the well, the being of the sky* seemed to enfold itself and yet release itself like the unravelling, ravelling petals of a flower. (29–30; my emphasis)

The image of awakening rocks or "sentient earth-sculpture[s]" ("Theatre of the Arts" 6) is further developed from *Tumatumari* to *The Four Banks of the River of Space*. In the former novel, "she discerned upon the features of Rock an eye appear" (111) and gradually felt encircled in a "fantastic reciprocity of elements" (114). In *Four Banks,* the rocks in the waterfall also come alive, and Anselm, the protagonist, witnesses "a procession of draped bodies . . . rock sculptures that harness the river. The Macusis see them . . . as clothing inner bodies that wait to come alive, a living procession . . . a magical art born of 'live absences', a magical procession of living interior bodies sculpted at the heart of the Waterfall" (33–34).

Later, Anselm himself becomes "genuinely involved . . . in uplifted veil upon veil of darkness until [he] possessed a glimmering apprehension of the magic of creative nature, the life of sculpture, the genesis of art, the being of music" (39).

These passages clearly associate the creativeness of nature arising from an invisible, mysterious source (the "bloodstream of spirit" mentioned above) with humankind's creativity, which Harris never sees as an imposition of order on the so-called chaos of life. Art to him (and to his "dreaming" artist-protagonists) consists in capturing the free motion of elements in outer and inner landscape, in surrendering the self to this motion and thus allowing an untrammeled narrative structure to emerge into his consciousness. But the connection between outer landscape and inner psyche, the interweaving of these many-layered worlds, which Harris calls "composition of reality" ("Composition of Reality" 23), cannot be seized absolutely, only glimpsed through a multiplicity of images.

Harris has always attempted to merge the "two cultures" (art and science) and advocated a revolution in the humanities analogous to the shift from Newtonian to quantum physics. Plurality in both nature and man ("one is multitude" [*Jonestown* 5]), the notion of alternative or "parallel universes" (*Jonestown* 110), the rejection of all absolutes in favor of interconnected partialities, the dissolution of boundaries between life and death as between past, present, and future, all partake of a quantum approach to life developing through Anselm, the narrative medium and many-sided artist. He is indeed an "engineer, sculptor, painter, architect, composer" (x); another way of suggesting the multiplicity of art forms arising from a unified cross-cultural source. He gathers within himself and probes all these partial realities.

Like Anselm, Francisco Bone in *Jonestown* is "a vessel of composite epic" (5) in whose "Memory Theatre" and consciousness is reenacted the terrible Jonestown massacre that took place in Guyana on 18 November 1978.[14] Seven years later, Bone, who survived the massacre, remembers the day of the mass suicide and killings but also travels back to 1939 on the eve of World War II, when his mother was killed by a Carnival reveler disguised as a tiger, a recurring image in Harris's fiction. Thus contextualized in an individual act of violence (the mother's murder) and an impending holocaust, so representative of twentieth-century atrocities, the massacre is also paralleled with the extinction of pre-Columbian populations and civilizations and the mysterious disappearance of the Caribs in British Guiana suggesting that the Guyanese interior is also the seat of eclipsed cultures. But the setting here frequently extends from the Guyanese heartland to the cosmos and a vision of "archetypal oceans and skies" (51), a spatial arena in keeping with the Jonestown leaders' "celestial ambition" (52) to emulate the great conquerors of the past. The narrative analyzes the seldom-disclosed motivations of destructiveness and, among all of Harris's novels, is probably the one most concerned with the persisting tendency in men, even by resorting to genocide, to eliminate those different from themselves.

In spite of distinctly political motivations in his representations of tyranny, Harris's answer to these disasters is neither social nor political but moral and cultural. In his backward and forward psychological journey in the "womb of space and time," Bone traces "[a] map of the imagination that breaches the human-centered cosmos we have enshrined" (6). This breakthrough occurs through many different narrative features. One is the redeeming agency of the Virgin/Fury archetype. In classical European mythology, the furies were vessels of the revenge-syndrome, punishing doers of unavenged crimes.[15] As usual in Harris's fiction, the archetype cannot be apprehended in its wholeness and is broken into several personae,[16] women in the narrative being both concrete characters and partial faces of the archetype. One facet of the Virgin archetype is blended with a pre-Columbian approach to nature and men inspired by Maya culture and iconography.[17] Harris has drawn attention to a pre-Columbian tradition that implied "a profound and unusual treaty of sensibility between human presence on this planet and the animal kingdom" ("Imagination, Dead" 185). In this novel, as later in *The Dark Jester,* he borrows from that tradition the representation of natural and animal features in human faces. For instance, the predator in the novel, of which Jones is only one facet, is frequently represented as a tiger or jaguar, while the sun in Harris's fiction stands for a will-to-power and arrogance that can be broken and converted.[18] Thus when Bone builds the Virgin ship on which he travels (clearly a vessel of the voyaging imagination), he plucks the first nail of his ship "from the sun, from the tiger's killing weapon," and draws from

Jones "a fiery claw." Hence in his imaginative return to his childhood: "I sailed on the convertible claw of the sun as if I rode futuristic energy on the back of a tiger" (26–27).

Harris's expression "the womb of space and time" obviously identifies woman with the concrete nature in which his characters travel, while she is also the containing vessel of men's self-exploration. Bone's mother, another incarnation of the Virgin archetype, is equally the "mother of humanity" who bears the resurrection child. When in his dream-book he hears his mother say, "'One needs to break the charisma of conquest in oneself if one is to build a new Virgin ship,'" he ponders over the role of the furies, and at the end of his "epic of repentance" he sees in the Virgin archetype an expression of "the rhetoric of intercourse with reality shorn of violence" and a "transgression of frames of terror" (227).

The violence that led to the Jonestown massacre takes on many forms in the novel, among them the violence done to nature and sexual violence. The instinct of the predator in human, animal, and archetypal condition is an inescapable temptation that Bone himself shares and a menace. But he later perceives that violence, which has also been exerted on women by Jones, can be converted into a redeeming sexuality in both human beings and nature: "The act of penetration of space, of Virgin space, penetration of other worlds, was not in its mysterious origination an act of violence. It was an act of creation . . . of living diversities, the living orchestration of differing spaces, ages, realities" (128).

In a striking passage, Bone has a vision of an "incalculable spatial episode" (133), an intercourse between a log turned phallic tree and a "genesis cloud . . . in the womb of space" (132).[19] It enables him to visualize the possible rebirth of the pre-Columbian New World drowned like Plato's Atlantis, by the European conquest "in every mutilated landscape and catchment and lake": "The fate of Atlantis was laid bare as a counterpoint between rape or devastation and implicit freedom still to balance extinction with a renascence . . . of lost cultures whose vestiges and imprints could be orchestrated into the seed of the future" (136).

Nonviolent intercourse breaks the closure of eternity as conceived by Jones and at one stage by Deacon, Bone's friend and "adversarial twin,"[20] who saw himself "duel[ling] with eternity[21] . . . the Titans, the Tricksters of heaven" (52). The trickster, who frequently appears in Harris's fiction, is an ambivalent mythological Caribbean figure who embodies the divine, the animal (derived from the African spider god Anancy), and the human as the slave who eludes oppression by his cleverness. Harris also presents him as an artist who identifies "with the submerged authority of dispossessed peoples" (*History* 17).[22]

It is in this latter capacity, and not as god or the gods Deacon wants to confront,[23] that the trickster appears in *The Dark Jester* (2001) and dialogues with the Dreamer/narrator. The novel recreates the colonial encounter between Pizarro and the last pre-conquest Inca, Atahualpa. It is informed by the contrast between the cultures the two men represent while construing a worldview that counterpoints "a dominant cultural history" (102). Re-creating the meeting, the protagonist's dreaming psyche liberates it from history's closures into a natural, even cosmic dimension "across times" and relativizes man's position in the universe:

> Other facets, other faces, other sides to nature begin an immense liberation in breaking absolutes into partial organs. . . . Atahualpa . . . wears a garment of fire, ghostly spark of fire . . . which I partially understand . . . [a]s much and less than I understand the fleeting garment a bird wears when it sings and articulates a strand of greatest music, or a serpent whose wisdom is voiceless but wiser than the symbols of Eden, or a butterfly whose wings clap of a storm[24] unheard, unseen, or flying fish dancing on a wave. (vii–viii)

The Dreamer calls this extended existential reality "Atahualpan form" (2). To perceive it by moving beyond the separated categories of being erected by "Cartesian form" (16) is to draw inspiration from living nature to envision a transfiguration of the antinomic relation between dominant and dominated cultures, though Harris does not optimistically suggest that it takes place. Pizarro and the Bishop who forces conversion on Atahualpa practice "the art of the sword . . . [t]he art of political diplomacy exercised by tyrants." "Neither saw the mystery of wood and iron converted by a spark. Nor did they see the *life* of the land and water, the garden, the arteries of space and time. They saw nothing but reptilian gold, that fascinated them, the Beast and the Bird, which they loathed and melted, blindly, unseeingly" (11–12).

They are similarly indifferent to the lament of the landscape after Atahualpa's execution, which the narrator perceives retrospectively: "The music of nature, padded with loud tears of sorrow, comes across space and time. An orchestra peals in silence and then settles into tumbling rocks. The rivers and the waterfalls brazen it with sky-fall. I hear it all distinctly, however, silently, once again. I hear the voices of a great, ancient people come again from a body or rock and water and sky as they mourn the death of Atahualpa inflicted on him by the Conquistadores" (66–67).

After a dazzling vision of the "shadowy brilliance of elements within a black sky" (12–13), the Dreamer wonders "who had created such vision-ary and terrifying art (such terror and beauty and wisdom) before the times of Man in a Sky of Dream?" (13). In one of his talks, Harris asks:

> What is art? Sculpture appears to have existed long before Man existed in his present evolutionary shape. Out of the turbulence of the Earth the rocks ap-peared to sculpt bees, insects, animals and Man himself . . . in this long terrain of intuitive shapes . . . Man becomes a living work of art. He resembles the rock-hewn faces of creation which he shares with every creature long before he appears as he now is. ("Power of the Word" 3)

In *The Dark Jester,* the Dreamer also repeatedly questions himself about the nature of art.[25] The answer is woven into the narrative. As we have seen, the origin of Harris's own art lies in an upsurge of consciousness due to his sudden realization in the Guyanese heartland that the landscape was alive with the invisible presence of victimized peoples and their eclipsed history. In this novel, he reiterates the fictionalization of the source of art through the ruined configuration of the pre-Columbian Inca kingdom. The hidden inaccessible city of Vilcabamba[26] is clearly one embodiment of the never-discovered El Dorado (though, of course, the gold of Peru was an El Dorado for the Spanish conquerors). Already in his first essays, Harris had commented on the dual nature of El Dorado, both the object of "greed, cruelty and exploitation . . . [and] City of Gold, City of God" (*Tradition* 35). El Dorado, the gilded man, also disclosed "a living open tradition which realizes itself in an enduring capacity associated with the obscure human person" (*Tradition* 36). The obscure human person, whether in the Guyanese jungle or, more generally, in the underworld of the Amer-icas, still provides an answer to the question, "What is art?" When the narrator discovers beneath the glitter of the man of gold his suffering flesh in the hold of a ship sailing in the Middle Passage: "Then it was that I saw the *first* work of art (was it the first, had I forgotten the others?) in the Underworld of the Kings of America. Half-flesh, half-work-of-art. A stretched figure, cruelly placed on a plank, in the belly of a slave-ship . . . Within a global trading system a glitter on flesh preserves the allure of material value, the high price to be earned in buying and selling works of art that can labour, cut cane, create dams and canals. Art and flesh like myself" (98–99; my emphasis).

Although Harris is often said to be an "abstract" writer, his fictional language is obviously inspired by concrete reality. For both protagonist and reader, art has always meant an awakening to the dense inner life of the natural environment in close relationship with all living persons and creatures. His metaphysical perception of a world in the making has grown out of the landscape and the specific history of the Americas. Above all, what he calls a "cross-culturality between living nature and humanity" (*Mask of the Beggar* 50) generates his unique stylistic associations of all forms of life, as in the following passage that laments the death of Atahualpa:

> I hear a Bird's cry. It seems as distant as the Moon and yet closer than one can bear in its intensity and sorrow. . . . The Bird's cry returns pregnant and full of Andean sloping, slender rhythms woven out of silences in the Clock of the Sun. Radiant sparks, icy darts, that sail in the Ship of my Mind. It is consciousness aroused through the volcanic upheaval of the land that speaks with a people's sorrow across the ages. The call of aroused populations is nebulously lifted into a Bird's cry on the high Andes. (67)

Notes

1. *Palace of the Peacock* 26. For a complete, regularly updated bibliography on Wilson Harris, see http://www.ulg.ac.be/facphl/uer/d-german/L3/whone.html

2. In *Palace of the Peacock,* for instance, the narrator has the impression of being followed: "The forest rustled and rippled with a sigh and ubiquitous step. I stopped dead where I was, frightened for no reason whatever. The step near me stopped and stood still" (28). In *Heartland,* the protagonist feels he is being "watched." The three parts of the novel are entitled "The Watchers," "The Watched," and "Creation of the Watch."

3. Akin to John Keats's notion of "negative capability."

4. The strike lasted four and a half months in eight sugar estates on the east coast of Demerara in reaction to a change in the system of work from "cut-and-drop to cut-and-load." On 16 June, the police opened fire at a plantation, killing five workers and injuring twelve. On this subject, see Cheddi Jagan, *The West on Trial* 90.

5. "I do not believe any area of the world is historyless or a product of absolute historical accident" ("Fabric of the Imagination" 176). See also *Tradition the Writer and Society,* where he explains that witnesses of the conquest of the Caribbean "seem to exist in a terrible void of unreality" (31).

6. In *Caliban's Reason* 90–114.

7. The expression is borrowed from C. G. Jung's *Synchronicity.*

8. The expression "womb of space" first appears in the novel *Genesis of the Clowns* 177.

9. See his many comments on this in *The Radical Imagination.*

10. On this subject, see Maes-Jelinek, "'Carnival' and Creativity in Wilson Harris's Fiction."

11. See "Theatre of the Arts."

12. The name may have been inspired by Harris's great admiration for Titian's *Allegory of Prudence,* a painting in the National Gallery that represents the three ages of man with three animals under them, suggesting the link between the two species.

13. On the significance of this episode, see Harris's "Theatre of the Arts" 6.

14. The Jonestown "experiment" was a community and cooperative farm founded by a white American, Jim Jones, in the Guyanese heartland. Nearly a thousand people, including 276 children, who belonged to his sect of the "People's Temple" were forced to drink a sweetened cyanide soup or were shot on the spot. Jones's original purpose had been idealistic for his community of followers was multiracial and was meant to serve as a model of integration.

15. For a detailed analysis of their role, see Wilson Harris, "Apprenticeship to the Furies."

16. Cf. *The Four Banks of the River of Space,* in which the vengeful Homeric Ulysses is broken into several characters.

17. For a discussion of Harris's affinity with Maya culture in *Jonestown,* see Paula Burnett, "Memory Theatre and the Maya."

18. In *Palace of the Peacock,* Donne's will-to-power is at first associated with a pitiless sun (19). At the end of the novel, when he is at last humbled, the sun breaks into stars that become the peacock's eyes in "the palace of the universe" (146).

19. See the development of the whole passage (133–36).

20. In "Adversarial Contexts and Creativity," Harris explains that creativity and innovative form emerge from opposites or adversarial contexts. Both Deacon and Bone were born in 1930 and attended San Francisco College, where they met Jones, a fiction compatible with the real facts.

21. Harris has explained that eternity, which is usually conceived as an absolute, "is an implacable riddle . . . an extinction of birth and death in human creative terms" ("The Quest for Form" 22).

22. On this subject, see also Helen Tiffin, "The Metaphor of Anancy in Caribbean Literature."

23. However, in keeping with Harris's view that all kinds of fact, behavior, or motive potentially contain their reverse, the "tricksters of heaven" (dangerous messengers of eternity) later become "tricksters of spirit" (151). In *The Dark Jester,* the Jester or Trickster partakes of the sacred.

24. An allusion to the "butterfly effect," "the notion that a butterfly stirring the air today in Peking can transform storm systems next month in New York" (Gleick 8).

25. See also "What is Jest?" (ix), "What is history?" (1), "What is prophecy?" (24). The answers are all interlinked.

26. The city was the refuge of the last Incas. In 1911, the American historian Hiram Bingham went in search of this ghost city. What he eventually discovered in his obstinate exploration was the now-famous Machu Picchu (Bernand 113–22).

Epilogue

Theatre of the Arts

Wilson Harris

RECENTLY A COMMENTATOR, in a scientific program on genes, stated—I now paraphrase his remarks—that if we stripped away our pigmentations, we should find an African presence beneath the varying color of our skins. But, he went on to say, this has only been recently perceived and is still little understood. Furthermore, he implied, in the ages of *involuntary* migration of the original African presence—across landmasses, oceans, and rivers—the profoundest changes have occurred.

Our *immersion* in such changes has led us to conceive of absolute ethnicities or racial compartments. Thus, in the arts, we have *blocked* the flow of *measureless* cross-culturalities. We tend to claim fixed boundaries and to gain support for such absoluteness from animal habitats.

Ironically, the centuries have witnessed to gross conquests. Some of these occurred in the Americas five hundred years ago. European cultures invaded the Aztecs, the Incas, and others and appeared to destroy invaluable differences. Such differences, in my view, are the challenging foundations of universal possibilities woven from diversities.

By the way, I spoke, a moment ago, of our seeking support for *fixed boundaries* from animal habitats. What is animal habitat? Has it not been determined by the movement of landmasses, the changed shape of continents and oceans? Do we not see this in the incredible evolutionary detail that emerges in the animals of Australia, of the Andes, of the Amazon, and elsewhere? It is important to realize that animal habitat, though apparently grounded, at a particular moment, in absolute place, is itself partial *in the life of the earth*.

That is a message for art, for the way art bears on the human person, which we still have, it seems to me, to perceive very deeply if art is to speak to us beyond material fixtures and ornamentations, if art is to take us slowly, constructively, across the most sensitive boundaries.

Boundaries are *sensitive*, however *partial* they actually are. Their partiality may assist us to live and move in order to skirt or avoid earthquake regions by which we may be fatalistically trapped generation after generation. There is a *measureless* nature to the life of the earth in the midst of catastrophes, drought, and famine and flood that we blindly invite, a *precarious* freedom we need to understand if our cultures are to awaken from their "sleep" or "obliviousness" which seems so strong it is called realism.

Technical brilliance is at the core of realism. Realism, I would say, has undoubtedly been the fruit of the eighteenth- and nineteenth-century European novel-form which has influenced the twentieth-century theatre of the arts. But such realism, however sophisticated or satiric or comic, led the rulers of civilization, *unintentionally* perhaps into an "obliviousness" of the many diverse peoples under the umbrella of Empire. This may seem surprising. The British empire was one, it was said, on which the sun never set in the eighteenth and nineteenth centuries. Perhaps it was a trend or habit that ran from the "sleep" of conquest of the Americas making one people regard itself as absolutely superior to others who pursued different faiths. The *art* of Empire in the *novel-form* of the eighteenth and nineteenth centuries displayed all-white characters from all-white families and ignored all other peoples, diverse and peculiar, under the imperial umbrella.

Ruler and ruled never gained the mutual insight of creative and re-creative responsibility. The ruled were bracketed, as though they did not exist, upon the passivity of stages marked by the military crossings of the ruler.

There were a few American novelists of the nineteenth century such as, for instance, Herman Melville, whose black and white and brown characters (all playing major roles in his fiction) offered pregnant silences and room for speculation as to what lay beneath those silences. In a sense, the absolute domain of the ruling novel which Melville inherited was implicitly broken through such an array of speaking silences. *Benito Cereno* closes as follows: "Some months after, dragged to the gibbet at the tail of a mule, the black met his voiceless end . . . [his] head, [a] hive of subtlety" (307). It is possible also that we may find sketches of *the fluid life of the earth* in Melville's narratives. Critics, as far as I am aware, have not looked into these issues.

And this brings me to the question: *What does one mean by the life of the earth?* I am not speaking of a *description* of hills or valleys or plains or rivers that are *fixed* or *insentient* features.

In *Tumatumari*, a novel of mine published in 1968, we come upon a portrayal of *moving* landscape creating, I feel, a *measureless* dimension. The passage I have in mind runs as follows:

The clouds had vanished and the line of the mountains appeared now like a lofty crest of water breaking its own wave ceaselessly—undulating and refracting. It was a curious impression—the vast waving outline of the mountains and the transparent ocean of the sky within and beneath which fell away other exposures, shorelines, crests and seas . . . vegetation as well as sand—tier after tier, rank after rank of bush, descending balconies as in a submerged amphitheatre . . . fluid/solid—water/fire—cauldron of space . . . *In truth the ocean had once crawled here upon an ancient continental shelf and climbed still higher beyond Tumatumari to its farthest limit—the escarpment of Kaieteur.* (53–54)

In that passage is it not possible to visualize the ever-changing mobility of the earth, a mobility, a vulnerability, a curious infirmity, shall I say, that is born of land and water and fire and cloud through which we may create doors or windows, *sensitive* doors and windows, *sensitive* freedoms in the midst of fates?

When I speak of infirmity, I am referring to the infirmity of strength; the strongest fortresses have a hidden infirmity through which it is possible to build new architectures in space. The very *fixed* stages—upon which we build our cities—are *sentient* and *alive*. Sentience—and its veined and tributary variations—may be coming home to us at last as we find ourselves potentially overwhelmed by the threat of flood and drought that we, in part, visit on ourselves in our "obliviousness" of the life of the earth. May I emphasize again that the life of the *earth* is not *fixed;* it is not a description of *fixed* mountains or valleys divorced from the characters that move on it. The life of the earth needs to be seen *in fiction* as sensitively woven into the characters that move upon it, whose history, may I say, reflects a profound relationship to the earth, so that we may speak of a humanity whose feet are made of mud or land or water or any other element to attune us to our being on an earth that moves as we move upon it. This is the mystery of fiction if not of science. You may remember epic figures with one eye in the middle of their forehead and with feet of oats.

Tumatumari is an Amerindian word, somewhat anglicized, I would say, which means "sleeping rocks." In the novel I sought to bring the "sleep" of a traumatized people, traumatized by conquest, into league with sculptures that have sprung from the earth—sculptured crests, sculptured outlines, sculptured exposures—in order to engage in an awakening, within many-sided nature, from the brutalization of everyday place and person by conquistadorial legacies.

Let us remember that across the ages, before Man appeared in his present shape, the eruptive earth would have sculpted figures, in its *sentient* thrust and momentum, resembling Man and Beast and Bird before Man and Beast and Bird had actually appeared.

This, I feel, is the measureless origin of the arts, an apparently sleeping form imbued nevertheless with a subtle momentum, a subtle life within an apparent passivity.

We have seized on such passivity with what seems an all-powerful technology, we have brushed aside ancient legends of gods of the wind and the sea and the earth and the air without a thought of their *intuitive* depth, their intuitive bridle on the horses of the earth—horses of wind and sea— that needed a greater re-creative understanding and development.

Such horses, in the sculptures of the earth, may seem asleep, but they may teach us of our own "obliviousness," of our tendency to turn into *blocks* of flesh and blood. We are ourselves sculptures awaiting a *dream* of life that may dawn upon us when we engage differently with a pace that is secreted everywhere.

I can imagine someone pointing to philosophical concepts of alchemy —such as the *massa confusa* and the *prima materia*—which implicitly tell of the life of the earth and warn against assuming the earth is "passive" or "inanimate" or "dead."

This is true, but on reflection one cannot fail to see that the human person, by and large, is divided in himself or herself between *sentient earth-sculptures* (which appear to him or to her as *insentient*) and the *living work of art* that he or she is in *waking dream or play or action* in fiction. This division of two selves, in the theatre of the arts, may mark, I feel, the summit of division within ourselves, a blind summit that seems to me to be at the heart of feud and conflict that ravage our age. The earth we have wasted is our greatest ambivalent conquest and enemy. Perhaps we extend our will to conquer the earth into patterns of hate against human cultures for which we grieve in despair and terror that stir us out of our sleep.

Did C. G. Jung conceive of bridging this division between opposite selves in his *coincidentia oppositorum*? He may have, but it would have been intuitive.

In an article entitled *Merlin and Parsifal: Adversarial Twins,* I refer to Jung's statement that "a new conceptual language" is needed. But, as far as I was aware, he made no further statements and seemed afflicted by grave misgivings. As a consequence, he never pursued the psycho-physical medium he had raised. The novels he read were conventional in which an "obliviousness" rules the language and makes for an *insentient and fixed stage* on which character is built.

In *Tumatumari* I sought—through trials of the imagination—to create a theatre of the arts in which obliviousness is denuded and the two selves —sentient earth-sculpture and Man as a living work of art—actually come together in an astonishing way in a theatre of the arts.

Curiously enough, I see this clearly now as I look backwards and forwards across my fiction from the nineteen-sixties into the seventies, eighties, nineties, and into *The Dark Jester,* which has just been published. I can see now how they all have a *measurelessness* which I call the *unfinished genesis of the imagination.*

Let me return to *Tumatumari.*

Roi Solman dies in the Tumatumari waterfall. His wife, Prudence, sees him in a Dream descending into the waterfall and hunting the "wild boar of the rapids." The hunt which is normally pursued on land changes subtly and complexly in her Dream of the waterfall.

Everything changes subtly and complexly.

Who or what is the "wild boar of the rapids?" It is *sentient earth-sculpture.* It existed long before Roi possessed his present human shape. As a consequence, the stage of theatre on which Roi hunts moves and is alive in his consciousness. The rigid barriers of time are *partially* abolished within a *space* that *lives* in its own right. Prudence awakens, in some degree, to the life of her husband as *he* appears to awaken in her Dream to *his* life as a work of art. Such is, I feel, the *miracle* of fiction.

However one traces it—I have done so in different ways, different *fictions* across the years—the fact emerges obscurely at times, clearly at other times, depending on the intuitive scope of the writing, that each player in a work (if I may describe him or her as a player) needs to come into league with the earth on which he moves, in which he swims, into which he descends, as a *sentient living entity.* I feel that this requires a wholly different theatre of the arts to the one we now have, which may have sophisticated characterization but which is established on an *insentient stage.* This leads repeatedly to a *will to conquer* which divides people everywhere like a remorseless fate.

In *Tumatumari,* Prudence is a fictional player who sees her husband, Roi, in her Dream of his hunt of the "wild boar of the rapids," in a *fluid* combination of the earth and the "constitution of heaven [in the] raging spittle of the chase on the boar's lips which mingled now with hers . . . like the water[s] of life" (55).

What, may I ask, are "the waters of life"?

It is vitally important, it seems to me, to engage with this in the trials of the imagination that the novel discloses, however testing, however difficult, and *not* to divide one's attention by fastening on *pure* philosophical concepts: Philosophy is very important, but it needs to blend with the images in a work of art so genuinely, perhaps complexly, that we free ourselves from absolute restrictions in pursuing the *partial* nature of each image in its correspondences with other partial images.

Reason, as advanced by apparently sophisticated thinkers, leads to exercises that ignore the language of art in fiction. Such ignoring, such ignorance, reduces or measures flesh and blood as a *block,* and this inevitably, if unwittingly, leads to agencies of conquest. There are *reasons beyond reasons,* depths beyond surfaces. Such depths, such humilities, beyond a fixed or sovereign restriction, are the mystery of art, the true mystery of fiction.

Let me return now to the question I asked earlier on "the waters of life."

What are "the waters of life" which are gained from a wholly new approach to fiction and art as these may encompass inexplicable truth in multifarious life?

Is this not a question of *gnosis,* of *gnostic* understanding, of *knowledge* gained from extremities of living encounter with *earth-sculptures* that revise our approach to the nature of human-made sculptures, the nature of *human* art? How does sculpture live, how does art live, in subtle, curiously moving ways though it seems ornamental and inanimate?

Does such an approach to sculpture, to art, to the body and bodilessness of the Word in poem and fiction, point a way to the *veiled* meaning of *original spirit, original soul?*

Except that such knowledge—as I come, by intuitive degrees, to it— has no fortress location, no invulnerable location. In such apparently invulnerable fortresses lies a hidden vulnerability or infirmity we may see in mind and imagination. Such a vulnerability or infirmity may prove a complex window through our habits, beyond habitual discourse, beyond the cosmos, beyond the stars that we try to see, to place, within our galaxy.

The multifarious life of the earth, therefore, teaches us to pay the closest care and attention to variations and movements on the stage on which we live: and not to invest absolutely or fixedly on such a stage.

We are told of parallel universes by scientific speculations, parallel universes of which we know nothing except perhaps that there is a *Wound*— akin to the Wound of being and non-being we carry in ourselves—that may take us into the *spirit* of timelessness. A supreme paradox. We move through a *Wound* into *timelessness.*

Quantum "particle" and "wave"—in their apparent illogicality—may help us to sense a living spark reaching darkly and brightly perhaps from a true Creator. It reaches through the demiurgic and conquistadorial field with which we have to wrestle for precarious freedoms in the midst of implacable fates.

It is but a spark, a spark capable of multiple illuminations that take us into diverse potentials, diverse dangers, diverse hopes in cross-cultural ages.

It is but a spark, but it offers us an intensity of creative and re-creative imaginative and intuitive scope.

Without that "spark" what do we have but biased games or functions of uniform art and a clinging to science for masks to conceal our failures and our mortality?

Gnosis therefore—within the intuitions I have inserted in this talk— that there is no fortress locality to knowledge, that there is a complex window or infirmity within the strongest minds, the strongest imaginations— brings us to "the waters of life" as imbued by the spark of a true creation, a spark which assists us in contending with the demiurgic politics of our age. The demiurge is equipped to ride all who are oblivious of the *sentience* of the earth and the threshold such sentience provides into parallel universes of the imagination through a tree of life existing long before we arrived in our present shape and form.

I do not say this absolutely but as a Jest, a serious Jest, however, which permits us a glimpse of chasms between knowledge and ignorance we dream to cross.

Let me quote briefly from *The Dark Jester,* my most recent novel, to sustain a grasp, as it were, of the measureless spark that makes us, in fiction, *living works of art* in the ground on which we move and which moves with us.

This is the City of Cities, El Dorado. I bring to it the ruins of the past, the memories of places I know as mine but which are taken by Europe and Spain. El Dorado is the Troy of the Americas.

I walk in shoes of mist, I wear rock and water. Rock melts, water becomes a solidity or a desert. My bone and my garments fuse in world theatre.

"El Dorado is gold. I am a man of gold in a place of gold. This is the distinctive legend of flesh and gold." I cry the words boldly but my misgivings rise into space. There is a rumble. The Earth shakes. Shakes to Cassandra who comes across time to tell us in multiple ways of the fate of cultures. It is the heavy tread of my pursuers. Or is it my own bodiless step? A pulse beats fast as a drum.

. . . Troy collapses with the entry of a Wooden Horse which gives birth to a jealous many-headed enemy when everyone dances and celebrates in lust.

El Dorado hides on a saddle of ground on a Misty Animal in the Amazon. I swear I see it wrapped in elements of jealous enemy and lusty friend. I give a cry of joy, such joy, but how sprinkled with the desperation of unease. It is swept from me, so swiftly I am astonished. All that remains are the tears of the Animal like a shroud upon me. They materialize into my pursuers in jungled space, and leap and seize me. El Dorado vanishes. It is swallowed in the belly of a gigantic Horse or Animal of space . . .

Such is my wrestling with enemy and friend in the suspended heart of fate that edges into uneasy freedom.

They seize me.

I have a golden chain around my neck on a jungled body of land. My hair is like the hair of trees. They take me back to Cuzco, an outcast in my own land.

As I stand on the Scaffold, in world theatre, the Sea turns into the dramatization of slender hope spinning a path into desolate cities, desolate places. The land that is mine has become desolate. And yet I see a thread of water on which I cross. How can one come Home except upon threads of desolation one still carries?

The Sword of God coils into a Rope as it flashes to the wisdom of the Serpent.

I faintly hear the Bishop intoning a prayer.

I touch the Sword against which he leans. It hangs from a soldier's side or robe.

Will the Bishop's God, the Bishop's Sword, respond to a shape in me that turns as red as a feather in Air and Earth? It is a Wound in the body of art as delicate as a sail, a flimsy sail. Flimsy as it is it sings of a Ship, a hidden Ship in a Hidden City no one has yet found though it still endures with the promise of creation on Land and on the Sea. (107–9)

Note

This is a talk given at a conference in honor of Wilson Harris that took place at the University of Liège on 30 March 2001. The essay has been published in *Theatre of the Arts. Wilson Harris and the Caribbean,* edited by Hena Maes-Jelinek and Bénédicte Ledent, 1–10. Amsterdam and New York: Rodopi, 2002.

Bibliography

Accord, Clark. *De koningin van Paramaribo*. Amsterdam: Uitgeverij Vassallucci, 1999.

Achebe, Chinua. "The Novelist as Teacher." In *Hopes and Impediments: Essays 1965–87*, by Achebe. London: Heinemann, 1988.

Adamson, Joni, Mei Mei Evans, and Rachel Stein. "Introduction: Environmental Justice Politics, Poetics, and Pedagogy." In *The Environmental Justice Reader: Politics, Poetics, and Pedagogy*, edited by Adamson, Evans, and Stein, 3–14. Tucson: University of Arizona Press, 2002.

Adisa, Opal Palmer. "My Work Speaks to Those Other Women." In *Traveling Women*, edited by Palmer and Devorah Major, 28–29. Oakland: Jukebox Press, 1989.

Adler, Joyce Sparer. "The Evolution of Female Figures and Imagery in Wilson Harris's Novels." *Hambone*, no. 6 (fall 1986): 169–78.

Advertisement. "Elite Island Resorts and American Airlines." *New Yorker,* 11 November 2002, 119.

Alaimo, Stacy. "'Skin Dreaming': The Bodily Transgressions of Fielding Burke, Octavia Butler, and Linda Hogan." In *Ecofeminist Literary Criticism: Theory, Interpretation, Pedagogy*, edited by Greta Gaard and Patrick Murphy, 123–38. Urbana and Chicago: University of Illinois Press, 1998.

Alexis, Gérald. *Peintres haïtiens*. Paris: Editions Cercle d'Art, 2000.

Alexis, Jacques Stephen. *Les arbres musiciens*. 1948. Paris: Éditions Gallimard, 1957.

Allfrey, Phyllis Shand. *The Orchid House*. New Brunswick, N.J.: Rutgers University Press, 1997.

Alpers, Svetlana. *The Art of Describing: Dutch Art in the Seventeenth Century*. London: Penguin, 1989.

Alvarez, Julia. *A Cafecito Story*. White River Junction, Vt.: Chelsea Green, 2001.

Anker, Peder. *Imperial Ecology: Environmental Order in the British Empire, 1895–1945*. Cambridge: Harvard University Press, 2001.

Anonymous. "Jamaica, a Poem in Three Parts." In *Caribbeana: An Anthology of English Literature of the West Indies 1657–1777*, edited by Thomas W. Krise, 326–39. Chicago: University of Chicago Press, 1999.

"Antigua and Barbuda." *The Lonely Planet Online*. http://www.lonelyplanet .com/destinations/caribbean/ antigua and barbuda/printable.htm.

Antoine, Régis. "The Caribbean in Metropolitan French Writing." In *A History of Literature in the Caribbean: Hispanic and Francophone regions,* edited by James Arnold, 1:349–62. Philadelphia: John Benjamin's Publishing Co., 1994.

Armbruster, Karla. "A Poststructuralist Approach to Ecofeminist Criticism." In *The Green Studies Reader: From Romanticism to Ecocriticism,* edited by Lawrence Coupe. London and New York: Routledge, 2000.

Armbruster, Karla, and Kathleen R. Wallace, eds. *Beyond Nature Writing: Expanding the Boundaries of Ecocriticism.* Charlottesville and London: University Press of Virginia, 2001.

Arnold, David, *The Problem of Nature: Environment, Culture and European Expansion.* Oxford: Blackwell, 1996.

Arthur, Charles. "Confronting Haiti's Environmental Crisis: A Tale of Two Visions." In *Green Guerrillas: Environmental Conflicts and Initiatives in Latin America and the Caribbean,* edited by Helen Collinson, 149–57. London: Latin American Bureau, 1996.

Ashcroft, Bill, Gareth Griffiths, and Helen Tiffin, eds. *Key Concepts in Post-Colonial Studies.* New York and London: Routledge, 1998.

Ayala, César J. *American Sugar Kingdom: The Plantation Economy of the Spanish Caribbean, 1898–1934.* Chapel Hill and London: University of North Carolina Press, 1999.

Barker, David, and Duncan F. M. McGregor. "A Geographical Focus for Environment and Development in the Caribbean." Introduction to *Environment and Development in the Caribbean: Geographical Perspectives,* edited by Barker and McGregor, 3–17. Kingston: The Press, University of the West Indies, 1995.

Barnes, Fiona R. "Dismantling the Master's Houses: Jean Rhys and West Indian Identity." In *International Women's Writing: New Landscapes of Identity,* edited by Anne E. Brown and Marjanne E. Goozé, 150–61. Westport, Ct.: Greenwood, 1995.

Baud, Michiel. "The Origins of Capitalist Agriculture in the Dominican Republic." *Latin American Research Review* 22, no. 2 (1987): 135–53.

Bauer, George H. "Gay Incipit: Botanical Connections, Nosegays, and Bouquets." In *Articulations of Difference,* edited by Dominique D. Fisher and Lawrence R. Schehr, 64–82. Stanford: Stanford University Press, 1997.

Beckett, Samuel, and Georges Duthuit. *Proust: Three Dialogues.* London: Calder and Bogars, 1965.

Beckles, Hilary. *Black Masculinity in Caribbean Slavery.* St. Michael, Barbados: Pine, 1996.

Benítez-Rojo, Antonio. *The Repeating Island: The Caribbean and the Postmodern Perspective.* 2nd ed. Translated by James Maraniss. Durham, N.C.: Duke University Press, 1996.

Bennahmias, Jean-Luc, and Agnès Roche. *Des Verts de toutes les couleurs: Histoire et sociologie du mouvement écolo.* Paris: Albin Michel, 1992.

Bennett, Michael. "Anti-Pastoralism, Frederick Douglass, and the Nature of Slavery."

In *Beyond Nature Writing: Expanding the Boundaries of Ecocriticism,* edited by Karla Armbruster and Kathleen R. Wallace, 195–210. Charlottesville and London: University Press of Virginia, 2001.

Benveniste, Émile. *Problèmes de linguistique générale.* Vol. 2. Paris: Éditions Gallimard, 1974.

Berlin, Ira, and Philip D Morgan, eds. *The Slaves' Economy: Independent Production by Slaves in the Americas.* London: Frank Cass, 1991.

Bernabé, Jean, Patrick Chamoiseau, and Raphaël Confiant. *Éloge de la Créolité/ In Praise of Creoleness.* Bilingual edition. Translated by M. B. Taleb-Khyar. Paris: Gallimard, 1993.

Bernand, Carmen. *Les Incas peuple du soleil.* Paris: Découvertes Gallimard, 1999.

Berry, Wendell. *The Unsettling of America: Culture and Agriculture.* San Francisco: Sierra Club Books, 1996.

Bhabha, Homi. *The Location of Culture.* London: Routledge, 1994.

Bindé, Jérôme. "Toward an Ethics of the Future." *Public Culture* 12, no. 1 (2000): 51–72.

Bojsen, Heidi. "Entretien avec Patrick Chamoiseau." Interview. In *Frankofoni. Sprog, historie, litteratur og kultur,* edited by Inge Degn, 121–31. Aalborg: Aalborg University Press, 2003.

———. "L'hybridation comme tactique de résistance dans l'oeuvre de Patrick Chamoiseau." *Révue de littérature comparée* 2 (2002): 230–42.

Bongie, Chris. *Islands and Exiles: The Creole Identities of Post/Colonial Literature.* Stanford: Stanford University Press, 1998.

Botkin, D. B. *Discordant Harmonies.* New York: Oxford University Press, 1990.

Braidotti, Rosa. *Patterns of Dissonance: A Study of Women in Contemporary Philosophy.* Translated by Elizabeth Guild. New York: Routledge, 1991.

Brathwaite, Edward K. *The Development of Creole Society in Jamaica, 1770–1820.* Oxford: Clarendon Press, 1971.

Brathwaite, Kamau. *Contradictory Omens: Cultural Diversity and Integration in the Caribbean.* Mona: Savacou Publications, 1974.

———. *Roots.* Ann Arbor: University of Michigan Press, 1993.

Brathwaite, L. E. "Gold." In "Guyana Independence," edited by George Lamming and Martin Carter, special issue, *New World* (1966).

Braziel, Jana Evans. "Jamaica Kincaid's 'In the Night'—Jablesse, Obeah, and Diasporic *Alterrains* in *At the Bottom of the River.*" In "Re-Thinking Postcoloniality," special issue, *Journal x: A Journal in Culture and Criticism* 6, no. 1 (autumn 2001): 79–104.

Braziel, Jana Evans, and Anita Mannur, eds. *Theorizing Diaspora: A Reader* (London: Blackwell, 2003).

Breeze, Jean "Binta." *Spring Cleaning.* London: Virago Press, 1992.

Brodber, Erna. *Myal.* London and Kingston: New Beacon, 1988.

Browne, Janet. *The Secular Ark: Studies in the History of Biography.* New Haven: Yale University Press, 1983.

Bruni, Sergio de Almeida. "Dutch-Brazil. A Glimpse of Paradise." In *Brasil-Holandês. Dutch-Brazil,* edited by Cristina Ferrâo and José Paulo Monteiro Soares, 21–22. Rio de Janeiro: Editora Index Ltda., 1995.

Buell, Lawrence. "The Ecocritical Insurgency." *New Literary History* 30, no. 3 (summer 1999): 699–712.

———. *The Environmental Imagination: Thoreau, Nature Writing, and the Formation of American Culture.* Cambridge and London: Belknap Press of Harvard University Press, 1995.

———. *Writing for an Endangered World: Literature, Culture, and Environment in the U.S. and Beyond.* Cambridge and London: Belknap Press of Harvard University Press, 2001.

Bundy, Andrew, ed. *Selected Essays of Wilson Harris: The Unfinished Genesis of the Imagination.* New York: Routledge, 1999.

Burnett, Paula. "Memory Theatre and the Maya: Othering Eschatology in Wilson Harris's *Jonestown.*" *Journal of Caribbean Literatures* 2, nos. 1–3 (spring 2000): 215–32.

Burton, Richard D. E. *Le roman marron: Études sur la littérature martiniquaise contemporaine.* Paris: L'Harmattan, 1997.

Cabort-Masson, Guy. "De Glissant et Chamoiseau: Vrai ou faux projet de société?" *Antilla,* 28 April 2002, 22–25.

Cabrera, Lydia. *El monte: Igbo, finda, ewe orisha, vititi nfinda: Notas sobre las religiones, la magia, las supersticiones y el folklore de los negros criollos y el pueblo de Cuba.* Miami: Ediciones Universal, 1975.

Cairo, Edgar. *Lelu! Lelu!: Het lied der vervreemding.* Haarlem: In de Knipscheer, 1984.

Camargo, Aspásia. "The picture of biodiversity." In *Brasil-Holandês: Dutch-Brazil,* edited by Cristina Ferrâo and José Paulo Monteiro Soares, 9–10. Rio de Janeiro: Editora Index Ltda., 1995.

Carpentier, Alejo. "America's Marvelous Reality." In *Magical Realism: Theory, History, Community,* edited by Lois Parkinson Zamora and Wendy Faris. Durham, N.C.: Duke University Press, 1995.

———. *The Kingdom of This World.* Translated by Harriet de Onís. 1949. New York: Noonday Press, 1957.

Casteel, Sarah Phillips. "New World Pastoral: The Caribbean Garden and Emplacement in Gisèle Pineau and Shani Mootoo." *Interventions* 5 (2003): 12–28.

Certeau, Michel de. *The Practice of Everyday Life.* Translated by Steven Rendall. Berkeley and Los Angeles: University of California Press, 1984.

Césaire, Aimé. *Cahier d'un retour au pays natal.* Edited, with introductory commentary and notes by Abiola Irele. Paris: Présence Africaine, 1983. Ibadan: New Horn Press Limited, 1994.

———. *The Collected Poetry.* Translated by Clayton Eshleman and Annette Smith. Berkeley and Los Angeles: University of California Press, 1983.

———. *Logboek van een terugkeer naar mijn geboorteland.* Translated by Simon

Simonse. Bilingual edition of *Cahier d'un retour au pays natal.* Haarlem: In de Knipscheer. Paris: Présence Africaine, 1956.

Césaire, Suzanne. "Le grand camouflage." *Tropiques* 14 (1945): 267–73. Reprint, Paris: Jean-Michel Place, 1978.

———. "Malaise d'une civilisation." *Tropiques* 5 (April 1942): 43–49. Reprint, Paris: Jean-Michel Place, 1978.

———. "Misère d'une poésie." *Tropiques* 4 (January 1942): 48–50. Reprint, Paris: Jean-Michel Place, 1978.

Chamoiseau, Patrick. *Biblique des derniers gestes.* Paris: Gallimard, 2002.

———. *Écrire en pays dominé.* Paris: Gallimard, 1997.

———. *Solibo Magnifique.* Translated by Rose-Myriam Réjouis and Val Vinokurov. London: Granta, 1999.

———. *Texaco.* Paris: Gallimard, 1992.

———. *Texaco.* Translated by Rose-Myriam Réjouis and Val Vinokurov. London: Granta, 1998.

Chamoiseau, Patrick, Gerard Delver, Édouard Glissant, and Bertène Juminer. "Manifeste pour refonder les DOM. *Le Monde,* 21 January 2000; 24 August 2003.

Chamoiseau, Patrick, and Raphaël Confiant. *Lettres créoles: Tracées antillaises et continentales de la littérature 1635–1975.* Paris: Hatier, 1991.

Chauvet, Marie. *Amour, colère, et folie.* Paris: Gallimard, 1968.

———. *Fonds des nègres.* Port-au-Prince: Imprimerie Henri Deschamps, 1960.

Cheney, Jim. *Nature/Theory/Difference.* In *Ecological Feminism,* edited by Karen J. Warren, 158–78. London and New York: Routledge, 1994.

Comvalius, Th.A.C. "Een der vormen van de Surinaamse lied na 1863." *De West Indische Gids* 20, no. 22 (1939): 350–60.

Condé, Maryse. "Unheard Voice: Suzanne Césaire and the Construct of a Caribbean Identity." In *Winds of Change: The Transforming Voices of Caribbean Women Writers and Scholars,* edited by Adele S. Newson and Linde Strong-Leek, 61–66. New York: Peter Lang, 1998.

Connor, Randy, David Hatfield Sparks, and Mariya Sparks. *Cassell's Encyclopedia of Queer Myth, Symbol, and Spirit.* London and New York: Cassell, 1997.

Cooper, Carolyn. *Noises in the Blood: Orality, Gender, and the "Vulgar" Body of Jamaican Popular Culture.* Durham, N.C.: Duke University Press, 1995.

Corzani, Jack. *Splendeur et misère: L'exotisme littéraire aux Antilles.* Pointe-à-Pitre, Guadeloupe: G.U.R.I.C., Centre d'enseignement supérieur littéraire études et documents, June 1969.

Coupe, Lawrence, ed. *The Green Studies Reader: From Romanticism to Ecocriticism.* London and New York: Routledge, 2000.

Crocker, John. *The Centaur Guide to the Caribbean and El Dorado.* Fontwell: Centaur, 1968.

Crosby, Alfred W., Jr. *The Columbian Exchange: Biological and Cultural Consequences of 1492.* Westport, Ct.: Greenwood Press, 1972.

———. *Ecological Imperialism: The Biological Expansion of Europe, 900–1900.* Cambridge: Cambridge University Press, 1986.

Cunningham, Richard L. "The Biological Impacts of 1492. In *The Indigenous Peoples of the Caribbean,* edited by Samuel L. Wilson, 29–35. Gainesville: University Press of Florida, 1997.

Cuomo, Christine J. "Ecofeminism, Deep Ecology, and Human Population." In *Ecological Feminism,* edited by Karen J. Warren, 88–105. London and New York: Routledge, 1994.

Dabydeen, Cyril. *Coastland: New and Selected Poems 1973–1987.* Oakville, Ontario: Mosaic Press, 1989.

———. *Dark Swirl.* Leeds: Peepal Tree Press, 1989.

Dacal Moure, Ramón, and Manuel Rivero de la Calle. *Art and Archeology of Pre–Columbian Cuba.* Translated by Daniel H. Sandweiss. Edited by Daniel H. Sandweiss and David R. Waters. Photographs by Kristine Edle Olsen. Pittsburgh: Pittsburgh University Press, 1996.

D'Aguiar, Fred. "Adam's Other Garden: Derek Walcott's Exploration of the Creative Imagination." *Caribana* 3 (1992–93): 67–77.

Dance, Daryl Cumber. *New World Adams: Conversations with Contemporary West Indian Writers.* Leeds: Peepal Tree Press, 1992.

Daniel, Elie, "Le Cap Haïtien: Évolution structurelle et images urbaines." *Chemins critiques; Revue Haitiano-Caraibeenne* 1, no. 4 (July 1990): 89–108.

Dash, J. Michael. "Le cri du Morne: La Poétique du paysage césairien et la littérature antillaise." In *Soleil éclaté: Mélanges offerts à Aimé Césaire,* edited by Jacqueline Leiner, 101–10. Tübingen: Gunter Narr Verlag, 1984.

———. *Edouard Glissant.* Cambridge: Cambridge University Press, 1995.

———. Introduction to *Caribbean Discourse,* by Édouard Glissant, xi–xlvii. Charlottesville: University Press of Virginia, 1989.

———. Introduction to *The Ripening,* by Édouard Glissant, 1–17. Portsmouth: Heinemann, 1985.

———. *The Other America: Caribbean Literature in a New World Context.* Charlottesville: University Press of Virginia, 1998.

Dayan, Joan. *Haiti, History, and the Gods.* Berkeley and Los Angeles: University of California Press, 1995.

"The Declaration of Basse-Terre/La Déclaration de Basse-Terre." In *Le guide politique de la Martinique: Nationalisme,* edited by Max Cantinol. http://perso.wanadoo.fr/martinique.politique/Pages/.

"The Declaration of Cayenne/La Déclaration de Cayenne." In *Le guide politique de la Martinique: Nationalisme,* edited by Max Cantinol. http://perso.wanadoo.fr/martinique.politique/Pages/.

Degras, Priska, and Bernard Magnier. "Édouard Glissant, préfacier d'une littérature future: Entretien avec Édouard Glissant." *Notre Librairie* 74 (1984): 14–20.

Deleuze, Gilles, and Félix Guattari. *Mille plateaux: Capitalisme et schizophrénie.* Paris: Les Éditions de Minuit, 1980. Translated by Brian Massumi as *A Thousand*

Plateaus: Capitalism and Schizophrenia. Minneapolis and London: University of Minnesota Press, 1987.

De Lisser, Herbert George. *Revenge: A Tale of Old Jamaica*. Kingston: Gleaner, 1919.

DeLoughrey, Elizabeth. "'The litany of islands, The rosary of archipelagoes': Caribbean and Pacific Heterotopias." In "Small Cultures: The Literature of Micro-states," special issue, *Ariel* 32, no. 1 (2001): 21–51.

———. "Tidalectics: Charting Caribbean 'Peoples of the Sea.'" *SPAN: Journal of the South Pacific Association for Commonwealth Literature and Language Studies* 47 (October 1998): 18–38.

Deren, Maya. *Divine Horsemen: The Living Gods of Haiti*. Kingston, N.Y.: McPherson and Company, 1991.

Descourtilz, M. E. *Voyage d'un naturaliste en Haïti 1799–1803*. 1809. Paris: Librairie Plon.

Díaz-Brisquet, Sergio, and Jorge Pérez-López. *Conquering Nature: The Environmental Legacy of Socialism in Cuba*. Pittsburgh: University of Pittsburgh Press, 2000.

DiGennaro, Ralph. "Winged Wanderlust." Special advertising section. *New Yorker,* 11 November 2002, 85–86, 88.

Dixon, Melvin. *Ride Out the Wilderness: Geography and Identity in Afro-American Literature*. Chicago: University of Illinois Press, 1987.

Dodd, Elizabeth. "The Great Rainbowed Swamp: History as Moral Ecology in the Poetry of Michael S. Harper." In *Beyond Nature Writing: Expanding the Boundaries of Ecocriticism,* edited by Karla Armbruster and Kathleen R. Wallace, 177–94. Charlottesville and London: University Press of Virginia, 2001.

Dodds, Paisley. "Deforestation at Root of Devastating Haiti Floods." *Los Angeles Times,* 6 June 2004.

Drake, Sandra. *Wilson Harris and the Modern Tradition: A New Architecture of the World*. Westport, Ct.: Greenwood Press, 1986.

Dumont, René. *Cuba ¿Es Socialista?* Caracas: Editorial Tiempo Nuevo. 1970.

Dye, Alan. *Cuban Sugar in the Age of Mass Production: Technology and the Economics of the Sugar Central, 1899–1929*. Stanford: Stanford University Press, 1998.

Edmond, Rod. "Home and Away: Degeneration in Imperialist and Modernist Discourse." In *Modernism and Empire,* edited by Howard J. Booth and Nigel Rigby, 39–63. Manchester and New York: Manchester University Press, 2000.

Elder, John. *Imagining the Earth: Poetry and the Vision of Nature*. Athens: University of Georgia Press, 1996.

Eichner, Bill. Afterword to *A Cafecito Story,* by Julia Alvarez, 39–45. White River Junction, Vt.: Chelsea Green, 2001.

Fonkoua, Romuald. "Discours du refus, discours de la difference, discours en 'situation' de francophonie interne: Le cas des écrivains antillais." In *Convergences et divergences dans les littératures francophones—Actes du colloque* 8–9 (February 1991), edited by D. Delte, 55–80. Paris: Éditions L'Harmattan, 1992.

Foucault, Michel. *Discipline and Punish.* Translated by Alan Sheridan. New York: Pantheon, 1977.

———. *The Order of Things: An Archaeology of the Human Sciences.* New York: Vintage, 1973.

Gaard, Greta, and Partick Murphy, ed. *Ecofeminist Literary Criticism: Theory, Interpretation, Pedagogy.* Urbana and Chicago: University of Illinois Press, 1998.

Galeano, Eduardo. *Open Veins of Latin America: Five Centuries of the Pillage of a Continent.* New York and London: Monthly Review, 1973.

Garrido, Orlando H., and Arturo Kirkconnell, illust. *Field Guide to the Birds of Cuba.* Oak Ridge: Comstock Publishing, 2000.

General Council of Martinique. http://www.cg972.fr/DIRmot3.HTM11/14-02.

Gerbi, Antonello. *Nature in the New World: From Christopher Columbus to Gonzalo Fernández de Oviedo.* Translated by Jeremy Moyle. Pittsburgh: University of Pittsburgh Press, 1985.

Gilkes, Michael. "The Landscape of Dreams: Extract from a Conversation between Wilson Harris and Michael Gilkes." In *Wilson Harris: The Uncompromising Imagination,* edited by Hena Maes-Jelinek, 31–38. Mundelstrup, Denmark: Dangaroo Press, 1991.

———. *Wilson Harris and the Caribbean Novel.* London: Longman Group Limited, 1975.

Giuliano, Alan. "The Myth of Ecotourism." *Environmental News Service,* September 2001. http://ens-news.com/ens/sep2001/2001L-09-07g.html.

Gleick, James. *Chaos: Making a New Science.* London: Abacus, 1987.

Glissant, Édouard. *Caribbean Discourse: Selected Essays.* Translated by J. Michael Dash. 1989. Charlottesville: University Press of Virginia, 1999.

———. "Creolization in the Making of the Americas." In *Race, Discourse, and the Origin of the Americas: A New World View,* edited by Vera Lawrence Hyatt and Rex Nettleford, 268–75. Washington, D.C.: Smithsonian Institution Press, 1995.

———. *Le discours antillais.* 1969. Paris: Seuil, 1981. Paris: Gallimard, 1997.

———. *Faulkner, Mississippi.* Paris: Éditions Stock, 1996. Translated by Barbara Lewis and Thomas C. Spear as *Faulkner, Mississippi.* New York: Farrar, Straus, and Giroux, 1999.

———. *Introduction à une poétique du divers.* Montréal: PUM, 1995.

———. *La Lézarde.* Paris: Gallimard, 1997.

———. *Poetics of Relation.* Translated by Betsy Wing. Ann Arbor: University of Michigan Press, 1997.

———. *Poétique de la relation.* Paris: Gallimard, 1990.

———. *Traité du tout-monde.* Paris: Gallimard, 1997.

Glotfelty, Cheryl, and Harold Fromm, eds. *The Ecocriticism Reader: Landmarks in Literary Ecology.* Athens and London: University of Georgia Press, 1996.

———. "Literary Studies in an Age of Environmental Crisis." Introduction to *The*

Ecocriticism Reader: Landmarks in Literary Ecology, edited by Cheryl Glotfelty and Harold Fromm, xv–xxxvii. Athens: University of Georgia Press, 1996.

González-Wippler, Migene. *Santería: The Religion.* New York: Harmony Books, 1989.

Goodison, Lorna. *To Us, All Flowers Are Roses.* Urbana: University of Illinois Press, 1995.

Gosson, Renée K., and Eric Faden. *Landscape and Memory: Martinican Land-People-History.* Directed by Renée Gosson and Eric Faden. 2001. Videocassette. Third World Newsreel, 2003.

Grainger, James. "The Sugar Cane: A Poem, In Four Books." In *Caribbeana: An Anthology of English Literature of the West Indies 1657–1777,* edited by Thomas W. Krise, 166–260. Chicago: University of Chicago Press, 1999.

Grove, Richard H. *Green Imperialism: Colonial Expansion, Tropical Island Edens, and the Origins of Environmentalism, 1600–1860.* Cambridge: Cambridge University Press, 1995.

Guillén, Nicolás. *Obra poética, 1922–1958.* Edited by Angel Augier. Havana: Editorial Letras Cubanas, 1980.

"Haiti's Deforestation Led to Deadly Floods." 10 June 2004. http://www .terradaily.com/2004/040529001428. 7w5797hv.html.

Hallward, Peter. *Absolutely Postcolonial: Writing between the Singular and the Specific.* Manchester and New York: Manchester University Press, 2001.

Hambuch, Doris. "Displacements in Contemporary Caribbean Writing." PhD diss., University of Atlanta, 2000.

Hamel, the Obeah Man. London: Hunt and Clarke, 1827.

Handley, George B. "A Postcolonial Sense of Place and the Work of Derek Walcott." *Isle: Interdisciplinary Studies in Literature and Environment* 7, no. 2 (summer 2000): 1–23.

"Hands off Piton: Walcott Threatens to Get Physical." *Weekend Voice,* 19 May 1990.

Harris, Wilson. "Adversarial Context and Creativity." *New Left Review* 154 (November/December 1985): 124–28.

———. "The Age of the Imagination." *Journal of Caribbean Literatures* 2, nos. 1–3 (spring 2000): 17–25.

———. "Apprenticeship to the Furies." *River City: A Journal of Contemporary Culture* 16, no. 2 (summer 1996): 104–15.

———. *Carnival.* London: Faber, 1985.

———. *Companions of the Day and Night.* London: Faber, 1975.

———. "The Composition of Reality: A Talk with Wilson Harris." Interview by Vera M. Kutzinski. *Callaloo* 18, no. 1 (winter 1995): 15–32.

———. "Creoleness: The Crossroads of a Civilization." In *Selected Essays of Wilson Harris: The Unfinished Genesis of the Imagination,* 237–47. New York: Routledge, 1999.

———. *The Dark Jester.* London: Faber, 2001.

———. *Da Silva da Silva's Cultivated Wilderness.* London: Faber, 1977.

———. *Eternity to Season.* 1954. London: New Beacon Books, 1978.

———. *Explorations: A Selection of Talks and Articles 1966–1981.* Edited by Hena Maes-Jelinek. Mundelstrup, Denmark: Dangaroo Press, 1981.

———. *The Eye of the Scarecrow.* London: Faber, 1965.

———. "The Fabric of the Imagination." *Third World Quarterly* 12, no. 1 (January 1990): 175–86.

———. *The Far Journey of Oudin.* London: Faber, 1961.

———. *The Four Banks of the River of Space.* London: Faber, 1990.

———. *Genesis of the Clowns.* London: Faber, 1977.

———. *The Guyana Quartet.* London: Faber, 1985.

———. *Heartland.* London: Faber, 1964.

———. *History, Fable, and Myth in the Caribbean and Guianas.* Georgetown, Guyana: National History and Arts Council. Ministry of Information and Culture, 1970.

———. "Imagination, Dead, Imagine: Bridging a Chasm." *Yale Journal of Criticism* 7, no. 1 (1994): 185–95.

———. Interview by Fred D'Aguiar. *Bomb,* no. 82 (winter 2002/2003): 75–80.

———. Interview by Helen Tiffin. *New Literature Review* 7 (1979): 18–29.

———. "Introduction to *Palace of the Peacock.*" Talk at the Festival Hall in London, 6 May 1998.

———. *Jonestown.* London: Faber, 1996.

———. *Merlin and Parsifal: Adversarial Twins.* London: Temenos Academy, 1997.

———. "New Preface to *The Palace of the Peacock.*" London: Faber, 1960.

———. *Palace of the Peacock.* London: Faber, 1960.

———. "The Phenomenal Legacy." In *Explorations: A Selection of Talks and Articles 1966–1981,* edited by Hena Maes-Jelinek, 43–48. Mundelstrup, Denmark: Dangaroo Press, 1981.

———. "The Power of the Word in Space and Place." Lecture delivered at the University of Cambridge in November 2000. Forthcoming.

———. "The Quest for Form." *Kunapipi* 1 (1983): 21–27.

———. "Quetzalcoatl and the Smoking Mirror: Reflections on Originality and Tradition." *Wasafiri* 20 (autumn 1994): 38–43.

———. *The Radical Imagination: Lectures and Talks.* Liège: Liège Language and Literature, 1992.

———. *The Secret Ladder.* London: Faber, 1963.

———. *Selected Essays of Wilson Harris: The Unfinished Genesis of the Imagination.* Edited by Andrew Bundy. New York: Routledge, 1999.

———. "A Talk on the Subjective Imagination," *New Letters* 40, no. 1 (October 1973): 37–48.

———. "Theatre of the Arts." In *Theatre of the Arts: Wilson Harris and the Caribbean,* edited by Hena Maes-Jelinek and Bénédicte Ledent, 1–10. Amsterdam/New York: Rodopi, 2002.

———. *Tradition, the Writer, and Society.* London: New Beacon Books, 1967.

———. *The Tree of the Sun*. London: Faber, 1978.

———. *Tumatumari*. London: Faber, 1968.

———. "The Unfinished Genesis of the Imagination." *Temenos* 13 (1992): 69–85.

———. "The Voyaging Imagination. (Undreamt-of Resources of Spirit)." Type-script. 12 pp.

———. *The Whole Armour*. London: Faber, 1962.

———. *The Wilson Harris Bibliography*. Edited by Hena Maes-Jelinek. University of Liège: Faculté de Philosophie et Lettres. http://www.ulg.ac.be/facphl/uer/d-german/L3/ whone.html.

Hauser, Nao. "On Idyll Time." Special advertising section. *New Yorker,* 11 November 2002, 115–16, 118, 120–21, 122.

Hay, Peter, *Main Currents in Western Environmental Thought*. Sydney: University of New South Wales Press, 2002.

Heller, Ben A. "Landscape, Femininity, and Caribbean Discourse." *MLN* 111, no. 2 (1996): 391–416.

Helman, Albert. *De laaiende stilte*. 1952. 7th ed. Amsterdam: Querido, 1981. Translated by Ineke Phaf-Rheinberger and Maria Roof as *Silence in Flames*. Review 68. *Literature and Arts of the Americas* 37, no. 1 (2004): 73–75.

———. *De stille plantage*. 1931. 22nd ed. Schoorl: Conserve, 1997.

———. "Volkswijsheid en orale literatuur." In *Cultureel. Mozaiek van Suriname: Bijdrage tot onderling begrip,* edited by Albert Helman et al., 82–115. Zutphen: De Walburg Pers, 1977.

Hemming, John. *The Search for El Dorado*. London: Michael Joseph Ltd., 1978.

Henke, Holger. "Mapping the Inner Plantation: A Cultural Exploration of the Origins of Caribbean Local Discourse." *Social and Economic Studies* 45, no. 4 (December 1996): 51–75.

Henry, Paget. *Caliban's Reason: Introducing Afro-Caribbean Philosophy*. New York and London: Routledge, 2000.

Herskovits, Melville, and Frances Herskovits. *Suriname Folk-lore*. New York: Columbia University Press, 1936.

Hintzen, Percy. *The Costs of Regime Survival Racial Mobilization, Elite Domination, and Control of the State in Guyana and Trinidad*. New York: Cambridge University Press, 1989.

———. "Reproducing Domination Identity and Legitimacy Constructs in the West Indies." *Social Identities* 3, no. 1 (1997): 47–75.

Hiss, Philip Hanson. *Netherlands America: The Dutch Territories in the West*. New York: Duell, Sloane, and Pearce, 1943.

Hochman, Jhan. *The Green Cultural Studies Reader: Nature in Film, Novel, and Theory*. Boise: University of Idaho Press, 1998.

Hoefte, Rosemarijn. "The Development of a Multiethnic Plantation Economy." In *Twentieth-Century Suriname: Continuities and Discontinuities in a New World Society,* edited by Rosemarijn Hoefte and Peter Meel. Kingston, Jamaica: Ian Randle, 2001.

Hollett, D. *Passage from India to El Dorado: Guyana and the Great Migration.* Madison, N.J.: Fairleigh Dickinson University Press; London: Associated University Presses, 1999.

Hoving, Isabel. "Hybridity: A Slippery Trail." In *Travelling Concepts,* vol. 1, *Text, Subjectivity, Hybridity,* edited by Joyce Goggin and Sonja Neef, 185–200. Amsterdam: ASCA Press, 2001.

———. "Remaining Where You Are: Kincaid and Glissant on Space and Knowledge." *Thamyris/Intersecting* 9 (2002): 125–40.

Hugo, Victor. *La légende des siècles.* Paris: Éditions Garnier Frères, 1974.

———. *Les rayons et les ombres.* In *Oeuvres poétiques,* vol. 1. Paris: Gallimard, 1964.

Hulme, Peter. *Colonial Encounters: Europe and the Native Caribbean.* London: Methuen, 1986.

Humboldt, Alexander. *Ensayo político sobre la isla de Cuba.* Havana: Publicaciones del Archivo Nacional de Cuba, 1960.

Jagan, Cheddi. *The West on Trial: The Fight for Guyana's Freedom.* Berlin: Seven Seas Publishers, 1975.

James, C. L. R. *Wilson Harris—A Philosophical Approach.* Trinidad and Tobago: University of the West Indies. Extra-Mural Department. Lecture given in 1965.

Jamieson, Ross W. "The Essence of Commodification: Caffeine Dependencies in the Early Modern World." *Journal of Social History* 35, no. 2 (2001): 269–94.

Johnson, Kerry Lee. "Translations of Gender, Pain, and Space: Wilson Harris's The Carnival Trilogy." *Modern Fiction Studies* 44, no. 1 (1998) 123–43.

———. "Vulnerable Figures: Landscape, Gender, and Postcolonial Identity in the Works of Wilson Harris, James Joyce, and Jean Rhys (Ireland, Dominica)." *DAI* 57–12A (abstract).

Jung, C. G. *Synchronicity: An Acausal Connecting Principle.* Translated by R.F.C. Hull. London: Routledge and Kegan Paul, 1955.

Kempadoo, Kamala. *Sun, Sex, and Gold: Tourism and Sex Work in the Caribbean.* Lanham, Md.: Rowan and Littlefield, 1999.

Kerridge, Richard, and Neil Sammells, eds. *Writing the Environment: Ecocriticism and Literature.* London and New York: Zed Books, 1998.

Keulartz, Jozef. *Strijd om de natuur: Kritiek van de radical ecologie.* Amsterdam: Boom, 1995.

Kincaid, Jamaica. *Annie John.* New York: New American Library, 1983.

———. *The Autobiography of My Mother.* New York: Farrar, Straus, and Giroux, 1996.

———. "A Fire by Ice." *New Yorker,* 22 February 1993, 65.

———. "Flowers of Evil." *New Yorker,* 5 October 1992, 156.

———. *My Garden (Book):.* New York: Farrar, Straus, and Giroux, 1999.

———. *A Small Place.* London: Virago Press, 1988.

Kirkman, Robert. *Skeptical Environmentalism: The Limits of Philosophy and Science.* Bloomington: Indiana University Press, 2002.

Kolfin, Elmer. *Van de Slavenzweep and de Muze.* Leiden: KITL, 1977.

Kutzinski, Vera M. "Improprieties: Feminism, Queerness, and Caribbean Litera-ture." In *International Feminisms: Divergent Perspectives,* edited by Ahmed I. Samatar, 165–206. Macalester Int., vol. 10. St Paul, Minn.: Macalester College, 2001.

Laguerre, Michel. *Afro-Caribbean Folk Medicine.* South Hadley, Mass.: Bergin and Garvey Publishers, 1987.

Lalla, Barbara. "Dungeons of the Soul: Frustrated Romanticism in Eighteenth- and Nineteenth-Century Literature of Jamaica." *MELUS* 21, no. 3 (autumn 1996): 3–23.

Lamartine, Alphonse de. *Méditations poétiques.* 1820. Paris: Hachette, 1891.

las Casas, Bartolomé de. *Brevísima relación acerca de la destrucción de las Indias.* 1522. Barcelona: Planeta, 1944.

———. *Historia de las Indias.* Turnhout, Belgium: Brepols, 2001.

Leopold, Aldo. *A Sand County Almanac, and Sketches Here and There.* New York: Oxford University Press, 1987.

Lerebours, Michel-Philippe. *Haïti et ses peintres de 1804 à 1980.* Vols. 1, 2. Port-au-Prince: L'Imprimeur II, 1989.

———. "Les premières étapes de la peinture haïtienne de 1804 à 1860." *Conjonc-tion,* no. 159 (April 1981).

Letchimy, Serge. *De l'habitat précaire à la ville: L'exemple martiniquais.* Paris: L'Harmattan, 1992.

Lévinas, Emmanuel. *Totalité et infini: Essai sur l'extériorité.* Paris: Kluwer Academic, 1971.

"L'heure de la modernisation." *France-Antilles Martinique,* no. 10202, 22 January 2001.

Licops, Dominique. "Redefining Culture, Politicizing Nature: Negotiating the Essentialism of Natural Metaphors of Identification in the Work of James Clifford, Paul Gilroy, and Aimé Césaire." *Thamyris/Intersecting* 8 (2001): 53–68.

Lier, R. A. J. van. *Frontier Society: A Social Analysis of the History of Surinam.* 1949. The Hague: Martinus Nijhoff, 1971.

Life and Debt. Directed and produced by Stephanie Black. Tuff Gong Pictures. New Yorker Films, 2001.

Long, Edward. *The History of Jamaica.* 3 vols. London: T. Lowndes, 1774.

Lorimer, Douglas A. Review of *Gothic Images of Race in Nineteenth-Century Britain,* by Howard L. Malchow. *Victorian Studies* 41, no. 4 (summer 1998): 681–84.

Love, Glen A. "Revaluing Nature: Toward an Ecological Criticism." In *The Ecocriticism Reader: Landmarks in Literary Ecology,* edited by Cheryl Glotfelty and Harold Fromm, 225–40. Athens and London: University of Georgia Press, 1996.

Lowenthal, David. *West Indian Societies.* New York: Oxford University Press, 1972.

Loxley, Diana. *Problematic Shores: The Literature of the Islands.* New York: St. Martin's Press, 1990.

Loy, Harry Jong. "No-Meri-Mi-Kondre." In *Sirito: 50 Surinaamse vertellingen,* edited by Michiel van Kempen and Jan Bongers, 60–63. Paramaribo: Kennedy Stichting, 1993.

Ludwig, Ralph, ed. *Écrire la parole de nuit.* Paris: Gallimard, 1994.

MacDonald, Alexander. "Home from the Fields." In *The Poets of Haiti 1782– 1934,* translated and edited by Edna Worthley Underwood, 122. Portland, Me.: Mosher Press, 1934.

MacPhee, Ross D. E. "Cuba Past/Cuba en el pasado." In *Natural Cuba/Cuba natural,* edited by Alfonso Silva Lee. Saint Paul: Pangaea, 1996.

Maes-Jelinek, Hena. "'Carnival' and Creativity in Wilson Harris's Fiction." In *The Literate Imagination: Essays on the Novels of Wilson Harris,* edited by Michael Gilkes, 45–61. London and Basingstoke: Macmillan, 1989.

———. *The Naked Design: A Reading of "The Palace of the Peacock."* Mundelstrup, Denmark: Dangaroo Press, 1976.

———. *Wilson Harris.* Boston: Twayne, 1982.

Marrero, Leví. *Cuba: Economía y sociedad.* Vols. 1–10. Madrid: Editorial Playor, 1971–84.

"The Martinique Project/Le Projet Martinique." In *Le guide politique de la Martinique: Nationalisme,* edited by Max Cantinol. http://perso.wanadoo.fr/martinique.politique/Pages/.

Marx, Karl. *The Poverty of Philosophy: Answer to the "Philosophy of Poverty" by M. Proudhon.* Beijing: Foreign Languages Press, 1978.

McCook, Stuart. *States of Nature: Science, Agriculture, and Environment in the Spanish Caribbean, 1760–1840.* Austin: University of Texas Press, 2002.

McLeod, Cynthia. *De vrije negerin Elisabeth: Gevangene van kleur.* Schoorl: Uitgeverij Conserve, 2000.

Melas, Natalie. "Re-imagining the Universal." In *Unpacking Europe: Towards a Critical Reading,* edited by Salah Hassan and Iftikhar Dadi, 134–51. Rotterdam: Museum Boijmans Van Beuningen/Nai Publishers, 2001.

Melville, Elinor G. K. *A Plague of Sheep: Environmental Consequences of the Conquest of Mexico.* Cambridge: Cambridge University Press, 1994.

Melville, Herman. "Benito Cereno." In *Billy Budd, Sailor, and Other Stories.* Harmondsworth: Penguin, 1970.

Merchant, Carolyn. *The Death of Nature: Women, Ecology, and the Scientific Revolution.* 1980. San Francisco: Harper and Row, 1983.

———. *Earthcare: Women and the Environment.* New York: Routledge, 1995.

———. "Reinventing Eden: Western Culture as a Recovery Narrative." In *Uncommon Ground: Rethinking the Human Place in Nature,* edited by William Cronon, 132–59. New York: Norton, 1996.

Merleau-Ponty, M. *Phénoménologie de la perception.* Paris: Gallimard, 1945.

Mitchell, W. J. T. "Imperial landscape." In *Landscape and Power,* edited by Mitchell, 5–34. Chicago: University of Chicago Press, 1994.

Mitsch, Ruthmarie H. "Maryse Condé's Mangroves." *Research in African Literatures* 28, no. 4 (1997): 54–70.

Montero, Mayra. "The Great Bonanza of the Antilles." Translated by Lizabeth Paravisini-Gebert. In *Healing Cultures: Art and Religion and Curative Practices in the Caribbean and its Diaspora,* edited by Margarite Fernández Olmos and Lizabeth Paravisini-Gebert, 195–202. New York: Palgrave, 2001.

———. *Tu, la oscuridad.* Barcelona: Tusquets, 1995. Translated by Edith Grossman as *In the Palm of Darkness: A Novel.* New York: Harper Collins, 1997.

Mootoo, Shani. *Cereus Blooms at Night.* Vancouver: Gang Press Publishers, 1996.

Moreau de Saint-Méry, Médéric-Louis-Elie. *A Civilization That Perished; The Last Years of White Colonial Rule in Haiti.* 1797. Edited and translated by Ivor Spencer. Lanham, Md.: University Press of America, 1985.

Moreno Fraginals, Manuel. *Cuba/España, España/Cuba: Historia común.* Barcelona: Grijalbo Mondadori, 1995.

———. *El ingenio: El complejo económico y social cubano del azúcar.* Vols. 1, 3. Havana: Editorial de Ciencias Sociales, 1978.

Mungroo, Albert. "Het weeklagen van de kankantrie." In *Nieuwe Surinaamse verhalen,* edited by Michiel van Kempen, 55–82. Paramaribo: Uitgeverij De Volksboekwinkel, 1986.

Musset, Alfred de. "La nuit d'août." 1835–37. In *Poésies,* 316–19. Paris: Gallimard, 1957.

Naess, Arne. "Deep Ecology." In *Key Concepts in Critical Theory: Ecology,* edited by Carolyn Merchant, 120–24. Atlantic Highlands, N.J.: Humanities Press, 1994.

Naipaul, V. S. *The Enigma of Arrival.* London: Penguin, 1987.

———. *A House for Mr. Biswas.* London: Andre Deutsch, 1961.

———. *The Middle Passage.* New York: Vintage Books, 1962.

Nonon, E. "La faune précolombienne des Antilles françaises." *Tropiques* 10 (February 1944). Reprint. Paris: Jean-Michel Place, 1978.

O'Brien, Susie. "The Garden and the World: Jamaica Kincaid and the Cultural Borders of Ecocriticism." *Mosaic: A Journal for the Interdisciplinary Study of Literature* 35, no. 2 (June 2002): 167–84.

O'Gorman, Edmundo. *The Invention of America: An Inquiry into the Historical Nature of the New World and the Meaning of Its History.* Bloomington: Indiana University Press, 1961.

Ormerod, Beverley. "French West Indian Writing since 1970." In *French and West Indian: Martinique, Guadeloupe, and French Guiana Today,* edited by Richard D. E. Burton and Fred Reno, 167–87. Charlottesville: University Press of Virginia, 1995.

————. *An Introduction to the French Caribbean Novel.* London: Heinemann, 1985.

Ortiz, Fernando. *Cuban Counterpoint: Tobacco and Sugar.* Translated by Harriet de Onís. 1947. Durham: Duke University Press, 1995.

Pané, Ramón. *Relación acerca de las antiguedades de los indios, las cuales, con diligencia, como hombre que sabe su idioma, recogió por mandato del Almirante.* 1571. Mexico: Siglo XXI, 1977.

Paravisini-Gebert, Lizabeth. "Caribbean Literature in Spanish." In *The Cambridge History of African and Caribbean Literatures,* 670–710. Cambridge: Cambridge University Press, 2003.

————. "Colonial and Post-Colonial Gothic: The Caribbean." In *The Cambridge Companion to Gothic Literature,* edited by Gerrold Hodges, 229–57. New York: Cambridge University Press, 2002.

————. "The Haitian Revolution in Interstices and Shadows: A Re-Reading of Alejo Carpentier's *The Kingdom of This World.*" *Research in African Literatures* 35, no. 1 (spring 2004): 114–27.

————. "*The White Witch of Rosehall* and the Legitimacy of Female Power in the Caribbean Plantation." *Journal of West Indian Literature* 4, no. 2 (1990): 25–45.

Pardo Tomás, José, and María Luz López Terrada. *Las primeras noticias sobre plantas americanas en las relaciones de viajes y crónicas de Indias (1493–1553).* Valencia: Universitat de València—CSIC, 1993.

Parry, John. "Plantation and Provision Ground: An Historical Sketch of the Introduction of Food Crops to Jamaica." *Revista de historia de América* 39 (1955): 1–20.

Pattullo, Polly. "Green Crime, Green Redemption: The Environment and Ecotourism in the Caribbean." In *Green Guerrillas: Environmental Conflicts and Initiatives in Latin America and the Caribbean,* edited by Helen Collinson, 176–86. London: Latin American Bureau, 1996.

Payne, Tommy. "Windows on Guyanese History." In *Co-operative Republic, Guyana 1970: A Study of Aspects of Our Way of Life,* edited by L. Searwar. Georgetown, June 1970.

Paz, Octavio. *The Other Voice: Essays on Modern Poetry.* Translated by Helen Lane. New York: Harcourt Brace Jovanovich, 1991.

Pedreira, Antonio S. *Insularismo.* Rio Piedras: Editorial Edil, 1992.

Perfecto, Ivette, Robert A. Rice, Russell Greenberg, and Marth E. Van der Voort. "Shade Coffee: A Disappearing Refuge for Biodiversity." *BioScience* 46, no. 8 (1996): 598–608.

Perfit, Michael R., and Ernest E. Williams. "Geological Constraints and Biological Retrodictions in the Evolution of the Caribbean Sea and its Islands." In *Biogeography of the West Indies Past, Present, and Future,* edited by Charles A. Woods, 47–102. Gainesville, Fl.: Sandhill Crane Press, 1989.

Phaf-Rheinberger, Ineke. "Caspar Barlaeus y la ética de una expansión global: 'Mercator sapiens' (1632) y 'Rerum per octennium in Brasilia . . . gestarum . . .

historia' (1647)." In *De litteris Neolatinis. America Meridionali, Portugallia, Hispania, Italia cultis,* edited by Theodoricus Briesemeister and Axelius Schönberger, 123–35. Frankfurt, Germany, 2002.

———. "'Und Dideldumdei und Schnedderedeng': Von der Black Atlantic nach Berlin-Brandenburg." In *Geschichte und Gegenwart,* edited by Gregor Wolff, 85–105. Die Berliner und Brandenburger Lateinamerikaforschung. Berlin: Wissenschaftlicher Verlag Berlin, 2001.

———. "La utopía moderna en Brasil en el siglo XVII: Los pinceles descriptivos y el diccionario visual de Frans Post." *Estudios Avanzados Inter@ctivos* 2, no. 4 (2003). http://www.usach.cl/revistaidea/.

Philip, Marlene Nourbese. "A Piece of Land Surrounded." *Orion* 14, no. 2 (1995): 41–47.

Phillips, Dana. "Ecocriticism, Literary Theory, and the Truth of Ecology." *New Literary History* 30, no. 3 (summer 1999): 577–602.

Platt, Kamala. "Ecocritical Chicana Literature: Ana Castillo's 'Virtual Realism.'" In *Ecofeminist Literary Criticism: Theory, Interpretation, Pedagogy,* edited by Greta Gaard and Patrick Murphy, 139–57. Urbana and Chicago: University of Illinois Press, 1998.

Poirier, Richard. *A World Elsewhere: The Place of Style in American Literature.* New York: Oxford University Press, 1966.

Poonai, N. O. "Wilderness and Wildlife in Guyana." In *Co-Operative Republic, Guyana 1970: A Study of Aspects of Our Way of Life,* edited by L. Searwar, 161–93.

Pratt, Mary Louise. *Imperial Eyes: Travel Writing and Transculturation.* London: Routledge, 1992.

Prest, John. *The Garden of Eden: The Botanic Garden and the Re-Creation of Paradise.* New Haven and London: Yale University Press, 1981.

Price, Sally, and Richard Price. *Two Evenings in Saramaka.* Chicago: University of Chicago Press, 1991.

Price-Mars, Jean. *Ainsi parla l'oncle.* 1928. Ottawa: Éditions Leméac, 1973.

Prieto, Eric. "Landscaping Identity in Contemporary Caribbean Literature." In *Studies in Francophone and Post-colonial Cultures,* edited by Kamal Salhi. 141–52. Lanham, Md.: Lexington Books, 2003.

———. "The Poetics of Place, the Rhetoric of Authenticity, and Aimé Césaire's *Cahier d'un retour au pays natal.*" *Dalhousie French Studies* 55 (summer 2001): 142–51.

Purdom, Judy. "Mapping Difference." *Third Text* 32 (1995): 19–32.

Ragatz, Lowell Joseph. *The Fall of the Planter Class in the British Caribbean, 1763–1833.* New York: Octagon Books, 1963.

Ramchand, Kenneth. Preface to *The Palace of the Peacock,* by Wilson Harris. London: Faber, 1968.

Ramdin, Ron, ed. *The Other Middle Passage: Journal of a Voyage from Calcutta to Trinidad, 1858.* London: Hansib Publications, 1994.

Ramos, Aarón Gamaliel. "Caribbean Territories at the Crossroads." Introduction to *Islands at the Crossroads: Politics in the Non-Independent Caribbean,* edited by Aarón Gamaliel Ramos and Angel Israel Rivera, xii–xxi. Kingston: Ian Randle Publishers, 2001.

Randall, Stephen J., and Graeme S. Mount. *The Caribbean Basin: An International History.* London and New York: Routledge, 1998.

Reed, T. V. "Toward an Environmental Justice Ecocriticism." In *The Environmental Justice Reader: Politics, Poetics, and Pedagogy,* 145–62. Tucson: University of Arizona Press, 2002.

Reid, Victor S. *New Day.* New York: Knopf, 1949.

Report of the Lords of the Committee of the Council Appointed for the Consideration of All Matters Relating to Trade and Foreign Plantations. London, 1789.

Rhys, Jean. *Wide Sargasso Sea.* New York: Norton, 1996.

Richardson, Alan. "Romantic Voodoo: Obeah and British Culture, 1797–1807." In *Sacred Possessions: Vodou, Santería, Obeah, and the Caribbean,* edited by Margarite Fernández Olmos and Lizabeth Paravisini-Gebert, 171–94. New Brunswick: Rutgers University Press, 1997.

Roach, Eric. *The Flowering Rock.* London: Peepal Tree Press, 1992.

Rochefort, Charles de. *Histoire naturelle et morale des îles Antilles de l'Amérique.* Amsterdam: Chez Arnould Leers, 1658.

Rodman, Selman. *The Miracle of Haitian Art.* Garden City, N.Y.: Doubleday, 1974.

Rodney, Walter. *A Short History of the Guyanese Working People, 1881–1905.* Baltimore: Johns Hopkins University Press, 1981.

Roemer, Astrid. H. *Was getekend.* Amsterdam: Arbeiderspers, 1998.

Rohlehr, Gordon. *Pathfinder: Black Awakening in the Arrivants.* Port of Spain: College Press, 1981.

Rosendale, Steven, ed. *The Greening of Literary Scholarship: Literature, Theory, and the Environment.* Iowa City: University of Iowa Press, 2002.

Roumain, Jacques. *Gouverneurs de la rosée.* 1946. Paris: Messidor, 1989.

———. *Masters of the Dew.* Translated by Langston Hughes and Mercer Cook. Oxford: Heinemann, 1997.

"Round Table of Caribbean Writers." Interview with Jamaica Kincaid, Edwidge Danticat, and Enrique Fernández, by Ray Suarez. *Talk of the Nation.* National Public Radio (Audiofile, 98 minutes), 3 April 1997. http://www.npr.org/templates/story/story.php?storyid=1011291.

Rouse, Irving. *The Tainos: Rise and Decline of the People Who Greeted Columbus.* New Haven: Yale University Press, 1992.

Said, Edward. *Culture and Imperialism.* New York: Vintage Books, 1993.

"Saint Lucia." *The Lonely Planet Online.* http://www.lonelyplanet.com/destinations/caribbean/saint-lucia/printable.htm.

Salkey, Andrew. *A Quality of Violence.* London: Hutchinson, 1959.

Sánchez Roa, Adriano. *Los dueños del café: 30 años de economía cafetalera.* Santo Domingo: Editora Corripio, 1990.

Schiebinger, Londa. *Nature's Body: Gender in the Making of Modern Science.* Boston: Beacon Press, 1993.

Searwar, L., ed. *Co-Operative Republic, Guyana 1970: A Study of Aspects of Our Way of Life.* Georgetown, June 1970.

Senior, Olive. *Gardening in the Tropics.* Toronto: McClelland and Stewart, 1994.

Sheller, Mimi. *Consuming the Caribbean: From Arawaks to Zombies.* London and New York: Routledge, 2003.

————. "Natural Hedonism: The Invention of Caribbean Islands as Tropical Playgrounds." In *The Society for Caribbean Studies Annual Conference Papers,* edited by Sandra Courtman, vol. 2, 2001: 28 paragraphs. http://www.scsonline .freeserve.co.uk/olvol2.html. Also in David Timothy Duval, ed. *Tourism in the Caribbean: Trends, Developments, Prospects.* New York: Routledge, 2004.

Shepherd, Verene A., and Glen L. Richards, eds. *Questioning Creole: Creolisation Discourses in Caribbean Culture.* Kingston: Ian Randle, 2002.

Sherry, Thomas W. "Shade Coffee: A Good Brew Even in Small Doses." *The Auk: A Quarterly Journal of Ornithology* 117, no. 3 (2000): 563–68.

Shiva, Vandana. *Biopiracy: The Plunder of Nature and Knowledge.* Boston: South End Press, 1997.

————. *Stolen Harvest: The Hijacking of the Global Food Supply.* Boston: South End Press, 1999.

————. *Tomorrow's Biodiversity (Prospects for Tomorrow).* New York: Thames and Hudson, 2001.

————. *Water Wars: Privatization, Pollution, and Profit.* Boston: South End Press, 2002.

Silva Lee, Alfonso. *Natural Cuba/Cuba natural.* Saint Paul: Pangea, 1996.

Smyth, Heather. "Sexual Citizenship and Caribbean-Canadian Fiction: Dionne Brand's In *Another Place, Not Here* and Shani Mootoo's *Cereus Blooms at Night.*" *ARIEL: A Review of International English Literature* 30, no. 2 (1999): 141–60.

Stedman, John Gabriel. *Narrative of a Five Years' Expedition against the Revolted Negroes of Surinam.* 1791. Edited with an introduction by Richard Price and Sally Price. Baltimore and London: Johns Hopkins University Press, 1988.

Stehlé, Henri. "Les dénominations génériques des végétaux aux Antilles françaises, histoires et légendes qui s'y rattachent." *Tropiques* 10 (February 1944). Reprint, Paris: Jean-Michel Place, 1978.

Stepan, Nancy Leys. *The Idea of Race in Science: Great Britain 1800–1960.* Hamden: Archon Books, 1982.

————. *Picturing Tropical Nature.* Ithaca: Cornell University Press, 2001.

Stephen, Henri J. M. *Winti: Afro-Surinaamse religie en magische rituelen in Suriname en Nederland.* Amsterdam: Karnak, 1985.

Stott, Annette. *Holland Mania: The Unknown Dutch Period in American Art and Culture.* New York: Overlook Press/Ambo/Anthos, 1998.

Thiong'o, Ngũgĩ wa. "In the Name of the Mother: Lamming and the Cultural Significance of 'Mother Country' in the Decolonization Process." In *Sisyphus and Eldorado: Magical and Other Realisms in Caribbean Literature,* edited by Timothy J. Reiss, 127–42. Trenton, N.J.: Africa World Press, 2002.

Thoby-Marcelin, Philippe, and Pierre Marcelin. *The Beast of the Haitian Hills.* Translated by Peter C. Rhodes. New York: Time-Life Books, 1964.

Tiffin, Helen "'Flowers of Evil,' Flowers of Empire: Roses and Daffodils in the Works of Jamaica Kincaid, Olive Senior and Lorna Goodison." *SPAN* 46 (April 1998): 58–71.

———. "The Metaphor of Anancy in Caribbean Literature." In *Myth and Metaphor,* edited by Robert Sellick, 15–52. Adelaide: Centre for Research in the New Literatures in English, 1982.

Tomich, Dale W. "The Other Face of Slave Labor: Provision Grounds and Internal Marketing in Martinique." In *Caribbean Slave Society and Economy: A Student Reader,* edited by Hilary Beckles and Verene Shephard, 304–18. New York: New Press, 1991.

Topik, Steven C. "Coffee Anyone? Recent Research on Latin American Coffee Societies." *Hispanic American Historical Review* 80, no. 2 (2000): 225–66.

Underwood, Edna Worthy, trans. and ed. *The Poets of Haiti 1732–1934.* Portland, Me.: Mosher Press, 1934.

United Nations. "Press Release GA/9320." 2 October 1997. http://www.un.org/ search.

———. "Press Release GA/9537: United Nations General Assembly Plenary-1d, 91st Meeting." 15 December 1998. http://www.un.org/search.

———. "Press Release SG/SM/6364." 17 October 1997. http://www.un.org/ search.

———. "United Nations Economic and Social Council Resolution 1998/40, 46th Plenary Meeting." 30 July 1998. http://www.un.org/documents/ecosoc/res/ 1998/eres1998-40.htm.

Valhodia, Jil. "La guerre doit être menée sur le terrain de l'imaginaire." Interview with Patrick Chamoiseau. *Les périphériques vous parlent* 10 (1998): 58–63.

Vidal, Beatriz, and Nancy Van Laan. *The Legend of El Dorado: A Latin American Tale.* New York: Knopf, 1991.

Vigny, Alfred de. *Oeuvres complètes.* 2 vols. Paris: Gallimard, 1948.

Viola, Herman J., and Carolyn Margolis, eds. *Seeds of Change.* Washington: Smithsonian Institution Press, 1991.

Walcott, Derek. "The Antilles: Fragments of Epic Memory." In *What the Twilight Says: Essays,* by Walcott, 65–86. New York: Farrar, Straus, and Giroux, 1998.

———. *The Bounty.* New York: Farrar, Straus, and Giroux, 1993.

———. *Collected Poems, 1948–1984.* 1996. New York: Farrar, Straus, and Giroux, 2000.

———. "A Frowsty Fragrance." Review of *Caribbeana: An Anthology of English Literature of the West Indies 1657–1777*, edited by Thomas W. Krise. *New York Review of Books*, 15 June 2000, 57–61.

———. "The Muse of History." in *What the Twilight Says: Essays*, by Walcott, 36–64. New York: Farrar, Straus, and Giroux, 1998.

———. *Omeros*. New York: Farrar, Straus, and Giroux, 1990.

———. "What the Twilight Says." In *What the Twilight Says: Essays*, by Walcott, 3–35. New York: Farrar, Straus, and Giroux, 1998.

Wallace, Alfred Russell. *Island Life*. 1880. New York: AMS Press, 1975.

Wallace, Kathleen R., and Karla Armbruster. "The Novels of Toni Morrison: 'Wild Wilderness When There Was None.'" In *Beyond Nature Writing: Expanding the Boundaries of Ecocriticism*, edited by Armbruster and Wallace, 211–32. Charlottesville and London: University Press of Virginia, 2001.

Waridel, Laure. *Coffee with Pleasure: Just Java and World Trade*. London: Black Rose, 2002.

Warren, Karen J., ed. *Ecological Feminism*. London and New York: Routledge, 1994.

Waswo, Richard. "The History That Literature Makes." *New Literary History* (spring 1987): 541–64.

Watts, David. *The West Indies: Patterns of Development, Culture, and Environmental Change since 1492*. Cambridge: Cambridge University Press, 1987.

Weiner, Tim. "Floods Bring More Suffering to a Battered Haitian Town." *New York Times*, 29 May 2004.

———. "A Haitian Village Gets a Barrage of Care." *New York Times*, 31 May 2004.

Weiner, Tim, and Lydia Polgreen. "Grief as Haitians and Dominican Tally Flood Toll." *New York Times*, 28 May 2004.

Wekker, Gloria. *Ik ben een gouden munt: Subjectiviteit en seksualiteit van creoolse volksklasse vrouwen in Paramaribo*. Amsterdam: Feministische Uitgeverij VITA, 1994.

———. "Of Mimic Men and Unruly Women." In *Twentieth-Century Suriname*, edited by Rosemarijn Hoefte and Peter Meel. Kingston: Ian Randle, 2001.

———. "Re: mati and literature." E-mail to Natasha Tinsley. 20 July 2001.

Williams, Brackette F. *Stains on My Name, War in My Veins: Guyana and the Politics of Cultural Struggle*. Durham, N.C.: Duke University Press, 1991.

Williams, Ernest E. "Old Problems and New Opportunities in West Indian Biogeography." In *Biogeography of the West Indies Past, Present, and Future*, edited by Charles A. Woods, 1–46. Gainesville, Fl.: Sandhill Crane Press, 1989.

Wimpffen, Alexandre-Stanislas de. *Haïti au XVIIIe siècle; Richesse et esclavage dans une colonie française*. 1797. Paris: Édition Karthala, 1993.

Wing, Elizabeth S. "Archaeological Implications for Lesser Antilles Biogeography: The Small Island Perspective." In *Biogeography of the West Indies Past, Present, and Future*, edited by Charles A. Woods, 137–52. Gainesville, Fl.: Sandhill Crane Press, 1989.

Woods, Charles A., and Jose Alberto Ottenwalder. *The Natural History of Southern Haiti.* Gainesville: University Press of Florida, 1992.

Wunderle, Joseph M., Jr. "Avian Distribution in Dominican Shade Coffee Plantations: Area and Habitat Relationships." *Journal of Field Ornithology* 70, no. 1 (1999): 58–70.

Wunderle, Joseph M., Jr., and Steven C. Latta. "Avian Resource Use in Dominican Shade Coffee Plantations." *Wilson Bulletin* 110, no. 2 (1998): 271–81.

———. "Winter Site Fidelity of Nearctic Migrants in Shade Coffee Plantations of Different Sizes in the Dominican Republic." *The Auk: A Quarterly Journal of Ornithology* 117, no. 3 (2000): 596–614.

Wynter, Sylvia. "Novel and History, Plot and Plantation." *Savacou* 5 (June 1971): 95–102.

Young, Matthew French. *Guyana, The Lost El Dorado: A Report on My Work and Life Experiences in Guyana, 1925–1980.* London: Peepal Tree Press, 1998.

Young, Robert J. C. *Colonial Desire: Hybridity in Theory, Culture and Race.* London: Routledge, 1995.

Zamora, Juan Clemente. *Indigenismos en la lengua de los conquistadores.* Barcelona: Universidad de Puerto Rico, 1976.

Zemon Davie, Nathalie. "Maria Sybille Merian. Metamorphoses." In *Women on the Margins: Three Seventeeth-Century Lives,* 140–202. Cambridge and London: Harvard University Press, 1995.

Contributors

ANTONIO BENÍTEZ-ROJO, renowned for *The Repeating Island,* is also author of numerous critical essays, short stories (including the collections *A View from the Mangrove* and *Tute de Reyes,* the latter of which won the Casa de las Américas Prize in 1967), and works of historical fiction (*Sea of Lentils,* among others). Before leaving his native Cuba in 1980, he worked in various capacities at Casa de las Américas. He was Thomas B. Walton Jr. Memorial Professor of Spanish at Amherst College until his unexpected passing on 5 January 2005.

LEGRACE BENSON holds a Ph.D. from Cornell University and an M.F.A. from the University of Georgia. Currently she is Director of the Arts of Haiti Research Project and an associate editor of the *Journal of Haitian Studies.* Author of a number of articles in scholarly journals concerning Haitian art, she has also contributed chapters to books concerning educational, environmental, and arts issues in Haiti and the wider Caribbean.

HEIDI BOJSEN is Assistant Professor at the Institute of Language and Cultural Studies, Roskilde University, Denmark. She is currently concluding her Ph.D. at the Institute of English, German, and Romance Languages at Copenhagen University. While her dissertation primarily concentrates on how cultural and national identities are represented in selected novels by Patrick Chamoiseau (Martinique) and Ahmadou Kourouma (Ivory Coast), her published articles cover questions on multiculturalism and hybridity in the Caribbean, conceptions of literature in Europe and Africa, and the politics of the French language.

JANA EVANS BRAZIEL is Assistant Professor of English at the University of Cincinnati. Braziel has published numerous articles and has also coedited three collections: *Race and the Foundations of Knowledges: Cultural Amnesia in the Academy* (forthcoming); *Theorizing Diaspora: A Reader* (2003); and *Bodies Out of Bounds: Fatness and Transgression* (2001). She is currently completing two book manuscripts: "Rethinking the 'Black

Atlantic': Race, Diaspora, and Cultural Production in Haiti and Haiti's Tenth Department," which explores Haitian diasporic cultural production as "arts of resistance" to U.S. imperialism and global capitalism; and "'Haiti's Gwo Nègs': Haïtiennité and the Trans-American Politics of Black Masculinity in Diaspora," which explores the cultural constructions and performative instantiations of black masculinity in diaspora through the Haitian Kreyòl concept of *gwo nègs*—or "big men."

RAPHAËL CONFIANT is an Assistant Professor of Regional Language and Culture in the Department of Applied Multi-Disciplinary Studies at the Université des Antilles et de la Guyane in Martinique, and one of the most recognized French West Indian writers. He is cofounder of the most recent identity theory to emerge from the French-speaking Caribbean: Créolité. In addition to teaching and writing (in French and in Creole), he is a member of several ecological associations on the island of Martinique. An ardent defender of Creole culture and the environment, he voices his opposition to the threat of French assimilation in both his writing and his action. His most recent work is *La Panse du chacal: roman* (2004, éditions Mercure de France, Paris).

CYRIL DABYDEEN, born in Guyana, is an acclaimed poet and short-story writer; he has written eight books of poetry, five books of stories, and three novels. He also edited *A Shapely Fire: Changing the Literary Landscape* and *Another Way to Dance: Contemporary Asian Poetry in Canada and the U.S.* His poetry and fiction have appeared in Canada, the United States, the United Kingdom, Australia, Asia, and the Caribbean, and are anthologized in over twenty volumes in five countries. A former Poet Laureate of Ottawa, he is an editor for the *Journal of Caribbean Studies*. His latest books are *Hemisphere of Love* (poetry); *Imaginary Origins: New and Selected Poems*; and *Play a Song for Me, Somebody* (fiction). He is with the Department of English, University of Ottawa, Canada.

ELIZABETH M. DELOUGHREY is Assistant Professor in the English Department at Cornell University. She has recently completed a comparative study entitled *Routes and Roots: Caribbean and Pacific Island Tidalectics* and has published in journals such as *Ariel, Interventions,* and the *Journal of Caribbean Literatures.*

RENÉE K. GOSSON is Assistant Professor of French and Francophone Studies at Bucknell University where, in addition to the French language, she teaches courses on the literature and culture of the French Caribbean. Her research concentrates on the neocolonial French presence in Martinique, read through various cultural sites: literature, landscape, commemorative statues, and music. She recently coproduced a film (with Eric Faden) entitled *Landscape and Memory: Martinican Land-People-History,* which juxtaposes Martinique's Creolists' ecological and ideological concerns with actual footage of symptoms of environmental and cultural distress on the island.

GEORGE B. HANDLEY is Associate Professor of Humanities at Brigham Young University, where he teaches literatures and cultures of the Americas and environmental humanities. A former director of Latin American Studies at BYU, he is the author of *Postslavery Literatures in the Americas* (2000) and of various articles on Caribbean and U.S. authors. He is currently writing a book-length ecocritical study of Walt Whitman, Pablo Neruda, and Derek Walcott.

WILSON HARRIS is one of the foremost writers and philosophers of our time. Born in Guyana and having resided for many years in England, he is the author of over twenty novels, including his best-known, *Palace of the Peacock* (1960), and his most recent work, *The Dark Jester* (2001). His visionary creative and nonfiction work has engaged in the broadest terms with questions of cultural literacy and the imagination, histories of conquest, indigenous and diasporic artistic production, western esotericism, literatures of the Americas, and the global necessity of engaging quantum landscapes in the ongoing project of cross-cultural and ecological sustainability.

TRENTON HICKMAN is Assistant Professor of English at Brigham Young University. He has published (and has essays forthcoming) on the writing of Jean Rhys, Cormac McCarthy, and the Nuyorican poets, as well as on the work of Julia Alvarez.

ISABEL HOVING is working in the fields of intercultural and postcolonial theory, cultural analysis, and gender studies. She is currently affiliated with the University of Leiden, where she works on a project on plant metaphors in Caribbean migrant writing. Her study *In Praise of New Travelers,* on Caribbean migrant women writing, was published by Stanford University Press in 2001. She is editor of *Thamyris/Intersecting: Place, Sex, and Race.*

SHONA N. JACKSON is Assistant Professor of English at Texas A&M, the founder and coeditor of the book series in Caribbean Studies at Lexington Books, and a member of the editorial board of *Wadabagei: A Journal of the Caribbean and Its Diaspora*. Her publications include "The Contemporary Crisis in Guyanese National Identification" in *Ethnicity, Class and Nationalism: Caribbean and Extra-Caribbean Dimensions* (edited by Anton L. Allahar, 2005) and "Guyana, Cuba, Venezuela and the 'Routes' to Cultural Reconciliation between Latin American and the Caribbean" in *Small Axe: A Caribbean Journal of Criticism* (forthcoming). Her research interests include twentieth-century (Anglophone) Caribbean, African, and African American literature, as well as postcolonial literature and theory and Caribbean history and culture.

HENA MAES-JELINEK, OBE, holds a B.A. from Brigham Young University, and a *licence* and a Ph.D. from the University of Liège. She is Emeritus Professor of the University of Liège and a member of the Belgian Royal Academy. She is the author of *Criticism of Society in the English Novel between the Wars; The Naked Design: A Reading of "The Palace of the Peacock";* and a monograph on *Heart of Darkness*. She has published extensively on British and postcolonial fiction (mainly Australian and Caribbean) and on postcolonial criticism inspired by Wilson Harris's concepts. She edited *Commonwealth Literature and the Modern World; A Shaping of Connections* (with Kirsten Holst Petersen and Anna Rutherford); *Wilson Harris: The Uncompromising Imagination; Crisis and Creativity in the New Literatures in English* (with Geoffrey Davis); and *A Talent(ed) Digger: Creations, Cameos and Essays in Honour of Anna Rutherford* (with Gordon Collier and Geoffrey Davis). She has published extensively on the work of Wilson Harris in various journals and collections of essays and edited *Theatre of the Arts: Wilson Harris and the Caribbean*. With Gordon Collier and Geoffrey she is general editor of the CROSS/CULTURES series published by Rodopi.

LIZABETH PARAVISINI-GEBERT is Professor of Caribbean Culture and Literature in the Department of Hispanic Studies and the Program in Africana Studies at Vassar College. She is the author of a number of books, among them *Phyllis Shand Allfrey: A Caribbean Life* (1996); *Jamaica Kincaid: A Critical Companion* (1999); *Creole Religions of the Caribbean* (with Margarite Fernández Olmos) (2003); and the forthcoming *Literatures of the Caribbean* (2005). She is at work on "Glimpses of Hell," a study of the aftermath of the 1902 eruption of the Mont Pelée volcano in Martinique, and on "José Martí: A Life," a biography of the Cuban patriot. She has coedited a number of collections of essays, most notably *Sacred Possessions: Vodou, Santería, Obeah, and the Caribbean* (1997). Her most recent edited volume, *Obsolete Geographies: Displacements and Transformations in Caribbean Cultures,* will be published in 2005.

INEKE PHAF-RHEINBERGER is an independent scholar in Berlin, Germany. She has published on Dutch- and Spanish-Caribbean as well as Latin American literatures. Her books include *Novelando la Habana* (1990); *Zur Architektur von Ricardo Porro in Vaduz und Havanna* (2004); *The Caribbean and Latin America* (ed. 1996); *Historia modernas, imaginarios urbanos, experiencias de fragmentación: El Caribe y América Latina* (ed. 2004); *A History of Literature in the Caribbean: The Dutch-speaking Area* (coed. 2001); and *Iconografía y ciencia: Estategias de la communicación en América* (coed. 2003).

ERIC PRIETO is Associate Professor of French at the University of California, Santa Barbara. His primary fields of interest are the relations between music and literature; twentieth-century modernism; and postcolonial Francophone literature. His publications include *Listening In: Music, Mind, and the Modernist Narrative* (2002) and a number of articles on postcolonial topics, including Aimé Césaire's *Cahier,* Martinican environmental fictions, the biguine, and the Belleville novel. The essay published here is related to his current book project on the poetics of place.

HELEN TIFFIN is currently Canada Research Chair in English and Postcolonial Studies at Queen's University. She is coauthor (with Bill Ashcroft and Gareth Griffiths) of *The Empire Writes Back: Theory and Practice in Post-Colonial Literatures* (1989) and *Key Concepts in Post-Colonial Studies* (1998); and (with Diana Brydon) of *Decolonising Fictions* (1993). She has edited or coedited five collections on postcolonial and environmental topics and is now researching the relationship between representation, colonialism, postcolonialism, and animals.

NATASHA TINSLEY is the Mellon Postdoctoral Fellow of Caribbean Literature at the University of Chicago. Her dissertation, *Thiefing Sugar: Reading Eroticism between Women in Caribbean Literature,* is the first book-length study of same-sex desire between women in the Dutch-, French-, and English-speaking Caribbean. Her articles have appeared in the publications of the Association of Netherlandic Studies, and she will also be published in the forthcoming anthology *Are All the Women Still White?* Her creative fiction appears in *Spirited,* an anthology of the work of black gay and lesbian writers edited by Lisa Moore.

DEREK WALCOTT was awarded the Nobel Prize for Literature in 1992. Born in St. Lucia in 1930, Walcott is well known internationally for his poetry, playwriting, and cultural criticism. His most recent book, *The Prodigal,* appeared in 2004.

Index

Vera M. Kutzinski, *Sugar's Secrets: Race and the Erotics of Cuban Nationalism*

Richard D. E. Burton and Fred Reno, editors, *French and West Indian: Martinique, Guadeloupe, and French Guiana Today*

A. James Arnold, editor, *Monsters, Tricksters, and Sacred Cows: Animal Tales and American Identities*

J. Michael Dash, *The Other America: Caribbean Literature in a New World Context*

Isabel Alvarez Borland, *Cuban-American Literature of Exile: From Person to Persona*

Belinda J. Edmondson, editor, *Caribbean Romances: The Politics of Regional Representation*

Steven V. Hunsaker, *Autobiography and National Identity in the Americas*

Celia M. Britton, *Edouard Glissant and Postcolonial Theory: Strategies of Language and Resistance*

Mary Peabody Mann, *Juanita: A Romance of Real Life in Cuba Fifty Years Ago*, Edited and with an introduction by Patricia M. Ard

George B. Handley, *Postslavery Literatures in the Americas: Family Portraits in Black and White*

Faith Smith, *Creole Recitations: John Jacob Thomas and Colonial Formation in the Late Nineteenth-Century Caribbean*

Ian Gregory Strachan, *Paradise and Plantation: Tourism and Culture in the Anglophone Caribbean*

Nick Nesbitt, *Voicing Memory: History and Subjectivity in French Caribbean Literature*

Charles W. Pollard, *New World Modernisms: T. S. Eliot, Derek Walcott, and Kamau Brathwaite*

Carine M. Mardorossian, *Reclaiming Difference: Caribbean Women Rewrite Postcolonialism*

Luís Madureira, *Cannibal Modernities: Postcoloniality and the Avant-garde in Caribbean and Brazilian Literature*

Elizabeth M. DeLoughrey, Renée K. Gosson, and George B. Handley, editors, *Caribbean Literature and the Environment: Between Nature and Culture*